**St. Louis Community College**

Forest Park
Florissant Valley
Meramec

Instructional Resources
St. Louis, Missouri

EUROPEAN HISTORICAL DICTIONARIES
Edited by Jon Woronoff

Historical Dictionary of Sweden

by
Irene Scobbie

European Historical Dictionaries, No. 7

The Scarecrow Press, Inc.
Metuchen, N.J., & London
1995

British Library Cataloguing-in-Publication data available

Library of Congress Cataloging-in-Publication Data

Scobbie, Irene.
    Historical dictionary of Sweden / by Irene Scobbie.
        p.   cm. — (European historical dictionaries ; no. 7)
    Includes bibliographical references.
    ISBN 0-8108-2922-3 (alk. paper)
    1. Sweden—History—Dictionaries. I. Title. II. Series.
DL643.S37   1995
948.5′003—dc20   94-20482

CONTENTS

EDITOR'S FOREWORD

Just like people, countries change. This applies most emphatically to Sweden. Once warlike and expansive, it has become neutral and somewhat standoffish. Once terribly poor and backward, it has become uncommonly rich and advanced. Once conservative and dominated by the nobility and men in general, it has become a prolific source of social experiments with particular stress on equality. This has put Sweden in the forefront in many sectors, indeed, so much so that the Swedish "miracle" was widely admired and emulated. Yet, even now that the limitations and failings are more evident, it remains a country from which much can be learnt.

These changes obviously took decades and sometimes centuries. And they can only be correctly appreciated by observing the longer trends. That is just one reason why this *Historical Dictionary of Sweden* is so useful. It does take a long view and it does show us where Sweden is coming from. But it also looks very carefully at the present situation, the problems as well as the achievements. The entries thus cover kings and nobles but also politicians, economists and writers. Others describe the leading political parties, trade unions and newspapers. The flow of events can be grasped more readily thanks to a handy chronology. And those wanting to learn more about any particular aspect can consult a substantial and well-structured bibliography.

This volume was written by someone who has devoted much of her life, initially, to learning about Sweden, and then to teaching about Sweden, Irene Scobbie. The learning was at Newcastle University, University College London, and also in Sweden. The teaching was, among other places, at the University of Cambridge, and at the Universities of Aberdeen and most recently Edinburgh, where Ms. Scobbie became Head of the Department of Scandinavian Studies. Before this book she also wrote a general work–*Sweden. Nation of the Modern World.*–and numerous articles, monographs and chapters on Sweden and especially Swedish literature. In 1985 she was awarded the Swedish Polar Star (1st Class) for services to Swedish culture.

Jon Woronoff
Series Editor

NOTE ON ALPHABETIZATION
AND SWEDISH NAMES

The Swedish alphabet has three extra characters, å, ä and ö, which come at the end of the alphabet. Here they are treated as if unmodified and placed alphabetically as a, a and o.

Swedish proper names have been used for the most part in this volume (e.g., Karl XII for Charles XII, Skåne for Scania) but there are a few exceptions (e.g., Gothenburg for Göteborg) where the English version is much more familiar than the Swedish.

The Swedish parliament is the *Riksdag,* a term used throughout this volume.

CHRONOLOGY

c.12,000–1500 B.C.   Stone Age.

c.12,000 B.C.   Nomadic tribes of reindeer hunters enter Sweden.

c.2500 B.C.   New tribes introduce agriculture and husbandry. Dolmens raised in western Sweden.

c.2000 B.C.–   Boat-Ax people's culture begins to spread in southern and central areas.

c.1500–500 B.C.   Bronze Age. Rich burial mounds and rock carvings on west coast.

c.400 B.C.–A.D.1   Early Iron Age. Iron used for tools and weapons.

c.A.D.1–400   Roman Iron Age. Trade links with Romans established.

A.D. 98   Tacitus mentions the *Suiones* in his *Germania.*

c.400–800   Later Iron Age. Svear gain supremacy over Götar.

c.800–1060   Viking Age. Swedish Vikings travel east and south to Russia, the Caspian and the Black Sea.

829   Missionary Ansgar visits Birka.

1008	King Olof Skötkonung baptized.
1080	King Inge driven from Uppsala for refusing to perform pagan rites.
1130s	Christian church built on site of Uppsala pagan temple.
1160	Death of Erik, later Saint Erik.
1164	(Old) Uppsala archbishopric established.
1187	Pirates sack Sigtuna.
1266	Death of Birger Jarl.
1303	Birgitta (St Birgitta) born at Finsta.
1313–64	Magnus Eriksson is King.
1323	Peace of Nöteborg establishes frontiers between Russia and Sweden-Finland.
c.1350	National law code introduced.
1364–89	Albrecht of Mecklenburg is King.
1397	Kalmar Union under Erik of Pomerania.
1412	Death of Queen Margareta.
1434	Engelbrekt Engelbrektsson's revolt.
1470	Sten Sture the Elder elected Regent.
1471	Sten Sture victorious at Battle of Brunkeberg.
1477	Uppsala University founded.

1512–20	Regency of Sten Sture the Younger.
1520	Stockholm Bloodbath.
1523–60	Gustav I Vasa is King of Sweden.
1527	Catholic Church property transferred to the Crown. Lutheranism introduced.
1541	Bible published in Swedish (Gustav Vasa Bible).
1560–68	Erik XIV is King of Sweden.
1563–70	Nordic Seven Years War.
1568	Johan III deposes Erik XIV.
1592–99	Sigismund is King of Sweden.
1599	Duke Karl becomes Regent.
1603–11	Karl IX is King of Sweden.
1611–1718	Age of Greatness.
1611–32	Gustav II Adolf is King of Sweden.
1617	Peace of Stolbova. Ingria and Southwest Karelia ceded to Sweden.
1617, 1626	Regulation of *Riksdag* and *Riddarhuset*
1621	City of Gothenburg granted its charter.
1632–54	Kristina is Queen of Sweden.
1632	New Sweden Colony on Delaware set up.
1654–60	Karl X Gustav is King of Sweden.

1658	Peace of Roskilde, Denmark cedes southern provinces to Sweden.
1660–97	Karl IX is King of Sweden.
1668	Lund University inaugurated.
1676	Battle of Lund.
1693	Declaration of Sovereignty, giving Karl XI absolute power.
1697–1718	Karl XII is King of Sweden.
1700	Battle of Narva, Swedes defeat Tsar's army.
1709	Battle of Poltava, Karl's army routed.
1718	Karl killed at Fredriksten, end of Great Northern War.
1718–72	Age of Liberty.
1719	Ulrika Eleonora, Karl XII's sister, elected Queen of Sweden.
1720–51	Fredrik I, Ulrika Eleonora's consort.
1731	Swedish East India Co. set up.
1735	Linnaeus publishes *Systema Naturae*.
1738	Arvid Horn resigns Chancellorship. Hat Party in office.
1739	Swedish Royal Academy of Sciences founded.
1741	Unsuccessful war against Russia.

1751–71	Adolf Fredrik is King of Sweden. His consort is Lovisa Ulrika.
1756	Court Party's abortive coup.
1756–63	Seven Years (Pomeranian) War.
1757	Land reform (*Storskifte*).
1765–72	Cap Party in office.
1771–92	Gustav III is King of Sweden.
1772	Gustav stages coup and introduces new Constitution. End of Age of Liberty.
1772–1809	Gustavian Period.
1782	Gustav establishes Royal Opera House.
1783	Maclean introduces land enclosures (*enskifte*) on his estate.
1786	Gustav founds Swedish Academy.
1788–90	War with Russia. Anjala League approaches Catherine the Great.
1789	Act of Union and Security gives Gustav almost absolute power.
1792	Gustav assassinated at masked ball.
1792–1809	Gustav IV Adolf is King of Sweden.
1808	War against Russia, France and Denmark.
1809	King deposed, and new Constitution enacted. In Peace of Fredrikshamn Sweden loses Finland and Åland.

1809–18	Karl XIII is King of Sweden.
1810	Jean-Baptiste Bernadotte elected Crown Prince.
1812	Karl Johan's (Bernadotte's) "1812 policy" supporting Tsar Alexander against Napoleon in exchange for Russian support in gaining Norway.
1814	Peace of Kiel, Denmark cedes Norway. Norway Assembly accepts new Constitution. Moss Convention, Norway accepts Union with Sweden under Karl XIII.
1818–44	Karl XIV Johan is King of Norway and Sweden.
1830	Lars Johan Hierta launches *Aftonbladet*.
1832	Göta Canal completed.
1837	Swedish Abstinence Society founded.
1840	Liberals force reform in composition of the Cabinet.
1842	Education Act makes primary education compulsory.
1844–59	Oscar I is King of Norway and Sweden.
1846	Guilds abolished and trade restrictions lifted.
1848	February Revolution has repercussions in Sweden in form of street riots. Per Götrek publishes the Communist Manifesto in Swedish.

1851	Swedish Order of Good Templars founded.
1853	Decision that state will build mainline railroads taken. Sweden's first telegraph line between Stockholm and Uppsala installed.
1855	November Treaty, Britain and France guarantee protection against Russia.
1859–72	Karl XV is King of Norway and Sweden.
1864	Sweden refuses to intervene in Dano-Prussian War. Pan-Scandinavian Movement doomed.
1865–66	Four-Estate *Riksdag* replaced by bicameral system.
1870	Women allowed to take *Studentexamen*.
1872–1907	Oscar II is King of Norway and Sweden until 1905. King of Sweden only until 1907.
1876	Office of Prime Minister (Statsminister) instituted. L. De Geer first incumbent.
1880	Sweden's first telephones in Stockholm and Gothenburg.
1882	Salvation Army started in Sweden.
1884	Fredrika Bremer Society founded.
1889	Social Democratic Party founded.
1892	Erik Gustav Boström resolves tax and defense problems.
1896	Alfred Nobel dies, bequeathing funds to establish the Nobel prizes.

1897	The first Social Democrat, Hjalmar Branting, takes his seat in *Riksdag*.
1898	Landsorganisationen (LO, Swedish Confederation of Trade Unions) founded.
1899	Kooperativa Förbundet (KF, Swedish Cooperative Movement) founded. Old defense system abolished. National Service introduced.
1902	Svenska Arbetsgivareföreningen (SAF, Swedish Employers' Confederation) founded.
1905	Union with Norway dissolved. Liberal Karl Staaff forms first ministry.
1909	Franchise extended for men to Second Chamber. General Strike.
1911–14	Staaff's second ministry.
1912	National subscription for F-ship. Death of August Strindberg.
1914	Gustav V's Palace Yard Speech. Staaff resigns, Hammarskjöld forms government.
1917	Edén-Branting government formed, Social Democrats represented for the first time.
1918–21	Universal suffrage and democratic parliamentary system introduced.
1920	Hjalmar Branting is first Social Democratic Prime Minister. Sweden joins the League of Nations.

1922	Kerstin Hesselgren becomes first woman member of *Riksdag.*
1925	Branting dies.
1931	Ådalen strike. Sweden hit by international depression.
1932	Ivar Kreuger commits suicide. Per Albin Hansson forms his first ministry.
1934	Alvar and Gunnar Myrdal publish *The Population Crisis.*
1936	Hansson forms his second ministry and 40 years of Social Democratic rule begins.
1938	Saltsjöbaden Agreement facilitating collective bargaining and labor relations.
1939	Sweden decides not to enter Finnish War. Wartime national coalition government formed under Hansson's premiership.
1940	German troops allowed transit through Sweden.
1941	German division allowed transit from Norway to Finnish front.
1943	Training camps for refugees from Norway and Denmark set up. Transit of German troops ceases.
1945	Coalition government dissolved, replaced by Social Democratic government under Hansson. Raoul Wallenberg disappears in Budapest.

1946	Hansson dies, succeeded by Tage Erlander.
1947	Karin Kock becomes Sweden's first woman Cabinet minister.
1948	Nordic defense negotiations fail. Sweden opts for neutrality in the Cold War.
1950	Bill to introduce comprehensive schools accepted by *Riksdag*.
1951–57	Social Democratic-Agrarian government.
1952	Stockholm Subway (Underground) opened.
1953	First meeting of Nordic Council.
1954	Beginning of Swedish Television.
1955	*Motbok* (alcohol ration book) abolished. Referendum on righthand driving.
1957	Referendum on ATP pension scheme.
1958	Women given right to be ordained.
1959	EFTA treaty signed in Stockholm. *Riksdag* accepts ATP by tiny margin.
1963	Four weeks holiday with pay introduced.
1964	Christian Democratic Party formed.
1967	Righthand traffic introduced.
1969	Olof Palme succeeds Erlander as Prime Minister. Strike at Kiruna.
1971	New Constitution, unicameral *Riksdag*.

1974   Tenure of employment law accepted.

1976   Trade Unions' Wage Earner Fund scheme
                accepted as Social Democratic policy. So-
                cial Democrats relinquish power. Three-
                party non-socialist coalition formed under
                Center Party leader Thorbjörn Fälldin.

1978   Government split over nuclear energy issue.
                Fälldin resigns, Ola Ullsten forms a Liberal
                minority government.

1979   Fälldin forms second three-party non-
                socialist government.

1980   Referendum on nuclear energy leads to law
                to phase out Sweden's 12 nuclear reactors
                by 2010.

1981   Moderate Party leaves coalition govern-
                ment, which becomes a Center-Liberal coa-
                lition under Fälldin. Environment (Green)
                Party founded.

1982   Social Democrats return to office under
                Olof Palme. Swedish krona devalued by 16
                percent. Kjell-Olof Feldt, Minister of Fi-
                nance, sets out "Third Way" policy.

1986   Palme assassinated on February 28 in
                Stockholm, when Sweden, an open society
                was said to have lost its innocence. Ingvar
                Carlsson becomes Prime Minister.

1987   Simplified income tax returns introduced.

1988   Environment (Green) Party represented in
                Riksdag for first time. Women's Party
                formed to further feminist interests.

1989   Social Democratic government introduces
             compulsory saving scheme. Abolition of
             foreign exchange controls. Kerstin Ekman
             resigns as member of the Swedish Academy
             in protest at her colleagues' feeble response
             to threats to Salman Rushdie and free
             speech.

1989/90   *Riksdag* pass Agriculture Deregulation Bill,
             allowing previously controlled food prices
             to be regulated by market forces.

1990   Social Democrats, Liberals and Center Par-
             ties agree not to fix a commencement date
             for phasing out nuclear reactors. Social
             Democrat government proposes statutory
             pay freeze and a ban on strikes, is defeated
             in parliament and resigns. Ingvar Carlsson
             returns as Prime Minister when non-
             socialist parties refuse to form an alterna-
             tive government. Swedish krona linked to
             the ECU. Liberals support Social Demo-
             crats' economic crisis package. Social
             Democrat government proposes cut in pub-
             lic expenditure after new crisis. Moderate
             leader Carl Bildt and Liberal leader Bengt
             Westerberg announce their intention of gov-
             erning together, unveil six-point program.

1990/91   Tax reforms introduced.

1991   Neo-Democratic Party founded under Bertil
             Karlsson and Ian Wachtmeister. Bildt and
             Bengt Westerberg publish ''A New Start for
             Sweden'' based on their six-point program
             announced in 1990.

1991   Sweden submits its application for member-
             ship of European Community. Social
             Democrats lose elections. Bildt, Moderate

leader, forms four-party non-socialist coalition. Neo-Democratic Party wins 23 seats. Environment (Green) Party fails to reach the four percent threshold and loses its representation in *Riksdag*. VAT on food reduced from 25 to 18 percent.

1992   Swedish krona floated, resulting in 25 percent fall in value.

1993   Volvo shareholders reject merger with French automobile company Renault. P.G. Gyllenhammer resigns.

April 1994   Ian Wachtmeister resigns from the Neo-Democratic Party. Newly-reorganized Women's Party registers for autumn general elections.

ABBREVIATIONS AND ACRONYMS

AB	Aktiebolag (Limited Company)
ABF	Arbetarnas bildningsförbund (Workers' Educational Association)
AMS	Arbetsmarknadsstyrelsen (Labor Market Board)
ASEA	Allmänna svenska . 'ektriska aktiebolaget
APK	Arbetarpartiet kommunisterna (Workers' Party Communists)
ATP	Allmän tilläggspension (General Supplementary Pension)
EC	European Community
EEC	European Economic Community
EFTA	European Free Trade Association
EU	European Union
HSB	Hyresgästernas sparkasse-och byggnadsförening (Tenants' Savings and Building Society)
IOGT	International Order of Good Templars
JO	Justitieombudsman
KB	Kungliga biblioteket (Royal Library)

KDS	Kristen demokratisk samling (Christian Democratic Alliance)
KF	Kooperativa förbundet (Cooperative Societies)
KFML	Kommunistiska förbundet Marxist-Leninisterna (Marxist-Leninist Communist Union)
LKAB	Luosssavaara-Kiirunavaara AB
LO	Landsorganisationen (Swedish Confederation of Trade Unions)
LRF	Lantbrukarnas riksförbund (Federation of Swedish Farmers)
NATO	North Atlantic Treaty Organization
NyD	Ny demokrati (Neo-Democratic Party)
OECD	Organization for Economic Cooperation and Development
OEEC	Organization for European Economic Cooperation
OPEC	Organization of Petroleum Exporting Countries
SAAB	Svenska aeroplan AB
SACO	Sveriges akademikers centralorganisation (Central Organization of Swedish Professional Workers)
SAF	Svenska arbetsgivareföreningen (Swedish Federation of Employers)
SAS	Scandinavian Airlines System
SJ	Statens järnvägar (Swedish Railways)

SKF	AB Svenska kullagerfabriken (Swedish Ball Bearing Company)
SR	Statstjänstemännens riksförbund (Federation of Government Employees)
SR	Sveriges Radio AB
TCO	Tjänstemännens centralorganisation (Central Organization of Salaried Employees)
TT	Tidningarnas telegrambyrå (Swedish News Agency)
UN	United Nations
VPK	Vänsterpartiet kommunisterna (Left Party Communists)
WEF	Wage Earner Funds

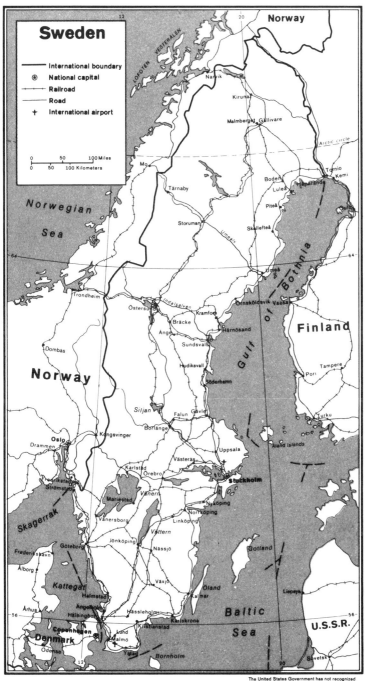

Sweden

International boundary
⊛ National capital
Railroad
Road
+ International airport

0   50   100 Miles
0   50   100 Kilometers

Norway

Norwegian

Sea

LOFOTEN
VESTERÅLEN

Narvik

Kiruna

Malmberget Gällivare

Arctic Circle

Tornio
Kemi
Boden
Luleå   Haparanda
Piteå
Mo
Tärnaby
Skellefteå
Storuman
Umeä

Gulf of Bothnia

64   64

Trondheim
Örnsköldsvik Vaasa

Finland

Östersund
Indalsälven
Kramfors
Bräcke
Ånge   Härnösand
Sundsvall
Dombas
Hudiksvall
Tampere
Norway
Söderhamn
Pori

Siljan
Falun Gävle
Borlänge
Kongsvinger
Turku

Oslo
Drammen   Uppsala
Åland Islands

Karlstad   Västerås
Fredrikstad Örebro
Strömstad   Stockholm

Mariestad
Vänern   Nyköping
Vänersborg   Norrköping
Linköping
Skagerrak   Vättern

Frederikshavn Göteborg Jönköping Nässjö
Gotland
Ålborg
Kattegat Halmstad
Ängelholm   Växjö   Öland
Århus   Kalmar   Liepaja
56   Hälsingborg Hässleholm   56
Copenhagen Lund Kristianstad Karlskrona
Denmark   Malmö   Baltic
Odense   Ystad   Sea   U.S.S.R.
Bornholm   Sovetsk

INTRODUCTION
SWEDEN: AN OVERVIEW

Geography

Sweden forms the eastern part of the Scandinavian Peninsula. Covering an area of 450,964 square kilometers (174,000 square miles), it is the fourth-largest country in Europe. An elongated country (55–69 degrees N., 11–24 degrees E.), it has a north-south axis of 1,610 kilometers (1,000 miles) and a breadth of 400 kilometers (250 miles approximately). It is bordered by the North Sea in the southwest, Norway in the west and northwest, Finland in the northeast, the Gulf of Bothnia in the east and the Baltic Sea in the southeast.

The climate is influenced by prevailing westerly winds and the Gulf Stream, which keep the country warmer than its northerly position would suggest. The mean February (winter) temperature is 7 degrees F (−14 degrees C) in the north to 30 degrees F (−1 degree C) in the south; the relative July (summer) figures are 57 degrees F (4 degrees C) and 63 degrees F (17 degrees C). Snow lies on the Norrland mountains for approximately eight months of the year and one month in Skåne. In the far north the midnight sun never sets during the summer (about six weeks).

There are four main physical regions: the mountainous region of the north (Norrland), where the largest deposits of Sweden's mineral resources, iron ore, copper lead, pyrites and some gold are found, as well as extensive forests and fastmoving rivers; the central lowland lake region (Svealand and Götaland); a relatively low highland area (Småland); and the rich agricultural plain in the south (Skåne). The natural vegetation ranges from Alpine (moss, lichen, dwarf birch) in the very far north, to coniferous (pine, spruce, aspen) down to deciduous (beech, sycamore, elm, etc.) in the south. There are herds of domesticated reindeer in the northern

1

mountains, while elk, badger, fox and roedeer are common in central and southern Sweden. The brown bear is still found as far south as Dalarna, but the wolf and most other predators have become almost extinct.

Population

In 1991 Sweden's population was 8,590,630. One and a half million people live in greater Stockholm, the capital, 740,000 in greater Gothenburg (Sweden's second largest city) and over 85 percent of the population live in the southern half of the country. In Malmöhus in the extreme south there are 151 inhabitants per square kilometer, while in Norrbotten in the far north there are only three. Life expectancy is high—80 years for women and 74 for men.

Ethnically Sweden is still a fairly homogeneous country, with about 90 percent of the population native Swedes. The Lapps were the earliest inhabitants, pre-dating the Swedes; in the Middle Ages Germans settled in Swedish towns; Walloons arrived later to work in the mines or set up businesses; Scottish and German soldiers were drawn to Sweden's warrior kings. This century has seen a much greater influx of immigrants. Migrant workers began to arrive in the 1950s, and the numbers reached a peak in the late 1960s and early 1970s. In 1970 there were 73,000. Since then the figure has been between 20,000 and 48,000. The number of emigrants since 1974 has fluctuated between 20,000 and 30,000 per year. Many of the immigrants and emigrants are from other Scandinavian countries. Others went to Sweden from southern Europe to find a higher standard of living, or as political refugees (often from Latin America) seeking asylum.

The official language is Swedish, a Germanic language, and the Swedish State Church, to which 95 percent of the population belong, is Lutheran.

Economy

Sweden has few natural resources, but they include an abundance of iron ore and extensive forests. There was also a plentiful supply of hydroelectric power until Sweden became highly industrialized. Now electric energy covers only one-third of requirements, less than imported oil. Conversely, modern farming methods have turned the 19th century shortage of arable land into a surplus. In this century, and increasingly from the 1960s, Sweden has developed her natural resources, and manufactures specialized goods with world markets in view. Virtual self-sufficiency in certain vital sectors is preserved (e.g., food), but on the whole as an advanced trading nation Sweden is exposed to international market forces and must keep exports competitive if present high living standards are to be preserved.

AGRICULTURE, FISHING AND FORESTRY.

In 1992 only 3.1 percent of the total labor force was employed in these three industries. Eight percent of Sweden is under cultivation, covering the fertile plains of Skåne in the south, the central plains of Västergötland and Östergötland, the district around Lake Mälaren, and some fertile coastal plains and river valleys in the north. The chief crops are oats, barley, wheat, sugar beet and potatoes. About 75 percent of the total crop yield provides fodder for livestock: cattle, pigs and sheep. Most farms are small and privately owned but they are highly mechanized and efficient, and Sweden is self-sufficient in dairy produce, potatoes, grain, sugar, vegetables and meat products.

The fishing industry has lost much of its economic significance recently. There are still large catches off the west coast and in the Baltic, and herring, cod, North Sea prawns, eel, salmon, haddock and mackerel are the most important fish. Many Swedish trawlers land their catch directly in foreign ports, but Sweden imports even more in the form of processed and tinned fish.

About 58 percent of Sweden's land area is afforested, with conifers predominating. The largest forests are in Norrland and Dalarna, but since the growth rate is faster in the warmer south, forestry is gaining in importance there. The forestry industry is involved today not just in timber but in pulp, paper and board, and by-products such as rayon, dyes, resins and turpentine.

MINING

Sweden is rich in metals, especially iron, but not fossil fuels. The most important iron ore deposits are at Kiruna and Malmberget in northern Sweden. They are worked by LKAB, a state-owned company. Aitik in the Kiruna area has Sweden's largest copper mine, owned by Trelleborgskoncern (Boliden). Sulphide ore deposits are found near Skellefteå. Silver and gold deposits have also been discovered.

Sweden's steel-making is traditionally sited in central Sweden, Avesta and Sandviken producing most stainless steel. Recession and foreign competition brought about radical changes in the 1980s. Some 60 percent of finished steel is now special high quality steel.

MANUFACTURING INDUSTRIES.

Engineering is now Sweden's most important industry. The leading manufactured goods include motor vehicles (Volvo, Saab-Scania, which makes airplanes, too), which in 1992 accounted for 9 percent of the GDP and represented 16 percent of Sweden's exports. In 1970 Sweden had 10 percent of the world's shipbuilding market, the largest yards being Götaverken and Eriksberg in Gothenburg and Kockums in Malmö, but this fell rapidly after the oil crisis. In 1977 a state-owned holding company, Swedyards, took over to save the industry, which was greatly reduced in capacity, and now specializes in more sophisticated constructions such as roll-on roll-off ferries, large floating platforms, off-shore hotels and bridge components.

Light engineering, 10 percent of industrial output in 1992, centers on electronics and telecommunications. ASEA produces electric generators and motors, transmission equipment and industrial robots, while the Ericsson group specializes in telecommunications and personal computers. Electrolux produces household machinery, electric components for office machinery, etc.

The chemical industry produced 13 percent of the total industrial output in 1992. Its largest company is Nobel Industries, covering everything from basic chemicals, explosives and plastics to soap, toothpaste, candles and fertilizers. A large investment program has led to a great expansion in the Swedish petrochemical industry, especially in plastics. Pharmaceuticals have also been developed extensively.

Other thriving industries include food and beverages, graphics, textiles and glass blowing, Boda, Orrefors and Kosta enjoying international recognition for their design.

Sweden still has a mixed economy despite half a century of socialist governments. On the whole they have managed the economy through social and fiscal legislation rather than state ownership. Nearly 90 percent of industrial output comes from private firms, the State and cooperative companies accounting for the rest. Public-sector businesses are found mainly in such services as the post office, telecommunications, roads and railroads and energy production.

Despite recession, Sweden is a relatively rich country, and a fairly even distribution of wealth has put Sweden near the top of such living standard indicators as automobiles, refrigerators, freezers, telephones and newspapers.

History

STONE AGE (c. 12,000–1500 B.C.)

Archeological evidence shows that the first migration into Sweden started towards the end of the last Ice Age, c. 12,000 B.C., when reindeer hunters and fishermen crossed the land bridge joining Sweden with the Continent. These nomadic tribes used implements made of flint and bone. From about 2500 B.C. new tribes introduced agriculture and cattle-rearing, which allowed a more settled existence. Dolmens, great stone monuments to the dead, have been found in west Sweden from that time, evidence of a belief in some form of afterlife. A form of peasant culture spread in south and west Sweden in what are now the provinces of Skåne, Halland, Bohuslän and Västergötland. From 2000 B.C. there are traces of the Boat-Ax People (so-called because of their boat-shaped stone ax), a warlike people who had trading links with Europe. Their culture quickly spread in the southern and central areas, and archeologists believe that these tribes formed an élite. The wealth of decorative objects found in the richer graves suggests that there was some kind of nobility in the country. It is difficult to ascertain whether there were successive migrations into Sweden or whether (less likely) one culture developed out of another.

BRONZE AGE (c. 1500–500 B.C.)

Trade links with Europe and with the British Isles were maintained during the Bronze Age. Bronze was not produced in Scandinavia but bronze objects, both implements and weapons, reached Sweden along European trade routes. Burial mounds containing rich metal objects for use in the afterlife also date from this time. Most numerous on the west coast, they show the existence of an aristocracy, perhaps Boat-Ax People. Rock carvings, most impressively in Bohuslän on the west coast, have also survived from this period. They depict boats, humans, animals, tools, weapons and disks and other designs suggesting sun cult and fertility rites. For most of the Bronze Age Sweden had a mild climate, but towards the end of the period this deteriorated. The paucity of finds from this time coincides with the upheavals on the Continent and the spread of the Celtic peoples across Europe, which endangered the old trade routes.

EARLY IRON AGE (c. 400 B.C.–A.D. 1)

The colder climate and increased isolation caused Scandinavians to produce warmer clothing and habitations and to improve agricultural methods, and the foundations of Scandinavian culture were laid. An important step forward came with the use of iron for tools and weapons. Iron implements were at first imported, but gradually Swedish smiths learnt to manufacture them from indigenous bog iron.

ROMAN IRON AGE (c. A.D. 1–400)

As the Romans penetrated into Gaul they came into contact with, and influenced, the Germanic tribes, including the Scandinavians. Trade links with the Roman Empire were established during this period, and a great many Roman coins found their way into Scandinavia. Written sources began to mention Scandinavia. Pliny the Elder (A.D. 23–79) refers to an island far to the north, and Tacitus in his *Germania* (A.D. 98) mentions for the first time the *Suiones,* i.e., Swedes, "strong in men, arms and their fleets."

LATER IRON AGE (c. A.D. 400–800)

This was a period of unrest in Sweden, out of which emerged the first Swedish state. At some stage the Svear, whose kingdom lay in Uppland and around Lake Mälaren with Uppsala as its center, must have gained supremecy over the powerful Götar and other independent tribes. The Svear kings extended their rule until by the beginning of the Viking period it embraced the whole of Sweden, except the extreme south, and even settlements on the southeast coast of the Baltic. The Svear gave the country its name: *Sverige,*, i.e., *Svea rike,* the Svear Kingdom.

VIKING AGE (c. A.D. 800–1060)

Suddenly the Scandinavians emerged from their relative obscurity, making their name as intrepid merchant warriors, pirates, plunderers and/or settlers. Danish and Norwegian Vikings raided western European settlements while most Swedish Vikings journeyed eastwards through Russia and down to the Black Sea and the Caspian Sea, seeking out lucrative trade with the Arab world. They established strongholds in Novgorod and Kiev and ruled much of European Russia. Gradually Swedish settlers in Russia were assimilated by the Slav population, and by the end of the Viking era the Swedes had returned to their former isolation. Little is known about the political situation in Sweden at this time. The country appears to have been loosely united under the Svear King Erik the Victorious of the Yngling dynasty, who ruled until c. 994. His son Olof Skötkonung was the first Swedish King to accept Christianity, but his two sons who succeeded him were the last of the line, and the Yngling dynasty died with them in 1060.

Sweden resisted Christianity longer than most European countries. The missionary Ansgar visited Sweden in 829 and set up a church at Birka with little lasting effect. Uppsala's heathen temple, the great center for the Old Norse gods (Odin, Thor and Frej), survived until the llth century. By the 1130s when, symbolically, a Christian church was built on the old heathen temple site at Uppsala, Sweden had became a Christian country.

12th, 13th, AND 14th CENTURIES

Over a century of turmoil followed the death of Olof Skötkonung and his sons towards the end of the llth century as two families, the Sverkers and the Eriks, struggled for supremacy. A pretender, Erik Jadvardsson, according to legend went on a crusade to Finland, which became part of the Swedish kingdom. Little is known about Erik except that he died violently in 1160 and became Sweden's patron saint. Sverkers and Eriks succeeded each other until Erik Eriksson, the last of his line, died in 1250, when his brother-in-law Birger of the Folkung family became jarl (earl) and virtual ruler until his death in 1266. Birger jarl subjugated the rebellious magnates, gave laws securing the Church and the Thing (Assembly), and helped establish trade links with Europe. He fortified Sweden's coastal defenses, one of the forts forming the foundation of Sweden's capital, Stockholm. Birger's son Valdemar became King but was deposed in 1275 by his brother Magnus Ladulås. Magnus set up a Council of the Realm comprising representatives of the nobles, bishops and lawmen, plus three officials: the Lord High Steward, the Chancellor and the Marshal. In 1279 he exempted magnates serving in his cavalry from taxes and extended the exemption to include Church lands in 1281. Despite these moves towards a feudal system, the Swedish peasants were not subjected to serfdom.

Magnus's son Birger succeeded him in 1290. The nobility, gaining rapidly in authority, deposed Birger in 1319, preferring his nephew Magnus, already King of Norway. During Magnus's reign a national code of law replaced the old provincial laws, laying the foundation of Sweden's first constitution; and in 1323 the Peace of Nöteborg established the frontiers between Russia and Sweden-Finland. Magnus's power was largely illusory, for he had crippling debts, was unable to raise taxes without the Council's consent, and was dogged by Council members determined to retain their privileges. In 1364 Magnus was deposed by the nobility, who elected instead Albrecht of Mecklenburg. When the latter proved less amenable than expected the magnates deposed him too and appealed to the remarkable Queen Margareta, Regent of both Norway and Denmark, to name a successor. Her 15-year-old great-nephew Erik of Pomerania, already heir to Norway and Denmark, was accepted as King of Sweden and was crowned in Kalmar in 1397, ushering in the Kalmar Union, a Scandinavian union of crowns.

KALMAR UNION

As long as Queen Margareta was in control the Union held, but after her death in 1412 Erik quickly made himself very unpopular in Sweden. A successful revolt led by Engelbrekt Engelbrektsson in 1432 led to Erik's downfall. Engelbrekt called a national assembly in 1435 and was elected regent. He had been used as a tool by the magnates to depose Erik and, having served his purpose, he was murdered in 1436. Erik's nephew Christopher of Bavaria was chosen as his successor to all three Scandinavian crowns in 1440, but when he died without an heir in 1448, the Union began to crumble. The Swedish magnates elected Karl Knutsson as their Regent, but the Danes chose Christian I of Oldenburg.

Dissension within Sweden grew, Council members of both the nobility and the clergy preferring a distant Union monarch, others wanting a national leader to defend Sweden's interests. The Sture family emerged in the 1470s to represent the anti-Union faction. On Karl Knutsson's death in 1470, his nephew Sten Sture the Elder was elected Regent, and at the Battle of Brunkeberg outside Stockholm he defeated Christian's forces. Sweden was virtually ruled by Regents for the next 40 years, but there was internal strife, with some Swedish magnates supporting Christian. When Sten Sture the Younger became Regent in 1512, he determined to assert Swedish independence but was opposed by the forceful Archbishop Gustav Trolle. He had Trolle removed from office, which prompted a Danish attack in the name of the Church as well as the Kalmar Union. In 1520 Christian II killed Sten Sture, entered Stockholm and, despite promises of amnesty, executed 82 of Sture's leading supporters, in the so-called Stockholm Blood-bath. His actions spurred anti-Unionist Swedes, especially the men of Dalarna for whom Engelbrekt was a hero, into rallying behind Gustav Eriksson Vasa, a nephew of Sten Sture's widow, who expelled the Danes. In 1523 he was elected King of an independent Sweden, and the Kalmar Union was defunct.

THE EARLY VASAS (1523–1611)

The 27-year-old Gustav Vasa had borrowed heavily from Hansa merchants, the royal coffers were empty, he was considered by many to be an usurper, and he had taken over a country that had been torn by civil strife for centuries. The Catholic Church was the richest single institution in Sweden. In 1527 Gustav persuaded *Riksdag* to transfer Church property to the Crown and to make Bishops responsible to the King. He appointed Olaus Petri, a Lutheran pastor, Secretary of Stockholm and his brother Laurentius Petri, Archbishop of Uppsala. The Swedish Lutheran Church was established within a few years and Gustav's most pressing economic problems were solved. He reorganized his kingdom with vigor, using German jurists to establish a central administrative office, had a series of castles built to defend strategic points, and helped Sweden's trade. Gustav survived several rebellions and by 1544 was able to proclaim the Swedish crown hereditary. By the time of his death in 1560 he had turned Sweden into an independent, well-ordered Lutheran state with a stable economy.

Gustav's defense policy had been to secure existing boundaries, but his sons Erik XIV (1560–68), Johan III (1568–92) and Karl IX (Regent and then King 1592–1611) sought to make Sweden a Baltic power, which brought them into conflict with Denmark, Poland and Russia. When in 1561 Reval (now Tallinn, Estonia) acknowledged Swedish rule in exchange for protection, Sweden was committed to an expansion policy which led to the Nordic Seven Years War (1563–70), in which neither Sweden nor Denmark established superiority, and to further wars with Poland, Denmark and Russia. On the sudden death of Karl IX in 1611 Sweden was threatened on all sides, and the immediate task for Karl's son and heir, Gustav II Adolf (1594–1632), was to save his country, which he did through diplomacy and military force.

Caught in internal troubles Russia was prepared to evacuate Ingria and southwest Karelia in 1617 (Peace of Stolbova), and so Sweden emerged in possession of Finland and overland communications with Estonia.

AGE OF GREATNESS (1611–1718)

When the Thirty Years War broke out in Europe in 1618 Gustav II Adolf emerged as Protector of the Protestant faith. He landed in Pomerania in 1630, defeated Tilly's Catholic forces at Breitenfeld, Saxony, and marched triumphantly into southern Germany. In 1632 he defeated Wallenstein at Lützen but fell in battle. Before embarking on a full-scale foreign war Gustav Adolf had, with his Chancellor Axel Oxenstierna, introduced an effective system of government based on a Council, appointed by the King, and "colleges" equivalent to modern government departments. After his death the system continued to function well, and Oxenstierna guided Sweden successfully to the end of the war and through peace negotiations. In the Peace of Westphalia (1648) Sweden gained western Pomerania, Verden and Bremen (thus controlling the mouth of the Oder and being a German power) and five million *riksdaler* to pay off her armies.

Gustav Adolf's only child, Kristina, ruled until 1654, when she abdicated in favor of her cousin Karl X Gustav, who followed an expansionist policy. In 1658 (Peace of Roskilde) he forced the Danes to relinquish the provinces of Blekinge, Skåne, Halland and Bohuslän, but his sudden death in 1660 cut short his grand design of a united Scandinavia under his rule. His son Karl XI fought successfully one desperate battle in 1676 for the retention of the southern provinces, but then devoted his energies to internal affairs. During two long regencies the nobility had increased their land holdings. Karl XI reclaimed estates for the Crown (the "reduktions"). He established himself as absolute monarch, and in a period of peace he carried out far-reaching reforms in the field of the economy, the penal code, the Church, education and defense.

The Age of Greatness started with one soldier king and ended with another. Karl XII succeeded his father in 1697. He was an untried 15-year-old and, assuming a disaffected nobility after Karl

XI's "reduktions," Denmark, Poland and Russia prepared a triple attack. Demonstrating remarkable military skill Karl forced Denmark to leave the alliance, defeated Tsar Peter's numerically superior army at Narva in 1700 and forced the Poles to reject King August in favor of his own nominee Stanislav. In 1709 Karl overreached himself and was defeated by the Russians at Poltava. He fled to Turkey where he was held virtually a prisoner, but finally escaped to Sweden to recruit a new army. The myth of his invincibility had been exploded, however, and his enemies closed in. Defending his western borders, Karl was shot dead in 1718. The Swedish government sued for peace and in the ensuing treaties lost Bremen, Verden, Swedish Pomerania, Ingria, Estonia, Livonia and a large part of Karelia, and had to abandon dreams of a Northern Empire.

AGE OF LIBERTY (1718–1772)

The absolute monarchy died with Karl XII. His sister Ulrika Eleonora was elected Queen only after accepting a new constitution which reduced the role of the monarch to little more than a figurehead. Real power lay with the 24-member Council responsible to *Riksdag.* Two parties emerged, the Caps *(Mössor)* and the Hats *(Hattar),* which contended for political office. The Caps, led until 1732 by Arvid Horn, wanted a period of peace and moderation to help Swedish recovery. Horn's foreign policy was to establish friendly relations with Britain and Russia, while his home policy was mildly protectionist. The general peace in Europe allowed Sweden's merchant fleet to expand, especially in the Baltic, and by the 1730s trading companies were set up, including the Swedish East India Company (1731). The Hats were more actively mercantilistic, and they were also much bolder in foreign affairs, hoping that a French alliance would help them to regain foreign territories lost on Karl XII's death. In 1738 they ousted the Caps from office, and by 1741 they had launched a disastrous war against Russia. They clung to office until 1765 and were succeeded by the Caps, who in turn were defeated in 1769. The economy lurched from inflation to deflation, the country wearied of debilitating party squabbles, bribery and corruption, and the Age of Liberty foundered in 1772. Despite its flaws it fostered scientists of genius (e.g., Linnaeus, Celsius, Polhem and Swedenborg) and saw the birth of the Swedish Royal Academy of Sciences. It also paved the way for land reforms and was a first step in the direction of a true parliamentary democracy.

GUSTAVIAN AGE (1772–1809)

The Francophile Gustav III succeeded his father Adolf Fredrik in 1771 and tried to reconcile the Caps and Hats, but when this proved impossible he staged a bloodless coup and in 1772 introduced a new constitution which considerably increased his powers. Initially his reign was characterized by effective and humane measures, including a reform of the civil service and of the penal code. He stabilized the currency and strengthened Swedish defenses. A degree of religious freedom was introduced for Jews and others, and some trading restrictions were lifted. His wave of popularity began to ebb, and in 1788 Gustav attempted to unite the nation behind him by staging a glorious war. He attacked Russia, hoping to regain lost Finnish provinces. A group of Swedish officers who considered the war unconstitutional formed the Anjala Association and approached Catherine II of Russia, proposing negotiations. Gustav exploited the Anjala conspiracy to suppress the nobility and arouse his people's patriotism. The Danes chose that moment to declare war on Sweden, which had the effect of rallying the people behind the King. He determined to secure his authority at home and introduced the Act of Union and Security in 1789, a draconian measure giving him virtually absolute power. The nobility had long complained about the erosion of their privileges, and now a group of aristocrats plotted against him. In 1792 Gustav was assassinated at a masked ball in Stockholm. Culturally Gustav's reign marked a significant point in Swedish history. Royal patronage led to a flowering of Swedish poetry, painting, architecture and sculpture. Gustav established a Royal Opera House in 1782, the Swedish Academy in 1786, and the Royal Dramatic Theater in 1788, all of which have survived.

Gustav's son, Gustav IV Adolf, succeeded his father with no restriction of the monarch's power. Conscientious but untalented and lacking his father's charm, he proved unequal to the decisions necessary in a period of European revolution. From 1803 onwards he stubbornly supported Britain against France even after Tilsit in 1807 when Russia, Sweden's natural enemy, had reached an agreement with Napoleon. Tsar Alexander invaded Finland in 1808 and by 1809 had reached the northern borders of Sweden itself. Despairing of the King's ability to deal with the desperate situation, high-ranking Swedish army officers staged a coup and arrested the King, who was deposed and sent into exile. Russian peace terms were harsh, and Sweden lost the whole of Finland, which became part of the Russian Empire.

19th CENTURY

In 1809 a new constitution restored the balance of power between *Riksdag* and the Crown but retained the four Estates, and the deposed King's uncle, Gustav III's brother, was elected as King Karl XIII. Since he was senile and had no heir the selection of a crown prince was imperative. The choice fell upon Napoleon's marshal Jean-Baptiste Bernadotte. Although he did not accede to the throne, as Karl XIV Johan, until 1818, he was ruler in all but name from his first arrival in Stockholm in 1810. His supporters had assumed that a dynamic French soldier would secure Napoleon's backing and wrest Finland from Russia. Karl Johan's "1812 policy," however, entailed an alliance with Tsar Alexander against Napoleon in return for help in forcing Denmark to relinquish Norway to Sweden. He led Swedish troops against Napoleon in 1814 and then forced Denmark to cede Norway in return for Swedish Pomerania, Sweden's only remaining possession in Northern Germany (the Peace of Kiel, 1814). The Norwegians, however, had declared their independence and they accepted a union with Sweden only under military threat. The Union of Crowns allowed them to keep their new constitution and virtual independence in internal affairs, but foreign policy was run from Stockholm. This subordinate role caused Norwegian animosity from the very outset, and although the Union lasted until 1905 it often caused friction between the two countries.

Karl Johan's military actions while still Crown Prince were the last occasions on which Sweden was involved in a fullscale war. Despite his revolutionary background he was an autocratic ruler, appointing ministers of his own choosing and expecting them to be responsible to him, not *Riksdag*. He encountered increasing opposition from liberals demanding political, economic and social reforms, and when in 1830 L.J. Hierta founded *Aftonbladet,* Sweden's first modern newspaper, liberal journalists and politicians had a forum for their views. Faced with strong liberal criticism and with street riots when dissidents were arrested Karl Johan gave some ground.

By the time Oscar I succeeded his father in 1844 the pace of reform was already increasing. Oscar was more sympathetic to liberal ideas. In 1846 the guilds were replaced by much freer industrial and trade associations, and 1847 saw the removal of almost all restrictions on exports and imports. The tempo quickened in Sweden. The Göta Canal had been completed in 1832, and by 1854 a great railroad building project was started. There was social progress, too: women were given equal inheritance rights with men; legal reform made for a more humane penal code; and there was a greater measure of religious tolerance. When the 1848 revolutions in Europe sparked off disturbances in Stockholm, Oscar became more cautious.

It was not until 1866, under his son Karl XV (ruled 1859–72), that the four Estate *Riksdag* was replaced by a bicameral parliament. In his foreign policy Oscar initially allied himself with Russia, but by the time of the Crimean War (1853–56) he was ready to assist Britain and France in the Baltic if they would help restore Finland to Sweden. He signed the November Treaty with the Western allies in 1855, but the theater of war moved to the Crimea and nothing came of his scheme.

Karl XV was an enthusiastic Pan-Scandinavianist, but in the Dano-Prussian war (1864) the Swedish government refused to back up his promise of military support for Denmark. Sweden accepted a policy of neutrality, which she has endeavored to follow ever since. Karl's brother, Oscar II (ruled 1872–1907), who succeeded him, married a German princess and was sympathetic to the new German Empire, while several Swedish politicians were influenced by many of Bismarck's social measures. There was also a tendency to see Germany as a bulwark against the Russian Empire. Even so, these pro-German sentiments never developed into active political alignment with Germany.

In 1815 the Swedish population stood at 2.5 million, and by the end of the century it was over 5 million. Liberalized trade, modernization of agriculture, the rise of the middle classes and improved educational standards created conditions which transformed a backward rural country into a modern industrial state. A demand for Swedish timber in the mid-19th century was followed in the 1870s by an international need for Swedish pulp. Using new techniques, the iron industry expanded rapidly in Kiruna and in the Bergslagen area, and by the turn of the century Swedish steel was being exported on a large scale. Swedish engineering inventiveness and entrepreneurial energy led to the founding of firms exploiting such Swedish inventions as ball-bearings, telephones and dynamite. There was a great movement from the land to the towns. In 1850 90 percent of the population lived off the land, but by 1900 the figure was 50 percent and still rapidly falling.

Industrial development was not free from recessions and, during difficult periods, many Swedes emigrated, mostly to the United States.

In the second half of the 19th century many popular movements helped to bring about changes in society, such as the Free Church societies, the Fredrika Bremer Society for women's rights, the Cooperative Movement for consumers' rights, the Temperance Movement and the Swedish Order of Good Templars, aimed at reducing alcohol abuse. Folk High Schools began to raise educational standards, and all this coincided with the founding of several cheap, quality newspapers.

Even more fundamental to change in society was the setting up of the Social Democratic Party in 1889, with Hjalmar Branting as its guiding spirit. By 1898 Landsorganisationen (LO, Swedish Confederation of Trade Unions) was formed, which led to its counterpart, Svenska arbetsgivareföreningen (SAF, Swedish Federation of Employers) in 1902.

This dynamic picture contrasts starkly with a moribund *Riksdag,* where most members of the First Chamber were aristocrats and/or high-ranking civil servants, while the Second Chamber was dominated by the Farmers' Party, whose aim was simply to protect farmers' interests. The Farmers' Party finally split in the 1880s, leading to a regrouping. Liberal factions merged into the Liberal Union in 1900 and the various conservative groups formed a united union in 1904. Together with the Social Democratic Party, dating from 1889, this formed the basis of the main political parties active today.

20th CENTURY

Sweden remained neutral during World War I and was not seriously inconvenienced by it until 1917, when German unrestricted submarine warfare began. This led to serious food and fuel shortages and the introduction of rationing.

The Liberal leader Karl Staaff formed a government in 1905 and proposed franchise reforms. They were outvoted, and Staaff resigned. His successor, the Conservative Arvid Lindman, had modified proposals accepted. This compromise did not satisfy the Liberals or Social Democrats, and in 1917 a Liberal-Social Democratic coalition government's Universal Suffrage Bill was passed, coming into force in 1921, when Sweden became a true parliamentary democracy.

The Social Democratic Party's increased representation in *Riksdag* allowed its leader Hjalmar Branting to form a government in 1920. It lasted only a few months and heralded a period, lasting until 1932, of frequent changes of government and political instability. It was a time of industrial expansion but also of recessions, labor disputes and unemployment.

THE BEGINNING OF THE WELFARE STATE.

In 1932 the Social Democrats made electoral gains. Sweden had been caught in the Great Depression and the Social Democrats under Per Albin Hansson offered a comprehensive policy to combat unemployment and a social program. In Keynesian spirit, the State would invest in extensive public works that would offer well-paid employment and stimulate the economy. The investment would be paid for by national borrowing and higher taxes. To ensure a majority for his party Hansson made a pact with the Agrarian Party, promising aid for agriculture in exchange for support of his social program. The economic situation was improving internationally by 1933. The krona exchange rate was kept low, which stimulated exports, and Sweden's economic position quickly improved. Hansson started on his plan for *Folkhemmet*, a welfare state offering security for all. Disagreement on defense led to Hansson's resignation in June 1936, but the September elections that year returned him to office with further gains. He formed a coalition with the Agrarian Party and continued his move towards *Folkhemmet*, but then the outbreak of World War II interrupted progress.

WORLD WAR II

Sweden's trade was better organized in the Second World War than in the First, but she found it more difficult to preserve neutrality. She had joined the League of Nations in 1920 and reduced defense spending. After 1936 she began to strengthen her defenses, and in the spring of 1939 proposed a Nordic defense treaty, but the Scandinavians could not agree and nothing came of it. Sweden declared her neutrality. When the USSR attacked Finland (the Winter War) the Swedish government, a national coalition under P.A. Hansson, sent material aid and allowed volunteers to go to Finland but would not officially enter the war. Once Germany had occupied Norway and Denmark in 1940, Sweden deviated from neutrality by allowing German troops access to Norway via Sweden. Sweden provided a haven for Norwegians and Danes fleeing from the Nazis. When Hitler turned on the USSR he demanded access for German troops to Finland via northern Sweden (Finland's Continuation War). Permission was granted on a "once only" basis. As Hitler's position worsened Sweden cancelled all German transit agreements, but her neutrality was then threatened by the Allies demanding the cessation of all trading with Germany.

Count Folke Bernadotte rescued some 19,000 people from German camps during the war, and Raoul Wallenberg saved about 100,000 Hungarian Jews in Budapest before disappearing in 1945. In the final phase of the war thousands of refugees from Scandinavia and the Baltic states reached Sweden. After the war, Sweden retained her policy of neutrality and nonalignment, which allowed membership in the United Nations, Council of Europe and European Free Trade Association, but not in the North Atlantic Treaty Organization or European Community.

THE WELFARE STATE

At the end of the war P.A. Hansson, heading a Social Democratic government, started immediately on his social program. Hansson died suddenly in 1946, and his successor Tage Erlander carried on his policies. The program embraced full employment, increased real earnings, improved old-age pensions, unemployment and sickness benefits and child allowances, equal educational opportunities, a shorter working week and longer paid holidays. It had a strong socialistic flavor, but there was no nationalization, and financing the social program was done through taxation. In 1950 a comprehensive school system was accepted, and a national health insurance scheme became operative in 1955. In 1959 a controversial compulsory superannuation scheme (the ATP) was narrowly accepted. Finance ministers had levied high taxes in the past not just to cover expenditure but to distribute wealth more evenly. Despite vociferous opposition, the Social Democrats remained in office. The Saltsjöbaden Agreement (1938), which facilitated collective bargaining and almost eliminated harmful strikes, remained effective into the 1960s, Swedish industry was efficient and profitible, and if taxes were high so too were living standards. There seemed to be no credible alternative, for the non-socialist parties (Moderate, Liberal and Center Parties) appeared incapable of working together.

In 1969 Olof Palme succeeded Erlander. The first main issue he faced, constitutional reform, had all-party backing. *Riksdag* voted in 1970 to replace the bicameral parliament with a single chamber *Riksdag* elected through proportional representation every three years. The monarchy was retained, but the King's duties became little more than ceremonial. King Gustav VI Adolf had succeeded his father Gustav V in 1950. His eldest son Gustav Adolf was killed in an air crash in 1947, and he was succeeded in 1973 by his grandson, Carl XVI Adolf, the first King to reign under the new Constitution.

Palme also encountered a combination of social, economic and ecological problems. Improved social benefits meant high taxation, and a security of tenure act made it difficult for employers to dismiss workers. When the Social Democrats adopted a scheme forcing large firms to place a percentage of profits into a fund to further workers' interests, Sweden seemed to be straying from "the middle way." Swedish industry was hard hit by the oil crisis of 1973–74. Ecology groups strongly opposed Sweden's alternative, nuclear energy. In 1976 Thorbjörn Fälldin, leader of the Center Party, campaigned for the closing down of Swedish nuclear reactors. This and dissatisfaction with the government's rising taxation and bureaucracy led to non-socialist coalition governments from 1976 to 1982. By then Sweden's economic position had deteriorated further and unemployment (4 percent in 1982) had risen. Palme was returned to power with a small majority in 1982.

With Kjell-Olof Feldt as Finance Minister, the Social Democrats embarked on a "Third Way" policy, i.e., a sound economy with a free market approach but with no reduction in social welfare and low unemployment without high inflation. The krona was devalued by 16 percent to spark economic growth based on rising exports. The policy proved successful initially, and exports rose, while domestic demand was restrained. Soon, however, labor costs began to rise, inflation was not brought down to OECD levels, resources were not transferred from the protected sector of the economy, and Sweden was again losing her competitive edge. The situation was not immediately evident, for between 1986 and 1988 international oil prices dropped sharply while pulp prices doubled, both very beneficial to Sweden, and unemployment remained low.

In 1986 Olof Palme was assassinated, for motives and by killers still unknown, and Ingvar Carlsson, his deputy, assumed the premiership. The circumstances of his appointment won him public sympathy and the economy seemed to have turned the corner, so he led the Social Democrats to victory in the 1988 elections, although with a reduced majority.

A less favorable picture emerged early in 1989 when inflation rose sharply and the economy looked vulnerable. When the government proposed an increase in VAT, the reaction was so strong, especially from trade unions, that a compulsory saving scheme was introduced instead. By the end of 1989, after substantial pay rises in the public sector, Sweden was again uncompetitive, the balance of payments position was as bad as in 1982, and the economy seemed out of control. Interest rates were raised to defend the krona, and in February 1990 the government proposed a crisis program, including a statutory pay freeze and a ban on strikes. This caused outrage among trade unionists, the backbone of Social Democratic support, and meanwhile the ban on strikes was defeated in *Riksdag* by 190 votes to 153. The Carlsson administration resigned, but since no other party leader could or would form a government while there was a socialist majority in parliament, Carlsson returned to office. Feldt, however, withdrew. His statements then and his memoirs published later showed that he felt the opportunity created by his ''Third Way'' had been frittered away in unjustified pay rises and an unwillingness to cut purposefully the public sector.

Carlsson's new administration, with Allan Larsson as Finance Minister, proposed a new crisis package in April 1990, looking to the Liberals for support. Several 1988 election promises were retracted (such as a sixth week statutory holiday) and the government declared that it would reexamine health insurance and reduce the high incidence of absenteeism. Cuts in public expenditure were also promised.

After much soul-searching the government also decided to seek membership in the European Union. As the Swedish economy fell into deeper recession and the balance of payments deficit worsened and—worst of all for a Social Democratic government—unemployment began to rise, Larsson said that devaluation was no longer an option. In May 1990 the *krona* had been linked to the ECU. In his January budget 1991 Larsson emphasized that Sweden must think in terms of international integration. His tax reforms tended to shift the tax burden onto goods and services rather than direct taxation. In a further step away from state control the government introduced a bill deregulating agriculture over a five-year period and allowing hitherto controlled food prices to react to market forces.

In threatening to curtail public spending, trim social benefits, seek EU membership and hold down inflation even if high unemployment ensued, the government was moving increasingly towards the middle ground. It differed with the nonsocialists fundamentally, however, on pensions, for it wanted to permit the ATP fund, a compulsory superannuation scheme, and the controversial WEF (Wage Earner Funds) to acquire shares on the stock market like private insurance companies. Nonsocialist parties saw this as a means of socializing the economy by putting financial power and influence into the hands of collectively-owned institutions.

Previous experience had shown up the non-socialist parties' difficulties in cooperating with each other, and their attempts at coalition in 1976–82 had ended in failure. In October 1990, however, Carl Bildt and Bengt Westerberg, leaders respectively of the Moderate and Liberal Parties, announced their intention of governing in tandem and put forward a joint six-point plan. In April 1991, in the runup to the autumn election, they consolidated this plan in their publication *A New Start for Sweden,* in which they advocated a strong market economy, increased competitive edge, individual ownership, a radical reform of the welfare state by encouraging freedom of choice, and a reduction in taxation, including VAT. All this would prepare Sweden for application for EU membership in 1994. To add to the Social Democrats' discomfort, protest parties were being formed, the Environment (Green) Party in 1981 and the Neo-Democratic Party in 1991.

In the 1991 general elections the combined Social Democrat and Communist percentage of votes fell to 42.6 percent, converting to 156 seats, the Moderate, Liberal, Center and Christian Democratic Parties polled 46.2 percent, 169 seats, the Environmentalists failed to reach the four percent threshold and so lost their parliamentary representation, while the Neo-Democratic Party, new to *Riksdag,* gained 24 seats. Carl Bildt, the Moderate leader, formed a coalition with the Liberals, Centerists and Christian Democrats. The Neo-Democrats were too right-wing to fit into the coalition, but their 24 seats gave them the balance of power. Since their program included the removal of restrictions and drastic rolling back of the public sector, however, Bildt could assume that they would not side with the socialist bloc.

The new coalition government, with Anne Wibble as Finance Minister, had in many respects similar aims as the outgoing government, to increase productivity and exports, to improve the balance of payments and prepare Sweden for EU membership. They were expected to be more zealous in providing incentives in the private sector through taxation, and in reducing the public sector (over 66 percent of the GNP shortly before they took office). They were determined to combat high inflation, a higher priority even than low unemployment. In their first full year of office the economic and labor situation worsened. Interest rates reached 10 percent, the krona was floated and lost 25 percent of its value. The public sector was squeezed and the welfare benefit system trimmed. Low unemployment rates and a generous welfare system, almost sacrosanct in Sweden in the postwar period, were proving too costly. Unemployment had reached 8.5 percent by 1993 and a further 5 percent of the work force were on state-sponsored training schemes. Unemployment benefits were reduced in September of that year from 90 percent to 80 percent of previous earnings for a maximum of 300 days, with a five-day delay before benefits were paid. It could be terminated if "suitable" work was refused. Tax relief on debt interest was removed, and this together with general uncertainty led to a drop in private consumption. By the end of 1993 there were signs of recovery. Exports rose by 2 percent (after a 3 percent fall in the coalition's first year in office); the krona steadied, and the discount rate came down to 5 percent. Early 1994 saw a slight improvement in the unemployment figures.

A three-year term of office is very short for a new government to make its mark, and public opinion figures suggest that Bildt's administration has not retained the level of support enjoyed in 1991. The government believes that a sustained improvement will result from EU membership, but it has also warned that a return to full employment cannot be guaranteed. Nor, it states, are present generous levels of welfare benefits sustainable, and voluntary insurance schemes are being suggested as one potential solution.

The electorate is faced with difficult choices in the coming election. Both major blocs seem to support membership in the EU, but opinion polls indicate that the majority is either opposed to it or quite frankly doesn't know. Similarly, both seem to be warning that the public sector must be slimmed down, that taxation is too high and that the welfare system is too costly. The Neo-Democratic Party has lost some of its credibility, its disillusioned leader Ian Wachmeister has resigned, and its survival is in doubt. The Left (Communists) has disagreed increasingly with the Social Democrats recently, holding rigidly to its views on full employment and drastic wealth distribution, but it has little to say about wealth creation or how Sweden would cope if she declined EU membership. All the main parties accept the need for continued rationalization in industry (and in this the trade unions have always proved cooperative), for investment in training, and in the country's infrastructure. They also respect the views of environmentalists but cannot see how to improve the economy while at the same time promising a definite timetable for the phasing out of nuclear reactors. Whichever parties are returned to power, they will have to struggle hard to preserve Sweden's international trading position and her social welfare system, and they will be dogged by uncertainty at least until the EU membership issue is settled.

THE DICTIONARY

-A-

ÅDALEN An area in Ångermanland, northern Sweden, at the center of the paper-pulp industry. Ådalen is associated with the labor unrest that came to a head there in 1931. Striking industrial workers were incensed when the employers enlisted strike-breakers. During noisy demonstrations, fuelled by communist agitators, the army was brought in and opened fire. Five civilians were killed. The incident was reported emotionally throughout Sweden and helped to bring about the fall of Carl Gustav Ekman's (q.v.) minority Liberal (q.v.) government in the ensuing election in 1932. The Social Democratic Party (q.v.) then gained power and continued to form the government for the next 40 years.

ADLERCREUTZ, CARL JOHAN (1757–1815) Swedish aristocrat and military general active in Finland (q.v.) during the Finno-Russian war of 1808–09. In March 1809, fearful that Russia would invade the whole of Sweden and aware of King Gustav IV Adolf's (q.v.) ineffectiveness, he sided with the revolutionaries, and helped to arrest the King and bring about the coup d'état that led ultimately to a new Constitution and the founding of the Bernadotte (q.v.) dynasty.

ADLERSPARRE, GEORG (1760–1835) Swedish aristocrat and military general. During the 1809 coup d'état, he moved his army from the Norwegian border to Stockholm (q.v.) to assist Adlercreutz (q.v.) and the revolutionary forces in deposing King Gustav IV Adolf (q.v.).

ADOLF FREDRIK (1710–1771) Swedish King, first King of the House of Holstein-Gottorp and descendent of Karl XI (q.v.).

After defeating Sweden in 1743, Empress Elizabeth of Russia imposed the condition that her favorite, Adolf Fredrik, be adopted as successor-designate to Fredrik I (q.v.), whom he succeeded in 1751. His reign coincided with the Age of Liberty (1718–72) when the Crown enjoyed little political power. He was dominated by his much more forceful wife Lovisa Ulrika (q.v.), sister of Frederick the Great of Prussia, but was personally uninterested in politics and played an insignificant role in the country's affairs. He was succeeded in 1771 by his much more charismatic son Gustav III (q.v.).

AFTONBLADET see NEWSPAPERS

AGRARIAN PARTY see CENTER PARTY

ÅLAND ISLANDS (Finnish AHVENANMAA). Now politically part of Finland (q.v.), this region, consisting of 6,554 islands, lies on the border of the Baltic and the Gulf of Bothnia almost exactly halfway between Sweden and Finland. There are some 22,000 inhabitants, over 96 percent of whom are Swedish speaking. As long as Finland was in union with Sweden, Åland's position was not in doubt, but at the end of the Swedish-Russian war of 1808–09 Sweden had to accept terms dictated by Tsar Alexander I, and in the Treaty of Fredrikshamn (1809) she lost one third of her territory, including all of Finland and the Åland islands.

Russia had two outlets to the west, the Baltic Sea and the Gulf of Finland. With a threat of war between Russia and Britain and France, Russian troops began to fortify Åland in 1833. As a prelude to the Crimean War, a French-British fleet entered the Baltic in 1854, and French troops landed on Åland and destroyed garrisons there. Hoping to involve Sweden in a war against Russia, the allies invited Oscar I (q.v.) to take over the Åland islands, but he declined unless given a guarantee that Finland would be restored to Sweden, a condition ignored by the allies. Ultimately, all Sweden got out of the affair was a guarantee that Russia would be prevented from regarrisoning Åland.

At the outbreak of the Russian Revolution in November 1917, Finland declared her independence from Russia, but by

January 1918 civil war had broken out between the White and the Red Finnish armies. The Åland islanders had expressed their wish, in August 1917, to be reunited with Sweden, but Russian troops invaded Åland in 1918. At the height of the Finnish civil war, Sweden sent two warships to evacuate any Ålanders wishing to leave. A Swedish garrison took over from the Russians until relieved by German troops aiding the Finnish White army. They left at the end of 1918, and in 1919 the islanders held a referendum in which 95 percent voted for reunion with Sweden. The Finnish government was opposed to this and in 1920 arrested two leading Åland islanders and installed a Finnish garrison on the islands. The language question played a part here. Swedish-speaking Åland was a necessary part of the Swedish-speaking Finns' shield against the Finlandization program being pursued with vigor in some quarters. Sweden referred the Åland question to the League of Nations and both Finland and Sweden agreed to accept the League's ruling. A three-man commission appointed by the League recommended in 1921 that the Åland islands should remain Finnish but that the Swedish language should be safeguarded and that the islanders should be given a measure of autonomy and guaranteed neutrality.

When Soviet Russia attacked Finland at the outset of the Winter War in 1939, the Finns set up military installations on Åland, but at the Moscow Peace talks the following year Russia insisted that they be dismantled. Finnish troops took up position on Åland again when the Continuation War started in 1941, but with the cease-fire in 1944 all fortifications were destroyed. In 1945 the islanders again requested reunion with Sweden, but Sweden declined. The Finnish parliament passed a new Åland law in 1961, approved by the Åland council, granting the islands virtual autonomy. Åland sends a representative to the Finnish parliament in Helsinki but runs its own internal affairs, has its own flag and issues its own postage stamps. The region's economy rests on shipping, agriculture and fishing, but increasingly on tourism. There are civil and commercial air links with Stockholm and Åbo (Turku) and frequent car ferry services from Sweden and Finland.

Despite despair and indignation at attitudes towards them in the past, the Åland islanders on the whole now consider that they have achieved the most a small territory could have hoped for.

ALLMÄN TILLÄGSPENSION (ATP, GENERAL SUPPLE-MENTARY PENSION) Most white collar and professional workers subscribed to private superannuation schemes to supplement the basic flat rate state pension established in 1947. In the early 1950s, the Social Democratic Party (q.v.) decided to introduce a national compulsory supplementary scheme with central pension funds administered by the state. This caused the dissolution of the Social Democratic-Agrarian coalition, for the Agrarians (q.v.) objected to the compulsory element in the proposal. The other non-socialist parties were afraid of the economic power a central fund would put into government hands. A national referendum on the issue held in 1957 was indecisive, giving the Social Democrats' scheme only 46 percent of the votes. The Second Chamber of *Riksdag* (q.v.) was dissolved, and after the ensuing election the Chamber was exactly balanced between the socialist and non-socialist parties. When Prime Minister Tage Erlander (q.v.) proposed his slightly amended pension scheme, one Liberal (q.v.) member defected and the proposal was accepted. ATP guarantees retiring employees up to 60 percent of their average income during their highest paid 15 years of employment.

ALMQUIST, CARL JONAS LOVE (1793–1866) Swedish author, journalist, polemicist and teacher. After graduating from Uppsala University in 1815 Almquist worked for seven years as a civil servant in the Ministry of Education and Church Affairs. In 1824 he married a peasant girl and moved to Värmland with like-minded friends to live the life of the ideal farmer. By 1825 he had returned to Stockholm (q.v.). Genuinely interested in education (q.v.), he taught at a new experimental secondary school in Stockholm and from 1829 was its headmaster. He wrote a number of textbooks while there, including a book on Swedish orthography in 1832, which had run to its fourth edition in 1854.

A prolific author of novels, plays, poems, essays and articles, Almquist wrote for most of his adult life, but dating his works is sometimes difficult, since their publication—mostly in volumes of collected works with the general title *Törnrosens bok* (The Book of the Wild Rose 1833–51)—was often much later than their completion. In the 1820s and early 1830s, Almquist's works were romantic, frequently with a tendency to the exotic. *Amorina* (1822) and *Drottningens juvelsmuycke* (The Queen's Diadem, 1832) mark the high point of his achievement in this period, and modern adaptations of them for the theater, opera and television have increased their popularity and underlined Almquist's strange but undoubted genius.

Almquist was anything but indifferent to the society in which he lived, however, and another aspect of his writing became more prevalent from 1838, the year in which he published his essay *Svenska fattigdomens betydelse* (The Significance of Swedish Poverty), a lively characterization of ordinary Swedish people and their temperament. There was a restlessness and unpredicability about Almquist which was very marked at this period. He became ordained so that he would be qualified for clerical posts, and he applied (unsuccessfully) for a Chair in Languages and Aesthetics at Lund University. Then in 1839 he began to contribute regularly to the new liberal paper *Aftonbladet* (q.v.), putting forward in a series of articles his program for the reform of society. That year he published *Det går an* (translated as *Sara Videbeck*), a lively, realistic novel dealing with an attractive, very capable young woman who has witnessed her mother's degradation in an unhappy marriage with a drunkard and is determined not to be caught in a similar trap. She agrees to live with her suitor Albert, but only on condition that they remain unmarried and retain full independence. The book profoundly shocked society and gave rise to a nationwide debate on the position of women (q.v.) in society and the sanctity of marriage.

By 1841 Almquist was forced to resign his teaching post and found other openings barred to him. He had to defend a charge of heresy, now had no hope of a church appointment and had to support himself and his family by his pen. He continued to write for *Aftonbladet* and joined its regular staff in 1846, while also contributing to other papers, including the radical *Jönköpingsbladet*. He grew ill and exhausted and became involved in dubious transactions, which came to a head in 1851. He was accused of embezzlement and the attempted murder by arsenic poisoning of a money lender, von Scheven, a case which has never been satisfactorily solved. He fled to America, travelled widely and in Philadelphia married bigamously the owner of a boarding house. In 1865 he returned to Europe as "Professor Carl Westermann" and died in Bremen, Germany, in 1866.

At the height of his career this enigmatic man produced some of the best literature (q.v.) in the Swedish language. He was also the most influential, if also controversial, polemical Swedish writer of his day, and he did much to advance Swedish liberal and feminist causes in the mid-19th century.

ALSTRÖMER, JONAS (1685–1761) Swedish manufacturer and farmer who epitomized the Age of Liberty's attitude to the economy. Having spent several years in England and Holland, Alströmer returned to Sweden in 1724 and founded a textile factory in his native Alingsås northeast of Gothenburg (q.v.), turning the government's mercantilistic approach to his advantage by obtaining large state subsidies. It was an ambitious scheme, employing English techniques, machinery smuggled out of Holland, and both Swedish and foreign labor, and the business became an important textile center. A government change of policy in the 1760s led to a withdrawal of subsidies, and the enterprise was not robust enough to survive. Alströmer was also enthusiastic about agricultural developments and was the first in Sweden to grow potatoes as a source of food on his farm, Nolhaga. He also improved Swedish sheep breeding by importing sheep for quality wool for his factory. He was ennobled in 1751.

ANCKARSTRÖM, JOHAN JACOB (1762–1792) Swedish officer and regicide. Gustav III's (q.v.) Act of Union and Security of 1789 reduced the Swedish aristocrats' privileges and gave the monarch almost absolute power. A group of disaffected aristocrats led by old General Pechlin branded

Gustav a tyrant and conspired against him. Anckarström, who had been accused of defaming the King's name in 1790 but had his case suspended through lack of evidence, bore Gustav a grudge. He was hired by the conspirators to assassinate the King. At a masked ball at the Royal Opera House in Stockholm (q.v.) on 16 March 1792, he shot Gustav, who died two weeks later. After the shot the doors were locked and the names of everyone present were recorded. When the police found Anckarström's discarded pistols on the premises the following day they arrested and charged him. Despite Gustav's deathbed request for clemency for his killer, Anckarström was publicly flogged for three days and then executed. The family changed its name to Löwenström in 1792.

ANJALA CONSPIRACY (1788) When Gustav III (q.v.) declared war on Russia in 1788, there was opposition within the officer corps on the grounds that it was unconstitutional. Major J.A. Jägerhorn, a Finland-Swedish officer, represented a group that wanted Finnish independence from Sweden. On his initiative, seven officers sent the so-called Liikala Note to Catherine II of Russia in August 1788, deploring the war and proposing negotiations between the Empress and "the nation's representatives." Meanwhile when Gustav demanded an oath of loyalty from his Finland-Swedish officers, 112 of them formed the Anjala League, signing a declaration on the illegality of the war, the necessity of peace negotiations and the recall of *Riksdag* (q.v.). Gustav's own brother Duke Karl (q.v.) was apparently implicated, although he escaped recriminations afterwards.

For Empress Catherine the salient point was the separation of Finland from Sweden, a thought alien to the majority of the Anjala signatories. Gustav's Russian campaign was going badly, but the Danes, ironically, helped him at this point by threatening to occupy Sweden via Norway. Gustav skillfully played upon the Swedes' hatred of the Danes and resentment of the nobility and officer class, and his people rallied behind him. Wishing to halt Russian expansion in the Baltic, Britain exerted pressure on Denmark to accept a ceasefire. At the beginning of 1789 the leaders of the Anjala

League were arrested (except for Jägerhorn who had gone over to Russia). They were treated leniently, but Colonel J.H. Hästesko was made the scapegoat and was executed in 1790.

ARBETARNAS BILDNINGSFÖRBUND (ABF, WORKERS' EDUCATION ASSOCIATION) Founded in 1912 on the initiative of Rickard Sandler (q.v.), ABF's aim was "by means of free voluntary educational activity independent of political party and religion, to educate its members for the Labor Movement and society, and to make cultural values available to all citizens." ABF is an association of political, cultural, trade union (q.v.) and cooperative (q.v.) organizations. Heavily subsidized by the state, it arranges lectures and study circles throughout Sweden. It publishes a series of educational pamphlets and a periodical *Fönstret* (The Window). It was particularly influential in the 1920s and 1930s, when formal education (q.v.) for most working class children ended at the age of 13 or 14.

ATP see ALLMÄN TILLÄGGSPENSION

-B-

BAGGE, GÖSTA (1882–1951) Swedish Conservative politician and Professor of National Economy. He was a member of *Riksdag* (q.v.) from 1932 until 1947 and leader of the Conservative Party (q.v.) from 1935 to 1947. At the outbreak of World War II (q.v.) Bagge pressed successfully for a four-party national government rather than a two-party coalition and served as Minister of Education in Per Albin Hansson's (q.v.) government from 1939 until 1944. He was more enthusiastic than most of his cabinet colleagues about assisting Finland (q.v.) in the Winter War, and he voted to allow German troops (the Engelbrekt Division) to pass though Swedish territory to support the Finns against Russia in the Continuation War. A highly respected academic, he founded the Institute of Social Policy in Stockholm (q.v.) in 1920.

BANÉR, JOHAN (1596–1641) Swedish general during the Thirty Years' War (q.v.). During his short but brilliant military career, King Gustav II Adolf (q.v.) had carefully trained a number of talented young officers, including Banér and Lennart Torstensson. In the attempt to secure Sweden's position in Germany after Gustav Adolf's death in 1632, Banér won a battle at Wittstock in 1636 and at Chemnitz in 1639. He was Governor General of Swedish Pomerania and from 1638 was also Commander of Swedish troops in Germany. He died in Germany and was succeeded by Torstensson. Banér's statue stands in Riddarholm Church in Stockholm (q.v.).

BERGMAN, INGMAR see CINEMA

BERNADOTTE, COUNT FOLKE (1895–1948) Oscar II's (q.v.) grandson and Gustav V's (q.v.) nephew. Count Bernadotte dedicated his life to humanitarian causes. In the last phase of World War II (q.v.), Sweden, as a neutral country, made great efforts to save Scandinavians and others imprisoned in Germany. Bernadotte was able to establish some kind of rapport with Heinrich Himmler, the SS leader, and through the Swedish Red Cross, whose delegate he was, Bernadotte succeeded in saving some 30,000 people, including 19,000 Scandinavians, from concentration camps. He also played an active part in arranging the peaceful withdrawal of German occupation forces from Norway in 1945. In 1948 Bernadotte was asked by the United Nations to mediate in Palestine, and he produced a partition plan, but he was murdered in Jerusalem that year by Jewish terrorists.

BERNADOTTE DYNASTY see KARL XIV JOHAN

BILDT, CARL (1949–) Swedish politician, leader of the Moderate Party (q.v.) and Prime Minister. Carl Bildt's family background is political. His father is a senior civil servant, and his great-great-grandfather, Gillis Bildt, was Prime Minister for one year in 1888–89. After studying politics at Stockholm University (1968–73), he served as Chairman of the Moderate Party's Students' Union (1973–74) and of the European Democrat Students (1974–76), then became an adviser to the Department of Economics (1976–78) and Under-Secretary of State (1979–81). He has been a member of *Riksdag* (q.v.) since 1979, and became leader of the Moderate Party in 1986. Learning from the difficulties experienced by previous non-socialist parties trying to cooperate with each other, Bildt and Bengt Westerberg (q.v.), leader of the Liberal Party (q.v.), declared their intention in 1990 of governing in tandem and put forward a joint six-point plan. They consolidated this plan in their publication *A New Start for Sweden,* which appeared in April 1991. In the elections in September of that year the socialist parties lost their majority and a four-party non-socialist government was established under Bildt's premiership. A fairly young politician, Bildt has tried energetically to move Sweden towards a strong market economy. In 1994 he negotiated successfully Sweden's application for membership of the European Union (q.v.). It is uncertain, however, whether he has persuaded the electorate to accept his views on the EU. In addition, rising unemployment since he came to office has caused some loss of support for his party, and opinion polls suggest that he may suffer defeat in the autumn elections in 1994. See also CONSERVATIVE (MODERATE) PARTY.

BIRKA A Swedish Viking (q.v.) town on Björkö in Lake Mälaren. Birka was Sweden's first important commercial trading center and had links with the whole of Scandinavia, Western Europe (many Frisian merchants visited and perhaps settled there) and Russia. Via the Baltic and Russian routes, its trading links reached the Byzantine Empire and the Arab world. Ansgar, the Christian missionary, visited it twice in the 9th century. Birka was active from c. A.D. 800 to 975, after which it declined and disappeared. The Baltic island of Gotland assumed the Baltic trade, the new settlement at Sigtuna (q.v.) dealt with Scandinavian goods, and Hedeby at the south of the Jutland peninsula dealt with northern Europe.

A large area of archeological remains, some 3,000 grave mounds, the vallum, harbor and fortification have been uncovered, and in 1990 Sweden's largest official archeological dig was started on Björkö. A team of 15 experts hope to reveal the full extent of the Viking town and its harbor.

BOHMAN, GÖSTA (1911–) Swedish Conservative (q.v.) politician. A law graduate, Bohman worked at the Stockholm Chamber of Commerce, becoming its Deputy Managing Director in 1948. In 1958 he entered *Riksdag* (q.v.) as a Conservative member. In 1971 he took over the Chairmanship of the Moderate (formerly Conservative) Party when it had been experiencing a poor showing in the polls and difficulty in finding a rallying leader. He succeeded in restoring the party's fortunes, clearly evident by the 1979 elections when it emerged as the largest non-socialist party. He was Finance Minister in 1976–78 in Thorbjörn Fälldin's (q.v.) first coalition government. He took up the same post again in 1979 but resigned in 1981 when the Moderates left the coalition. He also resigned his Chairmanship of the party but remained a group leader of Moderate members of *Riksdag*. A respected politician, Bohman increased substantially the influence of the Moderate Party at national level.

BOSTRÖM, ERIK GUSTAF (1842–1907) Swedish politician and estate owner who was a member of *Riksdag* (q.v.) from 1876 until 1907 and Prime Minister from 1891–1900 and 1902–1905. Boström's policies are closely linked with Protectionism, defense and suffrage. Sweden had enjoyed free trade since the 1860s, but by the 1880s competition from industrialized countries (e.g., Britain) and cheap grain-producing areas (e.g., America and Russia) led to the rise of a protectionist faction led by Boström, and the imposition of import duties. Boström met opposition in his efforts to strengthen Swedish defense but persuaded *Riksdag* to accept a defense reform in 1892, which led eventually to the abolition of the old *indelning* system. He was convinced by his last years as Prime Minister that the franchise must be extended and proposed in 1904 and 1905 an electoral reform which would have given the vote to all males over 25, but his proposals were linked to proportional representation and on those grounds voted down by the Liberals (q.v.) and the

Social Democrats (q.v.). Boström was also unsuccessful in saving the Norway-Sweden Union (q.v.). The Norwegians rejected his proposals in 1904, maintaining that he was treating Norway as a dependency, not an equal. The Union was dissolved the following year. An able parliamentarian, Boström often softened the more extreme elements in his government and initiated policies (defense, universal suffrage) that came to fruition after his death.

BRANTING, HJALMAR (1860–1925) Swedish politician, statesman, leader of the Social Democratic Party (q.v.) and three times Prime Minister. Branting's father was a school principal with professorial status. Branting studied science at Uppsala (q.v.) University from 1877–82 and while there associated with radical students who admired Karl Staaff (q.v.), the gifted lawyer who became Liberal leader. Branting became interested in social policy and economics, studied the social theories of Marx, and at this early stage of his career held Marxist views on the class struggle.

The 1880s and 1890s saw the birth of Swedish socialism, and Branting played a principal part in shaping it. In 1881 August Palm (q.v.), a Swedish tailor, had returned home from Germany via Denmark and begun to agitate for trade unions affiliated to the socialist movement. A Swedish Association was formed in Stockholm (q.v.) by 1884, and the following year *Social-Demokraten,* a socialist newspaper (q.v.), was founded. On leaving Uppsala, Branting worked for a few months at the Observatory in Stockholm but then turned to journalism. In 1886 he joined the editorial board of *Social-Demokraten,* founded by August Palm and Axel Danielsson, and from 1887 until 1917, with a few brief intervals, he was its chief editor. As such he bore responsibility for its contents and in 1889 was sentenced to three and a half months' imprisonment for an article written by Danielsson, a more committed Marxist than Branting. In 1889 Branting helped to form the Swedish Social Democratic Labor Party. Its program, formulated in 1897 mainly by Branting and Danielsson, was clearly inspired by the German Social Democrats' 1891 Erfurt program, but already in a modified form. Branting obviously believed that universal suffrage could be achieved by peaceful means, and that social reforms could be brought about by working within the legal system.

Branting's parliamentary career began in 1896 when he was elected to *Riksdag* (q.v.), the first Social Democrat to do so. Membership of his party was rising steadily. Landsorganisationen (LO, Confederation of Trade Unions) (q.v.) had been formed in 1898 and by 1901 all its members were affiliated to the party, but very few had a parliamentary vote. Universal suffrage was a vital part of Staaff's program and Branting supported him in *Riksdag*. As voting restrictions gradually eased Branting was joined in *Riksdag* by other Social Democrats. When Nils Edén (q.v.), Staaff's successor, became Prime Minister in 1917, Branting was appointed his Minister of Finance, and three other Social Democrats were also included in the government. Some of his Marxist colleagues, including Z. Höglund and F. Ström, who wanted to employ revolutionary means to effect change, considered this too revisionist and formed a left-wing splinter group, but thanks to Branting's standing in the party they remained a small minority. Turbulance after the Russian Revolution persuaded many Conservatives that universal suffrage would be the best means of preventing a Swedish revolution, and by 1921 all adults over the age of 23 were given the right to vote.

The Liberals had a good record on reform and until 1919 found little difficulty in working together with the Social Democrats. When in 1920 the latter drew up a program of far-reaching reforms, however, including unemployment benefits, higher taxes and some nationalization, Edén resigned and Branting became Sweden's first Social Democratic Prime Minister. His minority government lasted only a few months, but during that short time it set up commissions on the referendum, industrial democracy and socialization of natural resources, the findings of which were of great future value. In the first election based on the new electoral system, the Social Democrats emerged as the largest party, and in 1921 Branting formed his second ministry. He had no overall majority in a period punctuated by recession, labor disputes and unemployment. He survived until 1923 but was defeated when he tried to alter directives of the Commission on

Unemployment. The ensuing Conservative government lasted until October 1924, but then it was defeated on a defense issue, and Branting formed his third ministry. He was by this time an ailing man and had to resign in January 1925, and was succeeded by Rickard Sandler (q.v.). He died a month later. Young members of his last cabinet, including Per Albin Hansson (q.v.) and Ernst Wigforss (q.v.), built on the foundations he had laid to create the social welfare state (q.v.).

During his last years Branting was greatly interested in foreign affairs. A pacifist at heart, he took a leading role in the Peace Movement and attended the international conferences at Copenhagen in 1916, Stockholm in 1917 and Bern in 1919. Although his sympathies were with the Allies in World War I (q.v.), he criticized the Treaty of Versailles, maintaining that over-harsh treatment of Germany would be counter-productive. He had faith in the League of Nations and played an important part in negotiations. In 1921 he shared the Nobel Peace Prize (q.v) with the Norwegian Christian Lange.

BRATT, IVAN (1878–1956) Medical doctor, businessman, Liberal (q.v.) member of *Riksdag* (q.v.), Director of AB Stockholmssystemet and AB Vin- och Spritcentralen. Bratt took an active interest in social and medical issues and became prominent in the campaign against alcohol abuse. He maintained that private and commercial financial interests should be divorced from the alcohol trade and gave his name to a system, the Bratt system, to that end. There had been mounting pressure since before World War I for total prohibition on alcohol in Sweden, but the Bratt system, which was introduced first in Stockholm (q.v.) in 1914 and three years later was extended to the whole country, severely restricted the sale and consumption of alcohol instead. All alcohol sales were channelled through the state monopoly AB Vin- och Spritcentralen, which in 1917 introduced the alcohol ration book *(motbok)*. Catering companies were also added to the state monopoly. Results of a referendum on prohibition held in 1922 were inconclusive, and the Bratt system remained until 1955, when the *motbok* was abolished and restrictions on serving alcohol in public were reduced. The state monopoly remains, however, a retail outlet that actively discourages its customers from purchasing its wares. See also TEMPERANCE MOVEMENT.

BREMER, FREDRIKA (1801–1865) Swedish feminist writer. F. Bremer was born on an estate near Åbo in Finland, but when she was only three the family moved to the Stockholm (q.v.) area. An emotional, impressionable child, she suffered under a strict conventional upbringing with a tyrannical father and formal relations between parents and children. She began her literary career with *Teckningar utur hvardagslifvet* (Scenes from Everyday Life, 1828) which she published to raise money for charity. It aroused great interest and brought her almost instant recognition. One of the stories, *Familjen H* (The H. Family), is credited with being Sweden's first realistic novel. F. Bremer's own upper-class background provided the setting and the characters in her stories, which are all about the home life of educated people. In 1834 she produced *Presidentens döttrar* (Daughters of the President). Then followed *Nina* (1835), *Grannarne* (The Neighbors, 1837) and *Hemmet* (The Home, 1839). By this time she was known internationally through translations of her work.

Always interested in people, social conditions and politics, she embarked in 1849 on a journey alone to the United States. For two years she travelled widely in America, meeting leading cultural figures of the day and seeing conditions for herself. She wanted, as she said, to see things ''from within.'' She was disappointed in some aspects of American society, deploring slavery in the South, but she was suitably impressed by America's youthful vigor, and above all she approved of the many educational opportunities it offered and of institutions of higher learning open to women (q.v.). She recorded her impressions in *Hemmen i den nya verlden* (Homes in the New World, 1853–54).

In 1856 F. Bremer published the novel *Hertha,* which constitutes an attack on the male-dominated society that Sweden then was. She criticized the lack of provision for women's education (q.v.) and training. There are strong autobiographical traits in the portrayal of a domineering father who denies his daughter her independence and thwarts her development. Women's subordinate position in society and the plight of unmarried women in middle or upper-class homes are underlined. From a purely literary point of view the novel is too tendentious to be wholly successful, but sociologically it had the desired effect, for it inspired widespread debate on women's rights, and two years later, in 1858, unmarried women legally attained their majority at the age of 25.

An inveterate traveller, F. Bremer visited Switzerland, Belgium, France, Italy, Palestine, Turkey and Greece, a journey described in *Lifvet i gamla verlden* (Life in the Old World, 1860–62). On her return to Stockholm she devoted herself to women's education and welfare and other social causes. A prolific writer with a strong, independent and persevering character, she was an important pioneer not only in literature (q.v.) but in the Swedish feminist movement. Her disciple, the aristocratic Sophie Adlersparre, founded the Fredrika Bremer Society (q.v.) in her honor.

-C-

CAP PARTY (MÖSSPARTIET) see HAT PARTY

CARL XVI GUSTAV (1946–) King of Sweden and son of Prince Gustav Adolf and Princess Sibylla of Saxe-Coburg-Gotha. His father was killed in an air crash in 1947, so Carl Gustav succeeded his grandfather Gustav VI Adolf (q.v.) in 1973. The new Constitution, although not officially in place until 1975, was acted upon and he became a "democratic monarch." As such he is Head of State but not Commander of the Armed Forces, does not preside over Cabinet meetings or appoint the Prime Minister. His specially-tailored courses at Sigtuna (q.v.), and Uppsala and Stockholm universities, plus extensive travel throughout Sweden, have given him an insight into the government and the fabric of Swedish society. He is a keen sportsman, yachtsman and skier and is interested in nature conservation and the environment, all of which brings him close to his subjects. In 1976 he married

Silvia Renate Sommarlath, daughter of a German business-man. The young couple quickly became popular, quelling fears of a republic after the death of the greatly respected Gustav VI Adolf. They have three children, Victoria (b. 1977), Carl Philip (b. 1979) and Madeleine (b. 1982). Under the new Act of Succession of 1980 Crown Princess Victoria is heir to the throne.

CARLSSON, INGVAR (1934–) Swedish Social Democratic politician. From a working-class background, Carlsson graduated in politics at Lund University in 1958. He was a secretary in the Prime Minister's office (1958–1960) and has been a member of *Riksdag* (q.v.) since 1965. He was a member of the government from 1969 to 1976 and from 1982 to 1991, and was Minister of Education and of Housing before becoming Olof Palme's (q.v.) deputy in 1982. Carlsson took over the leadership of the Social Democratic Party (q.v.) and the premiership in 1986 after Palme's assassination. He led his party to victory in the polls in 1988, although with a reduced majority, but was soon under pressure. By 1990 rising inflation, adverse balance of payments and substantial pay rises were seriously threatening the economy. Carlsson proposed a crisis package, including a pay freeze and a ban on strikes, but it was rejected by *Riksdag,* and Carlsson resigned. No other party leader would form a government, however, and Carlsson returned to office. He proposed new measures to curb spending in the public sector, which proved unpopular with the trade unionists (q.v.). Despite his efforts the recession deepened and unemployment rose, and in the 1991 elections the socialist parties lost their majority and Carlsson resigned as Prime Minister. He was succeeded by Carl Bildt (q.v.), the Moderate (q.v.) leader, who formed a four-party coalition government. Carlsson remains leader of the Social Democrats and became leader of the Opposition in *Riksdag* in 1991.

CELSIUS, ANDERS (1701–1744) Swedish astronomer. Celsius was born in Uppsala (q.v.) of an academic family, his father and both grandfathers having held Chairs at Uppsala University. In 1730 he followed in their footsteps and became

Professor of Astronomy there. This was a remarkable period in the history of Swedish science, which saw the rise of such men as Linnaeus (q.v.) and Swedenborg (q.v.) and the founding, in 1739, of the Swedish Royal Academy of Science (q.v.). Celsius made a study of the earth's magnetism and the aurora borealis. In 1740 he became the first director of the observatory at Uppsala that had been built in his honor. Two years later he developed the centigrade ("Celsius") thermometer now in universal use.

CENTER PARTY (CENTERPARTIET) In 1913 the Farmers' Union (Bondeförbundet) was formed to protect the agrarians' political, social and economic interests. In 1921 it united with the Agrarians' National Union (Jordbrukarnas riksförbund). It changed its name in 1957 to the Farmers' Union Center Party (Centerpartiet Bondeförbundet), abbreviated the following year to Center Party (Centerpartiet). Representing a specific section of the community, it had a small but constant following, but its political influence increased from the 1930s, when no one party was assured of an overall majority in *Riksdag* (q.v.). In 1933 when Per Albin Hansson's (q.v.) new social welfare proposals seemed doomed to be outvoted, the Agrarian Axel Pehrsson-Bramstorp (q.v.) did a deal with Hansson, which guaranteed the farmers' interests while securing Hansson's support. After the 1936 election Pehrsson-Bramstorp accepted Hansson's invitation to join a Social Democratic-Agrarian coalition which lasted until World War II. In the war years the Agrarians were part of the national coalition government.

In the postwar years the party continued to guard predominantly farmers' interests. However, under Gunnar Hedlund (q.v.), party leader from 1949 to 1971, it began to gain urban support too, and described itself as a social-liberal party. In practice it tended more towards the Social Democrats (q.v.) than the Liberals (q.v.) in the 1950s, entering a coalition with the Social Democrats in 1951 when the latter had lost their overall majority. By 1957 the coalition was causing both parties unease, and the Social Democrats' ATP (q.v.) compulsory pension scheme killed it off. The Agrarian, or rather, Center Party, sought to stop the move from the country to the expanding towns, which was leading to large deprived sparsely populated areas, and to prevent the exploitation of the environment.

With the increase of nuclear energy (q.v.) their environment policy was thrust into prominence. Thorbjörn Fälldin (q.v.), leader of the party since 1971, made the dismantling of nuclear power stations a key issue and in the 1976 elections the Center Party emerged as the largest non-socialist party. Fälldin formed a non-socialist coalition government but by 1978 he resigned, finding it impossible to phase out nuclear energy as quickly as intended. He returned to office after the 1979 elections, promising a referendum on the nuclear question, and remained head of a coalition, but his party's popularity decreased and in 1982 the Social Democrats were returned to power. In 1985 Fälldin resigned as party leader and was succeeded by Karin Söder (q.v.) and then in 1986 by Olof Johansson (q.v.). Although not regaining the position enjoyed in the mid-1970s the Center Party was able to join a non-socialist coalition in 1991 under the premiership of Carl Bildt (q.v.), leader of the Conservatives.

Of the non-socialist parties the Centerists are closest to the Social Democrats, forming together with the Liberals the middle ground between socialism and a market economy and free enterprise. See also POLITICAL PARTIES.

CHRISTIAN DEMOCRATIC ALLIANCE (KRISTEN DE-MOKRATISK SAMLING, KDS) Three new political parties won seats in *Riksdag* (q.v.) for the first time in the 1980s and 1990s, one of which was the KDS. It was founded in 1964 on the initiative of Lewi Pethrus, a Free-Church clergyman. It considered itself neither socialist nor non-socialist but aimed at dealing with social issues in a Christian spirit. In 1985 the party gained a seat in *Riksdag* for the first time. It increased its support, and after the 1991 elections the KDS leader Alf Svensson was offered a cabinet post in Carl Bildt's (q.v.) four-party non-socialist coalition. See also POLITICAL PARTIES

CINEMA IN SWEDEN With beautiful scenery, good lighting and a population appreciative of the visual arts the Swedish film industry got off to a good start. The largest film company, Svensk Filmindustri (Swedish Film Industry), began making films in 1907 and enjoyed a golden period during the silent movie era, with Victor Sjöström (1879–1960) and Mauritz Stiller (1883–1928) the best directors. Sjöström won acclaim for his film *Ingeborg Holm* (1913) which made a realistic statement on poor social conditions, and between 1916 and 1921 he produced a number of masterpieces, notably *Terje Vigen* (1916), based on a narrative work by Henrik Ibsen, and *Ingmarssönerna* (The Ingmarssons, 1918) and *Körkarlen* (The Phantom Carriage, 1920), both based on stories by Selma Lagerlöf. Stiller also filmed Lagerlöf works, including *Herr Arnes penningar* (Sir Arne's Hoard, 1919), *Gunnar Hedes Saga* (1922) and *Gösta Berlings Saga* (1924). In the latter he launched Greta Gustavsson, soon to become famous as Greta Garbo.

The Swedish Film Industry's international reputation suffered with the advance of sound pictures, Stiller and Sjöström were lured to Hollywood, and the company fell back on a series of comedies for home consumption. *Hets* (Frenzy, 1944), directed by Alf Sjöberg (1903–1980) with a script by Ingmar Bergman (1918–) marked the rise of quality films in Sweden again. It was followed by Sjöberg's *Fröken Julie* (Miss Julie, 1951), based on Strindberg's (q.v.) play, and a series of films by Bergman. The latter's *Det sjunde inseglet* (The Seventh Seal, 1956) and *Smultronstället* (Wild Strawberries, 1957) quickly gained international recognition, and Bergman went on to produce such classics as *Såsom i en spegel* (Through a Glass Darkly, 1961), *Höstsonaten* (Autumn Sonata, 1978) and *Fanny och Alexander* (1983). He assembled a group of Swedish actors who became internationally famous—Max von Sydow (1929–), Bibi Andersson (1935–), Harriet Andersson (1932–), Ingrid Thulin (1929–), etc. and lured back to Sweden Sjöström and Ingrid Bergman, the leading actress in *Autumn Sonata*.

Bergman's metaphysical searching was not always popular in Sweden, and with increasing competition from television from the 1950s the Swedish film industry was in financial trouble. It was rescued by the state-supported Swedish Film Institute, founded in 1963 at the instigation of

Harry Schein, with the aim of supporting the making of Swedish feature films, marketing them abroad, arranging film clubs, etc. It distributes financial aid annually and awards prizes for artistic merit. Schein was its Director from 1963 to 1970 and Chairman from 1970 to 1978. Production of Swedish films rose to about 25 per year and young directors were given a chance to prove themselves. The result was a number of internationally successful films, sometimes experimental and often socially critical. Jan Troell (1931–) produced *Här har du ditt liv* (This is Your Life, 1966), a brilliant evocation of Sweden early in this century based on an autobiographical novel by Eyvind Johnson. He subsequently made the equally successful *Utvandrarna* (The Emigrants, 1971) and *Nybyggarna* (The Immigrants, 1972), a dramatization of Vilhelm Moberg's novels about Swedish emigration to America, and *Ingenjör Andréns luftfärd* (The Flight of the Eagle, 1982), based on P.O. Sundman's documentary novel describing Andrén's attempt to reach the North Pole in a balloon. Bo Widerberg (1930–) proved equally successful with *Elvira Madigan* (1967), *Ådalen 31* (1969)—a critical account of the Ådalen incident (q.v.) that brought down a government—*Joe Hill* (1974) and *Ormens väg på hälleberget* (The Serpent's Way, 1987) based on Torgny Lindgren's social and psychological novel. Vilgot Sjöman (1924–) gained artistic approval for his experimental *491* (1963), *Jag är nyfiken-gul* (I am Curious-Yellow, 1967) and *Jag är nyfiken-blå* (I am Curious-Blue, 1968).

Even with state support, new talent was not always forthcoming, and the 1980s were lean years. 1993 showed signs of recovery. Five film consultants were appointed to distribute the Swedish Film Institute's grants, and with the worst period of financial uncertainty over, promising directors are emerging, such as Åke Sandgren, Agneta Fagerström-Olsson, Clas Lindberg and Colin Nutley, an Englishman living in Sweden whose film *Änglagården* (House of Angels, 1992) has already won acclaim.

The majority of films screened in Sweden are of foreign origin, mostly American, a situation likely to persist. A report completed in 1993 for the Swedish Film Institute showed that Sweden has more cinemas per capita than any other European country, and even if it were desirable, domestically-produced films could never meet this demand. Swedish interest in cinematic art is demonstrated in its most concentrated form at the annual Gothenburg Film Festival, which lasts ten days and nights and shows hundreds of films from Scandinavia and all over the world.

COMMUNIST PARTY (SVERIGES KOMMUNISTISKA PARTIET; VÄNSTERPARTIET KOMMUNISTERNA) Although the Social Democratic Party (q.v.) did not have as many factions as the other major parties, Hjalmar Branting (q.v.) did have to cope with left-wing rebels who objected to his lack of revolutionary fervor. In 1917 Hinke Bergegren and other anarchistic members broke away from the party to form the Swedish Social Democratic Left Party (Sveriges socialdemokratiska vänsterparti). By 1921 some of these dissidents returned to the fold, while others formed the Swedish Communist Party (Sveriges kommunistiska parti). In its ideology this new Communist Party identified itself closely with the Soviet Union and wanted Swedish industry and natural resources to be brought under state control by revolutionary means. Its support came mainly from the large industrial towns and among poor farmers in Northern Sweden, but its violence deterred many potential voters. During World War II (q.v.), sympathy for Russia helped to swell party support, and in the first postwar elections the Communists won 15 seats in the Lower Chamber, but during the Cold War support waned.

After 1953 the party began to adopt a more independent attitude to Moscow. In 1967 it changed its name to Left Party Communists (Vänster-partiet kommunisterna, VPK), at which a Maoist group left the party and formed the Marxist-Leninist Communist Union (Kommunistiska Förbundet Marxist-Leninisterna, KFML). Ten years later a few other members left to form the Moscow-faithful Workers' Communist Party (Arbetarpartiet Kommunisterna, APK) Neither they nor KFML won a single seat in Riksdag (q.v.). Lars Werner became leader in 1976 of the main Communist Party, and while still believing in socialism he stressed that this aim would be achieved by democratic, not revolutionary, means.

In 1990 the party changed its name to Left Party (Vänsterpartiet), discarding the "communist" tag altogether. The party's following was still to be found mainly among industrial workers, but Werner, a popular figure, also enjoyed a certain amount of support among intellectuals and in universities. In elections in the 1970s and 1980s they won between 17 and 20 seats in *Riksdag,* rising to 21 in 1991. With neither the Social Democrats (q.v.) nor the non-socialist bloc able to achieve an overall majority this has occasionally given the Communists the deciding vote, but such influence is perhaps more apparent than real, for a party aiming at public ownership and power to the workforce is hardly likely to vote with Conservatives (q.v.) against Social Democrats. See also POLITICAL PARTIES.

CONSERVATIVE (MODERATE) PARTY (MODERATA SAMLINGSPARTIET) After the 1865 Parliamentary Reform, a very conservative body formed a large majority in the Upper Chamber of *Riksdag* (q.v.). These members were critical of Norwegians wanting to break away from the Union (q.v.) with Sweden; they wanted a strong defense; they supported industrialists and landowners; and were against social and political reforms. In the Lower Chamber the conservative Lantmannapartiet (Farmers' Party) had split over the question of tariffs but by the turn of the century had reformed with conservative tendencies intact. Political views were polarizing, the Social Democrats (q.v.) and Liberals (q.v.) had both established a national organization, and in 1904 the various conservative groups united in the Allmänna valmansförbundet (General Voters' Union). The government until Karl Staaff's (q.v.) successful efforts to change things consisted of the King and his Council of Ministers whom the King appointed and dismissed as individuals. Oscar II (q.v.) and Gustav V (q.v.) would turn naturally to conservatives in the first instance when appointing a Prime Minister.

The Liberals and Social Democrats had universal suffrage first on their list of priorities; the Conservatives preferred the status quo but were strong on defense. The two issues became inextricably linked early in the century. General compulsory military service led to the slogan "One man, one gun, one vote,'' which eventually even the Conservatives in the Upper Chamber could not ignore. They agreed to accept a measure of reform provided the other parties accepted proportional representation. This provision was rejected and wrangling over the issue continued during the premierships of the Conservatives Erik Gustaf Boström (q.v.) and then Christian Lundeberg (1905), and the Liberal Karl Staaff (1905–06). Finally the Conservative leader Arvid Lindman (q.v.) (Prime Minister 1906–11) persuaded *Riksdag* to accept a modified proposal for universal male suffrage and proportional representation. In the first ˙election to reflect the changes in 1911, the Liberals emerged as the largest party in the Lower Chamber with 102 seats, and the Conservatives lost heavily and had exactly the same number of seats as the rising Social Democrats, 64 each. Staaff, appointed Prime Minister, had the Upper Chamber dissolved, and the ensuing elections to it reduced its conservative majority. The Conservatives had by now organized themselves under Lindman into a united party, Högern (Right), and the move to party politics as understood today was complete.

Staaff's refusal to increase defense spending in 1914 and his subsequent resignation let in the Conservatives, and Hjalmar Hammarskjöld (q.v.) served as Prime Minister from 1914 to 1917. Their mismanagement of Swedish neutrality (q.v.) and food supplies during the war, plus the rising support for the Social Democrats now that voting rights were being extended, accelerated the decline of the party's authority. In the 1917 elections they won only 57 seats, the Liberals 62 and the Social Democrats 87, and except for two brief periods (1923–24 under Ernst Trygger [q.v] and 1928–30 under Lindman) during the unsettled years of social unrest and high unemployment, they were never again able to form a single party government. In 1938 they changed their name to Högerriksorganisation (National Right Organization), abbreviated officially in 1952 to Högerpartiet (Right Party).

During World War II (q.v.) the Conservatives, led by Gösta Bagge (q.v.), joined a national coalition government under Per Albin Hansson (q.v.), and party politics were in abeyance. In the postwar elections in 1945 the Social Democrats were returned with a majority and the non-socialist parties were in opposition. The Conservatives were critical of the government on many scores, including its neutral stance during the Cold War, its refusal to join NATO and its retention of wartime controls and high taxation. They also objected vociferously to the ATP (q.v) compulsory insurance scheme, which put vast sums into the hands of the state, calling it nationalization by the back door.

In Swedish politics there has been some erosion of clear-cut party lines, reflected for instance in 1969 when the Conservative (Right) Party became Moderata samlingspartiet (Moderate Alliance Party) to discard its reactionary image. All parties now accept equal opportunity and social welfare, the differences being in scope rather than principle. However, the Conservatives continue to support a strong defense force, a market economy (the Wage Earner Funds [q.v.] were anathema to them), lower taxation, a smaller public sector, freedom of the individual, the right to opt out of trade unions (q.v.), and less homogeneity in Sweden's schools.

In 1976 under Gösta Bohman (q.v.) the Conservatives joined a non-socialist coalition government formed by Thorbjörn Fälldin (q.v.), leader of the Center Party (q.v.), but withdrew in 1978 after disagreement on energy and economic policies. After the 1979 elections they tried again but left the coalition in 1981. The Social Democrats exploited the split and won the 1982 elections, retaining power until 1991.

Although in the 1991 elections the Social Democrats remained the largest single party, they fell far short of an overall majority, and it was the Conservatives who emerged as the most influential non-socialist party. Carl Bildt (q.v.), party leader since 1986, became Prime Minister, the first Conservative Prime Minister since 1930, and formed a four-party non-socialist coalition. The difficulties facing Bildt were the same as those Fälldin tried but failed to solve in the 1970s: how to prevent further state intervention while preserving high standards of living and a competitive Swedish industry. Even more fundamental is the problem of forging a workable government out of three or four parties with a common desire to prevent further increase in the public sector and erosion of freedom of the individual, but with divergent policies on the best means of doing so. See also POLITICAL PARTIES.

CONSTITUTION see *RIKSDAG*

COOPERATIVES In the second half of the 19th century many popular movements began to gather momentum in Sweden. Consumer cooperatives became widespread and a powerful factor in Swedish economic life. Influenced by the British socialist Robert Owen and by the first Cooperative Society established in Rochdale, England, in 1844, the first Swedish cooperative society was founded in Stockholm (q.v.) in 1850. Other societies followed suit in Sweden, but progress was slow, the members having small resources and little business experience. In 1899 a General Swedish Cooperative Congress was called by cooperative branches in Sweden's three largest cities, Stockholm, Gothenburg (q.v.) and Malmö (q.v.), and the Cooperative Union (Kooperativa Förbundet or KF) was founded.

By 1908 Swedish private retailers realized this union was potentially formidible and formed a national retailer association. They persuaded cartels of manufacturers of certain commodities, such as margarine, to boycott KF. KF members retaliated by becoming manufacturers themselves. It became an idealistic as well as financial campaign, led by dedicated, gifted KF managers, most notably Axel Gjöres and, from 1924 to 1957, Albin Johansson. Johansson's classic victory was the breaking of a price monopoly on electric light bulbs by having KF start up the LUMA factory outside Stockholm. From the 1920s KF became an important industrial as well as wholesale cooperative and by 1980 had 60 productive units and over 300,000 member families, its own publications *Kooperatören* and *Vi,* correspondence courses and a folk high school. It bought up PUB, a prestigious department store in Stockholm, and set up DOMUS to add to some 150 department stores throughout the country.

The cooperative spirit spread into other fields, including OK union, an oil consumers union, Reso, a travel agency, and FOLKSAM, which KF started in 1905 to insure against fire and which by the 1970s had become the third largest insurance company in Sweden. In 1923 the Tenants' Savings and Building Society (Hyresgästernas Spar- och Byggnadsförening, HSB), was established in Stockholm. It spread rapidly and had branches in 60 towns by 1940. In that year a similar kind of cooperative housing scheme, Riks-byggen (National Building), was founded by KF, Landsor-ganisationen (LO, Swedish National Trade Union Con-federation) (q.v.) and the National Union of Construction Workers. These two cooperatives together are responsible for about two thirds of housing in Sweden.

Other cooperatives that affect the whole nation are farm-ing cooperatives. The first one dates from 1850, but it was the 1880–1940 period that saw the development of farming cooperatives in earnest. By today over 80 percent of all Swedish farmers belong to one. Lantbrukarnas Riksförbund (LRF, Federation of Swedish Farmers) is responsible for negotiations with the government on prices and other agri-cultural matters. KF and LRF work closely together to ensure quality for consumers and fair prices for producers.

The cooperative movement did not eliminate private enterprises, and the zeal prevalent in the first half of this century has declined, but KF and other cooperatives remain a powerful force and have influenced standards directly or indirectly in most segments of the Swedish economy (q.v.).

CULTURE see CINEMA; LIBRARIES; LITERATURE; MU-SIC; RADIO AND TELEVISION; SWEDISH LAN-GUAGE; THEATER; VISUAL ARTS

-D-

DAGENS NYHETER see NEWSPAPERS

DAHLBERGH, ERIK (1625–1703) Swedish count, architect, engineer and field marshal. As a young officer Dahlbergh fought in Karl X Gustav's (q.v.) army during the Polish and

Danish wars. Sweden had expanded her territory during the Age of Greatness, and it was important to consolidate her defenses. Dahlbergh was given several important commissions during the reign of Karl XI (q.v.), including the building of fortifications. Although best known as a military engineer he was also an architect, the extant town hall in Jönköping being an example of his work. Karl XII (q.v.) was only 15 when he came to the throne, and his enemies prepared to regain territory previously lost to Sweden. Dahlbergh was Governor-General of Livonia from 1696 to 1702 and successfully repelled the Polish attack on Riga at the outbreak of the Great Northern War (1700–21). Becoming a European power had aroused Sweden's self-awareness and pride as a nation, and Dahlbergh, a man of many parts, was commissioned in the 1660s to prepare and edit a collection of illustrations showing Swedish cities and castles. The result was the handsome *Suecia antiqua et hodierna,* comprising almost 500 engravings of Swedish towns and stately buildings dating from Sweden at the height of her European power.

DE GEER, LOUIS GERHARD (1818–1896) Swedish Prime Minister, statesman and academician. Born into an aristocratic, influential family, De Geer studied law and went on to write novels and essays. He entered *Riksdag* (q.v.) as a member of the Nobility Estate in 1853 and by 1858 was invited by King Karl XV (q.v.) to become Minister of Justice, which in practice made him leader of the Cabinet, a post which he held until 1870 and which he succeeded in adapting into the premiership. His period as Minister of Justice is associated with several liberal reforms, including improved rights for unmarried women (q.v.), religious tolerance and the removal of restrictions on internal trade. He is best remembered for his Parliamentary Reform Bill, accepted in December 1865, which replaced the four Estates with a bicameral *Riksdag* elected by common vote. Although his Bill included many restrictions on eligibility to vote and resulted at first in an extremely conservative *Riksdag,* it led gradually to a more genuinely democratic system. De Geer was out of office from 1870 until 1876, when he became

Sweden's first Prime Minister. He was unsuccessful in his efforts to improve the Union (q.v.) between Norway and Sweden and also ran into difficulty over defense issues. In 1880 he resigned and ceased to play a leading role in Swedish politics. In 1891 he published his memoirs, *Minnen.*

DE LA GARDIE, MAGNUS GABRIEL (1622–1686) Swedish Chancellor. He gained Queen Kristina's (q.v.) favor and was richly rewarded but later fell from grace. On the death of Kristina's successor Karl X Gustav (q.v.) in 1660, a group of Regents headed by De La Gardie ruled during Karl XI's (q.v.) minority. As in other regency periods the Swedish magnates increased their power and their wealth, and for several years De La Gardie was one of the richest and most influential men in Sweden. His country seat, Läckö Castle, on a promontory in Lake Vättern, vied with the King's royal castle. In 1670 De La Gardie persuaded the Swedish Council to form an alliance with France and accept French subsidies. His policy backfired in 1674, when Sweden was obliged to support France in her war against Brandenberg and lost the Battle of Fehrbellin in 1675. This proof of the Swedish army's vulnerability encouraged Denmark and Holland to attack Sweden. The hard-won Battle of Lund, 1676, in which the young Karl XI acquitted himself well, repelled a Danish invasion, but De La Gardie and his fellow Regents were in disgrace. His goods were confiscated, including Läckö, which became Crown property. It was restored in 1926 and is now a museum and a fine example of the lifestyle of a Swedish magnate in the Age of Greatness.

DESIDERIA (DESIRÉE) (1777–1860) Queen of Sweden-Norway. The beautiful daughter of a wealthy Marseilles merchant François Clary, Desirée was engaged to Napoleon in 1794–95 but instead married Marshal Jean Baptiste Bernadotte in 1798. In 1810 Bernadotte accepted the unexpected invitation to become Crown Prince of Sweden, adopting the name of Karl Johan (q.v.). Desirée joined him in Stockholm (q.v.) in 1811 with their son Oscar (q.v.) but soon returned to Paris, which she found much more congenial. She remained in France for several years, even though from 1818 she was the consort of

the King of Sweden and Norway. The marriage of her son
Crown Prince Oscar in 1823 persuaded her to return to
Stockholm (q.v.) where she remained, but she was too essen-
tially Gallic to settle happily in her adopted country.

DROTTNINGHOLM PALACE AND THEATER lie on Lövön in
Lake Mälaren, approximately 13 kilometers from the center
of Stockholm (q.v), a Versailles in miniature. Appropriately,
Drottningholm means Queen's Island, for Queen Katarina,
Johan III's (q.v.) consort, gave it its name, Queen Hedvig
Eleonora, wife of Karl X Gustav (q.v.), built a palace there,
and Queen Lovisa Ulrika (q.v.), Gustav III's (q.v.) mother,
improved it. The first palace burnt down in 1661, and the
present building was designed and started by Nicodemus
Tessin the Elder, and completed by his son Nicodemus
Tessin the Younger in 1681. It is a charming Baroque
building set off by formal gardens. In 1753 Kina, a Chinese
pleasure pavilion, was erected as a betrothal gift to Lovisa
Ulrika. It was destroyed by fire and replaced by a larger
pavilion designed by C.F. Adelcrantz in a blend of Rococo
and oriental style. The court took up residence in the palace
in the summer, and recently the present royal family has
made it a permanent residence, using the Royal Palace in
Stockholm for more official occasions.

Lovisa Ulrika was greatly interested in the Arts, and in
1754 opened the first Drottningholm theater. It burnt down in
1762, and C.F. Adelcrantz designed a new one, which was
inaugurated in 1766. Gustav III took it over in 1777. His
strong enthusiasm for the theater led to great activity when
he was in residence, with performances of operas by Gluck,
Handel, Uttini and other contemporaries as well as Swedish
artists. On Gustav's death in 1792 the theater was closed and
neglected. It was used only twice in the 19th century, in 1854
and, to celebrate the birth of Prince Gustav, later Gustav V
(q.v.), in 1858. In 1921 Agne Beijer, looking for a painting,
discovered that the theater had been untouched, encapsulat-
ing intact the 18th century stage mechanism and costumes. It
was cleaned and put into operation on 19 August 1922, the
150th anniversary of Gustav III's coup d'état. Since then
public performances have been given every summer, the

repertoire being works suited to the 18th century setting, and the original sets and costumes being used. In rooms surrounding the auditorium a unique collection of theatrical exhibits has been arranged based largely on the Drottningholm originals and tracing European theater history of the 16th, 17th and 18th centuries.

-E-

ECONOMY Sweden is richly endowed with extensive forests and large copper and iron deposits, but until the 19th century she was essentially a rural, almost self-sufficient country with a primitive economy. Essential imports (especially salt, and grain in years of poor harvests) were paid for by copper, tar and pitch exports until the 18th century and then mostly by iron exports. Transport costs and adverse tariffs made Swedish timber less attractive than Norwegian and Canadian timber until the mid-19th century.

Rapidly-growing demand abroad for Sweden's raw materials from the mid-19th century began the great transformation. To meet advanced industrial countries' need for sawn timber, steamdriven sawmills sprang up along the Norrland coast and exploited the vast forests of the north. When by the turn of the century the ruthless exploitation had exhausted the supply of virgin forests, the pulp industry opened up. The world's first chemical pulp factory was set up in Bergvik in northern Sweden in 1872, but it was in the 1890s that the industry developed on a large scale. All this coincided with the large railroad program, which revolutionized transportation (q.v.). New techniques in the iron and steel industry led to the founding of the Sandviken Ironworks and the mining of ore around Kiruna beyond the Arctic Circle and Grängesberg in the Bergslagen area. Small iron foundries amalgamated or closed down, leaving the way open for mass-produced iron and then steelworks.

Agriculture was mechanized, which helped the engineering industry to expand. It was an exciting period for Swedish engineers when industries exploiting Swedish inventions were founded. G. de Laval (q.v.) invented the mechanical cream-separator in 1878; Sven Wingquist invented the ball-bearing, and in 1907 SKF (Swedish Ball Bearing Company) was set up; F.W. Lindquist's Primus cooker, G. Dalén's acetylene gas units, C.E. Johansson's precision instruments were all developed in this period. By the 1890s electro-technology had become an important branch of the Swedish engineering industry. L.M. Eriksson's telecommunications firm started making telephones in 1876, and in 1883 the firm subsequently called ASEA began making electrical machinery. Gustav Pasch's safety match led to the foundation of the match industry in Jönköping. Alfred Nobel (q.v.) had patented his invention, dynamite, in 1867. He also improved firearms and in 1894 began producing munitions at Bofors.

A reliable banking system was a necessary adjunct to this growth of industrialization, and in the second half of the 19th century the important Swedish banks were formed, including Stockholm's Enskilda Bank, founded by André Oskar Wallenberg (q.v.), still one of the most powerful names in Sweden.

Progress was not unimpeded. The international economic scene had repercussions in Sweden, leading to recessions and even depressions as well as booms, and there were also many labor disputes. With the Saltsjöbaden agreement (q.v.) in 1938, however, industrial peace became the norm. From the end of World War II, with the state encouraging investment, a well educated population and great scope abroad for Swedish manufactured goods, Sweden became one of the most industrialized countries in the world. In the 1950s and 1960s the automobile and aircraft industries made great strides, as did the petrochemical industry and packaging and food processing industries. Mechanization, computing and the use of industrial robots arrived in the 1960s, marking a move towards capital-intensive, not labor-intensive concerns. It also led to mergers and concentration of control in fewer hands, with the three largest banks playing a central role. As industry has become more international and competition fiercer, many large Swedish companies (e.g, ASEA, Electrolux, Volvo, SKF, etc.) have established factories overseas where costs are lower, and Swedish capital has increasingly been invested abroad.

EDÉN, NILS (1871–1945) Swedish historian and politician. Edén, a professor of history at Uppsala (q.v.) from 1903 to 1920, was also a member of *Riksdag* (q.v.) from 1908 until 1924. He was appointed leader of the Liberals (q.v.) on the death of Karl Staaff (q.v.) in 1915. In the disturbed period during the Russian Revolution and World War I (q.v.) there were frequent changes of government in Sweden. Edén led a Liberal-Social Democratic coalition from October 1917 to March 1920, with seven Liberal and four Social Democratic (q.v.) ministers, including Hjalmar Branting (q.v.). During Edén's premiership universal suffrage was accepted by *Riksdag.* After the passage of that legislation the Social Democrats wanted to introduce more socialistic measures, at which point Edén resigned. He went on to be Provincial Governor of Stockholm (q.v.) (1920–1938).

EDUCATION Until the Reformation, education in Sweden was largely in the hands of the Catholic Church, which ran cathedral schools. Even after the founding of Uppsala (q.v.) University in 1477, potential clergymen continued to study abroad. After the Reformation, education was still closely linked with the Church, but, much impoverished, that body had little to spend on education. Uppsala University became defunct. There was a slight improvement under Gustav Vasa's sons Erik XIV (q.v.), who reopened Uppsala University, and Johan III (q.v.).

More substantial developments followed under Gustav II Adolf (q.v.), who required and trained civil servants as Sweden's influence in Europe grew. He supported Uppsala and established a new university at Dorpat, Livonia (1632), and Åbo, Finland (opened officially in 1640). With the School Acts of 1611 and 1620 secondary schools and a German-type *gymnasium* were established. The 1686 Church Law decreed that every parish clerk should teach children of the parish to read, but education remained limited to the Nobility, Clergy and Burghers.

More universal in its effect was the 1842 Education Act, which led to the founding of an elementary school in every parish and compulsory attendance. Every province was to have a teacher training college, and minimum salaries for teachers were to be set. It took time to implement such measures, but by 1880 some 60 percent of Swedish children attended elementary school. In 1882 attendance for six years (7–13) became compulsory, and in 1937 a compulsory seven-year period was established.

Until the mid-19th century, most working-class children attended the elementary school, while children from professional or wealthier homes attended secondary schools and *gymnasia,* which led to university entrance and the professions. In 1950 the egalitarian free nine-year comprehensive school was introduced, at first experimentally, and by 1962, nationally. From that date almost all Swedish children had to attend a comprehensive school from the age of seven to 16 and were given a grounding in Swedish, mathematics, social subjects, science subjects, English and the Arts. Formal examinations gave way to continual assessment. In 1966 the different types of *gymnasia* (academic, technical and commercial) were combined to offer courses for pupils not necessarily aiming at tertiary education, and by 1971 all *gymnasia,* vocational and technical schools were subsumed in the general *gymnasium-*school offering two, three and four-year courses of either a general or a more specialized or technical nature. These were not compulsory, but once the system was running smoothly about 90 percent of the pupils opted to attend.

To Uppsala University were added the universities of Lund (q.v.) (1668), Gothenburg (q.v.) (1954), Stockholm (q.v.) (1960), Umeå (1963) and Linköping (1965). During this period of great educational expansion university colleges were also set up in Växjö, Karlstad and Örebro. The 1977 Act divided Sweden into six higher education regions, while an Office of the Chancellors of Swedish Universities was established to coordinate and plan the higher education system.

Adult education has been important in Sweden since the 19th century. Workers' study circles formed the nucleus of early trade unions (q.v.) in the mid-19th century, and later in that century other movements and societies sprang up, notably the Temperance (q.v.), Free Church and Cooperative (q.v.) Movements, which offered working-class people educational courses and library facilities. Even after the establishment of comprehensive schools, adult and continuing educational courses have continued to thrive. The Folk High School, a nonprofit-making residential adult education institution established to offer all citizens a general education free from formal examinations, was introduced from Denmark in 1868. It rapidly gained in popularity, and there are now 120 in Sweden offering short courses in the liberal arts. They are state-subsidized, and at least half of them are sponsored by specific organizations, such as the Temperance, Labor, Free Church and Cooperative Movements.

EKMAN, CARL GUSTAF (1872–1945) Swedish politician and journalist. When the Liberal Party (q.v.) split in 1923 over the issue of prohibition, Ekman became leader of the anti-prohibition Independent Liberals (Folkfrisinnade). The 1920s were a period of considerable political unrest, with frequent government changes. In 1926 Rickard Sandler's Social Democratic (q.v.) government fell when it failed to prevent an opposition motion on strike-breaking. With only 32 seats in the Lower House of *Riksdag* (q.v.), Ekman became Prime Minister. He became known as "Master of the Balancing Act" *(Vågmästaren),* seeking support from either the Social Democrats or the non-socialist parties, depending on the issue. He survived from June 1926 to October 1928 and succeeded in the passage of the important Education Act of 1927, making six year primary schooling compulsory for all.

After the 1928 election, a Conservative (q.v.) government was formed but it fell in 1930 when trying to raise tariffs on food imports to assist farmers, and Ekman formed his second ministry. He had even fewer seats in *Riksdag* than in 1926, and the world recession had caused a slump in Sweden with rising unemployment and falling wages. A crisis was reached in 1931 in Ådalen (q.v.) when troops fired on a crowd demonstrating against strike-breakers and five people were killed. Ekman's government was blamed. The final blow came in 1932, when Ivar Kreuger (q.v.), the Match King and international financier, committed suicide. It emerged that Kreuger had at least twice donated large sums to the Liberal government and to Ekman personally in exchange for Bank of Sweden authorization to the financially hard-pressed Kreuger. Ekman was forced to resign and in the ensuing

election of 1932 the Social Democrats won. Per Albin
Hansson (q.v.) formed his first government and began a
period of Social Democratic domination of Swedish politics
that was to last 44 years.

EMIGRATION Migration is a constant thread running through
Swedish history, but it was at its most intensive during the
period 1850–1930, when over 1.2 million Swedes (i.e, one
fifth of the population) emigrated, 97 percent of them to the
United States, 1.6 percent to Canada and most of the
remainder to Australia. The five main causes were: 1. The
growth of the Swedish population in the early 19th century,
said succinctly by the poet Tegnér to be the result of "peace,
vaccination and the potato"; 2. A scarcity of farming land
(farmers' younger sons were particularly vulnerable); 3.
Harvest failure (living close to the breadline, many peasants
were in danger of starvation if crops failed); 4. Religious
persecution (the State Church opposed Free Church movements and prohibited their form of worship); 5. Military
service (able-bodied Swedish men were obliged to do their
national service at a time when conditions for men in the
ranks were brutalizing). To these five points could be added
the development of steamships and railroad systems, making
it easier to cross the Atlantic and to get to and from ports.
      The first Swedish emigrants during this period went to
North America for religious reasons. Gustaf Unorius
founded a new settlement in Wisconsin and wrote several
articles for the Swedish liberal paper *Aftonbladet* (q.v.),
praising America as a land of equality and opportunity. He
preached in Free-Church communities before returning to
Sweden. Other Swedish Free-Church members followed his
example, most notably the Erik Jansson sect. They had taken
their name from a grain merchant from Uppland, Sweden,
who considered himself a prophet. From 1840 onwards he
railed against the Swedish clergy, and in 1845 he decided to
move to America with his faithful flock. Eight hundred of
them set off, mostly reasonably well-to-do farmers. Other
Jansson groups followed, 1,500 souls in all, to worship freely
in the USA. Jansson went first to New York but then bought
land in Illinois. There he set up the religious community

Bishops Hill (i.e., *Biskopskulle,* Jansson's birthplace). The hardworking, competent members built up a self-sufficient commune run on communist principles, but then ill-luck befell them. Two ships from Sweden with new sect members foundered, while inadequate diet and the unusual climate killed many of those already at Bishops Hill. Other members wearied of Jansson's tyrannical regime and left. In 1848 Jansson was shot when trying to retain a woman against her will. His successor Jonas Olason kept the colony running smoothly for five years, but all the profits went on unsuccessful business ventures and by 1860 the Bishops Hill colony collapsed. It remains today as a kind of museum to the Swedish emigrants of this pioneering period. Brigham Young's Mormons also persuaded hundreds of young Swedes to join them in Utah. They were lent money for the outward journey but had to repay it with interest.

After 1850 emigration changed character and the increasing stream of emigrants were most often landless peasants or farmers' younger sons, between the ages of 15 and 35, leaving Sweden for economic reasons. There is a correlation between poor Swedish harvests and the rise in emigration to America, with a rise, for instance, after the crop failure in 1868, a falling off during the good harvests in the 1870s, and then a sharp acceleration in the bad harvests of 1887, when over 50,000 left. By the end of the 1860s there were five large travel companies dealing with single Atlantic crossings. The Homestead Act of 1862, which allowed emigrants to purchase land cheaply in the USA, played a large part in Swedish emigration. Large numbers from south and southwest Sweden went to fulfil a dream of owning their own farms. They spread over the Mid-West, settled in Iowa, Wisconsin, Minnesota, Kansas and Nebraska, breaking new ground, and building settlements with schools, churches and mission houses. Some emigrants remained in the towns, especially Chicago, but also Minneapolis, Seattle and New York.

Emigration figures culminated in the 1880s and early 1890s, when the Swedish agricultural and iron industries suffered a setback. There was very little during World War I, but then came the final upsurge in 1923, coinciding with another decline in the Swedish iron industry. The American depression discouraged emigration after that, and by the early 1930s Swedish manpower was beginning to find opportunites at home as the welfare state (q.v.) began to evolve. In 1965 a Swedish Emigration Institute was established in Växjö, Småland, where archives, public and private records, correspondence, a museum and Sweden's largest library concerning Swedish emigration are now housed. The Foundation deals with the documentation of Swedish settlements abroad, mostly North America and Australia. Towards the end of the 19th century the scale of emigration had become a worrying factor for the Swedish government, as so many energetic young people left the country.

In retrospect it seems likely that emigration helped the campaign for extending the franchise, while the channelling of this energy perhaps prevented the extreme social unrest leading to revolution in some countries. Another compensation was that about 200,000 Swedes returned, often with capital and new initiatives, while others who did well in their adopted country sent money to relatives back home, thereby helping the Swedish economy in a small way.

ENGELBREKT ENGELBREKTSSON (c. 1390–1436) Swedish rebel and Guardian of the Realm. A member of the lesser nobility, Engelbrekt was a mineowner from Dalarna. The grand design of Erik VIII of Pomerania (q.v.), King of Denmark, Norway and Sweden by virtue of the Kalmar Union (1397)(q.v.), to rule a united Scandinavia at the heart of a Baltic Empire, led to constant warfare and hardship for many of his subjects. When an alienated Hanseatic League blockaded Swedish ports and prevented the export of iron and copper, members of Engelbrekt's own class, the miners of Dalarna and hard-pressed peasants united behind Engelbrekt and rebelled successfully against Erik. Engelbrekt was elected Guardian of the Realm at Arboga. By tradition that assembly in 1435 is the first meeting of the Swedish *Riksdag* (q.v.). Swedish magnates were soon afraid of the new forces that were emerging and conspired towards Engelbrekt's murder in 1436. One of the great figures in Swedish medieval history, he was soon considered by the ordinary people to be a saint, and his grave became a place of pilgrimage. To Swedish romantic historians of the 19th century he was a patriot struggling to free his people from the Kalmar Union, but what evidence there is suggests that he simply wanted to stop Erik's incessant wars and the subsequent misery of the people.

ENVIRONMENT (GREEN) PARTY (MILJÖPARTIET DE GRÖNA) This political party was formed in 1981, and, with its roots in the campaign against nuclear energy (q.v.), it felt it had no allegiance to the traditional left-right formation. Instead it wanted to be a pressure group advocating ecological balance, cultural diversity and an alternative economy. Succeeding at first only in local elections, the new party surprisingly won 20 seats in the 1988 elections to *Riksdag* (q.v.). It was not able to sustain this level of support in the 1991 elections and remains something of an unknown factor on the party political scene.

ERIK VIII OF POMERANIA (1382–1459) The great nephew of Queen Margareta (q.v.), he was proclaimed her heir on the death of her only son Olof in 1387. Erik was crowned King of three Scandinavian countries in Kalmar in 1397. As he was only 14 years old, power remained in Queen Margareta's hands, and under her skillful guidance the Kalmar Union (q.v.) functioned well enough, but on her death in 1412 when Erik came to power there was soon discord. Extremely ambitious, Erik planned to build up a Baltic empire with his three Scandinavian countries at the center. This involved him in constant warfare, which led to high taxation and hardship for his people. His tendency to ignore Sweden, which he rarely visited, and the appointment of Danes and Germans to command Swedish fortresses increased his unpopularity among his Swedish subjects. Finally the lesser nobility, miners and peasants rebelled under Engelbrekt (q.v.), and Erik was deposed in 1434. Swedish magnates reinstated him conditionally after Engelbrekt's murder in 1436, but he was deposed definitively in Sweden in 1439. He lost control in the rest of the Scandinavian mainland too and withdrew to the island of Gotland, which served as a base for acts of piracy against Swedish and Danish vessels. In 1446 Erik abandoned Gotland to the Danes and spent the next ten years of his life in Pomerania. It was Erik who introduced Sound dues on ships passing through Öresund and who made Copenhagen the capital of Denmark.

ERIK XIV (1533–1577) Swedish King, eldest son of Gustav I Vasa (q.v.) and Katarina of Sachsen-Lauenburg, and one of the most fascinating, unpleasant and ultimately pathetic of the Vasas. Educated as a Renaissance prince, Erik was gifted, widely read, and interested in the Arts. He wrote poetry, sketched, sang and played the lute. He had inherited his father's energy and interest in government. He also held Gustav's views on defense, and speedily strengthened Swedish forces and built up the strongest fleet in the Baltic. Unfortunately he also inherited the Vasa's suspicious temperament to such an extent that it became paranoia and eventually brought about his downfall.

His half-brothers Johan (q.v.) and Karl (q.v.) had been granted independent duchies by Gustav, but in 1561, a year after his succession to the throne, Erik brought them firmly under the authority of the Crown. When Duke Johan planned an ambitious independent foreign policy, Erik had him arrested. His suspicion of the Nobility led him to appoint commoners to the highest offices, and when he set up an efficient spy system and a Royal Supreme Court the Nobility grew antagonistic. The situation deteriorated further when Erik arrested members of the influential Sture (q.v.) family on charges of treason. Before their trial was concluded Erik, in a fit of madness, had them murdered in his presence. When he recovered his sanity he tried to make amends, but the Stures and the Nobility remained unappeased. Erik had sought unsuccessfully the hand of Elizabeth of England and then of Mary, Queen of Scots. When, shortly after the Sture murders, he legitimized his relationship with the low-born Karin Månsdotter in 1567, the aristocracy was outraged. By 1568 they were prepared to support a rebellion led by Duke Johan. Erik was officially deposed in 1569 and succeeded by Johan (III). Erik was held prisoner until his death, caused, it was rumored, by poison administered on Johan's orders. An examination of his remains in 1958 revealed traces of arsenic, but there is no evidence against his half-brother.

Erik's reign coincided with the disintegration of the Teutonic Order, when Baltic countries were looking for territorial gain. Influenced by Machiavelli's writings, Erik hoped to benefit from the unsettled situation. In 1561 Reval was persuaded to acknowledge Swedish rule in return for Swedish protection. Frederik II of Denmark formed an alliance with Poland and Lübeck against Sweden in 1563, and the brutal Northern Seven Years War was launched. It ended inconclusively after Erik's dethronement with the Peace of Stettin (1570), but it can be seen as the beginning of Sweden's struggle to become a European power.

ERLANDER, TAGE (1901–1988) Swedish politician, leader of the Social Democratic Party (q.v.) and the longest-serving Prime Minister in Swedish history. Born in Ransäter, Värmland, the son of an organist, Erlander graduated from Lund University in 1928 and worked for a publisher before entering *Riksdag* (q.v.). From 1938 to 1944 he was an under-secretary in the Social Department, entered the government in 1944 as a Minister without portfolio and went on to become Minister of Education in 1945. When Per Albin Hansson (q.v.), the Social Democratic Prime Minister, died suddenly in 1946, the party's rather surprising choice as his successor was the politically inexperienced Erlander. It was a difficult time to assume leadership. In 1944 the party had drawn up a 27-point plan of postwar reforms aimed at industrial democracy, a positive employment policy and increased state control of the economy, and Erlander had now to deal with this on a slender majority—and sometimes no majority at all—in *Riksdag*.

Several economic problems arose. Predicting a postwar depression, Gunnar Myrdal (q.v.), Minister of Commerce, had prepared to stimulate the economy. There was instead a boom, imports rose sharply, and by 1947 anti-inflationary restrictions on consumer goods were imposed. Myrdal had also entered into a trade agreement offering Russia favorable credit to buy Swedish goods up to a staggering 20 percent of her total exports. The opposition complained also that wartime emergency restrictions were not being removed quickly enough. Ernst Wigforss (q.v.), the Finance Minister, introduced extremely high taxation in 1947: a steeply-graded income tax, corporation tax, capital tax, death duties and estate duties were all introduced or raised with the intention of distributing wealth more evenly as well as financing state services. It was, said the opposition, socialism by the back door.

Erlander kept his nerve. He lost three parliamentary seats in the 1948 elections but remained as Prime Minister of a minority government. He had a temporary respite—Myrdal resigned and Wigforss had retired, inflation was falling and the standard of living was improving for most Swedes. His position was unstable, however, and in 1951 he persuaded the Agrarian Party (q.v.) to join in a coalition. Although there was vociferous opposition to the Social Democrats' fiscal policy, there was often consensus on their social reforms, and Erlander was able to raise the Old Age Pension (1946), introduce a Child Allowance scheme (1948), a statutory three weeks holiday with pay (1953) and, more importantly, a National Health scheme (effective from 1955). By 1951 the first steps towards a Comprehensive School system were taken, and in 1954 a Commission to draft a new constitution was set up.

The most critical point in Erlander's career concerned the ATP (q.v.), a compulsory state-run superannuation pension scheme. The Opposition disliked the compulsory element and were afraid that the vast contributions to be placed in state funds would allow the government to manipulate the economy (q.v.). A consultative referendum on the issue was indecisive, the Agrarians left the coalition and Erlander was defeated in *Riksdag*. Before the ensuing elections in 1957 he slightly amended the ATP proposal and was returned as Prime Minister of a government with exactly half the parliamentary seats. In the event one Liberal (q.v.) member felt obliged to support the proposal and the ATP was duly accepted. From then until his voluntary retirement in 1969 Erlander remained firmly in control, skillfully drawing attention to the non-socialist parties' inability to cooperate in forming a credible alternative government.

In 1953 Harpsund (q.v.), an estate north of Stockholm, was placed at the Prime Minister's disposal. By nature a consensus politician, Erlander often invited to this Swedish Chequers or Camp David leading trade union officials and industrialists to discuss informally a kind of tri-partite state-employer-employee system. It led to industrial peace, but the "Harpsund Democracy" was increasingly encroaching on the power of *Riksdag* and, maintained its critics, could lead to a one-party state with power concentrated in perpetuity in the Social Democrats' hands. By 1964 the Harpsund meetings were drastically reduced. With industrial peace, a thriving economy and high living standards Erlander completed the passage of important social legislation through *Riksdag*. The Comprehensive School was in place by 1962, and the Constitutional Commission's recommendations of a unicameral *Riksdag* and elections every three years were accepted in 1967. Measures bound to increase state interference even further in the running of the economy were emerging in the Social Democrats' program, such as the establishment of the State Investment Bank in 1967. State expenditure and the public sector were rising rapidly, and the non-socialist parties were beginning to show signs of a willingness to cooperate and present a united front.

When Erlander handed over the reins to his successor Olof Palme (q.v.) in 1969, however, he was still a popular national leader. At the outset of his premiership this rather gangling inexperienced figure with no talent for fiery oratory was judged by some to be a nonentity, but his irony, dry humor, pragmatic approach and sheer common sense gradually won the country's affection. After retiring he published his memoirs in six volumes (1972–82).

ESTONIA A small Baltic state with vulnerable national boundaries, Estonia has a long history of invasion and exploitation. Compared with the German and Russian occupations, the period of Swedish soveignty from 1561 to 1710 was considered benign. Swedish Vikings (q.v.) raided Estonia, but by the 12th century Estonians had the reputation of being Baltic pirates. Danish kings made several crusades against Estonia, and in 1219 Valdemar II (the Victorious) partially conquered it and founded the town of Reval (present-day Tallinn). The Teutonic Order of Knights had acquired large parts of Estonia, and in 1346 they purchased the Danish-owned territory from Valdemar Atterdag and reduced the Estonian peasantry to serfdom.

By the early 16th century, with the dissolution of the Teutonic Order and the jockeying for supremacy in the Baltic, Estonia was coveted by various states in the Baltic area. In 1558 Ivar IV of Russia captured Narva, and Reval appealed to Sweden for help. Gustav Vasa (q.v.) was reluctant to engage in foreign ventures, but his son and heir Erik XIV (q.v.) promised Reval and adjacent Estonian provinces protection if Swedish soveignty was accepted. Swedish troops defended Reval and blockaded Narva. In 1581, in the reign of Johan III (q.v.), General Pontus de la Gardie captured Narva, and the three main Baltic ports, Narva, Reval and Viborg (in Sweden-Finland) were thus in Swedish hands. The Peace of Teushina in 1595 between Russia and Sweden confirmed Sweden's hold on Estonia.

Gustav II Adolf (q.v.), wanting an educated populace from which to draw competent, trained secretaries and officials, founded a university at the inland town of Dorpat (Tartu) in 1632. It was attended by students from the Baltic states and also by Swedish students who subsequently sought office in Estonia. When Gustav Adolf regularized the legal system throughout his realm he established a court of appeal at Dorpat as well as Stockholm (q.v.), Jönköping, and Åbo (Finland). Sweden's empire had been built up at the expense of neighboring states, which were always waiting for a chance to regain lost territory.

The sudden death of Karl XI (q.v.) in 1697 and the accession of his untried 15-year-old son Karl XII (q.v.) seemed to offer Tsar Peter I an opportunity for reprisals and for gaining access to the west. At the outset of his remarkable military career, Karl XII defeated the Russian army at Narva in 1700 and deterred further Russian encroachments. Tsar Peter was biding his time, however. After defeating Karl at Poltava (q.v.) in 1709, he pushed home his advantage and in 1710 occupied the whole of Estonia. The Treaty of Nystad between Russia and Sweden confirmed that Sweden had ceded Estonia to Russia.

After two centuries of Russian domination Estonia became a republic in 1920, but soon lost its independence. In

1939 it was forced to allow Soviet naval and air bases on its territory, and then became caught up in the Soviet-Nazi conflict. In 1940 it was declared part of the USSR, but was then occupied by German troops from 1941 to 1944, after which Soviet authority was reestablished. Hundreds of Estonians fled and found refuge in Sweden, a country always well disposed towards them. At the end of World War II a separate group of Estonians sought asylum in Sweden. These refugees were wearing German uniform, having been forcibly conscripted into the German army, and Stalin insisted on their being returned to the Soviet Union as prisoners of war. This caused a great outcry in Sweden, but Per Albin Hansson's (q.v.) government acceded to the Soviet demand on the grounds that it was justified in international law.

With the dissolution of the USSR Estonia once again declared itself a republic, and Sweden has helped with both material and diplomatic aid. Carl Bildt's (q.v.) government speedily recognized the new republic and has tried to mediate between the many Russians, resident in Estonia since the period when it was part of the USSR, and the hard-line Estonian conservatives wishing to expel them.

EUROPEAN UNION (EU) Formerly called the EUROPEAN ECONOMIC COMMUNITY (EEC) and then the EUROPEAN COMMUNITY (EC) As an advanced trading nation Sweden has for a long time approved of international cooperation. On the other hand, the Swedes have preserved their neutrality (q.v.) since 1814 and avoided any international treaties or agreements that would oblige them to put that policy of neutrality at risk. In the immediate postwar period they joined the Council of Europe and the United Nations, but not NATO. There were many internal discussions on whether Sweden should apply for membership of the EEC, as it then was, but they always were stranded on the neutrality issue, the Swedes fearing that a European common defense policy could lead them into an armed conflict. As long as the rest of Scandinavia and Britain remained outside the Community, the matter seemed to lack urgency. Sweden was happy to join Britain, Denmark, Norway, Iceland, Austria and Switzerland in 1959 in forming the European

Free Trade Association (EFTA), an organization that facilitated trade without unforseen obligations. The situation changed when Britain and Denmark joined the EEC. The Swedish government refused to reconsider applying, but it was soon clear that the Swedish economy and cultural life would eventually be at a disadvantage. Many large Swedish concerns began to circumvent EC regulations by setting up subsidiaries in member states, but most companies were unable to do so, and although in 1972 Sweden entered a free trade agreement with the EC, it was becoming increasingly difficult to keep Swedish exports competitive. Sweden had prided itself justly on being in the forefront of scientific, medical and technological research, but exclusion from European educational exchanges arranged through ERASMUS, for instance, was also causing concern.

With the relaxing of tension between East and West, defense and neutrality seemed less important, and there was also a realization that Swedish neutrality was in any case effective only so long as other countries were prepared to acknowledge it. In 1990 negotiations between the EC and EFTA were undertaken (the European Economic Space [EES] agreement), and in July 1991 Sweden decided to apply for full membership in the EC. Negotiations were begun in 1993 and successfully concluded in March 1994, when Sweden, together with Finland and Austria, were invited to join the EU. As a result of the referendum on 13 November 1994, Sweden became a full EU member in 1995.

EXPRESSEN see NEWSPAPERS

-F-

FÄLLDIN, THORBJÖRN (1926–) A Swedish sheepfarmer from the North of Sweden who became Prime Minister. He became a member of *Riksdag* (q.v.) in 1958 and went on, in 1971, to become Chairman of the Center Party (q.v.) (formerly the Agrarian Party). In 1976 there was general discontent with the Social Democratic (q.v.) government. The oil crisis had hit the Swedish economy and punitive taxes were driving famous Swedes into exile. What particularly won support for Fälldin, however, was his opposition to nuclear energy (q.v.). A three-party non-socialist coalition government was formed after the 1976 elections with Fälldin as Prime Minister. He discovered when in office that scrapping nuclear power plants already in operation was almost impossible and a compromise on further building inevitable, but, feeling he could not go back on his word to the electorate, he resigned, and Ola Ullsten (q.v.), the Liberal (q.v.) leader, ran a minority government until the 1979 elections. In the election campaign Fälldin promised a referendum on the vexed nuclear issue. He was reelected and became Prime Minister of a non-socialist coalition until 1982. The economic situation had not improved, the Moderates (Conservatives) (q.v.) had withdrawn from the coalition and the Social Democrats were returned to power under Olof Palme (q.v.).

Fälldin is generally regarded with affection as that rare bird, an honest politician. In a televised debate in 1976 his brilliant opponent Olof Palme was seemingly scoring all the points, but Fälldin's quiet bucolic performance won voters' confidence. He resigned as Center Party leader in 1985 and was succeeded by Karin Söder (q.v.) and, in 1986, by the present leader Olof Johansson (q.v.).

FARMERS' PARTY see POLITICAL PARTIES

FELDT, KJELL-OLOF (1931–) Swedish Social Democratic politician. Feldt graduated in politics at Uppsala University in 1956 and completed a post-graduate degree in national economy in 1967. He had been active in the Students' Social Democratic Association, and from 1962 to 1964 he edited the socialist periodical *Tiden.* He was a member of the Social Democratic Party's (q.v.) council from 1978 and was on the executive committee from 1981 to 1990. Feldt was Minister of Trade 1970–75, and a Minister of State in the Finance Department 1975–76. When the Socialists returned to power in 1982 Feldt was appointed Minister of Finance, a post he held until 1990. He devalued the Swedish krona by 16 percent and initiated his policy of the "third way," i.e.

stimulating the economy without large public cutbacks. The Swedish economy improved and remained buoyant in the 1980s. Feldt attempted to hold down inflation by low wage agreements and restraint in the public sector, but this caused dissension within his own party and disagreement with Landsorganisationen (LO, Swedish Trade Union Confederation) (q.v.). Nor was he enamored of LO's Wage Earner Funds (q.v.). Feldt won support from his own party and from the Liberals (q.v.) for a tax reform, but when in 1990 against a background of increasing costs his introduction of economic restrictions did not meet with general approval, he resigned. He published *Den tredje vägen: en politik för Sverige* (The Third Way: a Policy for Sweden) in 1985, in which he propounded his economic views.

FERSEN, AXEL VON, THE ELDER (1719–1794) Swedish aristocrat and politician. The family, whose name was originally von Versen, came from Estonia. Von Fersen served in the French army for ten years. He joined the Hat Party (q.v.) in the *Riksdag* (q.v.) of 1751–52, and helped to quash the Court Party's attemped coup in 1756. He was Marshal of the Realm in 1755–56, 1760–63 and 1767–70. By 1769, when the incompetence of both the Hat and the Cap Parties was causing instability in the country, von Fersen urged an increase in royal authority, incurred heavy debts in his political campaign and left *Riksdag*. He was, however, a defender of liberty. He was recalled to the Council after Gustav III's (q.v.) coup in 1772 but resigned from it after only seven months in protest against what he considered to be the King's absolutist tendencies, and led the opposition to the King in *Riksdag*. His views were moderate, but when in 1789 Gustav introduced an amendment to the Constitution which virtually gave him absolute power he had von Fersen arrested for a short time because of his opposition.

FERSEN, AXEL VON, THE YOUNGER (1755–1810) Swedish aristocrat, officer and statesman and the son of Axel von Fersen the Elder (q.v.). When at the French court, von Fersen won the favor of Queen Marie-Antoinette. Gustav III (q.v.), who followed with sympathy the fortunes of Louis XVI and his consort during the French Revolution, used von Fersen as his unofficial ambassador to the French court. In 1791 von Fersen helped to organize the royal couple's ill-fated flight to Varennes. The plot was uncovered but von Fersen was in Belgium by then. In 1799 he returned to Sweden. He was a royalist, and after Gustav IV Adolf (q.v.) was deposed von Fersen supported the candidature of Gustav Adolf's son as Crown Prince. Prince Karl August was elected instead, but when the latter arrived in Sweden in 1810 he suddenly collapsed and died. An autopsy showed that he had died of a stroke, but a rumor spread that he had been poisoned by von Fersen's sister, the aristocratic Sophie von Piper. At Karl August's funeral when von Fersen, as Earl Marshal, was leading the procession, he was dragged from his carriage by the mob and stoned to death, one of the least attractive episodes in Swedish history.

FINLAND Most of Finland was settled in the first century A.D. by Finnish tribes coming from the east and south, but coastal areas at that period were occupied by Swedes. There was a large amount of Swedish settlement of Finland in the 9th century, which then increased appreciably from about 1100 to 1300. Sweden's patron saint Erik (d. 1160) is said to have gone to Finland on a crusade against the pagan Finns and established Swedish rule there. A century later Birger Jarl and then Karl Knutsson waged successful crusades—or campaigns—and brought Finland under the Swedish crown. The border with Russia was first drawn with the Peace of Novgorod (1323), although the boundaries were disputed for a long time, and it was the Peace of Tevsina (1595) that established the frontiers.

By dint of its geographical position Finland was inevitably the theater of war in disputes between Russia and Sweden. Gustav II Adolf (q.v.) was able to exploit Russia's weakened position after civil unrest in the Peace of Stolbova (1617) by the terms in which Russia ceded Ingria and southwest Karelia to Sweden-Finland. This gave Sweden a land link between Finland and Estonia (q.v.) and completely closed Russia's outlet to the Baltic. As Sweden lost her Great Power status at the beginning of the 18th century she progressively lost Finland to Russia in three stages. The first was the Peace of Nystad in 1721, in the aftermath of Karl XII's (q.v.) disastrous wars, when Viborg went to Russia. The second was after the Hat Party's (q.v.) ill-starred war on Russia in 1741. Poorly prepared for such a war, Sweden soon capitulated and had to accept the Peace of Åbo in 1743, losing southeast Finland. The third, in 1809, was the most disastrous of all, when Sweden became entangled in the ramifications of the Napoleonic wars. The meeting at Tilsit brought France and Sweden's archenemy Russia together, and Napoleon asked Tsar Alexander to force Sweden to join the Continental Blockade. Alexander attacked Finland in 1808. Work had been started on the Sveaborg fortification near Helsinki after the Peace of Åbo, and Gustav III (q.v.) had had this great bulwark completed during his reign. The Commander of Sveaborg overestimated Russia's strength in 1808 and was so pessimistic about the outcome of the war that he surrendered Sveaborg after a mere token resistance. Swedish troops tried to defend Finland, but there was no inspired leadership, Gustav IV Adolf (q.v.) proving inadequate in a crisis. By the end of 1808 all of Finland was in Russian hands. Dissatisfaction with the King reached its height, and he was deposed in 1809. With Swedish resistance in northern Sweden crumbling and the whole of Finland fallen, Sweden was forced to accept the Treaty of Fredrikshamn in September 1809, when Finland and the Åland Islands (q.v.) passed to Russia. Territory which Sweden had ruled for over 500 years was lost.

When the French Marshal Bernadotte was adopted as Crown Prince Karl Johan (q.v.) of Sweden in 1810 there were high hopes that he would regain Finland, but Bernadotte turned to Russia as an ally instead. By 1811 relations between Napoleon and Alexander had soured. In 1812 Karl Johan pledged Swedish troops to help defeat Napoleon in return for support in taking Norway as recompense for Finland. Under protest the Norwegians were forced into Union (q.v.) with Sweden in 1814, while Finland remained part of the Russian Empire.

Despite Karl Johan's ''1812 policy,'' Russia remained the traditional enemy, and in the 1850s Oscar I (q.v.), Karl

Johan's son, was tempted to get involved in British and French plans against Russia, his aim being the return of Finland to Sweden. The allies were not prepared to go that far in helping Sweden, however, and the Finns remained subjects of the Tsar. Strong emotional ties with Finland remained, but Sweden began to look upon it as a buffer state rather than Swedish territory waiting to be regained. This was still true in 1917, when Finland took the opportunity of declaring her independence at the start of the Russian Revolution.

With the growing threats from European totalitarian states in the 1930s, the Scandinavian countries made a joint declaration of neutrality (q.v.) in 1936. By 1938 a Swedish-Finnish agreement was reached on the protection of the Åland Islands, but this was cancelled under Russian pressure. The Hitler-Stalin pact gave Stalin a free hand in the East Baltic, and Russia demanded that Finland cede territory that would facilitate the defense of the approaches to Leningrad (St Petersburg). Finland refused and called for Swedish help. Russia attacked Finland, and Sweden declared herself non-belligerent, not neutral, allowing arms shipments and volunteers to Finland but not taking the final step of entering the war. After a heroic struggle against impossible odds Finland had to capitulate, and Sweden helped to broker the Peace of Moscow in 1940.

In 1941 Hitler turned on Russia, and Finland reentered the war as an ally of Germany, intending to regain territory lost to Russia. Again Swedish volunteers fought for Finland. After much soul-searching Sweden abandoned strict neutrality to allow a German division (the Engelbrecht Division) to cross through Sweden to reach Finland. As Germany faced defeat Finland ran the danger of being sucked into the Soviet Union against her will, but in 1944 Swedish diplomacy played a substantial part in arranging an armistice. Finland had to pay an enormous indemnity, lost territory in the north and had to lease a naval base near Helsinki to the Russians, but at least she preserved her independence.

During the Finnish wars many Finnish children were sent to Sweden for safety and were adopted by Swedish foster parents, and in the immediate postwar period hundreds of people moved from war-torn Finland to unspoiled Sweden and settled there. This form of immigration has continued for economic reasons but on a diminishing scale as the Finnish recovery was completed. In 1952 when the Nordic Council (q.v.) was set up to work for close cooperation among the Scandinavian countries, Finland joined. At first, Russian reactions had to be taken into consideration and certain areas, such as the economy, had to be avoided by Finland. Gradually, however, Finland played a full part in the Council, and since the collapse of the Soviet Union has been able to collaborate without reservation with Sweden and the rest of Scandinavia.

FOLKHEMMET See WELFARE STATE

FOLK HIGH SCHOOLS See EDUCATION

FREDRIK I (1675–1751) Swedish King from 1720, born in Kassel, Hesse, Germany. Fredrik married Karl XII's (q.v.) younger sister Ulrika Eleonora (q.v.) in 1715. Karl died without issue in 1718 and the Swedes, weary of war, seized the opportunity of abolishing the absolute monarchy. A new Constitution was drawn up, ushering in the Age of Liberty (1718–1772). Ulrika Eleonora was elected Queen only on acceptance of the new Constitution. She abdicated in favor of her husband in 1720. Having little interest in politics Fredrik was happy to play a puppet role. He had no legitimate issue and was succeeded by Adolf Fredrik (q.v.) of Holstein Gottorp.

FREDRIKA BREMER FÖRBUNDET (ASSOCIATION) Named for the feminist writer Fredrika Bremer (q.v.), this association was founded by Sophie Adlersparre, a disciple of F. Bremer, in 1884 with the aim of rallying women (q.v.), promoting their participation in social life and improving their position in society. Since its inception it has worked for women's suffrage, for improved educational and career openings and for revised marriage laws. From 1886 to 1913 it published the periodical *Dagny,* and from 1913 *Hertha,* a periodical taking its name from F. Bremer's socially most influential novel. As the association built up its reputation for reliability, government agencies began to turn to it for information on women's affairs. It established sub-committees to cover different areas of expertise. Its medical committee, since it was first set up in 1893, has been instrumental in improving health care for women, while the legal committee carefully vets and monitors government legislation, protecting and furthering women's interests. Improved education (q.v.) for women has always been a prime aim, and the association ran two vocational schools until 1962, as well as awarding thousands of scholarships to women over the past century. From its headquarters in Stockholm (q.v.) the association went on to establish branches in most Swedish cities and has become affiliated with the International Alliance for Women and the International Council for Women.

F-SHIP A Swedish armored vessel called *Sverige* (Sweden) finally launched in 1915, which caused a constitutional crisis. Worried by the arms buildup by European powers, the Swedish Conservative (q.v.) Prime Minister Arvid Lindman (q.v.) wished to improve Swedish defense forces and in 1911 succeeded with difficulty in gaining *Riksdag*'s (q.v.) approval for the F-ship. The Liberal (q.v.) leader Karl Staaff (q.v.) won the 1911 elections and as Prime Minister stopped work on the ship. A campaign was launched, supported by the nationalistic explorer Sven Hedin (q.v.), and funds amounting to 17 million kronor were collected privately to help pay for the ship. As part of the campaign a demonstration 30,000 strong marched into the Royal Palace Yard in Stockholm (q.v.), and Gustav V (q.v.) addressed them directly in a speech sympathizing with their cause and at odds with the views of his Prime Minister. Although by this time Staaff was beginning to realize that there was a strong case for strengthening Sweden's defenses, he was firmly committed to his belief in a constitutional monarchy and the authority of *Riksdag*. He insisted therefore that Gustav V must undertake not to express political views without first consulting the Prime Minister. This Gustav refused to do, Staaff resigned, a Conservative government was put into power, Swedish defenses were strengthened and *Sverige* was launched.

-G-

GEIJER, ARNE (1910–1979) Swedish trade unionist and Social Democratic (q.v.) politician. Geijer complemented his basic education by studying at the well-known Brunnsvik Folk High School in Dalarna, his native province. He became an official of the Metal Workers' Union, one of the most powerful in the country, and by 1948 was its Chairman. He went on to become Chairman of Landsorganisationen (Swedish Confederation of Trade Unions) (q.v.), an extremely influential post, which he held from 1956 to 1973. He was also a Social Democratic member of *Riksdag* (q.v.) from 1955 to 1976, withdrawing after the election that put a non-socialist coalition government into power under Thorbjörn Fälldin (q.v.). Geijer chaired a committee set up by the Social Democrats to persuade the electorate to accept their compulsory pension scheme in the 1957 referendum. A firm party man, Geijer nevertheless opposed the Social Democratic line in 1963 when it proposed to reduce Sweden's foreign aid to developing countries.

GEIJER, ERIK GUSTAV (1783–1847) Swedish historian and poet. Geijer was a leader of the neo-romantic Swedish poets active from the turn of the 19th century. Influenced by neo-Platonic philosophers and the German Romantic Movement they were interested in a spiritual, ideal world beyond the temporal one. They were also inclined to the nationalistic sentiments that became a feature of the early 19th century. Scandinavian poets of the period looked back to their Old Norse history, remembering the strength and independence of the Vikings (q.v.) and idealizing their other qualities. Geijer was a founder member of Götiska förbundet (Gothic Society, 1811), the aim of which was the reawakening of pride in the Old Norse ideals, and of its journal *Iduna,* in which he published poems extolling the virtues of the Vikings and the independent farmers of ancient times ("Vikingen" and "Odalbonden").

Geijer, a graduate of Uppsala (q.v.) University, was professor of history there from 1817 to 1847. His lectures attracted a huge audience from both town and gown. He is considered to be the first writer of a modern history of Sweden, *Svenska folkets historia* I-III (History of the Swedish People, 1832–36), in which, despite his obvious patriotism, he observed a degree of objectivity and based his work on a great deal of source material and research. A friend of King Karl XIV Johan (q.v.), Geijer was considered for about two decades to be a strong supporter of the conservative element in Swedish politics. Sweden's new Constitution of 1809 had clung to the old system of representation in *Riksdag* (q.v.) through the four Estates (Nobility, Clergy, Burghers, Peasants), a system opposed by a growing but unorganized number of liberal voices. The members of a conservative so-called historical school, Geijer among them, defended this form of representation on the grounds that the Estates had developed organically over a long historical period of development, represented different functions in society and were essential to the state.

In the 1830s a change of approach became evident, and the liberals became more organized and found more outlets for their views. The new liberal newspaper *Aftonbladet* (q.v.) (established 1830) and realistic literature by Fredrika Bremer (q.v.) and C.J.L. Almquist (q.v.) reflected and furthered liberal causes. Geijer roused great interest when in 1838 he felt obliged to announce that he could no longer support the Swedish class society and had become a liberal. He went on to advocate a bicameral *Riksdag,* a reform of suffrage and a liberalizing of the economy. His former allies described this as Geijer's apostasy *(avfallet)* and renounced him. More recently, however, it has been acknowledged that there had been an increasingly democratic approach to history and politics in Geijer's attitude, and his 1838 announcement was not a defection or volte face so much as part of a continuous development.

GENERAL STRIKE (STORSTREJKEN) 4 August–4 September, 1909. Landsorganisationen (LO, Swedish Confederation of Trade Unions) (q.v.) was formed in 1898 and within three years was affiliated with the Social Democratic Party (q.v.).

Many Swedish employers recognized the right of unions to negotiate for their members and in 1902 formed Svenska Arbetsgivareförenginen (SAF, Swedish Federation of Employers) (q.v.) as a countermeasure. It was a period of labor unrest, and when the international economic situation led in 1908 to a reduction in Swedish wages, a wave of strikes was triggered. The employers, in a concerted action in 1909, effected a general lockout, which was countered by a general strike. Many union leaders had avoided such a step as long as possible, but more radical groups in the labor movement had been spoiling for a fight, and hoped the strike would so disrupt society that a great leap forward towards socialism could be taken. Care of the sick, lighting, water and refuse services were maintained, and the railroad workers were not members of LO anyway. The strike lasted a month and was impressively well ordered, but society was able to cope quite well on voluntary labor. Union funds dwindled, and LO leaders were finally forced to advise their members to return to work. The more immediate result was that LO lost over half its membership and the Social Democratic Party suffered heavily too. On a longer timescale, LO leaders had demonstrated their organizational power to SAF and shown they were a force to be reckoned with. It was the more radical, anarchical members of LO who were discredited, and Hjalmar Branting (q.v.) and the more moderate Social Democratic leaders were able to push ahead with their plans for electoral reform.

GÖTA CANAL A waterway from Sjötorp on Lake Vänern to Mem in Östergötland. It joins the Trollhätte Canal in the west with the Södertälje Canal in the east, forming a 387 kilometer link between Gothenburg (q.v.) and Stockholm (q.v.). The canal is 182 kilometers long, on average 14 meters wide at the base and 26 meters at the surface, three meters deep, with 58 locks, and its highest point is 92 meters above sea level. It was built between 1810 and 1832, mostly under the direction of Count Baltzar von Platen (who died in 1829) with advice from Thomas Telford. The work was so well executed that no major repairs have been required. The project was first suggested for defense and transportation purposes by Bishop Hans Brask in the 16th century, but by the time it was finally realized in 1832 it was already in danger of being obsolete. The locks were designed with small wooden sailing ships in mind, Sound tolls were abolished in 1857, and the main railroads came into operation from the 1860s onwards. The canal benefitted inland areas, rejuvenating Söderköping port and helping Motala to expand as an engineering center, but it did not attract the volume of shipping anticipated. By the 1970s it was no longer viable financially and in 1978 the government took it over. The canal, a remarkable engineering feat, runs through beautiful country and has become a kind of national monument and a tourist attraction.

GÖTEBORGSPOSTEN See NEWSPAPERS

GÖTEBORGS SJÖFARTS OCH HANDELSTIDNING See NEWSPAPERS

GOTHENBURG (GÖTEBORG) (Population in 1991 433,042; Greater Gothenburg 739,945). Sweden's second largest city and largest seaport, Gothenburg is situated on the west coast in Västergötland at the mouth of the Göta River and is ice-free throughout the year. It had its origins in the 12th century settlement at Lödöse several kilometers north of its present location. In 1473 the Lödöse inhabitants were moved to the Göta River estuary. It was first called Götaholm and later Nya (i.e., new) Lödöse. In 1603 Karl IX (q.v.) moved the settlement again, this time to Hisingen (now a central part of the city) and called it Göteborg. The provinces north and south of the Göta were then part of Norway and Denmark respectively, and as Sweden's only outlet to the Atlantic, Gothenburg's position was strategically important—which was why the Danes destroyed it in 1611. Gustav II Adolf (q.v.) refounded it in 1619 and granted its charter two years later. He invited Dutch merchants and engineers to settle there, and the city plan to this day with its canals and fortifications shows their influence. The first town council consisted of ten Dutchmen, seven Swedes and one Scotsman. One of the first important civic buildings was Kronhuset

(Crown House), built in 1643–53. Karl X Gustav (q.v.) called a meeting of *Riksdag* (q.v.) there in 1660 but died suddenly, and the assembled *Riksdag* proclaimed his five-year-old son Karl XI (q.v.) instead.

Gothenburg's chief economic asset in the 17th century was the export of timber and iron, and the town developed quickly. The port suffered during Karl XII's (q.v.) wars, but flourished during the Age of Liberty, when it had a monopoly on the export of iron ore from Värmland, and when (in 1731) the East India Company (q.v.) was founded. A rich merchant class, often of Scottish descent, emerged and improved the city's architecture with elegant residences near the harbor. These merchants tended to be public-spirited and gained for Gothenburg the soubriquet the "donation city"— Sahlgren and Renström for instance helped fund hospitals, Chalmers a technical college, Fürstenberg a salon within the Art Museum, Keiller a public park, while Dickson's donation of books formed the nucleus of the City Library. Gothenburg prospered too during Napoleon's Continental Blockade early in the 19th century when Britain used it as a warehouse in northern Europe. A second prosperous period began with the completion of the Trollhätta Canal (1800), Göta Canal (q.v.) (1832) and the steady increase in transoceanic shipping. In 1845 the first docks were built and shortly afterwards the great shipyards Eriksberg, Götaverken and Lindholm started up. Once the Swedish industrial revolution got underway Gothenburg became an industrial city, the home of SKF (Swedish Ball Bearings), Volvo, Mölnlycke and branches of the textile and food-processing industries. It suffered from the recession following the oil crisis in 1973–74, shipbuilding being especially hard hit, but remains a thriving city.

Gothenburg is a bishopric. Its cathedral dates from 1633, although it was rebuilt in 1815–25 and restored in 1956–57. It is also an educational and cultural center, with a University, Chalmers University College of Technology, University Colleges of Social Studies and Teachers Training, a Music Academy, Oceanographic Institute, Botanical Gardens with a collection of flora from four continents, City Theater, Opera House, several museums, libraries, and the Ullevi sports stadium. Despite the recession, impressive new extensions to the University library, Arts, and Music Faculties have been completed recently, and a new Opera House financed largely by public subscription is nearing completion.

GOVERNMENT see *RIKSDAG*

GREAT NORTHERN WAR (1700–1721) See KARL XII

GREEN PARTY See ENVIRONMENT (GREEN) PARTY

GUSTAV I (GUSTAV ERIKSSON VASA) (1496–1560) After the Kalmar Union (q.v.) was established, successive Danish rulers attempted to unite Scandinavia under their sway. Christian II established his claim to the Swedish throne by force in 1520, killing the Swedish Regent Sten Sture (q.v.) and perpetrating the Stockholm Bloodbath (q.v.). Gustav Vasa, a relative of Sten Sture, was held hostage in Denmark, but escaped first to Lübeck, north Germany, where he was assured of financial assistance from the Hanseatic League, and then back to his native Sweden. He led a successful rebellion against Christian and by 1523 was elected King of an independent Sweden.

Gustav was faced with the formidable task of securing and reforming a backward country torn by decades of internal and external strife. He established the country's finances by confiscating, in 1527, the rich properties of the Catholic Church, in effect clearing the way for the establishment of the Swedish Lutheran State Church. This enabled him to discharge his debts to Lübeck. He transformed the neglected, antiquated system of government into a highly efficient, centralized administration, inviting skilled German lawyers to Sweden to assist in the work. Large sums were spent on building up military and naval forces loyal to the King, and a series of fortified castles were constructed at, e.g., Vadstena (q.v.), Gripsholm, Kalmar and Örebro, to defend strategic routes and waterways. Gustav secured the Vasa dynasty through the Succession Act of 1544, which converted Sweden into a hereditary monarchy.

Gustav was a gifted orator and an energetic, but ruthless ruler, feared and admired rather than loved. The leaders of four dangerous but unsuccessful risings against him (in 1525, 1527, 1531 and 1543) were executed mercilessly, even those who had previously risked their lives supporting his rebellion against Christian II. He held the reins of office firmly, was interested in every aspect of Swedish life, and ruled his country like a landowner running his private estates. On his death in 1560 his eldest son Erik XIV (q.v.) inherited a stable, solvent, well-organized and well-defended independent state, justifying Gustav's soubriquet "Founder of the Swedish State."

GUSTAV II ADOLF (1594–1632) King of Sweden. In 1611, on the death of his father Karl IX (q.v.), Gustav Adolf inherited a country at war with Denmark, Poland and Russia, and a fractious aristocracy. Although only 17 on his succession, he retrieved the situation resolutely and effectively. By granting certain privileges to the Nobility he was assured of their support. He fought off a Danish invasion and made a treaty with Denmark at Knäred in 1613. He was then able to deal with a Russia weakened by internal struggles, and by the terms of the Treaty of Stolbova (1617) he gained Ingria and southwest Karelia. The protracted war with Poland (1621–29), whose King Sigismund Vasa (q.v.) was Gustaf Adolf's cousin and had a strong claim to the Swedish throne, concluded in the Treaty of Altmark (1629), by which time Gustav Adolf was in possession of Livonia and important Prussian ports.

The attempts of Christian IV of Denmark to assist the Protestants against the Catholic League of the Habsburg Holy Roman Emperor, Ferdinand II, at this point failed, and Gustav Adolf decided he must come to the aid of the Protestants and enter the war. In 1630 he crossed to Pomerania, forced the hesitant rulers of Brandenburg and Saxony to join him and in 1631 defeated Count von Tilly's Catholic forces at Breitenfeld near Leipzig. This opened the way south and eastwards. It also gained Gustav Adolf great renown, and allies flocked to join the Swedish army. He first moved down the Rhine, defeating Tilly and capturing Augsburg and Munich. As he marched triumphantly along the Danube, meeting little resistance, the Emperor recalled Wallenstein, whose overbearing manner had aroused the German Catholic princes' animosity but whose brilliant military prowess now seemed essential. In 1632 the two armies met at Lützen. After a furious confrontation Wallenstein's troops retreated, but the Swedish King had been killed in the battle. Gustav Adolf's grand design had been to unite a powerful Protestant force in Germany under Swedish leadership. This was now shattered, but he had extended Swedish boundaries enough to lay the foundations of a Swedish Empire and the Age of Greatness, when Sweden was a powerful state in Europe.

   Gustav Adolf left his mark on Swedish internal affairs too. He reorganized government administration and the legal system. It was because it worked so well, and because he had the brilliant Axel Oxenstierna (q.v.) as his Chancellor, that he was able to absent himself from Sweden and campaign abroad so many years. He founded several Swedish towns, including Gothenburg (q.v.) in 1619, and encouraged industry. He established a standing army based on regional regiments. Uppsala (q.v.) University was revitalized and given the revenues of royal estates and the King's own library. Gustav Adolf had the intelligence and courage of previous Vasa monarchs, but possessed more charm and lacked their innate suspicion. He was also acknowledged to be a military genius, with ideas on strategy and tactics very advanced for his period. He was called the "Lion of the North" and hailed as the champion of Protestantism.

GUSTAV III (1746–1792) Swedish King, son of Adolf Fredrik (q.v.) and Lovisa Ulrika (q.v.), sister of Frederick the Great of Prussia. Gustav inherited in 1771 a country in economic and social turmoil, the result of a weak monarchy and a sustained struggle between the two political parties, the Hats (q.v.) and the Caps. His attempts at reconciling them having failed, he staged a bloodless coup in 1772 and introduced a new Constitution which gave greater authority to the monarch and brought to an end the Age of Liberty (1718–1772). This allowed him to tackle the country's more immediate problems. A foreign loan facilitated the stabilization of the currency; large imports of foreign grain alleviated the widespread deprivation caused by a series of disastrous harvests at a time of rising population; the Civil Service was reformed and many corrupt or incompetent officials were dismissed.

Reared in the spirit of the Enlightenment, Gustav instigated many reforms aimed at removing restrictions and at enhancing the rights of the individual. The penal code was revised and the death penalty for several offenses was removed; religious freedom was established for foreigners, and in 1782 Jews were allowed to live in large towns and have a synagogue there.

Gustav's initial enthusiasm began to wane and opposition, never wholly stifled, became more voluble. Hoping to unite his people behind him against a common enemy, he initiated a war against Russia in 1788. His campaign went badly, and a group of young officers in Finland (q.v.), the so-called Anjala League (q.v.), mutinied. Denmark invaded at that point, and Gustav, who possessed considerable histrionic skill, appealed successfully to his people's patriotism. The Danes were repelled and, in 1790, peace with Russia was established. Gustav equated the Anjala rebellion with the aristocracy, and in 1789 he pushed through a constitutional amendment, the Act of Union and Security, which was tantamount to establishing an absolute monarchy. Opposition among the aristocracy mounted, and in 1792 Gustav was assassinated at a masked ball in Stockholm by Anckarström (q.v.), a former guards officer. Gustav had married Sofia Magdalena of Denmark and was succeeded by their eldest son Gustav IV Adolf (q.v.).

Gustav's admirers saw him as a charming, gifted, enlightened monarch who loved and supported the Arts, especially the theater. His detractors considered him superficial, incapable of sustained effort, and they attributed even his reforms and magnanimous gestures to an egocentric desire for effect. Whatever his motives, Gustav's court, modelled on Versailles, attracted and inspired writers, painters and architects, and Gustav was a generous patron. Plays were performed in the beautifully proportioned court theaters in Drottningholm palace (q.v.) and Gripsholm castle. The Royal Opera House was opened in Stockholm (q.v.) in 1782, the Royal Theater in 1788, and Gustav helped found the Swedish Academy in 1786. All these institutions are extant and respected today.

GUSTAV IV ADOLF (1778–1837) Swedish King, son of Gustav III (q.v.). His uncle, Prince Karl, was Regent from 1792, after the assassination of Gustav III, until 1796, when Gustav Adolf reached his majority and ruled as an absolute monarch. He emerges as a pathetic figure, well-meaning and dutiful but of limited ability. His childhood had coincided with the French Revolution and the Reign of Terror, whilst his own father had been assassinated. He closed the Opera House, censured the theater and prohibited the importation of seditious literature—a wide category to this naturally suspicious King. He brought a measure of order into the country's finances, helped effect an important land reform, the General Enclosure Act (1803), and supported von Platen's plan for a canal across Sweden, the Göta canal (q.v.). In a calmer period of European history Gustav Adolf would perhaps have proved adequate, but Sweden was increasingly embroiled in the far-reaching consequences of the Napoleonic wars, requiring political and military skills beyond him.

He joined in an armed neutrality with Tsar Paul, Denmark and Prussia, but this was dissolved by Britain's attack on his fleet and the death of Tsar Paul. By 1805 Gustav Adolf had irrevocably allied himself with Napoleon's enemies, now deeming Napoleon to be the Beast of the Apocalypse, the Anti-Christ, and even when Napoleon's power was at its height he refused to compromise. It was alarming for Sweden when Tsar Alexander, Paul's successor, signed The Treaty of Tilsit (1807) and became an ally of Napoleon. The latter was happy to see Russia invade Finland (q.v.), still Swedish territory, hoping it would force Sweden to join the Continental Blockade against Britain. The whole of Finland was occupied by 1809, and northern Sweden was being invaded. Meanwhile, Denmark-Norway was poised to move into western Sweden. Still Gustav Adolf refused to meet Napoleon's demands or even to assemble *Riksdag* (q.v.). In desperation a group of high-ranking officers staged a coup, arrested the King and forced him to abdicate. He was formally deposed by *Riksdag* in 1809, and exiled with his family, Queen Frederika of Baden and their five children, who were barred from succeeding to the throne. He divorced his wife in 1812 and, as Colonel Gustafsson, lived a solitary, rootless life in Germany and Switzerland, where, in St Gallen, he died in 1837.

GUSTAV V (1858–1950) King of Sweden, son of Oscar II (q.v.) and Sofia of Nassau. Gustav came to the throne in 1907 and became the longest reigning monarch in Swedish history and the first to dispense with the coronation ceremony. As Crown Prince in 1905 he successfully urged the Swedes to accept the dissolution of the Union (q.v.) with Norway, arguing that a union that had to be maintained by force was worthless.

Conservative by inclination and anxious to preserve the monarch's personal authority, Gustav had strained relations with the Liberal leader Karl Staaff (qq.v.), who became Prime Minister for the second time in 1911. Gustav objected to Staaff's failure to build up Sweden's defenses, and he resented his Prime Minister's failure to consult with him before taking proposals to the *Riksdag*. When a rally of some 31,000 supporters of a strong defense force gathered in the Palace Yard in Stockholm (q.v.) in February 1914, Gustav addressed them directly and publicly sympathized with their views. Staaff objected to the monarch's public speech without prior consultation, resigned, and was replaced by the Conservative Hjalmar Hammarskjöld (qq.v.).

Although pro-German, Gustav believed in preserving Sweden's neutrality, and in 1914 on his initiative the three Scandinavian Kings met in Malmö (q.v.), Sweden, to underline their kinship and their neutrality (q.v.). In World War II (q.v.) Gustav again put his weight behind guarding Sweden's neutrality, and served as a unifying symbol for the nation.

In 1881 Gustav married Princess Viktoria, daughter of the Grand Duke of Baden. They had three sons, Gustav Adolf (q.v.), who succeeded him, Vilhelm and Erik. An increasingly popular figure, Gustav played competitive tennis as "Mr G." in to his nineties.

GUSTAV VI ADOLF (1882–1973) King of Sweden from 1950, eldest son of Gustav V (q.v.) and Viktoria of Baden. During his long period as Crown Prince Gustav Adolf devoted much time to the study of the humanities and became an acknowledged scholar, archeologist and international expert on Chinese art. He led excavations in Greece and the Far East and also took the initiative in founding the Swedish Arts Foundation (Humanistiska fonden). In 1905 he married Princess Margaret of Connaught (d. 1920), granddaughter of Queen Victoria, and in 1923 he married Lady Louise Mountbatten (d. 1965), the Duke of Edinburgh's aunt, thus veering influence away from Germany and towards Britain. Both as Crown Prince and as King, Gustav Adolf accepted the increasing limitations placed upon the power of the monarchy and was willing to cooperate in making Sweden a democratic monarchy with the King a largely representational figure. Towards the end of his reign a new Constitution was drawn up (but not formally enacted until 1975 after his death) and some demands were heard for a republic, but the King's attitude, together with the personal respect he commanded, undoubtedly helped in preserving the monarchy. In his first marriage he had four sons, Gustav Adolf, Sigvard, Bertil and Carl Johan, and a daughter Ingrid, who married King Frederik IX of Denmark. His eldest son was killed in an air crash in 1947, and he was thus succeeded by his grandson Carl XVI Gustav (q.v.), born 1946.

GYLLENBORG, COUNT CARL (1679–1746) Swedish aristocrat, politician and civil servant. After the death of Karl XII (q.v.) in 1718, President Arvid Horn (q.v.), leader of the Cap Party, adopted a moderate attitude towards Russia, was unwilling to support France in her campaign against Russia and was anxious not to antagonize England. The opposition Hat Party (q.v.), founded by Gyllenborg, was pro-French and had an increasing number of members too young to remember the miseries of Karl XII's disastrous wars who wanted vengeance on Russia. By 1738 the Hats were in the majority and Horn resigned. Gyllenborg became Chancellor, and as such bore a large share of responsibility for the subsequent war policy. Major Sinclair, a Swedish officer, had been sent on a mission in 1739 to Turkey to enlist support against Russia. His murder by a Russian patrol incited the revanchist members of Gyllenborg's party, and when French subsidies to Sweden were agreed to in a treaty in 1741 war seemed inevitable. The ill-prepared Swedish army was soon defeated, the Russians occupied the whole of Finland (q.v.), and Sweden had to accept Empress Elizabeth's peace terms.

In the event these were lenient. Sweden retained most of Finland on condition that Elizabeth's nominee Adolf Fredrik (q.v.) was accepted as Swedish Crown Prince. Gyllenborg used this, and internal squabbling amongst the Caps, to save face and remain Chancellor. He was succeeded in 1745 by Carl Gustaf Tessin. Gyllenborg, a cultured man, wrote the play *Swenska sprätthöken* (The Swedish Fop, first performed 1737), one of Sweden's first comedies.

GYLLENHAMMAR, PEHR GUSTAF (1935–) Swedish industrialist. After graduating in law at Lund University in 1959 Gyllenhammar studied maritime law in the United States and then aspects of industrialism in Geneva, Switzerland, in 1968. By 1971 he was Managing Director of AB Volvo, the world-famous Swedish automobile manufacturer, a post he occupied until 1983, after which he was Chairman of the Board until 1993. A well-known figure, Gyllenhammar is happy to debate in public the role of industry in society. A patriotic Swede, in 1978 he published *Jag tror på Sverige* (I Believe in Sweden). He also believes in Scandinavian and European cooperation, demonstrated in 1993 when he negotiated a merger between his company Volvo and the French automobile manufacturer Renault. His shareholders proved less enthusiastic about the deal and refused to accept its conditions. Convinced that merging with another large automobile company was Volvo's only chance of surviving as a company of international standing, Gyllenhammar resigned.

-H-

HAMMARSKJÖLD, DAG (1905–1961) Swedish statesman, academician and Secretary General of the United Nations. After completing his doctorate in national economy in 1934, he had a rapid diplomatic career as State Secretary in the Finance Department, then leading Swedish delegate to the OEEC (q.v.) from 1948–53 and Minister without portfolio from 1951–53. In 1953 he was appointed Secretary General of the United Nations, and in the best Swedish tradition of neutrality and public service he made the office independent of external political pressures. His active part in tackling international conflicts helped to set up a UN Emergency Force in the Sinai and Gaza in 1956, and he sent observers to Lebanon in 1958. His independence when trying to solve the Congo crisis displeased the USSR, with Kruschev demanding his resignation in 1960. He was killed near Ndola, Zambia, when his aircraft crashed in mysterious circumstances. He was awarded the Nobel Peace Prize (q.v.) posthumously in 1961. His reflections, *Markings*, were published in English in 1964.

HAMMARSKJÖLD, HJALMAR (1862–1953) Swedish Prime Minister. Hammarskjöld, father of Dag Hammarskjöld (q.v.), was Professor of Law at Uppsala (q.v.) University from 1891–96, Minister of Justice from 1901–02, Minister of Education in 1905, President of the Court of Appeal from 1902–1906, provincial governor of Uppsala from 1907–30 and a member of the Swedish Academy (q.v.) from 1918. When the Liberal leader Karl Staaff (qq.v.) resigned as Prime Minister in 1914 after Gustav V's (q.v.) Palace Yard speech (q.v.), the Conservative Hammarskjöld was invited to form a government. He strengthened Sweden's defenses but adhered to a policy of neutrality (q.v.). His pro-German sympathies often led to his interpretation of neutrality working in Germany's favor, especially in the area of trade. By 1917 food and other vital supplies were no longer reaching Sweden, but Hammarskjöld was reluctant to bow to British and American pressure to cease trading with Germany. Opposition to Hammarskjöld's inflexibility grew within his own government as well as in other political parties, and in March 1917 he was defeated in *Riksdag* (q.v.) and obliged to resign.

HANSSON, PER ALBIN (1885–1946) Swedish Social Democratic politician and one of the founders of the Swedish welfare state (q.v.). The son of a bricklayer, Hansson had only four years' formal schooling and worked as a messenger boy when only 12 years of age. He helped to form the Swedish Social Democratic Organization in 1903 and edited its journal *Fram* from 1905 to 1909. He joined the staff of the newspaper *Social-Demokraten* (q.v.) in 1910 and was its chief editor from 1917 to 1924. In 1918 he became a member of *Riksdag* (q.v.), a position he held until his death.

The period after World War I was politically unsettled with frequent changes of government, and the Social Democratic Party (q.v.) under Hjalmar Branting (q.v.) gradually increased its following. The first three Social Democratic governments lasted from March to October 1920, November 1921 to April 1923 and October 1924 to June 1926, and Hansson was Minister of Defense in all three—ironically, perhaps, since disarmament as well as socialism was one of his strongest tenets. He was largely instrumental in the controversial *Riksdag* decision in 1925 to reduce national service and disband some regiments.

Sweden enjoyed considerable industrial expansion in the 1920s, with goods produced by such firms as Electrolux, SKF and Swedish Matches entering world markets, but this also made her more vulnerable, and the Wall Street crash had serious repercussions in Sweden. All parties in *Riksdag* recognized the need to help the mounting numbers of unemployed, but no agreement was reached on how to do so. The Social Democratic government, under Rickard Sandler (q.v.) since Branting's death in 1925, resigned on the issue and was replaced by a Conservative (q.v.) and then a minority Liberal (q.v.) government under Carl Gustaf Ekman (q.v.). When Ekman's government fell in 1932, brought down finally by the Ådalen conflict (q.v.) and the scandal surrounding the Kreuger (q.v.) crash, Hansson's moment had come. He had been voted leader of the Social Democratic Party and after the 1932 elections was appointed Prime Minister. Together with Ernst Wigforss (q.v.) as Finance Minister and Gustav Möller (q.v.) as Minister of Social Affairs he set about forming what he called *Folkhemmet,* literally "the home of the people," which he defined optimistically in 1928 as "the good society which functions like a good home . . . where equality, consideration, cooperation, helpfulness prevail."

Along Keynesian lines his government prepared in 1933 to invest heavily in public works, mostly housing. The Social Democrats lacked an overall majority, but Hansson displayed the clever tactics which were a hallmark of his political career. He made a secret pact with the Agrarians (q.v.), promising protective measures for farmers in exchange for support for his reform program, a deal called the *kohandel* (literally "cowdealing," i.e., horsetrading). This secured the necessary majority and the proposed package was accepted. It was a turning point in the role of the state, for increasingly responsibility would lie with the community rather than the individual. Funds to meet that responsibility would be raised by taxation. Wigforss's budget introduced progressive income tax, a corporation tax as well as a tax on dividends, and indirect taxes on spirits, tobacco and coffee. Hansson had been an ardent socialist at the outset, but as Prime Minister he had no plans for nationalization. The international crisis was beginning to ease but conditions were still dire enough for crisis measures to be accepted. The Swedish krona was deliberately kept below parity. Swedish exports rose quickly, the government's building program had started an upward swing, unemployment fell, real wages rose and there was a general improvement in living standards.

This was a good climate for the introduction of Hansson's new social policy. A state-supported unemployment insurance scheme was introduced in 1934, followed in 1935 by an appreciable rise in the Old Age Pension. Hansson encountered difficulty over the defense budget in 1936. He attempted another deal: the Social Democrats would accept a slight increase in defense spending in exchange for support for a local cost-of-living pension. He was defeated and a minority Agrarian government held office until the 1936 elections.

With the slogans "Per Albin again" and "Welfare Policy" Hansson increased his party's number of seats in *Riksdag,* an endorsement of public support, but he still had no overall majority. He formed a coalition with Pehrsson-Bramstorp (q.v.) and the Agrarians, which gave him an unassailable majority, and the social program could continue. To counteract the low birth rate, publicized by Alva and Gunnar Myrdal (qq.v.) in their study *The Population Crisis* (1934), family allowances and government loans to newly-wed couples were introduced in 1937. Legislation on an eight-hour working day was extended to include farm laborers in 1937. To ensure industrial peace, vital to maintaining the great improvement in Swedish industry, Hansson persuaded Landsorganisationen (Confederation of Trade Unions) (q.v.) and Svenska Arbetsgivareföreningen (Swedish Federation of Employers) (q.v.) to accept the 1938 Saltsjöbaden Agreement (q.v.), where both sides of industry pledged themselves to regulatory collective bargaining. It led to harmonious labor relations free from damaging strikes.

The outbreak of World War II (q.v.) halted the social program. With Hansson fully in control as Prime Minister, a national government was formed in 1939 with representatives from all the major parties, and it ruled until July 1945. Sweden had declared her neutrality (q.v.) and by skill and good fortune was allowed to preserve it, although not without the occasional submission to pressure from the Nazis until 1943 and from the Allies from then until the end of the war. In 1944 the Social Democratic Party drew up a 27-point program for the postwar era, aiming at industrial democracy and increased state influence on the economy. The 1945 elections returned the Social Democrats as the largest party. Hansson was willing to have some form of coalition, but many of his party colleagues were impatient to embark on their new social program and so Hansson formed a purely Social Democratic government.

He died suddenly in October 1946 and was deeply mourned. A plain-spoken man who never forgot his working-class background, ''Per Albin'' had the common touch. A shrewd and yet in some ways visionary politician, he helped to create and to realize the concept of *Folkhemmet*. With increasing pragmatism he also successfully steered Sweden along the Middle Way between communism and capitalism towards an affluent, democratic welfare state.

HARPSUND An estate in Södermanland dating from the 14th century. The present house was built in 1914. It was donated in 1952 on the death of the owner C.A. Wikander to the nation as a residence and conference center for Sweden's Prime Ministers. In the late 1950s Tage Erlander (q.v.) arranged so many private discussions there between representatives of the government and both sides of industry that the opposition complained that this ''Harpsund Democracy'' was undermining *Riksdag*'s (q.v.) authority. Meetings there were greatly reduced by 1964.

HAT PARTY (HATTPARTIET) A political party which during the Age of Freedom (1718–72) wrestled for power with the Cap Party (Mösspartiet). After Karl XII's (q.v.) death in 1718 a new Constitution came into force which stripped the monarchy of much of its power. Arvid Horn (q.v.) became Chancellor and led a group (subsequently called Caps, i.e., Nightcaps) with peace as their first priority. Many Caps were from Finland or the east coast of Sweden and were interested in Baltic trade. They were mainly lower aristocracy, clergy and farmers. By 1738 the Hat Party was formed; the Hats were mainly from Stockholm (q.v.) and the west coast, from the upper aristocracy and large commercial concerns. The name refers to the officer's tricorn and was in direct contrast to the Nightcaps, a term used pejoratively to describe Horn's party and their cautious policies.

   The Hats, mostly too young to remember the misery caused by Karl's disastrous wars, pursued an anti-Russian, pro-French policy and wanted revenge for Sweden's humiliating defeat at Russia's hands. They also pursued a mercantilistic policy with high protective tariffs and state subsidies to trade and industry. Horn and the Caps lost power to the Hats in 1738. Despite an unsuccessful war against Russia 1741–43 the Hats remained in power until 1765. The Caps returned in 1765–69, the Hats from 1769 to 1771. By this time corruption was rife and both parties were discredited, and when Gustav III (q.v.) succeeded to the throne he was able to stage a bloodless revolution in 1772, when both Caps and Hats were disbanded.

HAZELIUS, ARTUR (1833–1901) Swedish philologist, ethnologist and museum curator. In his travels around Scandinavia Hazelius gathered together a fine ethnographic collection illustrative of the old peasant culture. These artefacts formed the basis of the Nordiska museet (Nordic Museum) in Stockholm (q.v.) dating from the 1870s. In Sweden there was a cultural reaction in the 1890s to the factual, realistic literature of the previous decade with its emphasis on social criticism and progress. Swedish authors began to extol the beauties of their home province (Selma Lagerlöf and Gustav Fröding wrote about Värmland, Erik Axel Karlfeldt about Dalarna, for instance) and to stress the importance of preserving traditions that were being seriously threatened by industrialization and population mobility. Swedish painters (e.g., Carl Larsson and Anders Zorn) reflected this trend. A spirit of nationalism began to spread, increased by the friction within the Union with Norway (q.v.) which seemed to put Sweden under threat.

It was in this atmosphere that Hazelius opened Skansen in Stockholm in 1891, the world's first major open-air museum, with the motto "Den dag skall gry då allt vårt guld ej räcker/att forma minnet av den svunna tid" (The day will dawn when all our gold will not suffice to create memories of things past). Skansen consists of over 125 buildings moved intact from various parts of the country. They include cottages, farm buildings, etc., arranged to present the life and culture of the Swedish people over the previous century and more, and are occupied by people in national costume. To the original collection of buildings Seglora church from Västergötland was added in 1917 and Skogaholm manor house from Närke in 1931. There are also collections of workshops demonstrating crafts from the 18th century onwards.

HEDIN, SVEN ADOLF (1834–1905) Swedish Liberal politician, historian and journalist. A graduate of Uppsala (q.v.) University, Hedin cut his teeth on the *Upsala-Posten* before moving to Stockholm (q.v.) in 1864 where he wrote for several newspapers and from 1874 to 1876 was editor of the liberal *Aftonbladet* (q.v.). He was elected to *Riksdag* (q.v.) in 1869 and except for two short periods in 1874–76 and in 1888 he remained a member until his death. He worked tirelessly for universal suffrage, an increase in *Riksdagen's* real power, the retention of free trade, the establishment of social welfare and the introduction of a general national service to replace the old unfair system of military service. His undoubted political gifts lay in effective opposition rather than in leadership, and it was Karl Staaff (q.v.) who led the Liberal

Party (q.v.) when it formed its first government. However, the liberal cause owed a great deal to Hedin. He was called a firebrand by conservative governments and administrations who feared his criticism and his brilliant debating skills.

HEDIN, SVEN ANDERS (1865–1952) Swedish explorer. His many travels to unknown and uncharted lands included three expeditions from 1893 to 1908 to Central Asia and Tibet, of which he made the first detailed map. A great national hero, he also took an active part in politics. In his pamphlet *Ett varningsord* (A Word of Warning, 1914), a million copies of which were distributed, he warned against Russian aggression and urged Sweden to join the Triple Alliance of Germany, Austria and Italy. He was largely the author of King Gustav V's (q.v.) Palace Yard speech (q.v.) in 1914, when the King, addressing over 30,000 pro-defense demonstrators, urged immediate action in strengthening the nation's defenses. Hedin retained his pro-German, anti-Russian attitude even during World War II (q.v.). He was the last Swede to be ennobled.

HEDLUND, GUNNAR (1900–1989) Swedish Agrarian politician. Hedlund succeeded Axel Pehrsson-Bramstorp (q.v.) as leader of the Agrarian Party (later called the Center Party [q.v.]) in 1949. The previous year the Social Democrats (q.v.) had approached the Agrarians with a view to forming a coalition government, but no agreement was reached. In 1951 Erlander (q.v.) leader of the Social Democrats, and Hedlund began negotiations again, and this time a coalition was formed with four Agrarians in the cabinet, including Hedlund who became Minister of Home Affairs. Both parties had much to gain, for Erlander had a slim majority and in his fight against inflation had to take unpopular measures, while Hedlund headed a party which essentially guarded the interests of people in rural areas, and with the move to urban areas gathering momentum it was a great advantage to have Ministers in the Cabinet when dealing with the problem of sparsely populated areas.

Hedlund held ministerial office until 1957, but then the coalition split over the issue of the ATP (q.v.), the state-controlled compulsory superannuation scheme. In the referendum on the ATP the Agrarians submitted an alternative to the Social Democrats' proposal which removed the compulsory element. In the 1958 elections the Agrarians won an extra 13 seats in *Riksdag* but the difference of opinion on the ATP, which Erlander succeeded in getting through, was too great for the coalition to continue. Hedlund, together with the Liberal leader Bertil Ohlin (q.v.), often expressed support for the Social Democrats' social welfare policy, however, and would not identify himself with what he considered the Conservatives' (q.v.) extreme policy, a fact which Erlander was happy to exploit, since it helped to keep his party in office.

Hedlund retired from politics in 1971 and was succeeded as party leader by Thorbjörn Fälldin (q.v.).

HESSELGREN, KERSTIN (1872–1962) Sweden's first woman member of *Riksdag* (q.v.). K. Hesselgren was a domestic science teacher and then a schools inspector. She entered *Riksdag* in 1922 immediately after the emancipation law had come into force and continued to be a member until 1944, sitting first as an independent and then, from 1936 to 1944, as a Liberal (q.v.). She was active nationally and internationally in the field of social work, and strove to improve social conditions, especially for women (q.v.). She was a leading figure in the women's emancipation movement and was chairman of various women's organizations, including the Liberal Women's National Association.

HIERTA, LARS JOHAN (1801–1872) Swedish politician and journalist who founded the liberal newspaper *Aftonbladet*. See also NEWSPAPERS.

HJALMARSON, JARL (1904–1993) Swedish Conservative politician. In 1929 Hjalmarson became secretary to the Conservative politician Arvid Lindman (q.v.) who was then Prime Minister. When Lindman resigned in 1930 Hjalmarson became Secretary and then Representative of the Conservative Party's (q.v.) national organization. In 1944 he was made Deputy Chairman of the party, and was its Chairman from 1950 to 1961. He was Provincial Governor of Gävleborg from 1963–71 and Chairman of the Swedish Red Cross from 1970–71. A man of charm and wit, Hjalmarson also had the reputation of being a skilled negotiator and a man of honor. He was often called the "Peacemaker" and in the 1960s when he had left party politics behind him he was often asked to mediate in labor disputes.

HORN AF EKEBYHOLM, ARVID (1664–1742) Swedish aristo- crat and politician. The son of a poor Finnish nobleman, Horn distinguished himself in Karl XII's (q.v.) early cam- paigns, rose to be a General and 1704 persuaded the Poles to depose their King Augustus and elect Karl's nominee Stanis- laus. In 1706 Karl sent him back to Stockholm (q.v.) to deal with affairs of state. He became a member, and then in 1710 President, of the Council. After Karl's death in 1718 and the acceptance of the liberating Constitution, Horn became Chancellor, leader of the Cap Party (q.v.) and Sweden's leading statesman. Realizing that Sweden needed above all a period of stability to recover from Karl's disastrous wars he followed a cautious policy. In foreign affairs he sought friendship with the European powers, especially Britain, and avoided antagonizing Russia, and at home he was mildly protectionist. It proved successful and Sweden made a good recovery in the 1720s and early 1730s. A younger generation with no memory of the misery of war grew restive and wanted revenge against Russia for Sweden's humiliating defeat. Others wanted a more adventurous mercantile eco- nomic policy. By 1738 the Hat Party (q.v.), which embraced these elements, had gained power and an old, exhausted Horn retired. He was praised even by his political enemies for his great contribution to Sweden's recovery.

HOUSE OF NOBILITY see *RIDDARHUSET*

-J-

JÄRTA, HANS (1774–1847) Järta was a Swedish politician with an independent mind and the courage of his convictions. A supporter of the French Revolution, he renounced his peerage in 1800, changing his name from the aristocratic Hierta with its conservative spelling to the more phonetic Järta. He was involved in the deposing of Gustav IV Adolf (q.v.) in 1809 and was secretary and the driving force of the constitutional committee set up immediately afterwards. He helped to draft the new 1809, Constitution which aimed at a balance of power between the monarch and *Riksdag* (q.v.). He was appointed Secretary of State in 1809, but in 1811 he resigned because during Karl XIII's (q.v.) illness the regency had gone not to the Council, as dictated by the Constitution, but to the new Crown Prince, Karl Johan (Bernadotte). He returned to office in 1815 but withdrew again in 1816, this time in disagreement over Karl Johan's economic policy. He was Provincial Governor in Dalarna from 1812 to 1832 and National Archivist from 1837 to 1844. He was also a member of the Swedish Academy (q.v.) from 1819. Although a vigorous opponent of Karl XIV Johan (q.v.) and popularly known as the Father of the Constitution, Järta became increasingly conservative. Ironically, as his friend the conservative poet and historian Erik Gustav Geijer (q.v.) turned to liberalism in 1838, Järta became from that time one of the Conservatives' (q.v.) most prominent allies against the Liberals (q.v.).

JOHAN III (1537–92) Swedish King, second son of Gustav Vasa (q.v.) and his second wife Margareta Leijonhufvud, and half-brother of Erik XIV (q.v.). Given the independent duchy of Finland by his father, Johan increased the suspicions of his paranoic half-brother Erik by marrying Katarina Jagellonica, sister of the King of Poland, Erik's rival for territorial gain in the Baltic area. Erik had Johan imprisoned, but with the help of his brother Duke Karl and the Nobility Johan staged a rebellion and in 1568 deposed the King. Johan, who lacked Gustav Vasa's practical, energetic character but was his most learned son, had Catholic leanings and a genuine interest in theology. He wished to reconcile Protestants and Catholics, but his attempts to impose a Catholic-inspired liturgy (the "Red Book") on the Swedish clergy had the opposite effect. Many of them preferred exile, and found asylum with Duke Karl, who had Calvinistic leanings.

Johan had his son Sigismund (q.v.), now Crown Prince of Sweden, educated as a Catholic and in 1587 successfully put forward his candidacy for the Polish throne. This led to a union of crowns on Johan's death, but it was short-lived, for Sigismund was soon deposed by his uncle, Duke Karl.

One of Johan's first actions as King was to negotiate with Denmark the Peace of Stettin (1570) which ended the Northern Seven Years War. Like Erik he struggled to stifle Russia's ambitions in the Baltic but with Poland as his ally. The war with Russia continued until 1597, several years after his death.

To gain backing in deposing Erik, Johan had made concessions to both the Nobility and to Duke Karl and enjoyed their support for many years, but towards the end of his reign he came into conflict with them, the Nobility wanting more political power and Karl trying to make his duchy an independent state within the state. On Johan's death Sweden was troubled economically as a result of incessant wars in the Baltic, politically as both the Nobility and Duke Karl jockeyed for increased power, and ecclesiastically as Sigismund, a Catholic, inherited a Protestant kingdom.

JOHANSSON, OLOF (1937–) Swedish politician. An active member of the Center (former Farmers') Party (q.v.), Johansson was Chairman of the Center Party Youth Organization from 1969 to 1971, and has been a member of *Riksdag* (q.v.) since 1971. During the non-socialist coalition governments under Thorbjörn Fälldin (q.v.) Johansson held cabinet office from 1976 to 1978, and from 1979 to 1982. Like Fälldin he was opposed to the proliferation of nuclear plants (q.v.) in Sweden, and became a well-known figure in the energy debates of the 1970s. He became Chairman of the Center Party in 1987, and in the four-party non-socialist coalition government formed by Carl Bildt (q.v.) in 1991, he was appointed Minister of the Environment.

-K-

KALMAR UNION (1397–1521) A Union of the Scandinavian countries. When the Danish King Valdemar Atterdag died

without male issue in 1375 his 23-year-old daughter Margareta (q.v.) was already married to King Håkon of Norway.
Their child Olov was elected King of Denmark with Queen
Margareta his official guardian. Håkon died in 1380, Olov
succeeded him and the two kingdoms were united. As Olov
was still a minor, Margareta, shrewd, resolute but flexible,
was effectively ruler. Meanwhile the Swedes' dissatisfaction
with their King Albrekt of Mecklenburg mounted until they
finally turned to Margareta for help, and Albrekt was deposed in 1389. Olov had died, only 17 years old, in 1387 and
Margareta adopted her great-nephew Erik of Pomerania
(q.v.) as her heir. In 1397 in Kalmar he was crowned King of
Denmark, Norway and Sweden; Norway included the
Faroes, Orkney, Shetland and Iceland; Sweden included
Finland. The actual treaty document was only in draft form
and was never ratified.

Erik was only 14 and Margareta was de facto ruler of a
united Scandinavia until her death in 1412. Erik lacked
her wisdom, patience and political flair, and the Union was
soon in trouble under him. He was involved throughout
most of his reign in a struggle with Schleswig and Holstein,
which caused friction, too, with the Hanseatic League. To
finance his wars he levied heavy taxes on Sweden and
installed there Danish and German officials, which the
Swedes resented. When a blockade of Swedish ports by the
Hanseatic League prevented the export of iron and copper,
resentment turned to rebellion under Engelbrekt Engelbrektsson (q.v.) who became Guardian of the Realm in 1435.
Erik was officially deposed in 1439 and succeeded by
Kristoffer of Bavaria.

The Union was in force again until his death in 1448, when
Sweden elected Karl Knutsson as King, while the Danes
favored Kristian of Oldenburg. This led to armed conflict,
with Karl Knutsson and then the Stures (Sten the Elder,
Svante and then Sten the Younger) (qq.v.) fighting to
establish Swedish independence, and Kristian I and then his
son Hans attempting to reimpose the Union. Hans's son
Kristian II invaded Sweden in 1518, defeated Sten Sture the
Younger and attempted to establish his rule forcibly by
summarily executing many of Sten's supporters (the Stock-

holm Bloodbath [q.v.] of 1520). It sparked a national rising under Gustav Vasa (q.v.) who by 1521 had united Sweden behind him, expelled the Danes and effectively brought the Kalmar Union to an end.

KARL IX (1550–1611) Swedish King, youngest son of Gustav Vasa (q.v.) and Margareta Leijonhufvud, half-brother of Erik XIV (q.v.) and uncle of Sigismund III Vasa (q.v.) of Poland and Sweden. Karl had inherited an independent duchy in central Sweden on the death of his father in 1560. In 1568 he joined his brother Johan in a rebellion against Erik, who was deposed and succeeded by Johan (III) (q.v.). Johan died in 1592 and during the absence of his son and heir, King Sigismund of Poland, Karl was de facto ruler of Sweden. A Protestant with Calvinistic leanings, Karl had already defied Johan's Counter-Reformation measures. Members of the Clergy who had refused to use Johan's Catholic-inspired liturgy, the "Red Book," had found a refuge in Karl's duchy. In 1593, before the Catholic Sigismund had returned from Poland to claim his Swedish kingdom, Karl called the Convention of Uppsala, which accepted the Augsburg Confession, thus reaffirming Sweden as a Lutheran country. Acting as Regent, Karl increased pressure on his nephew until finally defeating him in open war in 1598 and, the most ruthless of Gustav Vasa's sons, executing the leading Swedish supporters of King Sigismund in Linköping in 1600. He was formally proclaimed Karl IX in 1604, from which time Lutheranism has remained the state religion (q.v.), with the monarch as supreme administrator.

Having usurped Sigismund's crown Karl had made Poland his implacable enemy, and an inconclusive war was waged between them for a decade. In 1611 Christian IV of Denmark, seeing that Karl was engaged elsewhere, attacked a Sweden bereft of allies. At this point, with his country threatened on all side, Karl died of a stroke. He had married Maria of the Palatinate and was succeeded by their 17-year-old son Gustav II Adolf (q.v.), the legendary "Lion of the North," who speedily accomplished his immediate task of saving the country and then went on to establish Sweden as a European power.

KARL X GUSTAV (1622–1660) Swedish King, son of John Kasimir, Count Palatine and Catherine, daughter of Karl IX (q.v.), and cousin of Queen Kristina (q.v.). Averse to marriage, Kristina persuaded *Riksdag* (q.v.) to accept her cousin as heir to the throne in 1650. Immediately on her abdication in 1654 he became King. He recognized that too many royal estates had passed into the hands of the Nobility and set in train a scrutiny of the legality of their claims. Some estates were restored to the Crown, but the main recovery of alienated lands was left to his son Karl XI (q.v.). Trained at Sørø military academy in Denmark, Karl Gustav served with distinction during the Thirty Years War (q.v.) and was appointed Commander of the Swedish forces in Germany in 1648. Unlike Kristina, who wanted above all peace for her people, his inclination was always to settle a dispute by military force rather than diplomacy.

The struggle for supremacy in the Baltic was threatening Swedish interests, so in 1655 Karl Gustav went to war, first overrunning Poland. It proved easier to conquer than to hold, and the Poles rose up against the occupying forces, aided by the Dutch, who were alarmed at Sweden's increasing power, and by Russia. Hoping to exploit the situation, Denmark entered the war and Karl Gustav turned on the Danes, quickly occupying the whole of Jutland. His army was in danger of being completely cut off for he had no navy at his disposal, but early in 1658 he took a calculated risk and moved his entire army over the Belts, which in an abnormally cold winter had frozen over. Caught unawares, the Danes were obliged to accept the Treaty of Roskilde (1658), by the terms of which the hitherto Danish provinces of Halland, Bohuslän and the very fertile Skåne became part of southern Sweden. Trondheim and the island of Bornholm were also ceded to Sweden.

Although Sweden had emerged as the largest and strongest of the Scandinavian countries, Karl Gustav was not satisfied. A few months after signing the treaty he attacked Denmark again, this time intending to force Denmark-Norway into a Swedish-controlled Scandinavian kingdom. With Dutch help Fredrik III and the citizens of Copenhagen put up a stirring defense of their capital and warded off the

Swedish attack. Meanwhile, Swedish Pomerania was attacked, while the inhabitants of Trondheim and Bornholm rebelled, and guerrilla bands in Skåne embarrassed the authorities. At this critical point Karl Gustav suddenly died, in 1660, only 38 years old. However, since a quiescent Scandinavia was in the interests of France, England and Holland at this juncture, Brandenburg was persuaded to evacuate Swedish Pomerania, Russia returned Swedish territory in the Baltic, while Denmark was persuaded to accept the Treaty of Copenhagen (1660) in which Trondheim and Bornholm reverted to Denmark-Norway but Skåne, Halland and Bohuslän remained Swedish. Karl Gustav's legacy therefore was a reasonably secure country incorporating the southern provinces, which have remained Swedish ever since.

Karl Gustav married Hedvig Eleonora of Holstein-Gottorp in 1654 and had one son, Karl (XI) (q.v.), who was only four years of age when he succeeded his father.

KARL XI (1655–1697) Swedish King, son of Karl X Gustav (q.v.). When Karl X Gustav succeeded Queen Kristina (q.v.) he recognized the necessity of a "reduktion," i.e., reclaiming Crown estates and revenues from the Nobility, and started the process, but he was too occupied with foreign wars to pursue the matter. Karl XI was only five on his succession in 1660, allowing the Regents, headed by Chancellor Magnus Gabriel De La Gardie (q.v.), once more to strengthen the Nobility's position at the Crown's expense and to halt the "reduktion" process. On his sudden death Karl Gustav had left his country at war with Denmark, Poland, Russia and Brandenburg. The Regents obtained favorable terms in treaties with all of these and then turned to state finances. Reluctant to prejudice their own position, they weakened the monarchy further by the alienation of even more Crown lands. Sweden had expanded her boundaries at the expense of Denmark, while Holland saw Sweden as a threat to her maritime aspirations. De La Gardie saw an alliance with France linked to French subsidies as a free means of building up Swedish defenses. It was a miscalculation, for Brandenburg attacked France, and however reluctantly, Sweden was obliged by treaty to come to France's aid.

The Swedes were defeated at Fehrbellin (1675) which encouraged Denmark and Holland to declare war on Sweden. The Danes invaded and Karl, who had assumed power in 1672, was by great personal gallantry able to win the Battle of Lund (1676) and expel the Danes.

The young King's bravery was remembered, while the policies of the Regents and the Nobility were discredited. In Europe as a whole absolute monarchy was being accepted. In Sweden by 1682 Karl, with *Riksdag's* (q.v.) approval, was given absolute control and by 1693 it was even declared that he and his heirs were ''responsible to none on Earth for their actions.'' Karl used his divine right to carry out a full-scale ''reduktion,'' and by the end of his reign a third of all the land was in his hands and the peasantry had thus had the threat of serfdom removed. Karl was then able to build up Sweden's military forces again. He introduced the *indelning* system, a form of recruitment started by Gustav II Adolf (q.v.) but now taken much further. The larger provinces were made responsible for providing and equipping their own regiments, including cavalry, while the fleet was rebuilt and based at Karlskrona, more southerly and practical than Stockholm (q.v.).

In more romantic periods Swedes were fascinated by their great warrior Kings, such as Gustav II Adolf and Karl XII (q.v.), but in modern times Karl XI, the King who restored the country's finances, valued peace and preserved the peasants' traditional freedom, is more to their liking. He married Ulrika Eleonora of Denmark in 1680 and they had one son Karl (XII) (q.v.) and two daughters, Hedvig Sofia and Ulrika Eleonora (q.v.).

KARL XII (1682–1718) Swedish King, son of Karl XI (q.v.) and Ulrika Eleonora of Denmark, one of Sweden's warrior kings. Although only 15 on the death of his father in 1697, Karl was soon declared of age and assumed absolute power. It was a time of changes and realignments in Europe: the complicated Spanish succession exercised European leaders for most of Karl's reign; Augustus II of Saxony also became King of Poland; Peter became sole Tsar of Russia; and Karl's sister Hedvig Sofia married the Duke of Holstein-Gottorp, which the new King of Denmark, Frederik IV, saw as a threat. England and Holland were increasingly trading nations during this period, using their influence to keep the peace, while Louis XIV of France seemed best served if German states were warring against each other. Countries which had lost territory to Sweden during the 17th century thought that with an untried 15-year-old on the throne and the Nobility apparently disaffected, having lost lands and revenues under Karl XI, Sweden was vulnerable.

The Great Northern War broke out in 1700. Sweden's enemies Denmark, Saxony and then Russia formed an alliance. Karl XII soon displayed his great strengths—military genius, bravery and decisiveness. He invaded Denmark with the aid of an Anglo-Dutch squadron, and King Frederik sued for peace. He then moved quickly against Russia and with a numerically small but well-trained force he routed the Russian army at Narva (1700). It was then the turn of Augustus of Saxony-Poland. In 1702 Karl defeated the Saxons at Kliszow and in 1704 he occupied Warsaw, dethroned Augustus and forced the Poles to accept Stanislaus Leszcynski as their King. By 1706 at Altranstädt Augustus was forced to abdicate and withdraw from the alliance.

Karl now felt secure enough to deal decisively, as he thought, with Russia. In 1707 he moved on Moscow, expecting reinforcements from Finland, Poland, and also from Mazeppa, the Tsar's opponent in the Ukraine, to reach him. These troops did not appear in time. The Tsar pursued a scorched-earth policy, and then an exceptionally severe winter took its toll of the Swedish army. Karl moved south in 1709 and besieged Poltava in order to force Peter into a pitched battle. Although greatly outnumbered Karl might still have won, but he had been wounded in the foot two days earlier and contrary to his usual practice was unable to have overall control of the battle. The Swedish army fled, and Karl crossed with only a few hundred men into Bender, Turkey. Once news of Poltava spread, Sweden's enemies closed in. Augustus regained his Polish throne, the Danes invaded Skåne in southern Sweden and the Russians occupied Karelia and Viborg.

Karl remained a virtual prisoner for five years in Bender, repeatedly trying to persuade the sultan to attack Russia. He became an embarrassment until he broke out in 1713 amidst great confusion (the Kalabalik, i.e., fracas, in Bender). Travelling incognito Karl made an amazing ride on horseback to Stralsund in 15 days. Eventually he reached Lund (q.v.) in Skåne in 1715. Despite the dire state of Sweden's economy he raised a new army and tried to repel the invaders of the Swedish mainland. In 1718 he invaded Norway to prevent a Danish-Norwegian attack, but he was shot in the head on the battlements of Fredriksten fortress and died instantly. It was rumored that the bullet had come from his own lines, a claim impossible to confirm or deny despite historians' scrutiny of the site and Karl's cranium. The Swedes moved swiftly to obtain peace terms. Partly with English mediation they were able to salvage Wismar and Pomerania, but in the treaty with Russia (Nystad 1721) they had to accept the Tsar's terms and lost their eastern territory and part of Finland.

Karl's personality is an enigma that has fascinated many writers, including Voltaire. Romantics considered him to be a great hero and man of destiny; others saw him as an obstinate despot who brought about the downfall of the Swedish empire. He was uncommunicative, had no confidents and left few personal documents, and so his motivation and grand schemes are only speculation. Indisputably his death marked the end of absolutism. He left no direct heir, and his sister Ulrika Eleonora (q.v.) was elected monarch only after she had accepted a new Constitution depriving the monarchy of almost all its power. The country was exhausted, its economy near collapse and its defenses inadequate. The empire Karl had inherited had been acquired piecemeal and defending it in the 18th century required not just military prowess but diplomatic skills, which Karl singularly lacked. Ultimately he became an anachronism, attempting to solve Sweden's problems with drawn sword at the head of a small gallant army.

KARL XIII (1748–1818) King of Sweden from 1809 and of Norway from 1814, son of Adolf Fredrik (q.v.) and Lovisa

Ulrika (q.v.), and younger brother of Gustav III (q.v.). During his brother's reign Karl commanded the Swedish fleet against Russia in the 1788–90 war and for a brief spell commanded the army too. After Gustav's assassination in 1792 he acted as Regent until his nephew Gustav IV Adolf (q.v.) came of age in 1796. When his nephew was deposed in 1809 Karl was elected King but only on his acceptance of a new Constitution limiting the power of the monarchy. By this time Karl was old and his marriage to Charlotta of Oldenburg in 1774 had remained childless. When Bernadotte (Karl Johan [q.v.]) was elected Crown Prince in 1810, Karl adopted him and was content to remain in the background, leaving Karl Johan the de facto ruler. In 1814 Karl Johan forced Norway into a Union (q.v.) with Sweden and Karl became officially King of Sweden and Norway.

There is some ambivalence about Karl's loyalties. He was associated with the Anjala League (q.v.), a group of Finnish officers who rebelled against Gustav III in 1788 during the Russian war. The dying Gustav had specified that Karl was to be just a member of the Council acting as Regent during Gustav IV Adolf's minority but Karl had himself made sole Regent. However, during those four years he allowed himself to be dominated by Reuterholm, nicknamed the Grand Vizier, a mystic and Free Mason who exploited Karl's interest in occult sciences. After Gustav Adolf was deposed in 1809 Karl gave no support to those wishing to elect his nephew's son Gustav as Crown Prince, going on instead to show a touching faith in Bernadotte's judgement.

KARL XIV JOHAN (1763–1844) King of Sweden and Norway and founder of the present Bernadotte dynasty. Born Jean Baptiste Jules Bernadotte, he was the son of a lawyer from Pau in southeast France. An ardent supporter of the French Revolution, he joined the French army in 1780 and had a brilliant military career, rising to the rank of Marshal of France in 1804. In 1805 he was created Prince of Pontecorvo for gallantry in the Battle of Austerlitz. In 1810 he accepted an invitation, instigated by young radical Swedish officers, to become Crown Prince of Sweden, assumed the name of Karl Johan and became a Protestant. From the outset he was virtually in control, for King Karl XIII (q.v.) was already almost senile, childless and quickly developed a touching faith in this handsome, dynamic adoptive son.

Karl Johan confounded the supporters of his candidature (who had hoped he would use his French influence and regain Finland [q.v.], lost to Russia in the 1808–09 war), for his "1812 policy" was almost the exact reverse. He joined Russia against Napoleon and then forced Denmark to cede Norway to Sweden (Treaty of Kiel, 1814). The Union (q.v.) between Norway and Sweden lasted from 1814 to 1905. His supporters had also assumed that as a child of the Revolution he would favor reform, but in effect he resisted all efforts by the liberals to reduce the power of the Crown, and towards the end of his life he met increasing opposition to his conservative views. On inviting Bernadotte to Sweden it had also been assumed that as a friend of Napoleon and a brilliant soldier he would improve Sweden's standing militarily. In fact Napoleon neither liked nor particularly trusted Bernadotte. Karl Johan did improve Sweden's situation but he achieved this by keeping Sweden-Norway free from wars throughout his entire reign.

He married Desirée Clary (see Desideria), a merchant's daughter from Marseilles, in 1798 and was succeeded by their son Oscar I (q.v.) in 1844.

KARL XV (1829–1872) King of Sweden-Norway, and eldest son of Oscar I (q.v.) and Josefine of Leuchtenburg. Karl had acted as Regent for two years during his father's illness and succeeded to the throne in 1859. His reign coincided with many important reforms, carried through largely by his ministers Johan Gripenstedt and Louis De Geer (q.v.), including the removal of economic restrictions, the revision of the penal code and of local government, and increased religious tolerance. Most important of all was the *Riksdag* (q.v.) reform of 1865–66, when the old Four Estates gave way to a more democratic bicameral parliament. Karl was unenthusiastic about this measure but could not prevent it.

Karl was equally unsuccessful in his attempt to influence foreign policy. A zealous supporter of Pan-Scandinavianism (q.v.), he promised Frederik VII of Denmark assistance, but when the Dano-Prussian War started (1864) the Swedish government refused to honor this promise.

Karl was a popular monarch, handsome, outgoing, a patron of the Arts and a competent writer and painter. He was nevertheless unable to prevent the erosion of the authority of the Crown. He married Lovisa of the Netherlands. They had one daughter but no son and Karl was therefore succeeded by his younger brother Oscar II (q.v.).

KEY, ELLEN (1849–1926) Swedish author, educationist and champion of women's rights. The daughter of Emil Key, a well-known politician and member of *Riksdag* (q.v.), Ellen Key was given a good educational grounding at home. When her father lost his fortune in 1880 she began teaching in Stockholm (q.v.). She became a prominent lecturer, popular with workers' institutes and branches of the temperance movement (q.v.). From 1900 she was able to devote herself to her writings, which received recognition both at home and abroad, especially in Germany. At heart a liberal, she tried to unite her views with socialist ideas, fighting for freedom of expression and of the individual, and for the improvement of all citizens' lot. She was one of the first to demand votes for women (q.v.). She also criticized prevailing views on marriage and caused an outcry with her outspoken belief that love, not conventional morality, should be the deciding factor in a relationship.

Ellen Key's views on education were also radical for the period. Children, she maintained, should be allowed to develop freely under discreet maternal guidance, and she criticized schools for trying to make children conform. She advocated a school close to the present-day comprehensive system. Ellen Key believed that with the emancipation of women society would become gentler and war would no longer be feasible. Her views, expressed most importantly in *Barnets århundrade* (The Century of the Child, 1900) and *Lifslinjer* (Lines in Life, 1903–06), sometimes lacked clarity and were easily criticized by more trained minds, including philosophers and some writers, Strindberg (q.v.) among them, but her sincerity and her ability to communicate made her a most influential figure of the period.

KIEL, TREATY OF see KARL XIV JOHAN

KREUGER, IVAR (1880–1932) Swedish industrialist and financier, known as the Swedish "Match King." The son of a match manufacturer, Kreuger trained as a civil engineer and worked in America and South Africa before returning to Sweden in 1907. In 1913 he founded the United Swedish Match Company and set out to establish a world monopoly in match manufacture. With his partner Paul Toll he founded the international financial concern AB Kreuger & Toll (1924). By lending large sums to governments in deals involving monopolistic concessions he was able to control 75 percent of the world match industry by the late 1920s. He created a financial empire with great international influence, but was unable to withstand the world economic crisis, was in great difficulty in 1931, and finally committed suicide in Paris in March 1932.

The crash was followed by a wave of bankruptcies and suicides as the scale of his debts came to light. It took seven years to clear up his complex financial dealings, frauds and forgeries. In the aftermath of his death it emerged that he had secretly donated funds to the Swedish Liberal Prime Minister Carl Gustaf Ekman (q.v.). Ekman resigned in 1932 and the political scandal contributed to the fall of the government later that year. The Social Democrats (q.v.) came to power and remained in office either alone or in coalition for the next 44 years.

KRISTINA (1626–1689) Swedish Queen and only child of Gustav II Adolf (q.v.). She was only six when her father fell at Lützen in 1632, and Sweden was in effect governed by Chancellor Axel Oxenstierna (q.v.) until 1644 when Kristina came of age. The fortunes of the Nobility had greatly improved during Gustaf Adolf's reign, but mutual respect had ensured whole-hearted support for the King. After 1632 the Nobility acquired even more land and revenues, while the royal estates were being sacrificed to meet the costs of the Thirty Years War (q.v.). Many Swedish aristocrats had fought in Germany and the Baltic states where serfdom still prevailed, and they wished to impose such a system on the

Swedish peasantry, which had always enjoyed its freedom. Kristina inherited the Vasa intellect and personality, and was a gifted linguist and philosopher and patron of the Arts, but she was disinclined to tackle the country's economic and social problems. Indeed she exacerbated them by bestowing on her favorites royal estates the revenues from which had been earmarked for civil servants' salaries and other state expenses.

At her father's request Kristina had been educated as a male heir during her minority. She seems to have been bisexual by nature and found the idea of marriage and childbirth distasteful, although Oxenstierna urged her to produce an heir. She shrewdly played off the Nobility and the dissatisfied Peasantry against each other and had her cousin Karl Gustav (q.v.) accepted by *Riksdag* (q.v.) in 1648 as Commander of the Swedish Armies in Germany, and in the following year as her successor. She had by then decided to convert to Catholicism, which meant she could no longer be Swedish monarch and defender of the Protestant faith. In 1654 she abdicated, taking a tearful farewell of her people, and went via Innsbruck, Austria, where she officially embraced the Catholic faith, to Rome.

During her reign Kristina built up a cultural court life, was a generous patron to artists and philosophers, including the Swedish polymath Stiernhielm (q.v.) and the French philosopher Descartes, who spent four months in her capital—and died there of pneumonia. She did nothing to rescue the Crown's financial position, however, and in the eyes of many of her subjects, moreover, she had betrayed her country by abandoning her father's faith. Twice after her abdication she returned to Sweden, but found no enthusiasm for her reinstatement. She died in Rome and was buried there in St Peter's—an ironic end to the only child of the great Lion of the North and champion of Protestantism.

-L-

LAESTADIUS, LARS LEVI (1800–1861) Swedish revivalist preacher and botanist. Laestadius was a Lutheran (q.v.)

parson in Karesuando in northern Sweden from 1826 to 1849 and then in Pajola. He had felt that preaching was futile, but then in 1845 he underwent a great spiritual crisis and emerged with new insight and great revivalist zeal. His emotionally-charged preaching with its emphasis on public confession of one's transgressions attracted many people, including Lapps (q.v.), living in the harsh northern environment, and Laestadianism spread throughout the north of Sweden and Finland, but made little impact in central and southern Sweden. Since Laestadianism was based on the Lutheran doctrine it was no danger to the established Church theologically. Socially, however, it was more threatening to the hierarchy, for the revivalist preacher attracted large crowds who travelled great distances to hear him and broke with the old parish bonds. It was in effect one of the first of many popular movements in the 19th century that helped to bring about change in the social order when social reform in *Riksdag* (q.v.) had stagnated.

LAND ENCLOSURES Over the centuries Swedish farming land had been divided up among farmers' heirs until by the early 18th century the resulting small plots were uneconomic and a hindrance to progress. A peasant could own as many as 50 strips of land scattered over a large area, causing him to waste time travelling from one strip to another and making him dependent on other peasants. At the instigation of Jacob Faggot (1699–1777), Head of the National Land Survey, a scheme for the reallocation or exchange of land *(storskifte)* was introduced in 1757, aiming at forming larger units. The benefits of this agricultural reform were slight, for its actual scope was limited and its application less thorough than had been originally intended.

Inspired by enclosure reform in England and Denmark, Rutger Maclean, a Swedish landowner of Scottish descent, decided in 1783 to introduce a more drastic reform *(enskifte)* on his lands at Svaneholm in Skåne, the fertile south of Sweden. Despite strong opposition from farmers, he reallocated land following the principle of unitary holdings and one farm-house on each holding. This not only led to larger, more effective agricultural units, but also to the breakup of the old village communities. It was soon evident that the reform resulted in increased productivity, and a law passed in 1803 enabled the *enskifte* to be realized throughout the entire province of Skåne, followed in 1804 by Skaraborg county, and in 1807 the whole of Sweden with the exception of Kopparberg, Gävleborg, west Norrland and Finland. Farmers' travelling distances were reduced radically and they were made independent of other farmers. They were left to their own devices and could plow up meadow and grazing land. Within a few decades the reform had dissipated small farming communities and altered Swedish landscapes, especially in Skåne.

LANDSORGANISATIONEN (LO, Swedish Confederation of Trade Unions). A few trade unions (q.v.) were formed in Sweden during the 1860s and 1870s. It was the beginning of an unruly period in labor relations, exemplified in the 1879 Sundsvall strike involving 5,000 workers in the timber industry. The number of unions increased, and in 1898 they joined together to form LO. It was agreed that within three years all unions within LO would be affiliated with the Social Democratic Party (q.v.), which had been formed in 1889. In 1902 the employers formed their counterpart, Svenska Arbetsgivareföreningen (SAF, Swedish Federation of Employers). The first real trial of strength was in 1909 when SAF countered strikes with a lockout and LO responded with a General Strike (Storstrejken) (q.v.). It lasted a month, after which union funds ran out and members had to return to work, but despite its defeat LO had demonstrated its potential. By 1928 a new law on legally-binding collective bargaining was passed, leading in 1938 to the Saltsjöbaden Agreement (q.v.) between SAF and LO, which regulated procedures on collective bargaining and industrial action, and heralded a period of harmony in industrial relations.

LO's highest authority is its Congress, which meets every five years to set policy; there is then the General Council, which meets twice annually to effect Congress' decisions, and the National Executive, which meets weekly.

LO's central bargaining power was somewhat eroded by the 1980s, when some individual members of SAF began to deal directly with some of the large unions, including the Metal Workers' Union, LO's oldest and third largest union, but its role is still central.

Since 1974 boards of directors of large firms have had to include trade union representatives. In an attempt to increase wealth distribution and workers' influence further, LO accepted in the 1970s the Rudolf Meidner (q.v.) plan: 20 per cent of the profits of companies with a certain number of employees (50 or 100 was suggested) should go annually into funds to be administered by a union board. The funds (Wage Earner Funds, WEF) would be used to promote trade union activities among all members and for members' education and training, research, cultural and recreational facilities, etc. There was great opposition to WEF, not only among SAF members and non-socialist parties but even among more moderate Social Democratic supporters who felt socialism was being pushed too far. However, the WEF scheme was accepted as Social Democratic Party policy. The party lost the 1976 election, and by the time they were returned to power in 1982 the WEF scheme had been watered down to become innocuous. No further money was to be paid into WEF after 1990.

LO has become a powerful force in Swedish society. It embraces 23 unions, with a total membership of almost 2,270,000 in a country of eight and a half million. As well as guarding members' interests in collective bargaining, it encourages workers' education through the Arbetarnas Bildningsförbund (ABF, Workers Education Association) (q.v.) and its own schools. It is also represented on over 30 central agencies, including the powerful Arbetsmarknadsstyrelsen (AMS, Labor Market Board), the Occupation and Safety Board and the Immigration Board.

LANGUAGE see SWEDISH LANGUAGE

LAPPS (SAAMES) An ethnic minority, the Lapps, or Saame people as they are also called, stem from the oldest inhabitants in Scandinavia. There are references to them in ancient sources, and pollen analysis has dated a Lappish ski to as early as 2000 B.C. They were nomadic hunters, fishers and reindeer herdsmen, roaming the tundra, forests and coast-lines of Lappland (i.e., northern regions of Norway, Sweden, Finland and the Kola peninsula) long before those countries had been politically defined. Their Mongolian origins, Fenno-Ugrian language and culture are quite distinct from those of the Nordic peoples, and their way of life was traditionally adapted to the severe conditions of the very north of Europe. Approximately 2,000 Lapps live in Russia, 3,000 in Finland, 22,000 in Norway and 10,000 in Sweden.

Ideally suited to their natural habitat, the Lapps could cope with the harsh conditions in Lappland but were more vulner-able to threats from Scandinavian civilization spreading northwards. In the Middle Ages traders (called *birkarlar)* had a monopoly on trade with the Lapps, dealing in furs and even collecting taxes. In the 16th century Denmark-Norway, Sweden and Russia disputed the right to tax the Lapps and their reindeer herds. Another threat arose in 1673 when thousands of Finns were settled around Umeå in Lappland to hold it against Danes and Norwegians, and inevitably dis-turbed the Lappish herding patterns. Even so, they were still an exotic, almost unknown people when Linnaeus (q.v.) journeyed to Lappland in 1732 and published his *Iter Lapponicum.* The talks between Norway and Sweden in 1905 leading to the dissolution of the Union (q.v.) led *inter alia* to a treaty giving Swedish Lapps the right to graze their reindeer across the Norwegian border.

Advancing industrialization proved to be a severe hazard to Lappish culture: roads and railways interrupted Lapps' migration routes; waterfalls in Lappland were harnessed; electric power lines cut through forests. Perhaps the greatest threats, however, were government measures to regularize the Lapps' existence. They were obliged to think in the same monetary terms as the rest of the country, slaughtering and marketing their reindeer, often using modern farming meth-ods instead of the traditional seasonal migration. Increasing numbers of Lapps abandoned their ancient lifestyle, moved further south and settled in communities. By the 1970s fewer than one third of the Swedish Lapps were still dependent on their reindeer herds. The change was accelerated by the state insisting on every Lappish child having to attend school. In

1942 a folk high school for Lapps was established at Sorsele (removed in 1945 to Jokkmokk), where as well as general courses instruction in Saame language and culture was started.

In 1904 the first attempts were made to bring Swedish Lapps together. By 1918 a national meeting to discuss legal and cultural Lappish affairs could be held in Östersund. Individualistic by nature, the Lapps did not take easily to organization. By 1950 the National Swedish Lapp Assembly was formed in Jokkmokk, representing 44 Saame villages and 13 associations in Sweden. It meets annually and works to promote Lapps' economic, social, administrative and cultural interests. A Lappish newspaper founded in 1919 was taken over in 1960 by the highly respected Dr Israel Ruong, a Lapp and school inspector, and Lapp radio stations were established. In 1962 an *ombudsman* (q.v.) was appointed to deal with Lapp interests. The dilemma remains that measures to help preserve Lappish culture tend towards increased organization and therefore away from the traditional Lappish way of life.

LAVAL, CARL GUSTAV DE (1845–1913) Swedish engineer and inventor. One of several gifted Swedes whose creative work helped to further the industrial revolution in Sweden towards the end of the 19th century, Laval included among his many inventions a centrifugal cream separator (1878) and the first practical steam turbine (1883). He also invented milking machines and apparatus for gauging the fat content in milk. Laval was involved in founding several companies to exploit his own inventions, including AB Separator and AB De Lavals Ångturbin (Steam Turbine Co.) He was a member of *Riksdag* (q.v.) from 1888 to 1890 and from 1893 to 1902.

LIBERAL PARTY (FOLKPARTIET) In 1895 Folkpartiet, a party within *Riksdag* (q.v.), was formed. Five years later it amalgamated with the newly founded parliamentary party Liberala samlingspartiet (Liberal Alliance). It had a broader base than the Social Democratic Party (q.v.), embracing intellectuals, non-conformists, teetotallers and radicals, and counted several prominent politicians among its members, including Sven Adolf Hedin (q.v.), who had been advocating old age pensions from 1884, David Bergström, who pushed forward on the franchise issue, and above all Karl Staaff (q.v.), with a passionate belief in parliamentarianism. At first its program was wide but ill-defined: a state-supported home ownership plan, a factory inspection plan, pensions, suffrage, etc. When the energetic Karl Staaff was appointed its leader he worked for social improvements, including the setting up of a social welfare board and old age pensions, but above all he moved purposefully towards universal suffrage and an acceptance of *Riksdag*'s supremacy.

Staaff was Prime Minister from 1905 to 1906 and from 1911 to 1914, and in both periods he antagonized Gustav V (q.v.) by trying to make Ministers responsible to *Riksdag* and the electorate rather than the monarch, and to give more credence to the more democratically elected Lower Chamber than to the Upper Chamber. Matters came to a head in 1914 when Gustav openly sided with demonstrators against his Prime Minister's disarmament policy in his Palace Yard speech (q.v.). A furious Staaff tried to exact the King's promise never again to go over his Prime Minister's head, and resigned when the King refused. It was the end of Staaff's political career, although ironically no Swedish King ever again acted in such a nonparliamentarian way. A few years later, thanks to Liberal efforts, universal male suffrage was achieved, a pyrrhic victory for the Liberals, since it led to Social Democratic gains at their expense. In 1912 the Liberals held 102 seats in the Lower Chamber and the Social Democrats 64. Ten years later the respective figures were 41 and 93, and in 1932, when Per Albin Hansson (q.v.) launched his welfare program, 24 and 104.

In 1923 the Liberal Alliance split over prohibition, those opposing a total ban on alcohol forming Sveriges liberala parti (Swedish Liberal Party) and the others, in 1924, Frisinnade folkpartiet (Liberal Peoples' Party). In the unstable 1920s, a period of high unemployment and social unrest, neither left nor right parties commanded an overall majority, and Carl Gustav Ekman (q.v.), the Liberal leader, used this situation to keep a very minority Liberal coalition government in office from 1926 to 1928 and from 1930 to 1932. He sought backing from either side, depending on the issue, and earned the soubriquet "Master of the Balancing Act." The Social Democrats, for instance, supported his 1927 School Reform Bill, while the Conservatives accepted in 1928 the establishment of a labor court. A scandal ended Ekman's precarious premiership. Investigations after Kreuger's (q.v.) death in 1932 revealed undeclared financial aid to Ekman, and he was obliged to resign. In the elections that year the two Liberal Parties together won only 24 seats, and remained in the wilderness for many years.

In 1934 the two parties, with Gustaf Andersson i Rasjön as leader, amalgamated as Folkpartiet, its present name, and during World War II (q.v.) it joined in a national coalition government, with Andersson as Communications Minister and in 1944 with Andersson's successor, Bertil Ohlin (q.v.), as Minister of Trade. Ohlin forged as party policy a system which supported the welfare state (q.v.) but allowed businesses and their employees to work freely within a definite framework established by the state and local authorities. In the 1950s and 1960s Liberal support increased until it became the leading opposition party. By the 1970s this support declined in favor of the other non-socialist parties, but in a *Riksdag* balanced almost exactly between socialist and non-socialist members it retained its influence. In the 1976 elections the Liberals emphasized social welfare but opposed socialism and concentration of power. High taxation and increasing state interference plus an energy crisis contributed to the Social Democrats' defeat, and the Liberals joined the Center (q.v.) and Conservative (Moderate) (q.v.) Parties in a non-socialist coalition under the Center Party leader Thorbjörn Fälldin (q.v.).

Unable to realize his election pledge to phase out nuclear energy (q.v.), Fälldin resigned in 1978, the coalition was dissolved and the Liberals under their leader Ola Ullsten (q.v.) formed a minority government. After the 1979 elections a coalition was again formed under Fälldin, and when in 1981 the Conservatives withdrew the Liberals continued in office with the Center Party. Failure to revitalize the economy redounded on the Liberals in the 1982 elections when they lost heavily, winning only 21 seats as opposed to the Conservatives' 86, the Center's 56 and the Social Democrats' 166. The latter were in office from 1982 until 1991, but their socialist attempts to improve the economy ultimately proved no more successful and they were voted out of office in 1991. A non-socialist coalition including the Liberal Party was formed under the Conservative leader Carl Bildt (q.v.). Bengt Westerberg (q.v.), voted Liberal leader in 1983, became a member of the Cabinet and Deputy Prime Minister.

The constant thread running through the Liberal Party's policy since its inception has been a non-dogmatic social welfare system within a society free from heavy state control. With an electorate balanced fairly evenly between socialist and non-socialist views and with proportional representation, the party seems destined to be a respected, essential but always minority party of the middle ground. See also POLITICAL PARTIES.

LIBRARIES Sweden's library services can be traced back to the Enlightenment and to 19th century legislation on national literacy. In about 1800 the first parish libraries were set up, run usually by the pastor, and by 1868 there were 37 of them. In Gothenburg (q.v.) the Dickson public library, donated by James Dickson, a Gothenburg merchant, was established in 1861 and formed the basis of the city library there. By the turn of the century the Labor Movement and other popular movements were establishing libraries for their members, and in 1905 state aid was granted to public libraries for the first time. In the 1920s many small libraries amalgamated. Stockholm (q.v.) city library was the result of such an amalgamation, and its main building was inaugurated in 1928. There have been libraries for the blind since the 1910s, and the first children's library opened in Stockholm in 1911. A School of Librarianship was founded in 1926.

It was decided in 1930 that every county would have a central library, which would support branch libraries by lending them books, sending out mobile libraries and offering technical guidance. Financial aid was to come from both the state and the various county councils, and services would be free to the public. By 1954 the organization was complete, and there are now 24 central libraries covering the whole country.

Kungliga Biblioteket (KB, the Royal Library) in Stockholm serves as the national library. Since 1661 it has had the remit to collect, preserve and care for all Swedish books produced, which now totals some 265,000 items per year. The university libraries are also copyright libraries, and there is close cooperation between them and KB, not least in the preparation of a central catalog. Since 1953 KB has compiled lists of Swedish publications for the weekly *Svensk Bokhandel* (Swedish Book Trade) and the annual *Svensk bokförteckning* (Swedish National Bibliography). Since 1953 KB has also compiled a catalog of foreign acquisitions by Swedish research libraries. As well as KB and the university libraries, the Royal Swedish Academy of Sciences (q.v.) and the Academy of Literature, both from the 18th century, have specialized libraries.

In 1972 Bibliotekshögskolan (University College of Librarianship) was established at Borås and offers special two-year graduate courses.

LINDMAN, ARVID (1862–1936) Swedish Conservative (q.v.) politician, industrialist and rear-admiral. Lindman was a leading member of the conservative groups in *Riksdag* (q.v.) from 1906 until 1935, a period of great parliamentary and social change in Sweden. He was a member of the Lower Chamber, and was known as a more moderate, flexible and forward-looking politician than Ernst Trygger (q.v.), his ''dark-blue'' counterpart in the Upper Chamber. Lindman's first ministerial experience was as Minister of Naval Affairs in Christian Lundeberg's short-lived government in the autumn of 1905. When later that year the new Prime Minister, the Liberal (q.v.) leader Karl Staaff (q.v.), had had franchise reforms accepted in the Lower (directly elected) Chamber of *Riksdag* but rejected by the indirectly elected Upper Chamber, and the King refused to allow an election, Staaff resigned and Lindman formed a minority Conservative government, which remained in office until 1911. The franchise issue had been rumbling for many years, and Lindman too was anxious to introduce reform. His

Reform Bill, which with minor modifications was accepted by both Chambers in 1908, was a compromise on previous proposals: all tax-paying males over 24 could vote for the Lower Chamber; the property requirement for the Upper Chamber was lowered and plural voting, although retained, was reduced.

Unlike Staaff, a parliamentarian and reformer, Lindman and his government could easily cooperate with the King against radicalism. Lindman's social record as Prime Minister, however, is far from reactionary, as he carried through some liberal measures already initiated by Staaff and instigated others. In 1906 a law was passed severly restricting the acquisition of land by private enterprise in Norrland, where farmers, ruthlessly exploited by large timber companies, were in danger of losing their land and their living. In 1907 Lindman arranged for the state to purchase half the shares of the Grängesberg mining company, with an option to buy the remainder in 25 or 35 years. The state had already built a hydroelectric power plant at Trollhättan in 1906. In 1909 a Waterfalls Board was established to supervise the country's hydroelectric power reserves. In that year nightwork for women working in industry was banned and shop hours were limited.

Lindman had set up a Committee to examine national defense and was prepared to act on its recommendation to increase defense spending and extend military service. In 1911 the defense issue was beginning to concentrate on the ordering of a new, expensive battleship, the so-called F-ship (q.v.). The Liberals and Social Democrats (q.v.), who had a majority in the Lower Chamber, were strenuously opposed to it, the Conservative majority in the Upper Chamber supported it. Staaff wanted an election to decide the issue. By this time the franchise reforms had come into play, and in the 1911 elections the Social Democrats made great gains at the Conservatives' expense, and Lindman resigned. Staaff formed his second ministry, but in 1914 he resigned again, mainly on the issue of the King's right to express in public his disagreement with his Prime Minister.

With a major European war threatening, the Conservative Hjalmar Hammarskjöld (q.v.) formed a government, but by

1917 he had to resign and was succeeded by Carl Swartz, with Lindman as Foreign Minister. They speedily entered into negotiations with Britain, allowing desperately-needed foodstuffs to enter Swedish ports. Neutral Sweden, it emerged just before the 1917 elections, had allowed Count von Luxburg, the German chargé d'affaires in Buenos Aires, to use Swedish diplomatic channels to send coded telegrams to Berlin. The Luxburg scandal further embarrassed an already harassed government, and after the election a Liberal-Social Democratic government was formed. No government in the decade after World War I (q.v.) held office for more than two years, as the Social Democrats increased their following but no single party gained an overall majority.

There were electoral gains for the Conservatives in 1928, when the 66-year-old Lindman again formed a minority government. He promoted the King's view that Swedish defenses should be reinforced. It was a difficult period, as the European recession began to affect the Swedish economy. Farmers felt particularly vulnerable, and Lindman proposed imposing protective tariffs on grain and sugar imports. The Liberals and Social Democrats opposed measures that would raise food prices, and in June 1930 brought down the government. Lindman resigned. It was the last time he held ministerial office, but in 1935, only one year before his death, the two Conservative *Riksdag* groups, one in each Chamber, joined together under his leadership to form Riksdagshögern, known simply as Högern, i.e., the Right. Later that year Lindman handed over the Chairmanship to Gösta Bagge (q.v.).

LINNAEUS, CAROLUS (LINNE, CARL VON) (1707–1778) Swedish botanist, zoologist and medical doctor. Born in Småland, South Sweden, the son of a Lutheran pastor, Linaeus studied medicine at Lund (q.v.) and then botany at Uppsala (q.v.), where he was appointed lecturer in botany in 1730. He continued his studies in Holland, where he took his doctorate, and also visited England and France. While in Holland he was for two years in charge of the botanical gardens at Hartenkamp near Haarlem. Linnaeus (or von Linné after 1757 when he was ennobled), had an insatiable curiosity about people and nature and undertook a series of journeys in his native Sweden—to Lappland in 1732, Dalarna in 1734, Öland and Gotland in 1741, Västergötland in 1746 and Skåne in 1749. Many parts of these provinces, especially Lappland (see Lapps), were unknown, almost inacessible territory, and Linné's journeys were often adventurous. Each journey was recorded and published and did much to introduce Swedes to their own country. His factual, unembellished, immensely readable style also played an important part in the development of modern Swedish prose.

In Holland Linné published his system of botanical nomenclature in *Systema Naturae* (1735), followed by *Fundamenta Botanica* (1736), *Genera Plantarum* (1737) and *Critica Botanica* (1737), where he founded a sexual system of flora classification—to the dismay of some ''respectable'' members of society. He practiced medicine in Stockholm for a spell from 1738, and then in 1741 he was appointed Professor of Medicine at Uppsala. The post was enlarged to embrace natural history and botany and entailed the directorship of the botanical gardens at Uppsala. In 1745 Linné published *Flora Suecica* and *Fauna Suecica,* in 1750 *Philosophia Botanica,* and in 1753 *Species Plantarum.* Linné achieved a concise method of classifying plants and animals by introducing a binomial nomenclature of generic and then specific names, which forms the basis of modern classification. In 1758 he bought Hammarby, near Uppsala, and moved his considerable collection of specimens and other material there in 1766. After his death his collection was bought by Sir J.E. Smith, founder of the Linnaean Society (1788), and is now housed in Burlington House in London.

Linné belongs to a group of outstanding 18th century Swedish scientists, such as Polhem (q.v.), Scheele, Celsius (q.v.) and Berzelius, whose inventions brought them international fame. He was a founder member of the Swedish Academy of Sciences (q.v.) (1739) and was its first President. His birthplace, Råhult, in Skåne, was restored in 1935, and Hammarby, his Uppsala home, was inaugurated in 1939 as a museum.

LITERATURE No Swedish manuscripts predate the 14th century, although a literature closely related to the rich Old Icelandic literature almost certainly existed. The earliest preserved literature is mostly in Latin and influenced by the Church, the *Revelationes* of St Bridget (q.v.) providing the finest example. The first documents in Swedish were legal codes, culminating in King Magnus Eriksson's national *Landslag* (c. 1350). Ballads and romances were translated and adapted into the vernacular during the Middle Ages, but the unsettled political climate impeded cultural development.

Gustav Vasa (q.v.) brought political stability, but literature during the Reformation was mostly religious and didactic, and the most notable publications of the period were Swedish translations of the scriptures, first the New Testament (1526) and then the whole Bible in 1541. With Sweden's new status as a European power in the 17th century, a new confidence was reflected in her literature, led by Georg Stiernhielm (q.v.), who adopted classical poetic forms in his poetry. Swedish, not Latin, was chosen by Olof Rudbeck in his *Atland* (1679–1702), the apotheosis of Swedish Gothic ideology, which "proved" that Sweden was the cradle of Western civilization.

Olof von Dalin (1708–63) spread the ideas of the Enlightenment in his *Den svenska Argus* (The Swedish Argus, 1732–34), modelled on Addison's and Steel's *Tatler* and *Spectator* and written in flexible, modern prose. Important too were the travel descriptions of his contemporary Carl Linnaeus (q.v.). To Voltaire's impact on Swedish literature was added the influence of Rousseau, and a pastoral theme runs through the poetry of Fru Nordenflycht (1718–63) and her contemporaries. In the reign of Gustav III (q.v.), a patron of the Arts, poetry flourished, and J.H. Kellgren (1751–95) was the best of several writers invited to the royal court. Widely popular to this day is C.M. Bellman (1740–95) whose *Fredman's Epistles* and *Songs* combine Rococo charm and Baroque realism to conjure up in verse and music a lively but dissolute Stockholm (q.v.) in the late 18th century.

Romantic influences from England and Germany merged with nationalism in the poetry of several Swedish writers in the early 19th century. E.G. Geijer (q.v.) was the leading figure behind the Götiska förbundet (Gothic Society), formed to revive Swedish spirits after the loss of Finland to Russia in 1809 by looking back to their Viking (q.v.) ancestors. He and his colleagues chose Old Norse themes, a reminder of Scandinavia's illustrious past. Esaias Tegnér's *Frithiof's Saga* (1825), a romanticized version of an Old Scandinavian saga, achieved international fame. An equally rich source of inspiration was found in Platonic idealistic philosophy and German romantic poetry, reflected in P.D.A. Atterbom's and E. Stagnelius's mellifluous lyric poetry rich in symbol and mysticism.

In the mid-19th century the rise of the middle classes coincided with a more realistic writing, describing everyday life. The anarchistic C.J.L. Almqvist (q.v.) was a transitional figure, producing exotic, mystical works but also criticizing the Establishment. His most controversial novel, *Sara Videbeck* (1838), dealt with the status of women and advocated free sexual relationships. Revolutionary too in her way was Fredrika Bremer (q.v.), whose carefully observed sketches, novels and travel books described everyday life of the middle classes but also constitute a protest against an unfair male-dominated society.

For writers of the 1880s literature should not only record changes in society but also debate topical issues: clerical hypocrisy, scientific developments, heredity, education, the wretched conditions of the poor, voting rights were themes taken up in works by August Strindberg (q.v.) and his contemporaries. Such naturalistic writing was finally too gray and prosaic for writers starting out in the 1890s. V. von Heidenstam (1858–1940), soon joined by G. Fröding (1860–1911) and E.A. Karlfeldt (1864–1931), returned to the nature of their native provinces, to history and to folklore for inspiration and produced lyric poetry of great beauty. Better known internationally was a fourth writer of this neo-romantic group, Selma Lagerlöf (1858–1940). In imaginative novels often set in her native Värmland she treated universal themes of good and evil, sin and redemption and above all the power of unselfish human love. She also wrote educational books for children, the best known of which is *The Wonderful Adventure of Nils* (1906–7). A fin-de-siècle pessimistic mood is well characterized by the ironic novels and short stories of Hjalmar

Söderberg (1869–1941), a brilliant stylist and miniaturist at his best in *Historietter* (Short Stories, 1898).

The radical social changes in Sweden this century are reflected in its literature. Middle-class novelists, such as Sigfrid Siwertz (1882–1970), described different social strata in contemporary Sweden and often plotted the fortunes of a family through three or four generations. But then in the 1930s appeared the work of a generation of self-taught working-class authors whose use of autobiographical raw material brought something unique to modern Swedish literature. Eyvind Johnson (1900–1976), Ivar Lo-Johansson (1901–1990), Harry Martinson (1906–1978) and Vilhelm Moberg (1898–1973) all wrote moving series of novels depicting childhood poverty from within. Moberg's insight into the hard-working peasant's mentality was later used to great effect in his tetralogy, starting with *The Emigrants* (1949), which charts the fortunes of a group of Swedes who emigrated to the United States.

Two outstanding authors of this period do not fit easily into categories. Hjalmar Bergman (1882–1931) depicted a small middle-class community in central Sweden, but his amusing novels often moved into a world of fantasy and nightmare with considerable psychological overtones, and his drastic humor bordered on despair. Pär Lagerkvist (1891–1974) showed the individual alone in the universe struggling for a spiritual purpose in life, unable to accept a religious belief and yet unable to accept a world without one.

A rich vein of lyric poetry runs through Swedish literature, evident in this century in the verse of Karin Boye (1900–1941), Hjalmar Gullberg (1898–1961), Gunnar Ekelöf (1907–1968), Lars Forsell (1928–) and Tomas Tranströmer (1931–).

Sweden's literary response to World War II was a pessimistic, disillusioned and often obscure form of Modernism. Stig Dagerman (1923–1954) seemed to sum up his generation's Angst in his plays and prose work. By the 1950s there was a tendency towards provincialism, when both P.O. Sundman (1922–92) and Sara Lidman (1922–) wrote about small isolated communities in northern Sweden. By the 1960s, however, writers had entered the international stage. Pär Wästberg (1933–) and S. Lidman both visited and wrote about pernicious social conditions in Southern Africa. Jan Myrdal (1927–) began his literary career in the 1950s with satirical novels about the welfare state (q.v.) but then travelled widely in Asia and produced descriptions of China and Afghanistan. A polemicist, his *Report from a Chinese Village* (1963) and *Confessions of a Disloyal European* (1964) stimulated interest and admiration for China among Swedish left-wing intellectuals looking for an ideal to replace Stalin's tarnished image.

The last three decades have produced novelists capable of combining imaginative story-telling with deep psychological insight. Kerstin Ekman (1933–) achieved acclaim for a cycle of novels beginning with *Häxringarna* (The Witches Circles, 1974), in which she traced the rise of a whole Swedish community. A profound but never strident feminist, she showed the vital but unsung role played by hard-working women in the development of a community. P.C. Jersild (1935–), who trained as a doctor and social psychologist, satirized excessive rationalization in such novels as *The Animal Doctor* (1973) and *The House of Babel* (1978). Torgny Lindgren (1938–) made his mark with *The Way of the Serpent* (1982), a novel set in 19th century Västerbotten dealing with the power struggle in a small community. He has subsequently used biblical themes, most notably in *Bathsheba* (1984), a rewriting of David's love for Bathsheba. Most outstanding of all, perhaps, was Sven Delblanc (1931–1992), a writer with a wide range. In his epic Hedeby cycle (1970–1976) he depicted life in rural Sweden in the 1930s and 1940s, showing how the social structures and mores had changed. His Samuel cycle followed the fortunes of his own family from his grandfather, a wretchedly poor clergyman, to his father's failed farming venture in Canada, where Delblanc was born, back to modern Sweden. In addition to his humorous, even boisterous storytelling and autobiographical writing, Delblanc, an academic, also pondered on the ideal state, and his characters were sometimes caught between democratic liberty leading to licentiousness and strict discipline leading to dictatorship.

Sweden's tradition of good books for children, evident in works by Selma Lagerlöf and Elsa Beskow (1874–1953), has been maintained by many excellent writers, notably Astrid Lindgren (1907–), whose stories about Pippi Longstocking (from 1945) are internationally known; Tove Jansson (1914–), the Finland-Swede whose Moomin troll gives an endearing mirror image of the adult world; and Maria Gripe (1923–) who in her Josephine books (from 1961) treats her child readers seriously and writes sensitively about the adult world from the child's point of view. See also SWEDISH LANGUAGE; THEATER IN SWEDEN.

LO see LANDSORGANISATIONEN

LOVISA ULRIKA (1720–1782) Swedish Queen, daughter of Frederick Wilhelm of Prussia and sister of Frederick the Great. In 1744 she married Adolf Fredrik (q.v.), successor-designate to Fredrik I (q.v.) of Sweden. A talented, ambitious and forceful woman, she was educated in the spirit of the Enlightenment and unlike her much more passive husband found it difficult to accept the puppet-like role assigned to royalty during the Age of Liberty (1718–1772). When she became Queen in 1751 she took a leading part in the Court Party formed in that year to help increase the power of the throne, and in 1756 she even led an abortive coup d'état aimed at altering the Constitution in favor of the monarchy. She was active in the Arts, gathered leading cultural figures to the Court and in 1753 founded the Swedish Vitterhetsakademin (Academy of Literature). Although her son Gustav III (q.v.) found her overbearing and was eventually estranged from her, he was clearly influenced by her enlightened ideas, some of which he implemented during his reign from 1771.

LUND (Population in 1991 87,681). Together with Uppsala (q.v.), Sweden's most prestigious university town. The oldest settlement dates from c. A.D. 1000. In 1060 it became the seat of one of Skåne's bishops, and was soon the dominant one in the whole province, which was then part of Denmark. In 1100 Lund was the archbishopric of the whole of Scandinavia. Its twin-spired cathedral, built in sandstone, is Sweden's most outstanding Romanesque church. Its construction, led by the Italian Donatus, was completed in 1145 and has much in common with the great Rhineland cathedrals, for instance Mainz. It was restored by Adam van Düren at the beginning of the 16th century, and in the 1880s by Helgo Zettervall. The interior was restored in 1962. During repair work in 1941 the remains of a church dating from the 1080s was discovered. Lund lost some of its significance in 1154 and 1164 when Norway and Sweden respectively gained their own archbishoprics, but even so remained the most important spiritual Scandinavian center throughout the Middle Ages, when it boasted 23 churches and seven monasteries. With the Reformation it lost that role, the archbishopric was withdrawn, many churches were destroyed and their contents removed to Copenhagen and Malmö (q.v.).

In 1658 Karl X Gustav (q.v.) defeated the Danes, and by the terms of the following Peace of Roskilde Skåne became part of Sweden. Further battles ensued, but at the Battle of Lund (1676) Karl XI confirmed Skåne as part of his Swedish kingdom. Lund University received its charter in 1666 as a deliberate policy of Swedification. The University Library was founded that same year, but was not functional until 1671, when the book collection was transferred from the cathedral chapter to the university. In 1698 it became a copyright library.

In the post-World War II period Lund has acquired branches of the chemical, graphic, mechanical and food industries, but it preserves the atmosphere of an ancient academic town, which in addition to its august university houses a teaching hospital, the Botanical Gardens, an open-air Museum of Cultural History and several other museums.

LUTHERANISM see RELIGION

LÜTZEN, BATTLE OF see GUSTAV II ADOLF

-M-

MACLEAN, RUTGER see LAND ENCLOSURES

MALM, STIG (1942–) Swedish trade unionist (q.v.). In 1967 Malm was appointed representative of the Swedish Metal

Workers Union (one of the most influential in Sweden) in negotiations on wages and conditions. In 1977 he became Deputy Chairman of that union, in 1981 he was voted Deputy Chairman of Landsorganisationen (LO, Swedish Confederation of Trade Unions) (q.v.) and by 1983 had succeeded Gunnar Nilsson as LO's Chairman. In 1984 he became a member of the Social Democratic Party's (q.v.) executive committee. There has always been close cooperation between LO and the Social Democrats, and Malm's position was a powerful one, especially when a Socialist government was in office. There were occasional insinuations that in his efforts to get things done Malm was unethical in the use of that power, and he decided to resign in 1993.

MALMÖ (Population in 1991 233,887). Sweden's third largest city. There are references to Malmö from the 12th century, and the town received its privileges in 1353. Until the Treaty of Roskilde in 1658 during the reign of Karl X Gustav (q.v.) Malmö was part of Denmark and played an important part in Danish defense. Its influence receded after 1658, but the town was revitalized towards the end of the 18th century with the establishment of its harbor. It has become an important commercial center, with train links with the rest of Europe, an international airport (Sturup) and speedy ferry and hydrofoil services to Denmark.

The industrialist Frans Henric Kockum (1802–1875) founded a tobacco factory there in 1825 and engineering works in 1840. The company went on to produce trucks, forestry machinery and heating installation machinery, but it was above all its shipbuilding concern that gained most significance for Malmö.

In the oldest part of Malmö, Gamla Staden, stands St Peter's church from the 14th century, with a tower added in the following century, and the Town Hall, originating from 1546, and renovated by Helgo Zetterwall in 1864–96. There is a cobble-stoned square with restored 18th and 19th century town houses. A statue of Karl X Gustav was erected there in 1896, and there is also now the Form Design Center, which houses a permanent display of Swedish design and handicrafts.

MARGARETA, QUEEN see KALMAR UNION

MEIDNER, RUDOLF (1914–) National economist and trade union adviser. Meidner was head of the planning committee of Landsorganisationen (LO, Swedish Confederation of Trade Unions) (q.v.) from 1945 to 1966, Head of the State Institute for Labor Affairs from 1966 to 1971 and LO's official researcher from 1971 to 1980. Together with Gösta Rehn he was the main author of the LO document *Trade Unions and Full Employment* (1951). Meidner believed that to achieve full employment and therefore in their own interests, trade unionists should help promote greater efficiency in industry, but that profits should benefit the trade unionists, not the employers. This led to his proposal of setting up Wage Earner Funds (q.v.) (known popularly as "Meidner funds") to be built up from company profits but owned and managed collectively by wage earners who would with time own majority shares in the companies concerned. The LO Congress accepted the proposal, which then became official Social Democratic (q.v.) policy. The Social Democrats lost the 1976 elections, partly, it was said, because of the Wage Earner Funds, and by the time they had been returned to power in 1982 Meidner's scheme had been considerably watered down. No further money was paid into the funds after 1990. Meidner was given professorial status in 1983.

MODERATE PARTY see CONSERVATIVE PARTY

MÖLLER GUSTAV (1884–1970) Swedish Social Democrat, politician and journalist. Möller's name is closely linked with that of Per Albin Hansson (q.v.) and Ernst Wigforss (q.v.) as a founder of *Folkhemmet,* the Swedish welfare state (q.v.). In 1916 he became Secretary of the Social Democratic Party (q.v.) and he edited the daily newspaper *Social-Demokraten* (q.v.) from 1921 to 1924. He was a member of *Riksdag* (q.v.) from 1918 until 1951. Möller supported Hjalmar Branting's (q.v.) view that bringing about reform within the legal framework was preferable to revolution, and in 1918 he was one of those who urged acceptance in *Riksdag* of the Bill on universal suffrage.

When Branting formed his third government in 1924 he invited Möller to become Social Minister. That government fell in 1926, but in 1932 a Social Democratic government under P.A. Hansson, by then party leader, was formed and Möller was again Social Minister. Branting had died and the new team of Hansson, Wigforss, Rickard Sandler (q.v.) and Östen Undén (q.v.), all aged about forty, spear-headed policies which led to the welfare state. Wigforss imposed a heavy taxation burden partly to finance new social aims and partly to distribute wealth more evenly, while Möller initiated a series of social reforms aiming at "cradle to grave" security. Apart from a three-month interval in 1936 when the Agrarians (q.v.) were in office, Möller held the Social Services portfolio until 1951. On P.A. Hansson's sudden death in 1946 the older members of the party were said to favor Möller as Prime Minister, but the post went instead to the much younger Tage Erlander (q.v.).

MUSIC Music was important in Sweden at an early stage, as can be seen from folk songs, ballads and church music from the Middle Ages, and from student songs, post-Reformation hymns (many echoing plain song) and the ever-increasing popularity of choral societies today.

A more formal approach dates from the 16th century when Hovkapellet (the Royal Chapel) was founded. The first important Swedish composer of instrumental music was Johan Helmich Roman (1694–1750), called "the father of Swedish music," a prolific composer who, besides performing his own compositions, introduced the work of foreign composers. His music bridges the late Baroque and Viennese Classicism. Unfortunately there was no one of his calibre to take over his work.

Queen Lovisa Ulrika (q.v.) hired foreign opera companies to perform in Stockholm (q.v.), but it fell to her son Gustav III (q.v.) to establish Swedish opera. He founded the Royal Opera House in 1782 and also maintained a court orchestra of some 50 players. No Swedish composer of genius emerged, but the Royal Opera is still a respected institution and through the centuries has provided Swedish singers of international repute, such as "the Swedish nightingale" Jenny Lind (1820–1887),

Christina Nilsson (1843–1921), Set Svanholm (1904–1964), Jussi Björling (1911–1960), Birgit Nilsson (1918–), Nicolai Gedda (1925–), Elisabet Söderström (1927–) and Håkan Hagegård (1945–). Gustav's Drottningholm theater (q.v.) is also in operation and produces 18th century operas in authentic setting and costumes.

Franz Berwald (1796–1868), a member of the Royal Chapel, composed several symphonies and other orchestral works, but his talent was not recognized until the end of his life. He is now considered to be one of Sweden's best composers.

The Neo-Romantic movement in Swedish literature (q.v.) and the visual arts (q.v.) at the end of the 19th century was reflected in the music of Wilhelm Peterson-Berger (1867–1942), Hugo Alfvén (1872–1960) and Wilhelm Stenhammar (1871–1927).

In this century Swedish composers have largely followed Western musical traditions, Hilding Rosenberg (1892–), Dag Wirén (1905–1986) and Allan Pettersson (1911–1980) introducing Modernism into Swedish music. Lars-Erik Larsson (1908–) won popularity with his moving setting of *Förklädd gud* (Disguised God) based on a text by Hjalmar Gullberg. Karl-Birger Blomdahl (1916–1968) entered the space age with his opera *Aniara* (1959) a setting of Harry Martinson's epic about a space ship that is off course and moving into eternity. Lars Johan Werle (1926–) has based operas on texts by the 19th century writer C.J.L. Almqvist (q.v.).

Since Sweden's postwar economic boom music, like the other Arts, has been generously subsidized, the largest cities have their opera houses and symphony orchestras, and Swedish Radio (q.v.) broadcasts classical and pop music several hours a day. In addition, the government-funded Institutet för rikskonserter (Institute for National Concerts) was founded in 1968, since when it has arranged concerts throughout Sweden. Even in the recent recession, support for the Arts has been forthcoming. Work began in Gothenburg (q.v.) in 1991 on a new opera house, which was inaugurated with a production of *Aniara* in October, 1994.

Many young people in Sweden are attracted to rock and pop music, but since the 1960s there has also been a folk movement consciously combating foreign influences and arranging summer festivals with traditional fiddle music and other forms of ancient folk music.

MYRDAL, ALVA (1902–1986) Swedish Social Democratic (q.v.) politician, sociologist and peace reformer who from the 1930s onwards influenced Swedish thinking on social welfare, feminism, equality, peace and disarmament. She studied at Uppsala (q.v.), Stockholm (q.v.) and Geneva, and in 1924 married Gunnar Myrdal (q.v.). In her distinguished career she was *inter alia* a member of *Riksdag* (q.v.) from 1962 to 1972 and Minister without portfolio from 1967–73; Director of the United Nations Department of Social Services from 1950–56; Swedish Ambassador to India, Burma and Ceylon from 1955–61; and Swedish representative to the United Nations Disarmament Committee from 1962–73.

In 1934 she and her husband published *Kris i befolkningsfrågan* (The Population Crisis) which highlighted the dangers of the falling birthrate in Sweden. It led to a government commission the following year and the introduction of family allowances and state loans to newly-wed couples by 1937. In 1970 Mrs Myrdal chaired a joint Social Democrat-Landsorganisationen (q.v.) committee on equality. She stated that as social security and full employment had been achieved in Sweden it was time to turn to social equality. The committee's report was adopted as party policy and inspired many of the reforms of the 1970s, including parental leave, improved housing subsidies and day care. She also headed a commission that recommended the abolition of the State Church, but reaction was so hostile that the proposal was dropped. Alva Myrdal denounced roundly proposals in the late 1950s that Sweden should have nuclear weapons. She worked enthusiastically for peace, disarmament and women's rights. In 1982 she shared the Nobel Peace Prize (q.v.) with Alfonso Garcia Robles.

MYRDAL, GUNNAR (1899–1987) Swedish national economist and Social Democratic (q.v.) politician. He was a lecturer and then Professor of Economics at Stockholm University from 1927–50 and 1960–67. The economic crisis caused by the

Great Depression led to new economic thinking in Sweden: a Keynesian approach and a planned economy coupled with high taxation and social welfare. Myrdal was one of its chief spokesmen. His publication (written with his wife Alva [q.v.] whom he married in 1924) *Kris i befolkningsfrågan* (The Population Crisis, 1934) drew attention to the falling birthrate in Sweden and led to the introduction in 1937 of a family allowance scheme and state loans to newly-wed couples. In 1944 Myrdal chaired a joint Social Democratic-Landsorganisationen (q.v.) committee, which produced a 27-point plan aimed at offering a stronger socialist line and asserting the right to direct the economy (q.v.) in the interests of equality and if necessary to nationalize basic industries.

Myrdal was Minister of Trade in the Social Democratic government formed under Per Albin Hansson (q.v.) in 1945 and spoke optimistically of the Labor Movement approaching its harvest. His planning committee had predicted a postwar depression and planned to stimulate the economy, instead of which there was a boom and he had to deal with inflation and adverse balance of payments. His second miscalculation was a large-scale interest-free credit scheme agreed in 1946 to help the Soviet Union's recovery after the war. The enormous scale of the agreement was loudly criticized. At this point the hard-pressed Myrdal was offered the post of Executive Secretary of the United Nations Economic Commission for Europe and accepted it—with some relief, it was said. He occupied the post from 1947 to 1957. In his publications and lecturing Myrdal dealt with what he called the "Challenge of Affluence" and with the economics of the Third World. In 1974 he shared with F.A. Hayek the Nobel Prize (q.v.) in Economics, mainly for his work on the critical application of economic theory of Third World countries.

MYTHOLOGY see RELIGION

-N-

NEO-DEMOCRATIC PARTY (NY DEMOKRATI) This political party was formed in 1991 by Count Ian Wachtmeister and

Bert Karlsson with the specific aim of restricting state activities radically through privatization, deregulation and reduced taxation. Individual freedom was to be increased by a more frequent use of the referendum; immigration laws were to be tightened, while law and order would be pursued through severer punishment for violent crime. It is in many ways an expression of a rightwing backlash and did well in its first elections. It did not fit into Carl Bildt's (q.v.) non-socialist coalition government, formed in 1991, but in a delicately balanced *Riksdag* (q.v.) its votes could be crucial. As with the Communists (q.v.), however, voting against the party bloc closest to its ideology would allow the opposition into office, and its power is perhaps more apparent than real. See also POLITICAL PARTIES.

NEUTRALITY POLICY. At various times in her history Sweden had the reputation of being a belligerent nation, the military exploits of the Vikings (q.v.), Gustav II Adolf (q.v.) and Karl XII (q.v.) making their mark on the European stage. After the ignominious defeat of 1809, when Finland (q.v.) was lost to Russia, King Gustav IV Adolf (q.v.) was deposed and Napoleon's Marshal Bernadotte became Crown Prince of Sweden. The assumption by the Swedes who had engineered his candidacy was that he would conduct a glorious war against the Tsar and regain Finland. In the event Bernadotte, or by then Karl Johan (q.v.), offered the Tsar Swedish forces against Napoleon in exchange for help in annexing Norway. The Norwegians objected strongly enough to offer armed resistance in 1814 and Karl Johan imposed upon them by force the Convention of Moss and Union (q.v.) with Sweden.

This was the last time Sweden acted as a belligerent in any war, although this was fortuitous rather than deliberate policy on occasion in the 19th century. In 1854 Oscar I (q.v.) planned to join France and Britain against Russia in the Baltic, with a return of Finland as his reward. The allies found that price too high, the action switched in any case to the Black Sea and Sweden was spared involvement in the Crimean War. Karl XV (q.v.), a Pan-Scandinavian (q.v.) enthusiast, seemed equally ready to involve Sweden in Denmark's territorial disputes, but in the event the Swedish government was not prepared to enter the Dano-Prussian war in 1864, and again neutrality was observed.

Swedish foreign policy was revised in the 1870s, with a strengthening of ties with Germany, which was now seen as a shield against Russia. However, Sweden's official neutrality policy was beginning to emerge. In 1875 Oscar II (q.v.) made a state visit to Berlin, but he also visited St Petersburg and Copenhagen. Towards the end of the century Sweden's position seemed increasingly vulnerable. Finland was being subjected to a Russification program, Russia formed a treaty with France in 1894 and in 1907 joined the Entente countries. The Norwegians' growing discontent with the Union was leading to more militant threats, and the rather sluggish *Riksdag* (q.v.) was spurred into a reform of Swedish defenses in 1892 and 1901. The Union crisis came to a head in 1905, and the army and navy were mobilized. Common sense prevailed, however, and the dissolution was agreed without bloodshed.

As World War I (q.v.) loomed in 1914, Sweden's neutrality policy was fully formed. Hammarskjöld's Conservative (qq.v.) government declared Sweden's neutrality, supported by all sections of *Riksdag*. In November 1914 the three Scandinavian monarchs met in Malmö (q.v.) to mark Scandinavian neutrality. There were both pro- and anti-German feelings in Sweden, King Gustav V (who had married a German), the Conservatives, the military and senior civil servants favoring Germany and the Liberals and Social Democrats (qq.v.) sympathizing with the Allies, but Hammarskjöld, a legal expert, observed strict neutrality in accordance with international law. His refusal to join in any trade blockade against Germany led to a reduction in trade with the Allies, and Sweden suffered acute shortages of essential foodstuffs and oil as a consequence. This caused Hammarskjöld to lose popularity, and in 1917 he resigned in favor of the Conservative Carl Swartz. The ensuing elections in that year led to the Edén-Branting (qq.v.) Liberal-Social Democratic coalition government, which quickly reached a trade agreement with the Allies, securing much-needed supplies. When civil war broke out in Finland in 1917 it was easier for the Swedish government to maintain official neutrality, since sympathies within the coalition were fairly equally divided between the Red and the White factions.

Although the Edén-Branting government disapproved of the way the League of Nations was evolving it joined in 1920, feeling that Sweden must support an organization attempting to establish international justice and lasting peace. From 1922–26 and 1936–39 Sweden had a seat on the Council and guarded the interests of the small states against great powers, working always for international disarmament.

As faith in the League of Nations receded the Swedes became interested in Scandinavian associations, aiming at some kind of collective security, but not for the first time the interests of the various Scandinavian countries pulled them in different directions: Finland's natural enemy was Russia, Denmark feared Germany, Sweden feared both, and Norway, enjoying a false sense of security, feared neither, so no agreement was reached.

When World War II (q.v.) broke out Sweden declared her neutrality and strengthened defenses. When the Soviet Union threatened Finland the Finns asked Sweden for military aid, but the Swedes refused to be drawn into the conflict, promising diplomatic assistance only. When the Winter War erupted direct Swedish intervention was again refused, but Sweden declared herself ''non-belligerent'' rather than ''neutral'' and allowed humanitarian aid and Swedish volunteers to go to Finland. A French-British request in March 1940 to allow a task force to reach Finland via Narvik and Kiruna was also rejected on grounds of neutrality. That month Sweden helped to broker peace between Finland and the USSR.

The importance of Swedish iron ore was a constant threat to Swedish neutrality during the war. When Norway was occupied to ensure German supplies of ore via Narvik Gustav V assured Hitler in a personal letter (19 April 1941) that Sweden would observe strict neutrality in the conflict: no Swedish weapons or volunteers went to Norway's assistance, while permission to allow German access to Norway via Sweden was denied. This even-handedness was soon under great strain after Norway, Denmark and most of Europe had fallen into German hands, which led to some

Swedish appeasement. Unarmed German soldiers were allowed transit through Sweden, while outspoken criticism of Nazi atrocities in Swedish newpapers was avoided. Neutrality held, but until 1943 it was in Germany's favor. Another crisis point was reached during the Finnish Continuation War in June 1941, when Germany requested permission to send the Engelbrecht division to Finland via northern Sweden. It was finally granted but on a ''once only'' basis, and a similar request a month later was refused. As Germany's position deteriorated, the threat to Swedish neutrality came from the other side, with the United States in particular pressuring Sweden into restricting her trade with Germany. Under veiled threats the Allies insisted that Swedish exports of ore and ball-bearings to Germany must cease, a demand acceded to by 1944.

In the final stages of the war Sweden helped Finland to negotiate a cease-fire with Russia. A stream of refugees from Norway and Denmark entered Sweden, and by 1944 some 30,000 refugees from the Baltic states had also arrived. At the end of the war Swedish neutrality was again put to the test, for the Soviet government insisted that some Baltic refugees be returned to the USSR. Under protest the Swedes complied.

In the aftermath of the war Sweden tried to preserve her neutrality policy. Strictly speaking, joining the United Nations could perhaps be considered a break with that policy, but for Sweden the organization was a means of reconciling the Soviet Union and the Western powers. It has involved her in sending forces to Egypt, the Congo, Lebanon and Cyprus, but always under the authority of the United Nations. Once the Cold War became a hard fact Swedish policy was expressed as ''freedom from alliances in peacetime, leading to neutrality in the event of war.'' Membership of NATO was not sought. In 1948 on Swedish initiative talks began on a common Scandinavian defense policy, but this faced Norway and Denmark with a choice between Scandinavian defense and membership in NATO, and they felt safer inside NATO.

Swedish neutrality policy has remained consistant with international trade agreements, so Sweden joined the OEEC (later OECD) (q.v.). She also joined the Council of Europe in

1949, since it allowed international cooperation without military or defense commitments. Similarly, in 1959 she joined the European Free Trade Association (EFTA), but not the European Economic Community (EEC) (later European Community [EC] and then European Union [EU] [q.v.]), which was a more political organization aiming ultimately at a United States of Europe. However, by the end of the 1980s Sweden felt it was becoming impossible to be a competitive trading European nation outside the Community, and in 1991 she applied for full membership. Tacitly it was assumed that ways would be found, as with Ireland, to respect Sweden's neutrality, a policy that has kept her free from wars since 1814.

NEWSPAPERS The earliest Swedish newspapers were designed to convey news about the Thirty Years War (q.v.). The very first was in German and published by Gustav II Adolf (q.v.). In 1645 the first paper in Swedish, *Post- och Inrikes Tidningar* appeared. (It is still extant under the shorter title *Posttidningen,* now publishing legal announcements). The few government-supported papers in the 18th century were always restricted in scope and readership.

With increasing opposition to Karl XIV Johan's (q.v.) régime came *Aftonbladet,* founded by L.J. Hierta in 1830 and considered to be Sweden's first modern newspaper. Stimulated by the revolutions in that year in Europe, Hierta followed a liberal line. He combined speedy news coverage with ruthless polemics and entertaining articles. The government's persistent attempts to gag *Aftonbladet* is a measure of its success. Hierta outwitted the censors by producing *The New Aftonbladet* as soon as the original was impounded. When the *Twenty-Sixth Aftonbladet* appeared the government gave up. The paper steadily increased its readership while preserving the liberal line. In 1937 it was acquired by Torsten Kreuger, brother of Ivar Kreuger (q.v.), the financier, and then in 1956 by Landsorganisationen (LO) (q.v.), the trade union organization. It is now an evening tabloid and supports the Social Democrats.

Newspapers played an essential role in the late 19th century, when literacy was increasing after the 1842 Education Act, and popular movements were helping to increase political awareness in the population as a whole. Rudolf Wall founded *Dagens Nyheter* (DN) in 1864, charging only five öre a copy, within the means of most. DN became Sweden's most important liberal newspaper, debating and championing social and political reforms. Nowadays classing itself as independent, it has the largest circulation in Sweden. The Social Democratic pioneer August Palm (q.v.) founded *Social-Demokraten* in 1885. When the much more gifted Hjalmar Branting (q.v.) became its editor in 1887 it became the respected voice of the Social Democratic Party (q.v.). In 1944 it changed its name to *Morgon-Tidningen,* but by 1958 it had to cease publication.

Equally influential was *Stockholms-Tidning,* founded in 1889 by Anders Jeurling with a deliberate policy of getting liberal views across to a wide readership. Relying on profits from advertisements, he charged only two öre per copy, which, together with the spread of literacy, helped make the newspaper available to all. It became one of the most widely distributed dailies and reached its peak under E.B. Rinman's editorship. In 1931 it amalgamated with *Stockholms Dagblad.* It was bought by Torsten Kreuger and was a mouthpiece for the Liberals (q.v.) until 1956, when it was bought by LO. By 1965 it had ceased publication. An attempt to resuscitate it was made in 1981, but it quickly became defunct.

Svenska Dagbladet (SvD) was founded in 1884 originally to project conservative, protectionist views, but from 1897 under the influence of Harald Hjärne, Oscar Levertin and V. von Heidenstam it became a forum for more liberal views on universal suffrage and defense and above all a cultural daily. It remains a quality newspaper following an independent moderate line, and of the national dailies is second only to DN in the size of its readership. *Expressen* was founded in 1944 as a liberal evening paper. It has the largest circulation of all.

All these papers were Stockholm-based (q.v.), but in the provinces too newspapers had an important political and social function from the mid-19th century. In Gothenburg (q.v.) the illustrious liberal *Göteborgs Sjöfarts- och Handel-*

stidning (SHT) was founded in 1832. It fought for religious tolerance, educational and economic improvements and reform of *Riksdag* (q.v.). Like *Aftonbladet* SHT suffered from official harassment but overcame difficulties. Under the long editorship of Sven Hedlund (called ''an honorable man'' in Strindberg's *Red Room*) it became one of Sweden's leading dailies, whose contributors included Viktor Rydberg. Torgny Segerstedt's editorship (1917–45) included the difficult war years when Hitler's representatives pressured the Swedish government into censoring criticism of Nazi Germany. Segerstedt, a great defender of freedom of speech, often found himself and his paper in trouble. The postwar period was financially difficult, and SHT ceased production in 1973. In 1975 it reappeared as a weekly, but soon succumbed. In 1858 Gothenburg also acquired a Conservative daily, *Göteborgs Posten,* but from 1896 it has supported the Liberals and has become the leading west coast daily. *Sydsvenska Dagbladet* was founded in Malmö (q.v.) in 1870. Until 1966 it supported the Conservatives, but it then became and remains independent liberal.

Until the late 1930s newspaper circulation rose continuously but then began to decline. So too did the number of newpapers, mainly for financial reasons. The trend continued in the postwar years, when several medium-sized dailies closed down, unable to attract advertising revenues. Finally, with competition diminishing and fewer political views having an outlet, the government, genuinely believing that in a democracy citizens must have a choice of newspaper, decided that a danger level had been reached. In 1971 *Riksdag* accepted a plan to support so-called secondary papers, and by 1978 a Press Subsidy Board began to distribute subsidies. This measure appears to have stabilized the position without jeopardizing the freedom of the press, a freedom embodied in the Swedish Constitution.

NEW SWEDEN (1638–1655) Swedish colony on the Delaware River in North America. During Sweden's Age of Greatness (1611–1718) a ''Southern Company'' was formed to settle lands beyond Europe. In 1638 a Swedish expedition landed in Delaware Bay, bought land from the local Indians, and set up a colony entitled New Sweden, which embraced parts of present-day Delaware, Pennsylvania and New Jersey. Many Swedish settlers made a living from agriculture but the colony never became the important trading post that had been envisaged, not least through lack of support from the home country, and never enjoyed economic significance. In 1655 the Dutch overran the colony, and Swedish officials returned home. Most of the settlers, however, some 500–600, remained. Swedish clergymen were sent out to them and were active among them and their descendants. The Swedish language in the former colony finally became extinct at the end of the 18th century. The tercentenary of the colony's foundation was celebrated officially in 1936, when the Delaware monument by the Swedish sculptor Carl Milles was unveiled at Wilmington, Delaware.

NOBEL, ALFRED (1833–1896) Swedish chemist, industrialist, inventer and explosives expert. Nobel studied chemistry in Paris, worked with his father Immanuel in St Petersburg, Russia, on an underwater mine and with the Swedish-born engineer and inventor John Ericsson in the United States. In 1865 he invented dynamite and in 1875 gelignite. He bought the Swedish firm Bofors-Gullspång in 1894, where he produced munitions. He also set up factories in several European countries and in America, and amassed a considerable fortune. His inventions played a significant role in Sweden's industrial revolution, blasting passes through mountains and difficult terrain so that a network of roads and railroads could be built.

They were also used for destructive purposes, however, and to alleviate those effects Nobel bequeathed 33 million kronor for investment, the interest of which should be ''annually distributed in the form of prizes to those who during the preceding year shall have conferred the greatest benefit to mankind.'' See also NOBEL PRIZES.

NOBEL PRIZES After the death of Alfred Nobel (q.v.) in 1896, the Nobel Foundation was established in Stockholm (q.v.). Its aim, in accordance with Nobel's last will and testament, was to award Nobel Prizes in Physics, Chemistry, Medicine,

Literature and Peace to those who during the previous year had done most to benefit humanity. In 1968 the Bank of Sweden funded the addition of a prize in Economics in memory of Nobel.

The prizewinners in Physics, Chemistry and Economics are chosen by the Swedish Academy of Sciences (q.v.), in Medicine by the Caroline Institute of Medicine and in Literature by the Swedish Academy (q.v.), while the Norwegian *Storting* (Parliament) chooses the Peace laureates.

The prize money, which derives from investment of Nobel's original bequest, is managed by the Foundation and varies slightly from year to year. The value of the first prize, awarded in 1901, was 150,000 kronor but the current value is almost six times that amount. The award ceremony is held in Stockholm City Hall on 10 December, the anniversary of Nobel's death, and the prizes are presented by the King of Sweden.

Controversy has occasionally surrounded the Peace prize, as in 1973, when it was awarded to Henry Kissinger, and in 1978, when it was shared by Anwar Sadat and Menachem Begin. There has also been criticism of the Swedish Academy's choice of laureates over the years. Henrik Ibsen and August Strindberg (q.v.), for instance, were both ignored in favor of less significant candidates. More recently there have been suggestions that the Academicians have been more interested in achieving a global balance than in always selecting the best author. On the whole, however, the selection of recipients for such rich, international prizes has run smoothly.

Nobel prizes awarded to Swedes so far are as follows: Chemistry: Svante Arrhenius (1903), The Svedberg (1926), Hans von Euler-Chelpin (1929) and Arne Tiselius (1948); Physics: Gustaf Dalén (1912), Manne Siegbahn (1924), Hannes Alfvén (1970) and Kai Siegbahn (1981); Medicine: Alvar Gullstrand (1911), Hugo Theorell (1955), Ragnar Granit (1967), Ulf von Euler-Chelpin (1970), Torsten Wiesel (1981) and Sune Bergström and Bengt Samuelsson (shared, 1982); Literature (q.v.): Selma Lagerlöf (1909), Verner von Heidenstam (1916), Erik Axel Karlfeldt (1931), Pär Lagerkvist (1951), Nelly Sachs (1966), and Eyvind Johnson and Harry Martinson (shared 1974); Peace: Klas Pontus Arnoldsson (1908), Hjalmar Branting (q.v.) (1921), Nathan Söderblom (q.v.) (1930), Dag Hammarskjöld (q.v.) (1961) and Alva Myrdal (q.v.) (1982); Economics: Gunnar Myrdal (q.v.) (1974) and Bertil Ohlin (q.v.) 1977.

NORDIC COUNCIL (NORDISKA RÅDET) An organization designed to facilitate cooperation among the Nordic countries: Denmark, including Greenland and the Faeroes; Finland, including the Åland Islands (qq.v.); Iceland; Norway; and Sweden. In the immediate postwar period in the late 1940s there were differing opinions among Scandinavian countries on such issues as NATO and defense pacts, but there was also a feeling of kinship among Scandinavians. In 1952 Denmark proposed a Nordic Council which would allow for mutual discussion of economic, cultural and social issues free from any military commitments. The basis for such an organization had been in existence from 1919, when the non-governmental Föreningen Norden (Nordic Association) had been founded in Sweden to further Scandinavian cooperation in the cultural, economic, legal and social fields. Denmark and Norway introduced branches that same year, followed by Iceland in 1922, Finland in 1924 and the Faeroes in 1951.

The Nordic Council, established in 1953, is an advisory body to the parliaments in the Nordic countries. Its central organ, the Plenary Assembly, consists of 87 parliamentary members, elected by their respective parliaments, and non-voting government representatives nominated by the Nordic governments. Each elected member is assigned to the Presidium or to one of six standing committees which prepare questions of cooperation. The Council functions by either adopting recommendations from the standing committees or by passing declarations on specific issues. The general objectives for Nordic cooperation were formalized in the Helsinki Treaty of 1962. A further step was taken in 1971 with the establishment of the Nordic Council of Ministers, which has decision-making powers within the limits of the Helsinki Treaty. All decisions have to be taken unanimously, although a member-country can abstain. Each country appoints from among its cabinet members a minister to coordinate Nordic cooperation, thus ensuring high-level commitment, and permanent committees of senior officials have been set up in different sectors to prepare and implement the Council's decisions.

Great progress has been made in various fields, not least in legislation where the legal codes in the Nordic countries have been almost completely harmonized. Within civil and commercial law the various laws concerning marriage, parentage, contracts, purchase of goods, copyright, patents and transport are now almost identical throughout the Nordic area. On the employment and social front Scandinavian nationals can work and settle in another Scandinavian country without a work permit or residence permit. A Nordic convention on social security covers all forms of social benefits, and a Scandinavian is covered for medical care anywhere in the Nordic area. From 1987 Nordic citizens residing in another Nordic country have the right to communicate in their own language. From 1954 Scandinavians could cross Nordic frontiers without passports, although non-Nordic visitors must satisfy entry and residential requirements of each Nordic country. There are joint rules on customs control too.

In 1971 a Cultural Treaty was signed with the aim of furthering Nordic cultural interests and to increase the combined effect of investments in education and research. A plan projected in 1988 is to develop a single Nordic educational area and to improve mutual understanding of the Nordic languages. The *Nordic Plus* program was initiated to stimulate mobility of students and teachers, a Nordic Film Fund has been established to promote Nordic film production, and a Nordic Film Prize was added to the Nordic Council's Literature and Music Prizes. Since the 1960s the Nordic television companies have been exchanging and co-producing programs through Nordvision.

In 1982 a Nordic Project Export Fund was established to support feasibility studies of investment projects of Nordic interest abroad. In 1975 the Council agreed in principle to the joint Nordic Investment Bank for the purpose of financing investment and export projects of common Nordic interest.

There is also a Nordic Fund for Technology and Industrial Development. The power grids of Denmark, Finland, Norway and Sweden are interconnected and cooperate closely through the agency Nordel. Cooperation in transport and communications was assured in a treaty in 1973. There are uniform tariffs for rail goods traffic; a joint airline company, Scandinavian Airlines System (SAS), is operated by public and private capital from Denmark, Norway, and Sweden; and a postal union and a telecommunications union operate throughout the Nordic area.

As well as inter-Nordic joint ventures, the Council aims at reaching as far as possible similar approaches to international organizations, and there is often joint Nordic representation. In 1989 there was a detailed program on Nordic cooperation with the European Community (now European Union [EU] [q.v.]. It covered the period up to 1992, and dealt with such matters as transportation, education, environment policy and consumer issues. Another plan has been adopted for after 1992. The Nordic Prime Ministers have made a study of factors governing the Nordic area after 1996, when it is assumed that all the Nordic countries will have become members of the EU. Each national delegation of the Nordic Council has a secretariat, usually attached to its parliament, and the Nordic Council of Ministers has a joint secretariat in Copenhagen, Denmark.

NORWAY See UNION WITH NORWAY

NUCLEAR ENERGY An important factor in Sweden's industrial revolution at the end of the 19th century was a cheap supply of electricity from the harnessing of rivers, which compensated for the lack of indigenous mineral fuel. By the end of the 1950s, however, hydroelectric power could no longer meet industrial and domestic requirements. Coal, coke and above all oil were imported, but nuclear energy was also considered. A technologically highly developed country, Sweden was well abreast of modern research and has, moreover, large uranium deposits. A joint venture, ASEA-Atom, owned equally by ASEA and the state, was set up to deal with research and construction of nuclear reactors. The

Social Democratic (q.v.) government had planned to build 13 reactors ultimately, which would supply 35 percent of the country's energy requirements. In 1963, by which time imported oil met 75 percent of Sweden's energy needs, the first reactor came into service. The situation became more urgent when the OPEC countries suddenly raised oil prices steeply and Swedish industry looked vulnerable. The government invested heavily in the means of expanding electric power, including nuclear reactors, but public misgivings about radiation hazards were increasing.

In the 1976 elections, by which time five reactors were in service, Thorbjörn Fjälldin, (q.v.), leader of the Center Party (q.v.), made the phasing out of nuclear power a major part of his program, which won him many supporters. He formed a non-socialist coalition government, which was in difficulty from the outset because the other two parties, the Liberals (q.v.) and the Moderates (q.v.), saw no alternative to nuclear energy. Unable to reach an acceptable compromise, Fälldin resigned, but in the following elections in 1979, by which time six reactors were in operation, he promised a referendum on the nuclear question. He was returned to power and the referendum was held in 1980. While results were not clear-cut they showed a preference for keeping existing, or almost completed, reactors in use for their life time (calculated to be approximately another 25 years) but not replacing them. *Riksdag* (q.v.) decided that nuclear power would be phased out at a pace commensurate with an energy supply sufficient to sustain employment and social welfare. There are now 12 reactors in service, the last two of which came into service in 1985, but it is said that they will have ceased operation by the year 2010.

Sweden's energy policy is to transfer eventually from oil to indigenous, preferably renewable, sources of energy. By 1990 oil consumption had been reduced to approximately 38 percent of energy requirements, while electricity covered just over 32 percent, almost half of which came from nuclear sources. A huge investment has been made in wind and bio-energy and in an effective fuel-saving campaign. Meanwhile two commissions have led to proposals for increasing safety and for emergency training to tackle possible nuclear accidents.

-O-

OHLIN, BERTIL (1899–1979) Swedish Liberal politician and economist. Ohlin was Professor of National Economy at Copenhagen University from 1924–29. In 1929 he returned home to a Chair in National Economy at Stockholm (q.v.) University. He launched his political career as chairman of the Young Liberals in 1934–39. From 1944 to 1967 he was chairman of the Liberal Party (q.v.) (Folkpartiet). He entered *Riksdag* (q.v.) in 1938 and remained a member until his retirement in 1970. Coinciding with a period when the Social Democratic Party (q.v.) dominated Swedish politics his only Cabinet experience was as Minister of Trade 1944–45 in Per Albin Hansson's (q.v.) wartime national coalition government, but his influence as party leader gave the Liberal Party a new emphasis. His social liberalism was a middle way between the state control of the Social Democrats and the right-wing advocates of a completely free market, for he believed that the community had a responsibility to the individual. The state should set a framework within which the market economy would work freely. Ohlin was the main opposition politician throughout his leadership of his party.

A respected academic as well as politician, he was known internationally for his theories on international trade and was a guest professor at several European and American universities. In 1977 he shared the Nobel Prize (q.v.) for Economics (with James Meade) "for significant research in international trade and how it influences economic development."

OMBUDSMAN The office of the Swedish *ombudsman,* or more correctly *Justititieombudsman* (JO), dates from 1809 when, after Gustav IV Adolf (q.v.) had been deposed, a new Constitution was introduced. The *ombudsman*'s brief is to guard Swedish laws and the way they are applied, and to indict any officials, including judges, who have been guilty of negligence or unlawful behavior. In 1915 a military *ombudsman* was also appointed to deal with laws connected with defense matters, but this office was withdrawn in 1968 and its duties were subsumed by JO. Increased resources were then allocated and there are now four *ombudsmen.*

ORGANIZATION FOR ECONOMIC COOPERATION AND DEVELOPMENT (OECD). This organization had its origins in the immediate postwar period when American aid under the Marshall Plan was offered to help rebuild Europe after World War II (q.v.). It first included only the European recipients of Marshall Aid, but the United States and Canada then joined and later Japan, Australia and other industrial countries outside the Soviet bloc, and its aims widened to include aid to underdeveloped countries. Sweden was determined to preserve her neutrality in the postwar period and refused to join NATO and the incipient European Community (now European Union [q.v.]). She hesitated when offered Marshall Aid in 1947, knowing that the USSR had refused, but in reality she had become too dependent on foreign trade to remain isolated. Sweden accepted Marshall Aid and went on to cooperate fully in the OECD, the name of which was subsequently changed to Organization for European Economic Cooperation (OEEC).

OSCAR I (1799–1859) King of Sweden and Norway from 1844. He was born in Paris, the son of Jean Baptiste Bernadotte and Desirée Clary (see Desideria). When his father became Crown Prince of Sweden, assuming the name Karl Johan (q.v.), Oscar moved to Stockholm (q.v.) at the age of 11. Unlike his father, who never learnt Swedish, Oscar became wholly Swedish in both language and attitude. As Crown Prince of Sweden and Norway from 1818 until Karl Johan's death in 1844 Oscar supported several humanitarian and liberal causes, working for social, economic and educational reforms. He also tried to improve the spirit of the Union (q.v.) between Sweden and Norway, where he twice held the office of Governor, in 1824 and 1833. Through his connections with the Liberals (q.v.) Oscar endeavored to dampen opposition to his conservative father, and the Liberals expected to make rapid progress towards parliamentary reform after Karl Johan's death. As King, Oscar did indeed follow through several social reforms, including women's equal rights of inheritance in 1845, the Poor Law of 1847, the reform of the Legal Code and judicial system and the Education Act of 1849. After 1848, however, with the wave of unrest in Europe, including riots in Stockholm, it became obvious that Oscar was opposed to the surrender of any constitutional power and was unenthusiastic about reform of *Riksdag* (q.v.).

In his foreign policy Oscar favored the Pan-Scandinavian Movement (q.v.) and confirmed this by aiding Denmark in the Schleswig-Holstein war (1848–52). In contrast to Karl Johan's "1812 policy" he sought Western support as a defense against Russia. During the Crimean War he signed the November Treaty (1855) with Britain and France, which guaranteed their protection against Russia, but Russia accepted the Allies' terms in 1856 and Oscar gained no concessions from Russia except the demilitarization of the Åland Islands (q.v.), agreed at the Treaty of Paris. Support for Oscar waned. His subjects had enjoyed peace since 1814 and feared his foreign policy. They also wanted parliamentary reform.

Oscar was too ill to perform his duties from 1857 and allowed his eldest son Karl to act as Regent until his death. In 1829 Oscar married Josefine of Leuchtenberg. They had five children, Karl (XV) (q.v.), Gustav, Oscar (II) (q.v.), August and Eugenia.

OSCAR II (1828–1907) King of Sweden from 1872–1907 and of Norway from 1972–1905, younger son of Oscar I (q.v.) and Josefina of Leuchtenburg, and younger brother of Karl XV (q.v.), whom he succeeded. Although conservative in constitutional and social matters and eager to preserve residual influence that the Constitution allowed the monarch, Oscar had to recognize the inevitability of reform. He helped to bring about an improvement in Swedish naval and military defense, but it was in foreign affairs that his influence was strongest.

Oscar developed an increasing admiration for Bismarck and the new German Empire and a tendency to regard Germany as a bulwark against possible Russian aggression. His efforts to save the Union (q.v.) between Norway and Sweden were thwarted when he was opposed and then outmaneuvered by leading Norwegian politicians. In 1905 he accepted the Dissolution and surrendered the Norwegian

Crown to Prince Carl of Denmark, who was elected King and took the name Haakon VII.

In his more representational role Oscar was much more impressive. A highly intelligent, cultured man and a persuasive orator, he had a commanding presence and an awareness of royal dignity. Under the pseudonym Oscar Fredrik he was active as a writer and military historian. His memoirs were published posthumously in 1960–61. Like his contemporary Edward VII in Britain, he gave his name to an era, the Oscarian period. He married Sofia of Nassau in 1857 and had four children, Gustav (V) (q.v.), Oscar, Carl and Eugen.

OXENSTIERNA, AXEL (1583–1654) Swedish Chancellor, statesman and diplomat. After university studies in Germany, Oxenstierna, a member of a leading Swedish aristocratic family, returned home and at the age of 22 entered the service of Karl IX (q.v.). When only 26 he was appointed to the King's Council. In 1610 Karl suffered a stroke and Oxenstierna joined with the young Gustav Adolf (later Gustav II Adolf) (q.v.) to direct the government. When Karl died in 1611, Gustav Adolf's succession was not a foregone conclusion, for Karl had usurped the throne from his nephew Sigismund (q.v.), Gustav Adolf was still a minor and Sigismund's half-brother Johan was in Sweden and five years Gustav Adolf's senior.

Karl had treated the aristocracy harshly and Oxenstierna wanted to regain lost ground. Sweden was surrounded by enemies on Karl's death, and Oxenstierna realized that the lively, gifted Gustav Adolf would make a more effective defender of the realm than Johan. He skillfully extracted from Gustav Adolf a guarantee of privileges for the Nobility in return for being accepted as King, and the Nobility pledged their allegience to the 17-year-old monarch. The latter soon appointed Oxenstierna as his Chancellor, and there began one of the most fruitful partnerships in Swedish history. These two talented men complemented each other, Gustaf Adolf being extrovert, generous, impulsive and a brilliant soldier, Oxenstierna cautious, diplomatic and with a first-rate legal mind.

With Oxenstierna by his side Gustav Adolf built up a system of government administration which still forms the basis of Swedish government. The privileges granted to the Nobility included the right to the highest offices of state, including the posts of Steward, Marshal, Admiral, Chancellor and Treasurer. With Oxenstierna himself as Chancellor, the administration was run efficiently by well-educated— and highly rewarded—aristocrats who admired the King and served him loyally. It was partly because he had such an effective administration that Gustav Adolf was able to spend so many years away from his capital. In 1625, during the Thirty Years War (q.v.) when Gustav Adolf had captured parts of Prussia, he left Oxenstierna in charge of the conquered territories. When Gustav Adolf fell at Lützen, Oxenstierna was in Germany, and he remained in full charge of Swedish affairs there until his return to Sweden in 1636.

Gustav Adolf's heir was the six-year-old Kristina (q.v.), and until she became of age the country was run by a Council of five aristocratic state officials, including Chancellor Oxenstierna. The other four members deferred to his judgement and experience, and he was de facto Regent for many years. To finance the war, which continued until 1648, the regency sold or pledged Crown lands, which weakened the monarchy and strengthened the Nobility even further. Not least through Oxenstierna's efforts the centuries' long struggle between the Crown and the Nobility for power had quite decisively turned in the Nobility's favor. Oxenstierna was reluctant to relinquish power when Kristina came of age, but she wanted to free herself from his pervasive influence. She succeeded, against Oxenstierna's wishes, in having her cousin Karl Gustav (q.v.) accepted as the heir to the throne in 1650. It was said that Oxenstierna had hoped to persuade Kristina to marry his son, but she was disinclined to marry anyone. Oxenstierna's influence was now in decline. When Kristina abdicated in 1654 he was poised to take up a central position again, but he died that year.

In a period when the Nobility had found wealth and a new self-confidence, many new stately homes were built both in the capital and the country. Here too Oxenstierna led the way. He had a beautiful castle constructed in the late Renaissance style at Tidö, near Västerås, from 1625–1645.

-P-

PALACE YARD SPEECH see F-SHIP

PALM, AUGUST (1849–1922) Swedish pioneer of the Socialist movement. Palm was a tailor by trade, and on his travels as a journeyman in Germany (from which he was expelled in 1877) and Denmark he became inspired by socialist ideas. On returning to his native Skåne, south Sweden, he began to agitate for socialist reform and soon aroused the hostility of both the Church and the political establishment. In 1882 he published the first Swedish Social Democratic program, a translation from a Danish version that originated in the German Gotha program of 1875. In 1885 Palm moved to Stockholm (q.v.), where he founded and edited the newspaper *Social-Demokraten* (q.v.). Palm was an agitator with demagogic tendencies and was inclined to thunder against the Establishment, but he had little interest in theory and lacked the intellectual ability of a constructive political leader. By 1886 he was supplanted as editor of *Social-Demokraten* by the more intellectual Axel Danielsson and Hjalmar Branting (q.v.), and his influence on the Social Democratic Party (q.v.) he himself had helped to form quickly waned.

PALME, OLOF (1927–1986) A prominent Swedish politician, leader of the Social Democratic Party (q.v.) and Prime Minister from 1969–76 and 1982–86. Palme was one of the internationally best-known Swedish politicians of this century. Born of an upper-class Swedish family, he took a B.A. degree at Kenyon College, Ohio, and then a law degree at Stockholm University. He joined the Social Democratic Student Club in 1951, in 1952–53 was Chairman of the National Union of Students, and in 1955 became leader of the Social Democratic Youth Movement. By then he had attracted the attention of Tage Erlander (q.v.), the Prime Minister, and became his personal secretary. In 1956 he was elected a member of *Riksdag* (q.v.). In 1963 he was Minister without Portfolio, 1965 Minister of Transport, 1967 Minister of Education and in 1969, when the aging Erlander retired, Prime Minister.

The Social Democratic Party had then been in office for over 30 years and under Per Albin Hansson (q.v.) and then Erlander had established a welfare state (q.v.). Erlander had narrowly succeeded in having the ATP (q.v.) pension scheme accepted, a compulsory supplementary pension scheme that put vast sums at the disposal of the state. Taxation was already high by international standards, and there were rumblings of discontent, but Sweden had become the most affluent country in Europe and a successful example of the Middle Way between communism and capitalism. Palme even as a student opposed von Hayak's economic liberalism, praised the New Deal and was influenced by J.K. Galbraith. He is identified with the slogan "the discontent of rising expectations" and saw the roots of discontent in Swedish society not in poverty or unemployment (almost eliminated there by 1960) but in residual inequality.

Jämlikhet (equality) became the vogue word in the 1970s, and most of Palme's internal policies aimed at achieving it. As Minister of Education he not only favored the comprehensive school system but also introduced a reform of higher education (q.v.) and entrance qualifications, hoping to open tertiary education to all. As Prime Minister he helped to effect the Social Democratic program (drafted by a committee chaired in 1969 by Alva Myrdal [q.v.]), which sought equality in education, employment and social welfare, and equality between the sexes. It entailed the state playing an ever more regulatory role in all aspects of political and social life and a rapid expansion of the public sector. Palme countered increasing opposition with the conviction that in a dynamic society the state is not a restrictive factor but a means of providing security, full employment, higher welfare standards and infrastructure beneficial to all.

During his premiership Palme experienced a decline in support for the Social Democrats, and from 1973–76 he headed a minority government. In those years he skillfully carried through major constitutional reforms, including the transition in 1970 from a bicameral to a unicameral *Riksdag* and the new Constitution of 1974. Excessively high taxation to finance social welfare and meet the oil crisis made his balancing act precarious. To raise investment, but above all to increase workers' influence, the Landsorganisationen (q.v.) economist Rudolf Meidner (q.v.) had persuaded Social Democrats to accept the Wage Earner Funds (WEF), a plan whereby 20 percent of the profits of large companies would go annually into a fund to be administered by a trade union board. The threat of WEF becoming law helped topple Palme's government, and in 1976 a non-socialist coalition government took over. Dogged by the international economic crisis, the hotly debated issue of nuclear energy (q.v.), and their own inability to work together, the coalition parties just survived the 1979 election, but by 1982 Palme was again head of a minority Social Democratic government. A referendum had decided the nuclear energy question, and by rendering the WEF politically harmless and slightly improving the tax position Palme succeeded in being reelected in 1985. The following year Palme was shot dead while walking home from the cinema with his wife.

Palme's foreign policy and international career rested on his anti-communist and anti-colonialist views. He subscribed to Erlander's policy of Swedish neutrality (q.v.) and non-alignment, which precluded Sweden's membership in the European Community (now European Union [q.v.]), but he also believed in supporting national liberation movements. He caused concern in 1968 when he, a Cabinet minister, took part in an anti-American demonstration in Stockholm (q.v.) beside a North Vietnamese ambassador. When in 1972 he compared U.S. bombing of Hanoi to fascist and communist atrocities like Guernica and Treblinka, Swedish-American relations were strained even further. Palme worked for a just economic world order and for disarmament, taking part in the Brandt Commission with proposals on disarmament. In 1980 he was the UN peace envoy mediating in the Iran-Iraq war. He also kept in touch with leaders of the non-aligned countries. The international reaction to his assassination indicated the respect he commanded in the Third World. Neither the reason for the assassination nor the identity of the perpetrator has been found, and rumors persist of a cover-up in high places and of undercover lucrative arms deals with professedly peace-loving countries.

Palme was an energetic, intelligent and ambitious politician with an abrasive manner and a more ideological approach then his two immediate predecessors, and he naturally became a controversial figure. For many he was a
defender of the welfare state and an egalitarian society, but
for many others his policies were dangerous steps towards
the totalitarian state.

PAN-SCANDINAVIAN MOVEMENT (SKANDINAVISMEN)
The ultimate aim of this movement, which gathered strength
in Denmark and Sweden in the 1820s, was to unite all the
Scandinavian countries into one state. It drew a great deal of
support from the universities of Copenhagen, Uppsala (q.v.)
and Lund (q.v.), where the study of Old Norse literature
illuminated a time (often with a patina of 19th century
Romanticism) when Scandinavians were all "brothers."
Oehlenschläger, the Danish, Tegnér, the Swedish, and Ru-
neberg, the Finland-Swedish poet, all used Old Norse themes
and had a great influence on students and the more general
public. By the mid-19th century, when Germany constituted
a threat to Denmark and Russia a threat to Sweden, the
concept of Pan-Scandinavianism was a source of comfort. To
some extent Denmark was supported by Sweden in the
Schleswig-Holstein war of 1848–50, and when Prussia again
threatened Denmark in 1863 Karl XV (q.v.) of Sweden-
Norway promised aid to Frederik VII of Denmark in true
Scandinavian spirit. When the Dano-Prussian war broke out,
however, the Swedish *Riksdag* (q.v.) refused to honor Karl's
promise. Nor was any Norwegian assistance forthcoming.

Despite the rhetoric and indignant accusations of coward-
ice by individual Scandinavians, including Henrik Ibsen,
there was obviously not sufficient general support to realize
the political aim of the movement. Pan-Scandinavianism did
achieve several less obviously political aims, however. A
common postal area was established in 1865–69, for instance, and the 1880s and 1890s saw the harmonization of
several legal and economic measures within the Scandinavian area. Nordic cooperation in the 20th century was also
grounded in the Pan-Scandinavian Movement, especially the

founding of the Föreningen Norden (Nordic Association) in 1919 and the Nordic Council (q.v.) in 1952.

PARLIAMENT see *RIKSDAG*

PEHRSSON-BRAMSTORP, AXEL (1883–1954) Swedish politician and farmer, leader of the Agrarian Party (q.v.) from 1933 to 1949, and member of *Riksdag* (q.v.) from 1918 to 1921 and from 1929 to 1949. In 1933 Per Albin Hansson's (q.v.) first Social Democratic (q.v.) government was experiencing difficulty in getting through parliament its crisis program to deal with unemployment and economic depression. The government needed support from a non-socialist party, but the Right, Liberal (q.v.) and Agrarian Parties appeared to be opposed. Hansson entered negotiations with a young group of Agrarians, led by Pehrsson-Bramstorp, and reached a compromise known as *kohandeln* (literally "cow dealing", i.e., horse-trading, and a pun on *koalition*). The Agrarians would support the Social Democrats' Keynesian-type crisis package in return for the government abandoning its free trade policy and protecting farmers from cheap imports. The official leader of the Agrarian party, Olof Olsson, sided with the other non-socialist parties but had to resign. His successor was Pehrsson-Bramstorp. The *kohandeln* was a turning point in Swedish politics, for it allowed Hansson to progress towards the welfare state (q.v.) and led to over 40 years of Social Democratic governments in Sweden.

In June 1936 Hansson's government resigned on a defense issue and Pehrsson-Bramstorp was asked to form as broadly-based a government as possible. He himself became Prime Minister and Minister of Agriculture. His government is known as the "summer government," for in the autumn elections for the Second Chamber in 1936 the Social Democrats made substantial gains, Pehrsson-Bramstorp resigned, and Hansson started his second ministry. With no absolute majority Hansson decided to reinforce his position and invited the Agrarians to form a coalition. Pehrsson-Bramstorp remained as Minister of Agriculture. He continued to hold that office during World War II (q.v.) in a national coalition government under Hansson. After the 1945 elections Hansson was able to form a wholly Social Democratic government. Pehrsson-Bramstorp retired in 1949 and was succeeded as party leader by Gunnar Hedlund (q.v.).

PETRI, LAURENTIUS (1499–1573) Swedish reformer. Like his brother Olaus (q.v.), he studied under Martin Luther at Wittenburg and played a leading role in having the Reformation accepted in Sweden. On his return from Germany he became a professor at Uppsala University. Sweden's attitude to Rome had been left undefined after 1527 when *Riksdag* (q.v.) agreed to the confiscation of Church property, but when Gustav Vasa (q.v.), a widower in 1531, intended to remarry, he was anxious to have a Lutheran archbishop in place. Laurentius Petri was elected and became the first Lutheran Archbishop of Uppsala. As the other bishops left the country or died Lutheran bishops were appointed in their place. With Petri, therefore, the break with Rome and the Pope was tacitly effected.

Petri was a committed but comparatively conservative Lutheran and was much more flexible than his brother Olaus. He remained Archbishop under the ruthless, pragmatic Gustav Vasa, under Erik XIV (q.v.) who had Calvinist leanings, and under Johan III (q.v.), who inclined more to Catholicism. He collaborated in the Swedish translation of the New Testament in 1541, produced a new Church Ordinance in 1562, and a Swedish hymnal and catechism in 1567. Towards the end of his life he produced the Church Ordinance of 1571, which codified previous developments and formed the organizational framework for the Swedish Evangelical Church. See also RELIGION.

PETRI, OLAUS (1493–1552) Swedish reformer, clergyman and writer, and brother of Laurentius Petri (q.v.). After studying at Uppsala (q.v.) University, Olaus Petri went to Wittenburg, where he became a disciple of Martin Luther. After graduating in 1518 he returned to Sweden, where he was appointed secretary to Bishop Mattias of Strängnäs. He became a Deacon in 1520 and worked at Strängnäs as a preacher and teacher at the Cathedral school there. He was beginning to put forward Luthern ideas on the Reformation, caught the attention of

Gustav Vasa (q.v.) and was persuaded by him in 1524 to become Stockholm's (q.v.) Secretary and a member of the Stockholm Council, a post which he held until 1531. From 1531 until 1533 he was Gustav Vasa's Chancellor. Throughout these years he worked hard to promote and support the Reformation in Sweden. He cooperated in a Swedish translation of the New Testament, published in 1526, and produced a new hymnal, a new Church Ordinance and a book of homilies, all in Swedish. He represents the Reformation in its earlier, undogmatic stages, and a thread of tolerance and German humanism runs through much of his writing.

Gustav Vasa was less interested in doctrinal matters than in how to exploit Lutheranism (q.v.) in his struggle against the Church. Until 1527, when *Riksdag* (q.v.) consented to his confiscating Church property, he and Petri's interests coincided. Cooperation between them became increasingly difficult as Gustav's attitude towards the clergy hardened. In 1533 Petri fell from grace, and in 1540 he was condemned to death for high treason, a sentence commuted to a heavy fine. He had been ordained in 1539, and from 1543 he acted as Minister of the Stockholm Cathedral (Storkyrkan). As well as playing a key role in establishing a Lutheran state church in Sweden, Petri had a great influence on the Swedish language and literature (qq.v). He wrote in a clear, pithy, often ironic language which laid the foundations of modern Swedish. As well as Bible translations, hymns and religious tracts he produced *Domareregler* (Judges Rules), a collection of rules and advice to help judges avoid sophistry and excessive cruelty; he was presumably the author of the *Tobias Comedy*, a mystery play published anonymously in 1550; and he was the author of *Een swensk Crönika*, a Swedish chronicle in which the author insists that a historian must observe impartiality, respect truth irrespective of national prejudices, and seek for causes and connections in the unfolding of events. Such an approach was unlikely to meet with Gustav Vasa's approval, and the work was not published until 1818. See also RELIGION.

POLHEM, CHRISTOPHER (1660–1751) Swedish inventor, called ''the father of mechanics in Sweden.'' Having to earn his own living from the age of 12, Polhem worked first on a farm. His skill in arithmetic and mechanics soon became apparent, and he was allowed to use a workshop, making tools and clocks. When 25, he was able to study at Uppsala, (q.v.) where his mechanical genius was appreciated. The Board of Mines (Bergskollegium) and King Karl XI (q.v.) himself were impressed, and their support led to Polhem receiving a stipend that gave him independence and a study visit to Britain and Europe. In 1699 he founded the Stjernsund manufactory in Dalarna, which became famous for its clocks. Polhem's fertile mind and practical attitude produced a prodigious number of inventions large and small, including a siphon pump and a machine for raising ore for the mines at Falun, bridges, a dry dock, saw mills, textile machines, the padlock and household equipment. He also began construction work on the canal connecting Kattegatt with Lake Vänern. One of his most famous discoveries was a method of conveying over considerable distances energy generated by waterfalls. He taught mechanics to students, one of whom, Emanuel Swedenborg (q.v.), was his assistant at the College of Mines.

POLITICAL PARTIES Until the 19th century, parliamentary representation was effected through the four Estates, Nobility, Clergy, Burghers and Peasants. There were occasional groupings within these broad divisions, such as the Caps and Hats (q.v.) during the Age of Liberty (1718–72), but they had no clearly defined programs and disbanded as conditions changed. With the abolition in 1865 of the four-Estate system and the introduction of a bicameral *Riksdag* (q.v.), new political alignments were inevitable and led to the birth and development of modern political parties. At first they were fairly temporary alignments round specific issues. These groupings tended to be parliamentary, not national, and were often confined even to only one of the two Chambers of *Riksdag,* but by World War I (q.v.) the parties were becoming polarized. Louis De Geer's (q.v.) proposals for a bicameral *Riksdag* had contained so many restrictive measures that the composition of the first *Riksdag* after the new reform gave the Nobility and the Establishment control of the Upper Chamber, while well-to-do farmers had a compact majority in the Lower House.

These farmers formed a Farmers' Party (Lantmannapartiet), which defended agrarian interests and dominated the Chamber and yet had no interest in putting forward constructive policies. The result was many years of stagnation within parliament at a time when extra-parliamentary political activities were gathering momentum. The issue that finally split the Farmers' Party and led to changes in the composition of *Riksdag* was tariffs. Farmers wanted protectionist duties levied on cheap cereals from the United States and Russia. Many dairy farmers, however, who supplied the expanding towns, wanted to keep prices down. One faction of the Farmers' Party took up the cry "Sweden for the Swedes," the other "No starvation tariffs." This split in the main party on an issue that affected the general public coincided with growing pressure for increased suffrage and accelerated the formation of national parties. See also SOCIAL DEMOCRATIC PARTY; LIBERAL PARTY; CONSERVATIVE PARTY; CENTER PARTY; COMMUNIST PARTY; CHRISTIAN DEMOCRATIC ALLIANCE; ENVIRONMENT (GREEN) PARTY; NEO-DEMOCRATIC PARTY.

POLTAVA, BATTLE OF see KARL XII

POSSE, ARVID (1820–1901) Swedish count, estate owner and parliamentarian. After the 1866 parliamentary reform the new Second Chamber of *Riksdag* (q.v.) was dominated by the Farmers' Party (q.v.), which guarded the interests of well-to-do farmers in questions of taxes and defense. Louis De Geer (q.v.), the first Prime Minister under the new systems, was an administrator rather than a politician and showed no enthusiasm for a development towards parliamentarianism. He was defeated in 1880 on a defense issue and was succeeded as Prime Minister by Posse, leader of the Farmer's Party. There is reason to believe that Posse was behind De Geer's defeat and that he had parliamentarian leanings, wanting to limit further the power of the Crown. Although a decisive politician, Posse was unable to take his party with him on either defense or taxes and suffered the same fate as De Geer, resigning as Prime Minister in 1883. He remained a member of *Riksdag* until 1890.

-R-

RADIO AND TELEVISION Swedish radio and television programs are in the hands of Sveriges Radio (SR, Sweden's Radio), a corporation operating under government license. SR is jointly owned by various public organizations and popular movements (60 percent), the press (20 percent) and private industry (20 percent). Its Board of Governors has 15 members: the Director-General, the Chairman and six other members appointed by the government, five members representing shareholders, and two representing the staff. The Radio Act and an agreement between SR and the government stipulate that all broadcasting shall be impartial, objective and catering to a wide range of tastes, and that if persons or viewpoints are criticized there must be a right to reply. A Broadcasting Council ensures that the conditions of the Radio Act and agreement are met.

Broadcasting began, with only one channel, in 1925 and rapidly gained popularity. Program 2 was added in 1955, Program 3 in 1964 and Program 4 in 1993. Television broadcasting on a regular basis was introduced in 1956, and a second TV channel was started in 1969, the year that also saw the introduction of color TV. In 1979 SR was reorganized into four independent companies: Television, comprising TV1 and TV2; Riksradion (National Radio Network); Lokalradion (Local Radio Network); and Utbildningsradion (Education Broadcasting). They are all financed by license revenues, with the exception of the National Network's foreign broadcasts, which are financed by the state. A proposal in 1993 to cut the foreign budget by 20 percent has put some programs in jeopardy. The Swedish Foreign Office wants SR to discontinue broadcasts to France and Spain but retain programs aimed at Eastern Europe.

Program 1 covers news bulletins, current affairs, weather reports, talks, reports from home and abroad, plays, readings, literature and culture. Program 2 specializes in classical music but also broadcasts programs for immigrants. Program 3, which broadcasts 24 hours a day, covers popular music, sport and light entertainment, while Program 4, a new channel, broadcasts sports reports and some music from the national schedules, and has taken over from Program 3 programs aimed at listeners over 37 1/2 years old (sic!), allowing Program 3 to concentrate on entertainment for the younger listener. Local Radio has 24 stations and reports local news, current affairs and programs featuring local entertainers.

TV1 relays programs mainly from Stockholm (q.v.), while TV2 broadcasts programs produced mainly in the ten TV districts, Malmö (q.v.), Gothenburg (q.v.), Växjö, Norrköping, Örebro, Karlstad, Falun, Sundsvall, Umeå and Luleå. TV2 also reports regional news. Otherwise there is little difference between the two channels, both offering serious and light entertainment, sport and educational programs.

Education Broadcasting has the right to broadcast on both radio and television, and its programs appear on both national, regional and local radio and television networks. Its activities target preschool, school, university and adult education areas.

In 1986 cable TV was started and in 1991 parliament accepted a proposal for a commercial TV channel. Successful morning programs by the commercial channel sped up discussions on the advisability of breakfast TV, and in 1993 coverage of news and other items from all parts of the country was started on TV2 from 6:30 a.m. until 9:15 a.m.

In the past, *Riksdag* (q.v.) had set its face against advertising, but in addition to commercial TV it accepted in 1993 advertising on Swedish radio stations. Stations wanting to broadcast commercials must seek permission from a specially established board.

RELIGION IN SWEDEN Evidence of early religion in Sweden is mainly archeological. Weapons found in graves from circa 5000 B.C. and more elaborate finds in graves from the Bronze Age, such as precious objects possibly used as votive offerings, all suggest a belief in a deity and an afterlife. Some of the numerous rock carvings dating from circa 1500 B.C. indicate some form of sun worship. The Boat-ax people, so-called because of the shape of their favorite weapon, invaded Scandinavia early in the second millennium B.C. They may have been the Indo-European people known to have overrun Scandinavia at about that time. Germanic language, culture and religion are thought to have developed during the first millennium B.C., and Scandinavian gods are clearly related to deities worshipped in all the Germanic countries before Christianization. By the mid-6th century Old Uppsala had become the site for the Svear assemblies and also a religious center, the chieftains serving as priests as well as political leaders. To this day three great mounds remain there, the graves of three early Swedish kings. At the height of the Viking (q.v.) period the great temple at Old Uppsala had become a great heathen center for the whole of Sweden and beyond, and every nine years there was a special festival, with human sacrifices to Nordic deities.

The Scandinavians were polytheistic, but three gods came to dominate within the Northern pantheon: Odin (Woden and Wotan in the English and German versions), Thor and Freyr. Odin, who had sacrificed one eye for wisdom and could read magic runes, was giver of victory in battle and ruled over Valhall. His Valkyries, warrior maidens, chose warriors who had died in battle and carried them to Valhall. There is something mysterious about Odin, who was the god of cunning and knowledge. Thor, the thunderer, whose weapon was a hammer, was renowned for his great strength. Since he regulated the elements, sailors called on him when in peril. Freyr was the god of fertility, protecting the crops and the harvest. There were many other gods, including Baldr, Tyr and Ull (still preserved in Scandinavian place names), as well as elves, dwarfs, sprites and trolls, who inhabited mountains, forests, rivers and lakes.

Sweden held out against Christianity longer than the other Scandinavian countries. Ansgar, a Benedictine monk sent by King Louis the Pious, son of Charlemagne, was the first to preach the gospel among the Svear. He arrived at Birka (q.v.) on Björkö in Lake Mälaren in AD 829 and was well received by King Björn and allowed to build a church there, but when

Ansgar left, his successors were driven out or killed. Twenty years later, when Archbishop of Hamburg-Bremen, Ansgar returned to Birka and organized his congregation, but again with no lasting effect. Christian influences reached Sweden from the south along trade routes, while by the 11th century Norway and Denmark had accepted Christianity and were sending missionaries to Sweden. Olof Skötkonung was the first Swedish King to be baptized, in 1008, and during his reign a bishopric was established at Skara in Västergötland. In his son Stenkil's reign a further bishopric was founded at Sigtuna (q.v.). The old religion was remarkably tenacious in the heart of the Svear country, and in 1060 heathens drove out the Bishop of Sigtuna. Even at the end of that century the Christian King Inge was banished for refusing to perform pagan rites and supplanted by Blót (i.e., Sacrifice) Swein. It was the last large-scale act of defiance. Inge regained control, the temple at Old Uppsala was demolished and a Christian church was built on the site.

Swedish history of the Middle Ages is one of strife as chieftains of independent provinces struggled for power. After the Stenkils died out the Sverkers and the Eriks strove for supremacy. The first King Sverker (c. 1130–56), a religious man, donated land to allow the founding of Cistercian monasteries in Sweden, the first of which were built at Varnhem and Alvastra. Sverker was murdered and succeeded by Erik, a legendary figure said to have led a crusade against pagan Finland (q.v.). He was killed in 1160, became Sweden's patron saint and by 1220, when his remains were laid in Uppsala cathedral, had become both a national and an ecclesiastical rallying point. The Church in Sweden in the 12th and 13th centuries grew increasingly rich and powerful as it was granted not just land but exemption from land taxes. It had become the center for culture, education and teaching, with schools attached to cathedrals, and successive Kings turned to the Church for help in the administration of government. The office of Chancellor was held by a Bishop for most of the Middle Ages, while Bishops and Abbots also helped administer large areas of the kingdom. In 1120 there were six sees in Sweden: Skara, Sigtuna, Linköping, Eskilstuna, Strängnäs and Västerås. The see of Sigtuna was transferred to Old Uppsala and then, in 1276, to modern Uppsala (q.v.) where it became the archbishopric. Bishops had been royal nominees, but gradually the clergy alone elected them.

By the late 14th and early 15th centuries, when the Roman Catholic Church was weakened by internal division, the hegemony of the Church in Sweden began to decline slightly, for Swedish noblemen and lay men of culture began to study at European universities, and there was a rise in the standard of literacy. The crisis for the Swedish Church, however, arose in 1520, when under Gustav Vasa (q.v.) the Swedes rebelled against Kristian II of Denmark and seceded from the Kalmar Union (q.v.). Gustav needed funds desperately to repay debts incurred during the rebellion and to bring order into state finances. The Church owned over a fifth of all land in the country, an obvious source of wealth. By 1524 Olaus Petri (q.v.), a disciple of Martin Luther, was preaching the Lutheran doctrine in Stockholm (q.v.), and there were many others, including Gustav's own secretary Laurentius Andreae, Archdeacon of Strängnäs, who deplored the decadence of some clergy and supported a reformation.

The King made increasing demands on the Church for financial support, demands rejected by the Bishops, led by Hans Brask. In 1527 Gustav called *Riksdag* (q.v.) to Västerås and threatened to abdicate if he was not granted permission to claim a greater contribution from the Church. *Riksdag* consented to his confiscating the Bishops' castles and as much Church land as he deemed necessary. Gustav seems to have been uninterested in doctrinal matters and did not at first commit himself to Lutheranism (q.v.); nor was anything specific said about the standing of the Pope in Sweden. He was quick, however, to use the Västerås ruling, taking matters almost certainly further than *Riksdag* had intended. The clergy retained only sufficient lands to support their immediate needs, the rest becoming Crown lands. Many treasures belonging to the Church and to monasteries found their way into the royal coffers.

Gustav had appointed Olaus Petri Stockholm Cathedral preacher. In 1531 he made him Secretary of Stockholm and appointed his brother Laurentius (q.v.) Archbishop, and from then onwards vacant sees fell to Lutherans. Through Olaus Petri's strenuous efforts the first Swedish hymnbook and Swedish translation of the New Testament were published in 1526. By the late 1530s mass was heard in Swedish throughout the country, and the Bible in its entirety was published in Swedish in 1541. In 1544 *Riksdag* proclaimed Sweden an evangelical Lutheran kingdom; a Swedish hymnal appeared in 1549 and a Church Ordinance was ratified in 1571. A convocation at Uppsala in 1593 established that the Church of Sweden was founded on the Bible, the Apostolic Nicean and Athanasian creeds, the Augsburg Confession of 1530 and the 1571 Order of Service.

During Gustav's reign, followers of the new doctrine ranged from the conservative to the ardent reformist, with Gustav maintaining a kind of equilibrium. After his death in 1560, his heir Erik XIV (q.v.) favored the reformers, but his brother Johan III (q.v.), who usurped the throne in 1568, held contrary views. Johan had married a Polish Catholic princess and had himself Catholic leanings, but not so far as to acknowledge allegiance to Rome. In 1576 he had a new liturgy published, known popularly as the Red Book, which was virtually a translation of the Roman mass. His brother Duke Karl (q.v.), who had Calvinist tendencies, supported clergymen opposed to the Red Book. In 1587 Johan's son Sigismund (q.v.) was elected King of Poland, a Catholic country, and a Union of Crowns loomed.

Matters came to a head when Johan died in 1592. Karl was determined to resist any attempt by Sigismund to reintroduce Catholicism into Sweden. He called a meeting at Uppsala at which the Red Book was officially rejected and Sweden's allegiance to the Augsburg Confession was confirmed. Sigismund made ineffectual attempts to regain the upperhand, but by 1599 he had been deposed and in 1603 his uncle was proclaimed Karl IX (q.v.). Catholic worship in public was by then forbidden and the monasteries dissolved. Karl realized, however, that further moves towards Calvinism would meet opposition, and he remained content to be King of a Lutheran state where he was "supreme administrator."

Karl IX's son was the illustrious Gustav II Adolf (q.v.), who entered the Thirty Years War (q.v.) and for the Europeans was the Defender of the Protestant faith. Ironically, his only child, Queen Kristina (q.v.), went over to Rome, but she had to choose between the Crown and her faith, for Sweden by then was too firmly Lutheran to compromise.

Karl XI (q.v.) believed the Church had a role to play in integrating the southern Swedish states newly ceded from Denmark. The 1686 Church Law obliged every parish clerk to teach the children of the parish to read and the minister to examine their literacy. Education was particularly needed against ignorance and superstition in the late 17th century, when Sweden, like many other countries, fell prey to witch-hunts bordering on hysteria. Fifteen ''witches'' were burnt in Dalarna in 1669 alone, and the government set up a commission to investigate and restore sanity to this strange phenomenon.

The Lutheran Church saw the Pietist movement, which originated in northwest Germany in the 18th century and aimed at restoring moral fervor, as a threat. Many Swedes who had been prisoners of war in Russia after Poltava returned home convinced Pietists but were forbidden by the Conventicle Act of 1726 from holding private prayer meetings. Countering this bigotry was the spirit of the Enlightenment, embodied in some respects in Gustav III (q.v.). During his reign non-Lutheran Christians were allowed to worship and Jews were allowed to settle in large towns (1782). Liberal ideas in the 19th century took this further. Jews were permitted to settle anywhere in Sweden from 1854. Oscar I's (q.v.) consort Josephine was a Catholic, and Oscar supported a bill allowing non-Lutherans to hold public services. From 1860, leaving the State Lutheran Church could no longer lead to exile.

The 19th century was a period of popular movements in Sweden, and this included several religious movements. George Scott, a Scot who settled in Stockholm in 1830, brought Methodism to Sweden. He was forced to leave Sweden in 1842, but his disciples carried on his work, and when the Conventicle Act was repealed in 1860 Swedish Methodism was officially recognized. Carl Olof Rosenius helped to form the National Evangelical Foundation, which dates from 1856 and forms part of the State Church. In 1878 the Swedish Mission Society was formed under the guidance of Peter Paul Waldenström. 1866 saw the founding of the Swedish Baptist Free Church, based on the American Baptist movement and under the influence of American Swedes. It was a powerful movement, but lost many members to the Pentecostals, who began holding meetings in Stockholm in 1907 and under the leadership of Lewi Pethrus became one of the largest of the Free Church movements in Sweden. In 1882 the Salvation Army was introduced into Sweden, a branch of the international organization with its emphasis on practical social work.

Even so, the vast majority of Swedes, 88 percent of the population, or over seven and a half million people, belong to the Luthern Church of Sweden (although only about four percent attend church regularly) and the bond between State and Church remains intact. *Riksdag* alone make laws, including laws which govern the Church, but when it comes to questions of church membership the General Synod has to give its approval and has the right to make recommendations. There are now 13 dioceses, each headed by a Bishop, the Archbishop of Uppsala being considered primus inter pares.

Women (q.v.) became eligible for ordination in 1958, and the first women were admitted to the priesthood in1960. Thirty years later some 700 women priests were ordained, spread over the 13 dioceses.

Recent immigration policy has influenced the religious pattern in Sweden, bringing about a rise in the membership of the Roman Catholic Church (145,300 in 1991) and the Orthodox and Eastern churches (100,400). In that year there were also 16,000 Jews, 73,000 Muslims (mostly immigrants from Turkey, the Middle East and North Africa) 3,000 Buddhists and 3,000 Hindus.

RIDDARHUSET (HOUSE OF THE NOBILITY) The Palace of Swedish Nobles in Stockholm (q.v.). In 1617 Gustav II Adolf (q.v.), anxious to improve relations between the Crown and the Nobility, granted the Swedish aristocrats certain privileges, to be offset by stated obligations. The House of Nobility Ordinance (Riddarhusordningen) of 1626 defined the Nobility and how they would meet and conduct their business as the highest of the four Estates in *Riksdag* (q.v.). The names and crests of all the recognized noble families were entered in the House of Nobility, after which new names could be added only by the King's express consent. The 17th century was a period of Swedish expansion and for the Nobility a period of aggrandizement.

This is reflected in the magnificent building they commissioned to be built in the capital. It was begun by Simeon de la Vallée, an architect of French extraction, in 1641 and continued by the German Heinrich Wilhelm in 1646. The Dutchman Joest Vingboon designed the main section of the building in 1653–56, and de la Vallée's son Jean completed the work in 1675. The wings were added as late as the 1870s. The inside walls are adorned with the escutcheons of noble families. The parliamentary bill of 1866 to introduce a bicameral system was debated for four days in *Riddarhuset,* at the end of which the Nobility, together with the other three Estates, voted themselves out of existence. The building remains a beautiful monument to the Nobility's self-confidence and power during the Age of Greatness.

RIKSDAG The Swedish Parliament. In 1359 King Magnus Eriksson summoned national representatives, including burghers and peasants to Kalmar, but it is not certain that they actually assembled. The assembly at Arboga in 1435 under Engelbrekt (q.v.) is therefore regarded as Sweden's first *Riksdag,* but it was at Gustav Vasa's (q.v.) assemblies at Västerås in 1527 and 1544 that representatives from all four Estates (Nobility, Clergy, Burghers and Peasants) first attended, and the term *Riksdag* came into use in the 1540s. In the 17th century procedure became more formalized, with the *Regeringsform* (Instrument of Government) of 1634, and parliamentary committees began to evolve.

Under forceful monarchs the authority of *Riksdag* receded, but under weak monarchs and especially in regency periods it consolidated and spread. Karl XI (q.v.) and his son Karl XII (q.v.) made themselves absolute monarchs, but Karl XII's disastrous wars left Sweden exhausted and disgruntled. On his death in 1718 a new Constitution vested all real power in a *Riksdag* dominated by the Nobility. Corruption and economic crises weakened *Riksdag*'s position, and Gustav III (q.v.) began his reign with a coup and a new Constitution (1772) that allowed power to be shared among King, *Riksdag* and Council, but with a strong emphasis on the monarchy. In 1789 Gustav strengthened his position further, arrogating virtually absolute power to himself. His son Gustav IV Adolf (q.v.) was formally deposed after a coup in 1809, when a new Constitution was accepted by *Riksdag*.

Through the Instrument of Government, the Act of Succession, the *Riksdag* Act and the Freedom of the Press Act, power was shared between monarch and *Riksdag* (still comprising four Estates), while the judiciary was given independent status and the office of Parliamentary *Ombudsman* (q.v.) was established. This constitution lasted for 165 years, although with many modifications during that time. In 1865 the four Estate system was abolished in favor of a bicameral *Riksdag,* the Second Chamber directly elected, the First Chamber elected indirectly by provincial and local councils. The right to vote and to stand for election was severely restricted and only adult males were eligible. By 1909 all adult males were enfranchised, and the franchise was extended to women (q.v.) in 1921. By that time too the concept of parliamentarianism had been accepted, with the establishment of government departments each run by a Minister, and with a Cabinet answerable to *Riksdag.* Gustav V (q.v.) was the last King to oppose Parliament, but when in 1917 he attempted to appoint a Prime Minister unacceptable to *Riksdag* he had to give way.

As the gap between the written Constitution and actual practice widened, a commission was set up to examine all aspects of Swedish government. This resulted ultimately in a new Constitution accepted in 1971 and in place by 1974. *Riksdag* has now only one Chamber comprising 349 members elected directly in free elections. Elections are held every three years; the country is divided into 28 electoral regions, and all citizens 18 years of age or over are entitled to vote. Reorganization embraced government ministries too. There are now 16 standing committees covering essential areas of government: Constitution; Economy; Taxation; Justice; Legislature; Foreign Affairs; Defense; Social Insurance; Social Affairs; Culture; Education; Communications; Agriculture; Industry; Employment; and Housing. Membership reflects the political composition of *Riksdag*. In each area the Minister with that portfolio is responsible to *Riksdag*. The monarch's role became only representational, shedding such titles as, for instance, Chief of the Armed Forces. Immediately after an election *Riksdag* elects a Speaker from among its members, and it is the Speaker, no longer the monarch, who invites a party leader to form a government. In 1978 the Act of Succession was amended to allow the monarch's first-born child, whether male or female, to succeed to the throne. Carl XVI Gustav's (q.v.) heir to the throne is therefore Crown Princess Victoria.

ROSKILDE, TREATY OF see KARL X GUSTAV

-S-

SACO/SR An association formed in 1975 through the amalgamation of Sveriges akademikers centralorganisation (SACO, National Association of Swedish Academics) and Statstjänstemännens riksförbund (SR, National Association of Swedish State Employees). It has approximately 300,000 members and represents "white collar" workers, usually with university degrees.

ST BARTHÉLEMY, WEST INDIES For many years Gustav III (q.v.) (1746–1792) had wanted a base in the New World. In 1784 he was able to purchase from Louis XVI of France the West Indian island of St Barthélemy. It had only 950 inhabitants, 400 of whom were slaves, but was to be a trading station, centered on the port of Gustavia, for the Swedish West India Company (founded 1786) to exploit the slave trade. The Swedish frigate *Sprengtporten* left Sweden for St Barthélemy in 1784 to attend the inauguration of a Swedish colony on the island. The company prospered during the early stages of the Napoleonic wars, but had ceased trading by 1805. St Barthélemy was sold back to France in 1878.

ST BIRGITTA (BRIDGET, DEN HELIGA BIRGITTA) (1303–1373) Medieval Swedish visionary. Birgitta was born into one the most powerful families in Sweden. She was the daughter of Birger Persson, a knight and lawman, and Ingeborg of the royal Folkung family. At 13 she was married to the 18-year-old Ulf Gudmarsson, who also became a lawman, and for some years she was Mistress of the Robes for Queen Blanche of Namur, King Magnus Eriksson's consort. Birgitta and her husband had a reputation for doing good works. They went on a pilgrimage to Nideros (Trondheim) in Norway and to Santiago de Compostela. Ulf died shortly afterwards in 1344. When seven years old Birgitta had seen visions of the Virgin Mary. Now she experienced visions of Christ, who inspired her to found a new religious order. King Magnus was persuaded to grant her a royal estate at Vadstena (q.v.), where she planned to have a monastery for both sexes serving under an abbess. She went to Rome in 1349 to persuade the Pope to bless her enterprise and while there founded a Swedish hospice. In 1372 with her daughter Katarina and son Birger she went on a pilgrimage to Palestine and Cyprus, and on her return she died in Rome in 1373.

Meanwhile, in 1370 Pope Urban V granted her request, and the new Birgittian Order, a branch of the Augustinian Order but with rules drawn up by Birgitta, was established at Vadstena. It spread throughout Europe and at its height had 80 convents. Birgitta's body was carried from Rome to Vadstena where she lies buried. She was canonized in 1391. Her widely circulated *Revelvationes celestes* were collected and published in Latin in eight volumes in 1492 and in Swedish translation in 1857–80. A strong-willed and courageous figure, Birgitta influenced the Church and the political and cultural life of her day. Through her revelations she advised the Pope to return from his retreat in Avignon to Rome; she criticized the morals of King Magnus's court and the Swedish Church. She encouraged Swedish nobles to oppose the King, and her son Karl took part in a rebellion against him in 1362. Her recorded revelations have an important place in Swedish medieval literature and were retranslated into Swedish in 1958–59.

SALTSJÖBADEN AGREEMENT (1938) In the period after World War I (q.v.) and during the Great Depression labor relations were often strained, with damaging strikes and lockouts. As the industrial situation started to improve from 1932 and the Social Democratic (q.v.) government introduced its program for social reforms, both sides of industry were prepared to adopt a more conciliatory attitude, and this was reflected in the negotiations and final agreement reached in 1938 at Saltsjöbaden, a small Baltic town near Stockholm (q.v.). Leaders of Landsorganisationen (LO, Confederation of Trade Unions) (q.v.), and of Svenska Arbetsgivareföreningen (SAF, Swedish Federation of Employers) (q.v.) bound themselves to regulatory collection bargaining and industrial action. This agreement, together with the Labor Court, a non-political tribunal for unions and industry set up in 1929, afforded Sweden an unparalleled degree of industrial harmony and reduced appreciably the damage to the national economy caused in the past by strikes and lockouts.

SANDLER, RICKARD (1884–1964) Swedish Social Democratic politician. Closely associated with Per Albin Hansson's (q.v.) *Folkhemmet,* the Swedish welfare state (q.v.), Sandler was a member of *Riksdag* (q.v.) from 1912 until the year of his death and played a key role in Swedish politics. He taught at a folk high school and was Head of the Central Bureau of Statistics from 1926 until 1941. Like Hansson, his initial Cabinet experience was in Hjalmar Branting's (q.v.) first short-lived government in 1920, when he was Minister without Portfolio. In Branting's second ministry (1921–23) he was Minister of Trade. He returned to this post in Branting's third government in 1924, but on Branting's death in January 1925 he was promoted to Prime Minister. The Social Democrats were out of office from 1926 until 1932 when Hansson, not Sandler, became Prime Minister and leader of the party. Sandler was Foreign Minister in Hansson's Cabinet and worked enthusiastically with Hansson, Ernst Wigforss (q.v.) and Gustav Möller (q.v.) to create a welfare state. In 1939 he tried as Foreign Minister to form a loose Scandinavian defense union while preserving neutrality (q.v.) but Denmark, the Scandinavian country geographically closest to Nazi Germany, declined.

When the Soviet Union threatened Finland (q.v.) the latter looked to Sweden to help defend the Åland Islands (q.v.). Sandler thought Sweden was in honor bound to do so, but he was overruled by his Cabinet colleagues and he resigned on principle. From 1941 to 1950 he was Provincial Governor of Gävleborg county. In 1954 he was asked to chair the Constitutional Committee, which finally in 1963 presented me farreaching proposals that led to a new Constitution, a unicameral *Riksdag* and a further reduction of the monarch's powers.

SEGERSTEDT, TORGNY see NEWSPAPERS

SEVEN YEAR WAR (1756–1763) In this European war, also called the Pomeranian War (*pommerska kriget*) in Sweden, Prussia and Britain-Hanover were lined up against Austria, France, Russia and Saxony. The Hat Party (q.v.), which was pro-French, was in power and wished to enter the war. Pomerania was one of Sweden's very few remaining Baltic possessions, and the Hats, having learnt apparently nothing from the humiliating defeat at the hands of the Russians in 1741, hoped to regain lost territory. Queen Lovisa Ulrika (q.v.) of Sweden was the sister of Frederick the Great of Prussia. Her Court Party's abortive coup in 1756 still rankled with the government, and revenge was another motive for entering the war against Prussia. The Swedish army was no better trained or equipped than in 1741, the Swedes distrusted the Russians, ostensibly now their allies, and French subsidies to Sweden were lower than anticipated. By 1761 the Swedish economy was near collapse, inflation was rampant, and the Swedes had no stomach for the war. Axel von Fersen (q.v.), an influential member of the Hat Party, persuaded the Queen to use her influence with her brother to extricate Sweden. In exchange for improved financial support for the Court and an amnesty for those convicted of complicity in the 1756 coup she agreed. In May 1762 the Peace of Hamburg was signed, with no surrender of territory, and *Riksdag* (q.v.) expressed gratitude to Lovisa Ulrika.

SIGISMUND (1566–1632) King of Sweden from 1592 to 1599 and of Poland from 1587 to 1632. The son of Johan III (q.v.)

and the Polish Princess Catherine Jagellonica, Sigismund was born when his parents were imprisoned in Gripsholm on the instructions of his uncle Erik XIV (q.v.). He was brought up in the Catholic faith and was elected King of Poland (Sigismund III) when Crown Prince of Sweden. After his father's death he returned to Sweden, where he was hailed as King, but his hopes of restoring the Catholic faith in his northern kingdom foundered, not least because of the implacable opposition of his uncle, Duke Karl. In 1593, while Sigismund was still in Poland, Karl arranged the Uppsala Convention, which reaffirmed Sweden as a Lutheran (q.v.) state. At his Coronation *Riksdag* (q.v.) in 1594 Sigismund was unsuccessful in having religious freedom for Catholics introduced. On his return to Poland Sigismund tried to influence members of the Swedish Council to oppose Duke Karl. Animosity developed into open war in 1598, when Sigismund returned to Sweden with Polish troops. He was defeated that year at Stångebro and in 1599 was formally deposed. Duke Karl, now Regent, ruthlessly executed the leading Swedish supporters of Sigismund at Linköping in 1600.

Although Karl was formally proclaimed King Karl IX (q.v.) in 1604, Sigismund did not abandon his rights to the Swedish throne, which resulted in a protracted Polish-Swedish war that lasted until 1629, when Sigismund and his cousin Gustav II Adolf (q.v.) signed the Treaty of Altmark.

SIGTUNA (Population in 1991 31,485). Town in Uppland province on Lake Mälaren. Sigtuna assumed Birka's (q.v.) role as a trading center and was briefly the political capital of Sweden in the mid-10th century. It was also at the center of the Christian missionary activity round Mälaren and in 1060 was one of the sees established in that area by the Church. Its position was vulnerable, however, and after 1120 the see was transferred to Uppsala (q.v.). Sigtuna's reputation as an international trading post was also in decline by then, and it never recovered from a raid by Estonian or Finnish pirates in 1187. Stockholm (q.v.), where Birger Jarl had constructed defenses, took over Sigtuna's trading role. The ruins remain of St Per's, St Lars's and St Olof's churches from the 11th century. St Maria's church dating from the mid-13th century was restored in 1904–05, and the charming Town Hall dates from 1744. Sigtuna has also one of Sweden's few prestigious private boarding schools.

SKANSEN see HAZELIUS, ARTUR

SKÖLD, PER EDVIN (1891–1972) Swedish Social Democratic (q.v.) politician. Sköld was associated with Per Albin Hansson's (q.v.) ministries in the 1930s. He was Minister of Agriculture from 1932 to 1936 and Minister of Trade from 1936 to 1938. In the wartime national government from 1939 to 1945 he was Minister of Defense; in the postwar period, when the Social Democrats under Hansson and then Tage Erlander (q.v.) began to consolidate their plans for the welfare state (q.v.), he held from 1949 to 1955 the vital post of Minister of Finance.

SOCIAL DEMOCRATIC PARTY (SOCIALDEMOKRATISKA ARBETARPARTIET) The first political party to be formed on a national basis in Sweden. August Palm (q.v.) had been influenced by socialists when working in Germany and Denmark and on returning to Sweden he launched, in 1882, a journal *Folkviljan* (The Will of the People) in Malmö (q.v.) and in 1885 *Social-Demokraten* in Stockholm (q.v.). In 1889 he organized a conference, which led to the founding of the Social Democratic Party. Palm was essentially an agitator, unsuited to be the architect of a large organization. In 1892 he was ousted by Hjalmar Branting (q.v.), a much more intellectual and pragmatic character. As a student at Uppsala (q.v.) in the early 1880s Branting had embraced the socialist cause and Marxist views on the class struggle. He gradually realized, however, that a social revolution could be effected within the framework of the law and without bloodshed, a view which often led to his being at loggerheads with the left-wing extremists in his party. At Uppsala Branting was a younger contemporary of Karl Staaff (q.v.), a founder of *Verdandi,* a radical society which took up such issues as religious freedom, universal suffrage and the freedom of the individual. Staaff went on to be Liberal (q.v.) leader and then

Prime Minister. He and Branting had much in common and Branting was happy to support the Liberals, especially on universal suffrage, while his own new party was gathering strength.

Until the extension of the franchise, the Social Democratic Party's development was of necessity extra-parliamentary. Landsorganisationen (LO, Swedish Confederation of Trade Unions) (q.v.) was founded in 1898. At its first congress it voted to have all its associated unions become members of the Social Democratic Party within three years. Although this was slightly modified to remove the compulsory element, the links between the party and the unions remained very strong. Until the reform of voting rights, however, these supporters lacked a parliamentary vote. In 1896 Branting was elected to *Riksdag* (q.v.) but on a Liberal list, and he had to wait six years for other Social Democrats to join him. Together with Axel Danielsson, Branting put forward the Social Democratic Party's program. It owed much to German influence, demanding progressive taxation, some socialization of the means of production and above all universal suffrage, but from a Marxist point of view it was already "revisionist," for Branting and his followers aimed at better living conditions for the poor and improved security in the form of pensions, insurance, unemployment benefits, etc., not at ideologies and the class struggle.

Voting restrictions made an increase in parliamentary representation slow at first. Branting was joined in the Lower Chamber by three colleagues in 1902; by 1908 there were 34 Social Democratic members (out of 230) despite considerable grassroots support in the country at large. These members cooperated with Liberal members whose efforts finally in 1909 resulted in universal male suffrage. Cooperation was put under great strain during the General Strike (q.v.) in 1909. Staaff deplored these attempts to force changes on the government, and workers trying to muzzle the free press by strike action was to him a sign of anarchy. Social Democrats, however, felt loyalty to LO and the striking workers. In the 1911 elections, when the new voting rights were first exercised, the Social Democrats won 64 seats in the Lower Chamber, the Conservatives (q.v.) 64 and the Liberals 102.

Staaff became Prime Minister and invited Branting to cooperate in government, but Branting, while remaining sympathetic, preferred to remain on the sidelines, supporting the Liberals on social measures close to the Social Democrats' heart.

Swedish politics reacted at this point to international events. With World War I (q.v.) looming Staaff still refused to increase defense expenditure. His obstinacy brought about his downfall. In the 1914 elections the Liberals won only 70 seats, four fewer than the Social Democrats, while the Conservatives won 86 and formed the government. Branting meanwhile was facing growing opposition within his party. From the outset left-wing militant elements led by the anarchistic Hinke Bergegren had favored a more revolutionary approach to reform. In 1917, inspired by the Russian Revolution, left-wing dissidents, led now by Zeth Höglund, broke away and set up their own Communist Party (q.v.). Branting's authority proved strong enough to keep his party operating within the law. The Conservative government meanwhile had become very unpopular during World War I and in the 1917 elections won only 57 seats, as did the Liberals.

The Social Democrats now surged ahead with 87 and thus formed the largest party in the Lower Chamber. Gustav V (q.v.) invited Nils Edén (q.v.), Staaff's successor as Liberal Party leader, to form a government. The result was a Liberal-Social Democratic coalition which included Branting as Finance Minister and three other Social Democratic Ministers. In the Lower Chamber this coalition had a comfortable majority, but its wishes could be thwarted by the conservative Upper Chamber. There were still restrictions on voting for the Upper House and multiple voting. The coalition government was anxious to complete the move to universal suffrage. In this period of communist revolution and the abdication of the Kaiser there was fear of revolution in Sweden. Conservatives were persuaded to accept a democratic modification of the Constitution as the better course, both Chambers accepted universal suffrage, and women (q.v.) were given equal voting rights with men.

The Liberals had let a cuckoo into the nest. The Social Democratic Party wanted heavy taxation, the right to expropriate large estates and a republic, none of which the Liberals could accept. Edén resigned and Branting formed his first government. Having no overall majority it would obviously be short-lived, but its seven months in office gave experience to Branting's young team of Ministers, which included Per Albin Hansson (q.v.). It set up commissions to investigate such issues as state control of natural resources and production, and industrial democracy, invaluable for the future. After Branting's government fell the Conservatives held office until the 1921 elections, by which time the new electoral reforms were in place. The Social Democrats increased their majority but were still a minority government. This set the pattern for the next decade. Branting's second ministry lasted 18 months, followed by a Conservative, a Social Democratic, a Liberal, a Conservative and then a Liberal government, each falling ultimately on the unemployment issue.

P.A. Hansson, who had succeeded Branting as party leader in 1925, finally broke the cycle in 1932. His party had prepared a crisis package to counteract the ill effects of the Great Depression, allied to far-reaching social reforms. Public borrowing plus greatly increased taxes would finance a whole range of public works which would create employment while benefitting the country as a whole. (Ernst Wigforss [q.v.], Hansson's Finance Minister, held Keynesian views). Hansson promised the Agrarians (q.v.) support for agriculture too if they backed his program. A deal was struck and the Social Democrats embarked on a course which aside from a short break in 1936 kept them in office, either singly or in coalition, for the next 44 years. They began to build up *Folkhemmet,* the welfare state (q.v.), developing a system of social benefits such as child allowance, pensions, and sickness benefits, and they had a policy of full employment. Hansson, and after his death in 1946 his successor Tage Erlander (q.v.), negotiated a new Comprehensive School system (accepted in 1950) and a national health scheme. As with Wigforss's tax system, these measures aimed at equality of opportunity and the erosion of the class system as well as improving standards. Erlander's greatest test was the ATP (q.v.), a compulsory superannuation scheme, which *Riksdag* finally accepted by a majority of one in 1957, whereas proposals for a new Constitution were much more of an all-party decision in 1970.

Public disenchantment with the Social Democratic Party rose in the 1970s, not only because of ever-increasing taxes but because of growing state interference. The Wage Earner Fund (q.v.), for instance, accepted as party policy, would compel large companies to place 20 percent of their profits into funds to be administered by trade unions (q.v.). The oil crisis in 1973–74 brought matters to a head. Social legislation, trade union powers and job security were making Swedish products uncompetitive. With no indigenous oil supplies nuclear energy (q.v.) was to be exploited. Olof Palme (q.v.), who succeeded Erlander in 1969, found that the rising discontent now focused on environmental fears. In the 1976 elections the Center Party (q.v.) promised to cease production of nuclear fuel, while the non-socialist parties for once agreed to unite against the Social Democrats. This won them the election, but the alliance was short-lived and by 1982 Palme was back in office. Palme was assassinated in 1986 and succeeded as Prime Minister by Ingvar Carlsson (q.v.).

The Swedish economy had rallied for a short while but then declined and in 1991 a non-socialist coalition again defeated the Social Democrats, who became the Opposition. Although the Swedish electorate is almost equally divided between socialist and non-socialist views the three main non-socialist parties are not sufficiently homogeneous to form a lasting united front against a party so solidly supported by trade unions. The Social Democrats have had over 50 years experience of running the country this century and perhaps too easily tend to consider themselves the natural ruling party in Sweden. See also POLITICAL PARTIES.

SOCIAL-DEMOKRATEN see NEWSPAPERS; SOCIAL DEMOCRATIC PARTY

SÖDER, KARIN (1928–) Swedish politician. Mrs Söder was a teacher before becoming a member of *Riksdag* (q.v.), supporting the Center Party (q.v.). When Thorbjörn Fälldin (q.v.) formed his first non-socialist coalition government in 1976 he appointed her Foreign Minister, a post she held for two years, gaining general respect for her competent approach. She was Minister of Social Affairs in Fälldin's second coalition from 1979 to 1982. As Vice-Chairman of the Center Party she was Fälldin's deputy, and after his resignation as party leader in 1985 she was appointed Party Chairman. When she resigned the following year she was succeeded by Olof Johansson (q.v.).

SÖDERBLOM, NATHAN (1866–1931) Swedish theologian and Primate. Söderblom was a theology student at Uppsala (q.v.) at a time when the Swedish State Church had adopted a rigid attitude to change, condemning the many Free Church movements that flourished towards the end of the 19th century and what it considered the excessive materialism of the socialists. Although from a conservative, conformist religious family, Söderblom was attracted to Manfred Björkqvist's idea of a more ecumenical approach, an attitude reinforced when he attended a Christian student convention in Northfield, Massachusetts, in 1890. He voiced objections to the Church's association with the wealthy, and in the 1890s put forward his view that the Church should avoid taking sides in politics. Söderblom was the Swedish pastor in Paris in 1894, where he organized relief for August Strindberg (q.v.), who was living there almost destitute and friendless. He was appointed Professor of the History of Religion in Uppsala in 1901 and in Leipzig, Germany, in 1912. In 1914 he became Archbishop of Uppsala, Primate of Sweden, and in 1921 a member of the Swedish Academy (q.v.). A strong and inspiring personality, Söderblom exercised considerable influence on his students and on the Church.

Ecumenism led on naturally to peace promotion. Söderblom arranged an ecumenical meeting in Uppsala in 1917 during World War 1 with meager results. Undeterred he organized the Stockholm Ecumenical Congress in 1925, which had a much more positive outcome, for the Life and Work section of the World Council of Churches arose out of it. Söderblom was awarded the Nobel Peace Prize (q.v.) in 1930.

STAAFF, KARL (1860–1915) Swedish lawyer, radical Liberal politician and a leading figure in Swedish politics of his day. While still at Uppsala (q.v.) University in 1882, Staaff was a founder member and leading light of Verdandi, a radical society which debated such social issues as religious freedom, temperance (q.v.) and universal suffrage. He was a member of *Riksdag* (q.v.) from 1896 until 1915 and leader of the Liberal Party (q.v.) from 1905. In the 1905 elections the Conservatives (q.v.) emerged as a minority party and Staaff formed a Liberal government. He put forward his proposals for a reform of the franchise, which were approved by the Second Chamber but rejected by the First. King Oscar (q.v.) refused Staaff's requests for a dissolution of *Riksdag* and in 1906 Staaff resigned. Change was in the air, and Lindman's (q.v.) Conservative government passed a compromise Bill that gave a vote to all males over 24 for the Second Chamber but retained a form of plural voting for the First Chamber. Widening the franchise increased the Social Democratic (q.v.) vote in the 1911 elections: they won 64 seats, the same number as the Conservatives, but the Liberals with 102 were the largest single party and Staaff formed his second ministry. With Social Democratic support he embarked on his social program, a Social Welfare Board was established and a small state-supported Old Age Pension was introduced.

It was above all the constitutional question which exercised Staaff. Like Hjalmar Branting (q.v.), he eschewed political activities outside the law, but insisted that all adult citizens should be part of the legal process by having a vote. Staaff also believed in the sovereignty of *Riksdag* and frequently disagreed with King Gustav V (q.v.) on the extent of the monarch's authority. A crisis was reached over a defense issue. When still Prime Minister, Lindman, anxious about the military buildup in Europe, increased expenditure on defense and won *Riksdag*'s permission to build a cruiser, the so-called F-ship (q.v.). When Staaff came to power in 1911 he halted its production, wanting to channel money into his social reform program. The Social Democrats were pacifists and supported him, but the decision started a groundswell of opposition in the country. Public subscription quickly reached 15 million kronor towards the F-ship and some 30,000 demonstrators marched to the Royal Palace Yard in protest against Staaff. Gustav V addressed them without prior consultation with his Prime Minister and publicly sympathized with the protesters. Staaff made it into a constitutional issue, insisting that the King promise not to make political pronouncements without consultation. Gustav refused and Staaff resigned. In the ensuing elections his party lost badly, the Conservatives emerged as the largest party and ruled until 1917.

Staaff died in 1915 and it fell to his successor Nils Edén (q.v.) to form a Liberal-Social Democratic coalition in 1917 and steer the universal suffrage legislation through. In one respect Staaff was the architect of his own downfall, for he never attempted to reason with the King—indeed he frequently failed to consult with the monarch and to show common courtesy. It is largely due to Staaff and his friend Branting, however, that democracy was introduced without bloodshed and disruptive revolution.

STIERNHIELM, GEORG (originally OLOFSSON, GEORG) (1598–1672) Swedish poet, linguist, courtier and civil servant. Stiernhielm epitomizes his period, when Sweden was becoming a European power with a Baltic empire, and when Swedish language and literature (qq.v.) developed a patriotic self-confidence while also reflecting European Renaissance and Baroque influences. From 1614 Stiernhielm studied at foreign universities (Greifswald, Wittenberg and Leyden), since teaching at Uppsala (q.v.), Sweden's only university, was then in abeyance. Gustav II Adolf (q.v.) was eager to improve educational standards, for his new political system needed capable administrators. In 1626 Stiernhielm taught at Västerås *gymnasium,* a newly introduced type of school, and shortly afterwards he taught at an academy for young nobles established in Stockholm (q.v.) by the King's tutor. In 1630 he became Governor General of Livonia, part of the enlarged Swedish kingdom. He was elevated to the peerage in 1631 and held various government appointments, including that of Assessor in the newly-founded Crown Court at Dorpat (now Tartu) (1630), a member of the War Council (1663) and Director of the College of Antiquities (1667).

He is best remembered, however, as "the father of Swedish poetry." A court theater was founded at the castle in Stockholm and in the 1640s Stiernhielm wrote masques on classical themes to be performed before Queen Kristina (q.v.). He often adapted French libretti into Swedish, using a wide range of meters and verse forms. His greatest literary achievement was the didactic epic poem *Hercules* (published 1658), where he introduced the hexameter, the first Swedish poet to do so. The classical theme of Hercules at the crossroads, taken from Xenophón, was used to address contemporary young Swedish nobles who, intoxicated by newly-acquired wealth, were tempted to choose the primrose path. Stiernhielm's allegory praised sound Swedish virtues and urged a renunciation of harmful foreign trends. In his language studies too Stiernhielm exhorted the avoidance of foreign influences. He went back to Old Icelandic literature and incorporated original Old Swedish vocabulary into modern Swedish.

STOCKHOLM (Population in 1991 674,452; Greater Stockholm 1,641,669) The capital of Sweden, Stockholm is situated at Lake Mälaren's outlet into the Baltic and on a series of islands on the mainland of Uppland and Södermanland. It is Sweden's largest industrial city and second largest port. It was first mentioned as a town in 1252, although the oldest preserved privileges date from 1436. Birger Jarl (d. 1266) strengthened the country's defenses after pirates had burnt Sigtuna (q.v.), by erecting a series of fortifications around the coast. He built a fort on an island at the eastern end of Mälaren, around which Stockholm grew. German merchants were encouraged to settle under the walls of Stockholm castle, and the town became a commercial center to replace Sigtuna, which was abandoned after the pirate raid. It expanded rapidly as a result of trade agreements made with Lübeck, a Hansa town. Lübeck merchants were exempted from customs charges and granted the right to settle in the new town.

In the conflict between Denmark and Sweden in the final stages of the Kalmar Union (q.v.), Stockholm ,led by Sten Sture's (q.v.) widow, held out against Kristian II of Denmark until the Danes made their triumphal entry in 1520. Kristian's cruel reprisal, the Stockholm Bloodbath (q.v.), sparked a rebellion led by Gustav Vasa (q.v.) who in 1523 entered the capital victorious, expelled the Danes and brought the Union to a close. In 1524 Gustav appointed the Lutheran Olaus Petri (q.v.) as preacher in Stockholm Cathedral, the first Swedish church to hear protestant sermons.

With Gustav II Adolf's (q.v.) administrative reforms in the early 17th century Stockholm became the center of government. The Nobility's increasing wealth and involvement in government and political affairs led to their building town houses as well as country mansions. Some of these fine houses remain, although now in public hands. Wrangel's palace on Riddarholm, for instance, is now the Supreme Court, Bonde's palace houses the Court of Appeal, and the Tessin palace is the Provincial Governor's residence. Fire destroyed much of the city and from the 18th century stone buildings were constructed instead of the more vulnerable timber. The old castle *Tre Kronor* (Three Crowns) burnt down in 1697 and was replaced by the present Royal Palace, designed mostly by Nicodemus Tessin and finally completed in 1757.

Stockholm in the 18th century was a cultural center. The Swedish Royal Academy of Sciences (q.v.) was established there in 1739 and the Academy of Literature in 1753. In Gustav III's (q.v.) reign (1771–92) were added the Swedish Academy (q.v.), Royal Theater and Royal Opera. A city with a beautiful setting that seemed almost to float on water, Gustavian Stockholm was an important Baltic port and was alive with foreign and home-based sailing ships, ferries and barges. It was also a city of overcrowding, little sanitation and subject to outbreaks of cholera and even plague, and had a death rate almost on a par with that of Paris of that period.

In 1859–61 municipal cleaning and sanitation were introduced. With a rapid increase in population the old city plan from the 17th century was no longer able to cope and in 1861 a new city was drawn up, influenced by the Paris of Napoleon III. It was too ambitious to be wholly realizable, but the city did expand eastwards and acquire broad avenues and large sedate houses.

Industrialization from the late 19th century onwards brought a new period of development and prosperity. The city has expanded, and especially in the postwar era suburbs and satellite towns have been developed. An extensive subway (underground) system was started in 1950 and has been expanded to allow easy access to the city center from most suburbs and satellites.

Stockholm has become Sweden's leading industrial area, with emphasis on metal and machine manufacturing, paper, printing, foodstuffs and chemicals, but also the service industries. It is also the seat of government and most government agencies and an educational and cultural center, housing *inter alia* Stockholm University, teaching hospitals, University Colleges of Technology, Economics, Physical Training, Teacher Training, a military academy, a music academy, and an Arts college. It is the seat of the Swedish Academy, Academy of Literature, Nobel Institute, Royal Library, Wenner Gren Center, National Museum, Museum of Modern Art, Nordic Museum and Skansen Open Air Museum (q.v.), History Museum and Natural History Museum. When the *Wasa,* a Swedish naval vessel which capsized in Stockholm harbor on its maiden voyage in 1628, was raised in 1961 a specially designed museum was constructed around it.

Enthusiastic city planners removed and replaced large sections of the city center in the 1950s and 1960s but have subsequently adopted a policy of preservation. The result is that one can follow much of the city's history architecturally from Gamla Stan (the Old Town) to more recent projects, such as Ragnar Östberg's beautiful *Stadshus* (City Hall), completed in 1923, Vällingby, the first model satellite, built in 1952–56, and several large-scale housing estates in outlying areas.

STOCKHOLM BLOODBATH see GUSTAV I VASA

STRÄNG, GUNNAR (1906–) Swedish Social Democratic (q.v.) politician. Sträng began his working life as a farm laborer. At an early age he began to cycle round Uppland, his native province, trying to organize the rural workers. By 1932 he was an official of the Farm Workers' Union and by 1938 became its Chairman. In 1945 he entered *Riksdag* (q.v.), and that same year became a Minister without Portfolio. From 1948 to 1951 he was Minister of Agriculture and from 1951–55 Minister of Social Affairs. This was during the important postwar period when the Social Democratic Party was in office consolidating its social welfare policy, and as minister responsible for social affairs Sträng carried through the National Health scheme which came into force in 1955. In that year he took over the Finance portfolio which he held until 1976. During his term of office state income rose tenfold, a deliberate policy aimed at orchestrating incomes, employment and prices. Sträng was one of the veterans of the Labor Movement. He had great influence with the Social Democratic Party and his name is closely associated with the Swedish welfare state (q.v.).

STRINDBERG, AUGUST (1849–1912) Leading Swedish author. The son of a Stockholm (q.v.) steamship agent and a former waitress, Strindberg had a difficult childhood. His father was stern, his mother and grandmother pietistic, the large family had financial difficulties, Strindberg was aware of his mother's inferior social status and, a sensitive boy, he suffered from harsh discipline at school. Of his unhappy childhood he said that fear and hunger were the more memorable features, while Church and school were institutions for tormenting children, not preparing them for adult life. He acquitted himself well at school nevertheless and after matriculating in 1867 went up to Uppsala University. Strindberg was highly intelligent with a natural curiosity and mental energy, but the conservative university had little to offer him, and since he was struggling financially he left without graduating. He did casual tutoring in Stockholm where Dr Lamm, the father of one of his pupils, helped him to start medical studies, but he soon abandoned them. He also attempted, unsuccessfully, to become an actor.

Strindberg's first literary work of undoubted talent was the play *Mäster Olof* (Master Olof, 1872) whose eponymous hero was Olaus Petri (q.v.), the 16th century reformist. It is symptomatic that Strindberg chose a period of turmoil and a hero at odds with central authority, and characteristic that he was ahead of his time and that his innovative play was not appreciated. From 1874 to 1882 he was a librarian at the Royal Library in Stockholm (q.v.). He had married Siri von Essen in 1877, a marriage which was often acrimonious but which officially lasted until 1892. Siri's ambition was to be an actress and Strindberg wrote two fairly conventional plays with her in mind. The work which first made his name, however, was *Röda rummet* (The Red Room, 1879), a realistic novel in which he satirizes *Riksdag* (q.v.), hypocritical clergymen, the gutter press, unscrupulous business practices, the Establishment generally, and describes the wretched conditions in the Stockholm slums. His spirit of rebellion is tempered by humor inspired by Dickens and Mark Twain, which sugared the pill and made the novel popular. He followed it with *Svenska öden och äventyr* (Swedish Destinies and Adventures, 1882), stories which comment on modern Swedish society despite their historical settings.

As his marriage began to run into difficulties and he struggled against prejudice Strindberg's satire became more pointed and ill-humored. *Det nya riket* (The New Realm, 1882) has none of the boisterous humor of *The Red Room* and it offended the authorities. Sweden was becoming too restrictive, and he and his family began their nomadic life, living in France, Switzerland and then Germany. In 1884 when the feminist debate was in full swing Strindberg produced his contribution, *Giftas I & II* (Getting Married, 1884 and 1886). In a series of short stories he illustrates that a woman is first and foremost a wife and mother. He was now criticized by his fellow authors for these anti-feminist views but also by the Establishment for his radical opinions on other social issues. One of the *Giftas* stories offended the Church and Strindberg was indicted for sacrilege in 1884. He returned to Stockholm to face trial and was acquitted, but his nerves were badly affected, and he avoided Sweden for many years. In his short stories *Utopier i verkligheten* (Actual Utopias, 1885) he championed society's underdogs and defended socialism and pacifism.

Strindberg began at this stage the first of his important autobiographies, *Tjänstekvinnans son* (The Son of a Servant,

1886), where he traced his own development in relation to heredity, environment and the period. This naturalistic approach was evident in the plays which followed, *Fadren* (The Father, 1887), *Fröken Julie* (Lady Julie, 1888) and *Fordringsägare* (Creditors, 1889). His naturalistic novel *Hemsöborna* (The People of Hemsö, 1887) was surprisingly humorous—describing life on an island in the Stockholm archipelago had awakened happy memories of his holidays spent on Kymmendö.

Strindberg had reached a period of depression. His marriage finally ended in divorce in 1892, after which he moved to Berlin where he met and married an Austrian journalist, Frieda Uhl. This marriage lasted only a year, although the divorce was not finalized until 1897. During the period 1894–97 Strindberg was living in Paris, almost destitute, he missed his children, he was dabbling in pseudo-scientific experiments, trying to make gold and ruining his health in the process. He described these years in *Inferno* (1897). He also kept *Ockulta dagboken* (The Occult Diary) from 1896 to 1908, in which he documented his thoughts. They all showed how Strindberg the atheist was converted to a mystic Swedenborgian kind of religion.

The author who emerged from the so-called Inferno crisis had a greatly changed attitude from the naturalistic writer of the 1880s. Starting with *Till Damaskus* (To Damascus, 1898), he produced a series of symbolic, dream-like plays which plumb the psychological depths and inner life of the central character and ignore social conditions. *Advent* (1898), *Påsk* (Easter, 1900), *Dödsdansen* (The Dance of Death, 1900), *Ett drömspel* (A Dream Play, 1901) and five Chamber plays, including *Spöksonaten* (The Ghost Sonata, 1907), followed in rapid succession. In this prolific period Strindberg also produced a series of historical plays, including *Gustav Vasa* (1899), *Erik XIV* (1899), *Gustav Adolf* (1900), *Carl XII* (1901), *Kristina* (1901) and *Gustav III* (1902).

Strindberg had returned to Stockholm and there met the enchanting and ambitious actress Harriet Bosse, whom he married in 1901 (the third time this alleged misogynist had chosen to marry a professional woman) and divorced in

1904. Alone again he moved into *Blå Tornet* (The Blue Tower, an apartment still preserved and now housing the Strindberg Museum). In 1910, two years before his death, Strindberg wrote a series of newspaper articles, collected under the title *Tal till svenska nationen* (Speeches to the Swedish Nation), where he attacked the conservative elements in literature (q.v.), politics and religion in Sweden. The anarchistic streak in his youthful writing was still evident. He belittled the importance of the writers of the 1890s, especially Verner von Heidenstam and Oscar Levertin, compared with his own influence. He was often witty but sometimes unfair in these articles, and his targets spread beyond principles to personalities. Heidenstam was eventually driven to a counterattack with articles in *Svenska Dagbladet,* and the so-called Strindberg Feud began to rage.

In one sense Strindberg was right, for his stature eclipses his Swedish contemporaries. Nationally his works of the 1880s ushered Swedish literature into the modern period, where everything had to be examined honestly and without hypocrisy. He renewed Swedish prose with his lucid, buoyant language, which was a vehicle for his social criticism and naturalistic characterization and yet could also conjure up his mystical, occult experiences. Internationally he provided a guide to Naturalism in his plays of the 1880s and the preface to *Lady Julie*; a new approach to autobiography; and in his plays from *To Damascus* onwards he led world theater towards Expressionism. Since the Swedish Academy (q.v.) would not grant him the Nobel Prize (q.v.), his more radical admirers arranged a national subscription and awarded him an ''anti-Nobel Prize,'' and at his funeral procession great numbers of workers joined in to show their appreciation for the way he had defended their cause.

STURE, NILS SVANTESSON (1543–1567) A soldier and diplomat, he distinguished himself in the Northern Seven Years War (1563–70) against Denmark. There is little evidence to suggest disloyalty towards Erik XIV (q.v.), but the latter had him and his relative Svante Stensson Sture arrested for treason and in a fit of madness killed them.

STURE, STEN GUSTAFSSON (1440–1503) Known as Sten
Sture the Elder. Swedish Regent. Supported by commoners,
he tried to shrug off the Kalmar Union (q.v.) and defeated the
Danes at the Battle of Brunkeberg in 1471, an important date
for Swedish nationalism. His attempts to establish a strong
centralized state antagonized many Swedish nobles, who
preferred to have a distant Danish monarch. King Hans of
Denmark, with the help of Swedish magnates, was hailed as
King of Sweden in 1483, a decision Sten Sture had to accept,
but after a successful rising in 1501 he was once more elected
Regent, a post he held until his death. He was succeeded as
Regent by Svante Nilsson Sture, a distant relative, who met
increasing opposition from the Danish king and from ambitious Swedish magnates jealous of the Regent's power. He
died accidentally in 1512 and was succeeded by his son Sten
Sture (q.v.).

STURE, STEN SVANTESSON (1493–1520) Known as Sten
Sture the Younger. Swedish Regent. An energetic, ambitious
leader, he was said to have planned to become King rather
than Regent. He defeated the Danish king Kristian II at the
Battle of Brännkyrka in 1518 but was mortally wounded
when the Danes counter-attacked in 1520. It was left to his
relative Gustav Vasa (q.v.) to deliver the deathblow to the
Kalmar Union (q.v.) and seize the Swedish crown.

SVEABORG see FINLAND

SVENSKA ARBETSGIVAREFÖRENINGEN (SAF, SWEDISH
FEDERATION OF EMPLOYERS) The period from the end
of the 19th century up to the outbreak of World War I (q.v.)
was one of growing prosperity for Sweden, but it was
punctuated by recessions and labor unrest. Landsorganisationen (LO, Swedish Confederation of Trade Unions) (q.v.)
was founded in 1898, and as a countermeasure Swedish
industrialists formed SAF in 1902. A deep recession in 1909
gave rise to a series of strikes, and SAF decided to deal with
them by declaring a general lockout affecting over 100,000
workers. LO responded by calling a General Strike (q.v.).

This trial of strength lasted for a month, by which time union funds were exhausted and employees had to return to work. SAF members realized, however, that the workers had legitimate grievances and that LO, in organizing effectively a nationwide strike, had demonstrated that it was a force to be taken seriously. By 1938 relations between capital and labor had improved sufficiently for both LO and SAF to accept the conditions of the Saltsjöbaden Agreement (q.v.), thus committing themselves to collective bargaining and the honoring of long term contracts.

SVENSKA DAGBLADET see NEWSPAPERS

SVERIGES ARBETARES CENTRALORGANISATION (SAC, SWEDISH WORKERS' CENTRAL ORGANIZATION). This organization was formed by syndicalists in 1910 after the trade unions' reversals during the General Strike in 1909 (q.v.). Its membership, numbering over 15,000, is drawn mainly from workers in the forestry and building industries. It publishes a weekly paper called *Arbetaren* (The Worker).

SWEDENBORG, EMANUEL (1688–1772) Swedish scientist, theologian and mystic. His family name was Svenberg, but was changed to Swedenborg in 1719 when they were ennobled. Although associated mainly with mysticism, Swedenborg was first a scientist with the intellectual, all-embracing curiosity and technical ability found in many Swedish scientists of the 18th century, when the Swedish Royal Academy of Science (q.v.) was founded (1739) and Celsius (q.v.) and Linnaeus (q.v.) were establishing their international reputation. Swedenborg studied at Uppsala (q.v.) University and then travelled widely in Europe, interesting himself particularly in developments in technology and engineering. On his return to Sweden he became, in 1716, Assessor at the Royal Board of Mines. He was a prolific writer, dealing among other things with astronomy, docks, sluices, navigation and differential calculus. His prodigious treatise *Opera Philosophica et Mineralia* (1734) covered metaphysics and metallurgy, while the hefty *Oeconomia Regni Animales* (1740–41) dealt with anatomy and physiology.

In 1747 Swedenborg resigned his scientific post, following a religious crisis he suffered in 1743–44. He recorded his experiences in his *Journal of Dreams,* claiming a direct vision of the spiritual world. He remained a prolific writer but from 1747 devoted himself to themes touching upon mystical experiences and doctrines. He produced in Latin some 30 volumes of religious revelations, including *Arcana Coelestia* (1749–56), *De Coelo et eius Mirabilibus et de Inferno* (1758) and *Vera Christiana Religio* (1771). After his death his disciples formed a society in London called the Church of the New Jerusalem (1787) which gradually set up branches throughout the world. Swedenborg's mystical writings had a strong influence on many subsequent Swedish writers, including Almquist (q.v.) and Strindberg (q.v.) in his post-Inferno period.

SWEDISH ACADEMY (SVENSKA AKADEMIEN) This august institution, consisting of 18 members, was founded in 1786 by the Francophile Gustav III (q.v.) and was modelled on the French Academy. Its aim was to preserve and encourage the Swedish language (q.v.) and national Swedish literature (q.v.). It has published its *handlingar* (Proceedings) since 1786, and since 1893 has been publishing a dictionary of the Swedish language from 1521 to the present day. It has now reached the letter S. The first edition of *Svenska Akademiens Ordlista,* an authoratitive glossary of the Swedish language, appeared in 1874. Since then there have been twelve editions, the most recent dating from 1986. Since 1901 the Academy has selected the Nobel Prize (q.v.) winner for Literature.

Of the 18 original members Gustav selected 13. Since then the Academy itself has chosen its members who are elected for life. The first woman member was the writer Selma Lagerlöf, who first took her seat in 1914.

SWEDISH EAST INDIA COMPANY (OSTINDISKA KOMPANIET) (1731–1813) As Sweden recovered from the Great Northern War (q.v.) (1700–21) she began to build up her merchant fleet and encourage foreign trade. In 1731 the East India Company, founded in Gothenburg (q.v.) by a group of merchants, including the Scot Colin Campbell and the Gothenburg benefactor Niklas Sahlgren, was given its charter. Despite its name its activities were confined to the Chinese port of Canton. On the outward voyage their ships with a cargo mostly of iron would unload at Cadiz and other ports and carry home from Canton silk, porcelain, lacquer and mother of pearl, but above all tea, which it would then sell to European countries, especially Britain. To their first ship, the *Fredericus Rex Suecia,* was added a fleet of over 40 vessels, and all in all over 132 expeditions were made. The company was extremely successful for 30 years, bringing wealth to Gothenburg, which can still be discerned to this day in the fine well-preserved buildings near the harbor. By the turn of the century the company was struggling, it went bankrupt during the Napoleonic Wars and was finally dissolved in 1813.

SWEDISH LANGUAGE Swedish (svenska) is a Germanic language. The Germanic languages gradually branched into East Germanic (Gothic), West Germanic (Dutch, English, Frisian and German) and North Germanic. North Germanic (Common Norse) in turn developed into East and West Scandinavian, with Danish and Swedish on one hand and Norwegian and Icelandic on the other. By the Viking (q.v.) period (AD 800–1060) a distinctly Swedish language was evolving. It was at that time a highly inflected language (resembling Modern Icelandic which has preserved most of the Old Norse characteristics), but by the end of the medieval period Swedish had discarded much of the inflected system.

The broad periods of development of Swedish are

Old Swedish (c. 800–1526)
   a) Runic Swedish (c. 800–1225)
   b) Classical Old Swedish (1225–1375)
   c) Younger Old Swedish (1375–1526)
New Swedish (1526–)
   a) Early New Swedish (1526–1700)
   b) Modern New Swedish (1700–)

The few records from the runic period are mostly in the form of runic inscriptions carved on stones. The alphabet used is the futhark, the name taken from the first six letters of the alphabet. Its origin is uncertain but it apparently derived from the Latin alphabet with possible Greek influence. Writing, at first in Latin, came with Christianity, and Latin remained the language of the Church until the Reformation, and of scholars well into the 18th century.

To help those less familiar with Latin, Swedish translations of "legends," i.e., lives of the saints, appeared in medieval monasteries. By the 14th century chivalrous romances, lays and rhyming chronicles also appeared in Swedish. The oldest book in Swedish, however, is not derivative but is an original Swedish composition, the *Västgötalagen* (The West-Gautish Laws), dating from about the 1220s.

With the Reformation, the Petri brothers Olaus (q.v.) and Laurentius (q.v.) were able to use the new art of printing to produce copies of the Bible and other religious tracts in Swedish. The New Testament first appeared in Swedish translation in 1526, and the complete Bible in 1541, called the Gustav Vasa Bible. Linguistically it became an accepted model, and subsequent translations (the Gustav Adolf Bible, 1618, and the Karl XII Bible, 1703) did not alter it substantially. It was only in this century, with the Gustav V Bible of 1917 that more radical changes appeared. The standard language to emerge was based principally on the Svea dialect of Stockholm (q.v.) and the district around Lake Mälaren, but incorporated some features of the Göta dialect.

Many Swedish scholars strove to purify the language, and Gustav III (q.v.) established the Swedish Academy (q.v.) in 1786 to work for "purity, strength and sublimity of the Swedish language." The Academy produced a standard grammar in 1836 and began publishing the authoritative dictionary of the Swedish language in the 1890s.

Improved educational standards and popular cheap newspapers (q.v.) in the 19th century brought about a great measure of uniformity in the language nationally, and discrepancies between the spoken and the written language were reduced, a process that has increased in this century with radio and television (q.v.).

Changes in Swedish have reflected foreign cultural influences. With Christianity came an influx of Latin words, e.g., *skriva*<Lat. *scribere; präst<presbyter; biskop<episcopus; mässa<missa.* In the Middle Ages the German colony of

merchants in Stockholm introduced vocabulary associated with society (e.g., *fru, riddare*), local government (e.g., *borgmästare*) and trades (e.g., *skomakare, timmerman*). The Petri brothers had studied at Wittenberg, and the Gustav Vasa Bible, to which they contributed, shows the influence of Luther's German version. In the reign of the Francophile, theater-loving Gustav III (q.v.) French affected the upper strata of social life shown in such loan words as *salong, teater, pjäs* and *ridå* (Fr. *rideau*). Increasingly from the 19th century English loan words are prevalent, often connected with clothing (*blazer, jumper, shorts, jeans*) and food (*rostbiff, paj* <Eng. pie). Many railroad terms came with the techniques (*lokomotiv, räls, truck, tunnel*). Labor relations and business also reflect Anglo-Saxon influences (*lockout, strejk, clearing, service*), and sport even more so (*knockout, promoter, fotboll, golf, tennis, match, spurt,* etc.). Entertainment and technology have added greatly to the vocabulary (e.g., *jazz, blues, disco, hifi, video*).

Periodically there have been warnings against extensive borrowing and foreign influences, for example, from Stiernhielm (q.v.) in the 17th, Olov von Dalin in the 18th and Viktor Rydberg in the 19th centuries. Word-frequency studies suggest, however, that the most frequent and constant words in use are still native Swedish ones. Similarly, purists in the postwar period bemoan the informality of Swedish compared to the more rigid prewar language. This too reflects the change in society generally, but Swedish has retained its linguistic integrity and is still easily recognizable as the language of Olaus Petri and the Gustav Vasa Bible.

Swedish is closely related to the other Scandinavian languages and is generally understood in Norway and Denmark. It is also the native language of Finland-Swedes on the West coast of Finland and an area around Helsinki. It is still the second official language in Finland (after the Finno-Ugrian Finnish), but less than seven percent of the Finnish population are now naturally Swedish-speaking. Until World War II Swedish was also spoken in parts of Latvia and Estonia (q.v.), a relic of Sweden's former Baltic empire.

SWEDISH ROYAL ACADEMY OF SCIENCES (KUNGLIGA VETENSKAPSAKADEMIEN) The Age of Liberty (1718–

72), whatever its political and economic failings, was a golden age for the sciences, when Swedes of genius, such as Carl Linnaeus (q.v.), Anders Celsius (q.v.), Christopher Polhem (q.v.) and Carl Scheele won international renown. On the initiative of several scientists, in particular A.J. von Höpken and Linnaeus, the Royal Academy of Sciences was founded in Stockholm (q.v.) in 1739, with the aim of furthering the Swedish economy through research and invention especially in the fields of agriculture, medicine and mechanics. Its members exchanged reports on inventions and research with other learned societies abroad, including the Royal Society in London. Jöns Berzelius, the first to produce a table of chemical elements, was the Society's Secretary from 1818 to 1848 and gave it its present emphasis on science and mathematics. It is this society that selects annually the Nobel Prize (q.v.) winners in Physics and Chemistry.

SYDOW, OSCAR VON (1873–1936) Swedish lawyer and civil servant, and Provincial Governor of Norrbotten in 1911 and of Gothenburg (q.v.) from 1917–34. Twice von Sydow, a member of no political party, entered the political arena. He was Minister of Civil Service Affairs, serving under the Conservative Hjalmar Hammarskjöld's (qq.v.) premiership in World War I (q.v.) from 1914 to 1917. In the immediate postwar years no political party had a majority in *Riksdag* (q.v.). When Hjalmar Branting (q.v.) resigned in October 1920 a reform of the franchise had been passed but would not become effective until the autumn elections of 1921. In the hiatus no party wanted to form a government, and Louis De Geer (Jun.) a non-party man, formed a caretaker government consisting mostly of lawyers and civil servants. De Geer was unexpectedly defeated when trying to impose a duty on coffee; he resigned and von Sydow succeeded him in February 1921. In the ensuing election the Social Democrats (q.v.) improved their position, Branting formed his second government and von Sydow returned to his administrative duties as Provincial Governor.

SYDSVENSKA DAGBLADET see NEWSPAPERS

-T-

TELEVISION see RADIO AND TELEVISION

TEMPERANCE MOVEMENT For centuries Sweden had a problem with the consequences of excessive alcohol consumption. One of Gustav III's (q.v.) most unpopular measures, in 1775, was to prohibit private stills, a prohibition more often breached than observed. In 1800 home distilling was made legal again, and it was calculated that by 1829, when the population numbered about 2.5 million, there were some 173,000 private stills in use. Alcohol consumption per head was approximately 46 liters per annum (compared with nine liters today), and drunkenness was usual in all classes of society.

Inspired by an American temperance movement, it was decided in 1832 that to mark the 1000th anniversary of the missionary Ansgar's first visit to Sweden a temperance society should be set up in every parish. In 1833 Samuel Owen, a Stockholm (q.v.) industrialist and steamship builder, led the way in the capital by forming the Stockholm Temperance Society, and in 1837 the Swedish Temperance Society was formed. In 1833 Pastor Peter Wieselgren was appointed to the living at Västerstad in Skåne and had his first sermon interrupted by drunken members of his congregation, including women and his own parish clerk. He founded a temperance society at Västerstad in 1836 and travelled widely, lecturing on the evils of alcohol and gaining supporters. By the mid-1840s there were over 300 societies with over 100,000 members. The number of private stills had fallen in 1853 to 33,000, and alcohol consumption declined to 23 liters per head, but this, no doubt, was caused partially by potato blight and the high price of grain imports. In 1855 high taxes were imposed on the distilling of spirits, and by 1860 there was a ban on private stills.

From the 1870s, temperance societies changed in character and were modelled on the International Order of Good Templers (IOGT) which established its first lodge in Gothenburg (q.v.) in 1879, followed by the Blue Band, Swedish National Order of Templars, Verdandi Temperance organization, White Ribbon, Workers' Temperance Society and several others. This was a period of popular movements in Sweden, and the temperance societies played their part in educating the public and influencing public opinion. They did not merely negatively deprecate alcohol abuse but put other facilities at the disposal of workers, such as libraries and edifying lectures. Several working-class authors, including Vilhelm Moberg and Ivar Lo-Johansson, have testified to the important role temperance societies' libraries played in their lives. Many Swedish politicians were members of temperance societies, some of them with Cabinet status, such as Finance Ministers Ernst Wigforss (q.v.) and Per Edvin Sköld (q.v.), and the temperance movement's influence exceeds the size of its membership. It was calculated that in the late 1960s one third of the *Riksdag* (q.v.) members were also members of temperance societies, as opposed to only six percent of the population at large. Since 1939 the Swedish trade unions (q.v.) and the temperance societies have had a coordinating committee on alcohol issues.

Total abstinence was the issue that caused a split in the Liberal Party (q.v.), healed only after the 1922 referendum on the question. Since before World War I there had been mounting pressure for a total ban on alcohol, but on the initiative of Dr Ivar Bratt (q.v.) a rationing scheme was introduced instead, first in Stockholm in 1914 and three years later throughout the whole country. All alcohol sales were made through a state monopoly, the Vin- och- spritcentralen which introduced the *motbok* or ration book. A consultative referendum on prohibition held in 1922 meanwhile proved inconclusive, and the Bratt system continued until 1955, when the *motbok* was abolished but the state monopoly retained. There is presently concern that when Sweden becomes a member of the European Union (q.v.) such a monopoly will be illegal, and Sweden will lose this means of controlling alcohol consumption, but statements from Brussels suggest that Sweden will be allowed to retain her state monopoly.

THEATER IN SWEDEN Swedish theater originated from liturgical ceremonies, but there is a scarcity of material preserved today. After the Reformation, a number of didactic school dramas appeared, aimed at inculcating high morals in the young rather than achieving artistic standards. The unsophisticated *Tobias Comedy* (1550) attributed to Olaus Petri (q.v.) is a typical example. Plays by Plautus and Terence were performed by students, often in the vernacular. The Swedish historian Johannes Messenius (1580–1636) wrote a series of popular chronicle plays, but they are important as a reflection of a growing spirit of nationalism rather than for intrinsic merit.

With the rise of Sweden as a European power in the 17th century the court of Queen Kristina (q.v.) became a cultural center. Georg Stiernhielm (q.v.) produced the text for several allegorical plays performed in the Queen's honor. Outside court circles, strolling players from England, Germany and France exercised an important influence on the development of Swedish theater in the 17th and 18th centuries. A French troupe performed for some years from 1699 in Bollhuset (The Tennis Court) in Stockholm (q.v.), its repertoire including plays by Racine and Molière. A Swedish company formed in 1737 performed at Bollhuset, including in its repertoire the Swedish comedy *Svenska sprätthöken* (The Swedish Fop, 1737) by C. Gyllenborg (q.v.) and two plays by Olof von Dalin (q.v.), *Brynhilda* (1738) and *Den avundsjuke* (The Jealous Man, 1738).

Queen Lovisa Ulrika (q.v.) found Bollhuset too vulgar and had plays produced at Drottningholm (q.v.), her summer palace near Stockholm. Her son Gustav III (q.v.), an ardent theater-lover, set out to create a national theater. Believing that music would make this task easier, he first started on opera, calling on foreign composers such as Kraus, Naumann and Uttini. Bollhuset was used from 1773, but in 1782 an opera house was built in Stockholm where, in 1786, *Gustav Vasa* was staged, an opera which had been outlined by Gustav himself. It was the first of several historical nationalistic works associated with Gustav in the 1780s. His successful play *Siri Brahe och Johan Gyllenstierna* (1787) was in the repertoire of the Comédie Française for many years. In 1788 Gustav founded the Royal Dramatic Theater. There was also in this period a popular theater at Humlegården in

Stockholm that produced comedies and musicals. No great Swedish dramatist emerged, but the King's enthusiasm had created the right conditions for fostering talent. In 1792, however, he was assassinated and all theaters and other places of entertainment were immediately closed.

At the beginning of the 19th century Stockholm had only two theaters, the Opera House and the Dramatic Theater accommodated in the Arsenal, which was destroyed by fire in 1825. The New Theater was inaugurated in Kungsträdgården in 1842, in 1863 it changed its name to the Royal Dramatic theater, and in 1908 it moved to its present home at Nybroplan. There was a quickening of activity in the 1850s when four new theaters were opened in Stockholm. There were few Swedish plays to satisfy demand, and the repertoire consisted mostly of translations, works by Kotzebue, Scribe, Schiller and Shakespeare being most frequently performed. The Swedish writer Bernhard von Beskow (1796–1868) produced a series of plays based on Swedish history, while August Blanche's (1711–1868) comedies appealed to the middle classes.

By the 1880s Scandinavian dramatists associated with the "Modern Breakthrough" were being performed in Sweden, in particular Ibsen's *A Doll's House* and Björnson's *The Gauntlet.* August Strindberg (q.v.), Sweden's first dramatic genius, wrote a series of naturalistic plays, including *Fadren* (The Father, 1887) and *Fröken Julie* (Miss Julie, 1888), which were internationally recognized and finally performed in Sweden. Even more innovative were Strindberg's post-Inferno plays, *Till Damaskus* (To Damascus, 1898), *Påsk* (Easter, 1900), *Ett drömspel* (A Dream Play, 1902) and a series of Chamber plays from 1907. Using new scenic techniques, Strindberg turned from social drama and social psychology and sought to portray his quest for spiritual values and to understand the human condition by penetrating his own psyche. Strindberg joined a young director, August Falck, who established the Intimate Theater in Stockholm, where from 1907 to 1910 Strindberg's expressionistic plays were staged.

Strindberg cast a long shadow, and the three best-known Swedish dramatists this century show his influence. The experimental plays of Pär Lagerkvist (1891–1974) *Den svåra stunden* (The Difficult Hour, 1918) and *Himlens hemlighet* (Secret of Heaven, 1919) owe much to *A Dream Play* in the way Angst-ridden men search for the meaning of life. Hjalmar Bergman (1883–1931) became popular as a comic writer, and his plays *Swedenhielms* (1925), about the honor of a Swedish inventor hoping to win the Nobel prize (q.v.). and *Markurells i Wadköping* (his own adaptation of his novel; translated as *God's Orchid,* 1919), about a father's love for his son about to sit his matriculation examinations, have became almost a part of Swedish folk culture. It was, however, his *Marionette Plays* from 1917 that echoed Strindberg's expressionism in a dream world that slips into nightmare.

Stig Dagerman (1923–1954) epitomized the pessimism of the 1940s. In his play *Den dödsdömde* (The Condemned Man, 1947) the "hero" is condemned to death, reprieved, but still ends on the gallows. In *I skuggan av Mart* (In Mart's Shadow, 1949) an unprepossessing, cowardly young man is always overshadowed by the memory of his valiant, handsome brother. The dead Mart gradually becomes more real than when he was alive. Both plays conjure up a troubled world between dream and reality.

In the 1960s, when the Swedish economy was flourishing but taxation was very high, it was realized that the state must become the patron of the Arts. The Royal Dramatic Theater plus the municipal theaters in most of the large towns received subsidies, as did Riksteatern, the National Travelling theater set up to visit theaters, schools, hospitals and other public places throughout the country. Increased political activity in the late 1960s, usually of radical left-wing persuasion, led to the forming of theater groups outside the established theater to provoke debate and involve the public directly. The most successful was a lively group in Gothenburg (q.v.) under Kent Andersson (1933–) and Bengt Bratt (1937–). The most permanent of their social satires were performed in Gothenburg City Theater in 1967. In *Flottan* (The Raft), the raft of the title is a symbol of the all-embracing welfare state (q.v.). The home in *Hemmet* is a place for old people whom the welfare state has no use for.

The message in both plays is that the welfare state has lost a feeling for human dignity and values. These groups revitalized drama but by their very nature lacked permanency. The best directors went on to more conventional theater or television.

The most frequently performed Swedish playwright today is Lars Norén (1944–), whose most successful plays are *Natten är dagens mor* (Night is the Mother of Day, 1983) and its sequel *Kaos är granne med Gud* (Chaos is God's Neighbor, also 1983). Norén depicts a neurotic family, the father an alcoholic, the youngest son verging on mental breakdown. His method of confining the characters and increasing the tense atmosphere is in the Strindberg-Eugene O'Neill tradition. Per Olov Enquist (1934–) scored a dramatic success with *Tribadernas natt* (The Night of the Tribades, 1975), an unflattering portrait of Strindberg's relations with his first wife. His *Till Fedra* (To Phaedra, 1980) uses the Greek theme to highlight friction between generations, while *I lodjurets timma* (In the Hour of the Lynx, 1988) portrays a sensitive young man damaged by society and reacting violently to being treated as a "case."

With good subsidized theaters in Stockholm, Gothenburg and all the major provincial towns, a national travelling company and good television drama, most Swedes have access to proficient performances. The majority of plays produced are foreign, but there are excellent opportunities offered to Swedish authors. In 1993 a Swedish Academy of Theater was formed to promote and support the dramatic arts, an equivalent of the Swedish Academy (q.v.) and the Swedish Academy of Science (q.v.), both dating from the 18th century.

THIRTY YEARS WAR see GUSTAV II ADOLF

TINGSTEN, HERBERT (1896–1973) Swedish publicist and political scientist. Tingsten was Professor of Political Science at Stockholm University from 1935 to 1946. He had been a member of the Social Democratic Party (q.v.) from the early 1920s and was a leading theorist, demonstrated in his influential publications *Demokratiens seger och kris* (Democracy's Victory and Crisis, 1933) and *Den svenska social-demokratiens idéutveckling* I & II (The Development of Social Democratic Theory, 1941). His following book *Demokratiens problem* (Democracy's Problems, 1945) reflected his disillusionment, stating that socialism was not compatible with political freedom. From 1946 to 1960 he was editor of *Dagens Nyheter* (q.v.), an independent liberal daily with the largest circulation in Sweden, and made his mark, not least in the struggle against socialism. He was a consistent opponent of communist states and also criticized Sweden's neutrality and the decision not to join NATO. He believed, however, in social and economic equality, and came into conflict with the Bonniers, owners of the newspaper, over the issue of ATP (q.v.), a compulsory pension scheme. Tingsten was a prolific writer and a stimulating, if sometimes argumentative, personality who exercised a strong influence on Swedish political thought. As his memoirs show (*Mitt liv* I–IV, 1961–64), he felt increasingly isolated from the early 1960s onwards because of growing blindness.

TORSTENSSON, LENNART see BANÉR, JOHAN

TRADE UNIONS see LANDSORGANISATIONEN; SACO/SR; SVERIGES ARBETARE CENTRALORGANISATION; TJÄNSTEMÄNNENS CENTRALORGANISATION

TRANSPORTATION The railroad building program was initiated in the mid-19th century. In 1853–54, *Riksdag* (q.v.) decided that the state would finance the main lines while private enterprise would be responsible for branch lines. Nils Ericsson was in charge of the building of the state rail system. Since it was government policy to lay tracks through sparsely populated areas it opened up large, hitherto almost uncharted regions and led to the growth of new towns at junctions. By the 1930s, with ownership of private automobiles increasing, the railroads were in financial difficulty, and in 1939 the whole system was nationalized.

Nowadays, with large, more sophisticated trucks and an extensive road-building program, heavy goods are mostly transported by road. Ore mined in Kiruna and Malmberget in Norrland, however, is still sent by rail to the ports of Narvik and Luleå for shipment abroad. About 80 percent of all domestic passenger traffic is dealt with by the privately-owned automobile.

Shipping routes along the coasts and on lakes and canals, including the Göta Canal (q.v.), were previously extremely important in a country with a long coastline and thousands of lakes and islands, but thanks to modern bridge and road building they have been largely superseded by faster road transport. International shipping, however, is still important, the largest international ports being Gothenburg (q.v.), Stockholm (q.v.) and Malmö (q.v.).

Air travel has increased steadily since the 1950s. Services are dominated by the Scandinavian Airlines System (SAS), a consortium founded in 1951 and owned jointly by Sweden, Denmark and Norway. The main Swedish airports are at Stockholm (Arlanda), Gothenburg (Landvetter) and Malmö (Sturup).

Local transport is usually by municipal bus services, but Gothenburg and Norrköping have retained and improved their trolley (tram) services. Stockholm built a short subway (underground) line in 1933. In 1950 a modern system was introduced and has been extended gradually to include its suburbs.

TROEDSSON, INGEGERD (1929–) Swedish Conservative politician. Mrs Troedsson was Vice-Chairman of the Conservative Women's Association from 1965 to 1975, and has been a member of *Riksdag* (q.v.) since 1974. She was a Minister of State in the Social Department 1976–78, and appointed a Deputy Speaker of *Riksdag* in 1979. After the 1991 elections she made history by becoming the first woman Speaker.

TROLLE, GUSTAV ERIKSSON (1488–1535) Swedish Archbishop. In the final stages of the Kalmar Union (q.v.) Sten Sture the Younger (q.v.), the Swedish Regent, represented those wanting independence from Denmark, while Gustav Trolle led the Unionists on the Council. In 1515 Trolle visited Rome, where the Pope confirmed his appointment as

Archbishop. Deeply suspicious of Trolle's motives, Sten Sture persuaded a *Riksdag* (q.v.) to dismiss him and had his castle Stäket demolished. Trolle had Sten Sture and his supporters excommunicated by the Pope, which gave the Danish King Christian II's attack on Sweden in 1520 the character of a Holy War as well as an attempt to reassert his rights according to the Kalmar Union. Sten Sture was killed and, despite Christian's promise of an amnesty, over 80 of his supporters were executed in the Stockholm Bloodbath (q.v.). The massacre was said to have been at Trolle's instigation, but King Christian was probably using him to remove powerful Swedish enemies. Danish ruthlessness provoked a Swedish rebellion that carried Gustav Vasa (q.v.) to power and spelt the end of the Union. Trolle left Sweden in 1521, and accompanied Christian into exile when the latter was deposed by the Danes in 1523. Trolle supported Christian in his struggle to regain power, was imprisoned in Denmark from 1532 to 1533, was involved in the Danish "Count's Feud" and was mortally wounded in the Battle of Oxnebjerg in 1535.

TRYGGER, ERNST (1857–1943) Swedish lawyer and Conservative (q.v.) politician. Trygger was a Professor of Law at Uppsala (q.v.) University from 1889 and became a member of the Upper Chamber of *Riksdag* in 1898. In 1912 the various Conservative groups in the Upper Chamber united under Trygger's leadership. No association could be formed with the Conservatives of the Lower Chamber, led by Arvid Lindman (q.v.), however, the gulf between Tryggar, a "dark-blue" Conservative, and the more modern, flexible Lindman proving too wide. In 1914, in the furor caused by King Gustav's Palace Yard speech (q.v.) the ultra-conservative Trygger supported the King, but Lindman was more hesitant. When Hjalmar Hammarskjöld (q.v.) was forced to resign as Prime Minister in 1917, King Gustav asked Trygger to form a new government, but to his annoynace Trygger had eventually to admit his inability to do so and the more moderate Carl Swartz took over, with Lindman as his Foreign Minister.

In 1923 Trygger was able to form a minority Conservative government after the fall of Hjalmar Branting's (q.v.) Social

Democratic (q.v.) government. In 1924 he was defeated on a defense issue. Sweden, under Branting's premiership, had joined the League of Nations in 1920. Branting's party believed fundamentally in international peace and disarmament, and wanted to direct funds towards social welfare. Trygger had no such faith and wanted to keep Swedish defenses up to strength. *Riksdag* rejected his defense proposals. In October 1924, he resigned and Branting formed his third government. When Conservatives made electoral gains in 1928, Lindman became Prime Minister and invited Trygger to serve as Foreign Minister. When the government tried to introduce protective tariffs on grain imports to help the farmers, it was defeated, and in 1930 a Liberal (q.v.) government took office. Trygger never again held ministerial office, but he remained a member of the Upper Chamber until 1937.

-U-

ULLSTEN, OLA (1931–) Swedish Liberal politician. Ullsten was chairman of the Liberal Party's (q.v.) Youth Association from 1962 to 1964 and became a member of *Riksdag* (q.v.) in 1965. By 1975 he was on the party's national committee. After Thorbjörn Fälldin (q.v.) formed a non-socialist coalition government in 1976, Ullsten served as Foreign Minister from 1976 to 1978. On the resignation of Per Ahlmark, leader of the Liberals, in 1978, Ullsten became party leader and Deputy Prime Minister, and after Fälldin's resignation in that same year, he formed a Liberal government that was in power until the general elections in 1979. Fälldin formed his second non-socialist coalition government, which was in power from 1979 to 1982. During that time Ullsten was Foreign Minister and Deputy Prime Minister. The Social Democrats (q.v.) were returned to power in 1982, and the following year Ullsten resigned as Chairman of the Liberal Party. He withdrew from party politics and in 1984 was appointed Swedish Ambassador to Canada.

ULRIKA ELEONORA (1688–1741) Swedish Queen. The younger sister of Karl XII (q.v.), she was elected to the throne in 1719 only on acceptance of a new constitution which greatly restricted the power of the Crown and inaugurated the Age of Liberty (1718–72). She abdicated in 1720 in favor of her husband Fredrik I. Neither enjoyed any real power and were little more than royal figureheads. She died childless in 1741.

UNDÉN, ÖSTEN (1886–1974) Swedish Social Democrat (q.v.), lawyer, Professor of Civil Law at Uppsala (q.v.) University from 1917 to 1937, University Rector from 1928–34 and University Chancellor from 1937–51. Undén was first appointed as Minister without Portfolio in Nils Edén's (q.v.) Liberal-Social Democratic coalition of 1917–20 and was appointed Minister of Justice in Branting's (q.v.) short-lived government in 1920. He was associated with the group of very able young Social Democratic politicians whom Per Albin Hansson (q.v.) gathered around him after Branting's death in 1925, was Minister without Portfolio from 1932–36 and Foreign Minister from 1924 to 1926 and from 1945 to 1962. On Hansson's death in 1946 he acted as Prime Minister until a new party leader was elected.

Undén succeeded Branting in 1925 as Sweden's representative on the Council of the League of Nations. In that capacity he helped to solve an international crisis that arose when Poland, fearing German border activities, demanded a permanent place on the Council. Germany had already joined, and many members, including Undén, thought the Council should not be increased if it was to remain effective. Through Undén, Sweden offered its place to Poland. Undén was criticized strongly by Swedish Conservatives (q.v.) and Agrarians (q.v.), who felt he had succumbed to western pressures.

In the years after World War II Undén consistently supported Sweden's policy of armed neutrality (q.v.) and freedom from alliances, pressed successfully for Swedish membership of the United Nations and the OEEC (q.v.) but eschewed NATO. He was against Sweden's constructing strategic nuclear weapons and at the UN in 1961 he suggested setting up a club of nuclear free countries (known as the Undén plan). By 1963 the United States, Britain and the

Soviet Union had agreed on a test ban and Undén's "club" lost relevance. Undén published his memoirs in 1966.

UNION WITH NORWAY (1814–1905) By 1520 Sweden had left the Kalmar Union (q.v.), but Norway continued to be closely linked with Denmark and became virtually a Danish dependency. Finland (q.v.) had since the 13th century been considered part of Sweden, but in 1809, after a disastrous war, Finland became part of the Russian empire. Gustav IV Adolf (q.v.) was deposed in 1809 and succeeded by his uncle Karl XIII (q.v.). As Karl was old and childless, an heir apparent had to be elected, and the choice fell on the French Marshal Bernadotte, who took the name of Karl Johan (q.v.) on reaching his adoptive country in 1810. Many had hoped that this military campaigner would restore Finland to Sweden, but Karl Johan's "1812 policy" entailed an agreement with Tsar Alexander to help defeat Napoleon in return for support in taking Norway from Denmark. In 1813 Swedish troops were sent to Germany and took part in the Battle of Leipzig (though not, it was said, a very active part since Karl Johan was preserving his troops for the next part of his plan). The troops then moved towards Denmark and forced the Danes to accept the Peace of Kiel in January 1814. Norway was exchanged for Swedish Pomerania.

Norwegian self-awareness and national pride had been growing since the previous century, and Norway refused to accept the Danish King's right to cede their country to anyone. At a national assembly at Eidsvoll north of Oslo (or Kristiania as the capital was then called) Norwegians declared their independence and elected the popular Danish governor Prince Kristian Frederik as their King. A new Constitution was drawn up and on 17 May it was accepted at Eidsvoll. Its model was the French revolutionary constitution, and it gave only restricted authority to the King. Karl Johan insisted on the terms of the Kiel treaty and moved his troops into Norway. Although he had the military advantage, he was anxious to have the matter settled speedily before the Congress of Vienna convened, and he was ready for some degree of compromise. The result was the Convention of Moss in August 1814. Kristian Frederik surrendered the

Norwegian crown, while Karl XIII was appointed King of Norway on condition that he accepted the Eidsvoll constitution with some minor modificiatons. Norway was thus in union with Sweden not as a conquered province but as an independent state with its own laws and institutions. What the two countries had in common was the royal house and foreign policy, which was to be directed from the Foreign Office in Stockholm (q.v.).

Karl Johan, who succeeded Karl XIII in 1818, was fairly popular with the Norwegian public, and was twice, in 1832 and 1835, received enthusiastically by students when on a visit to Norway. The restrictions of the Norwegian Constitution chafed, however. It gave him only a suspensive veto, and if the *Storting* (the Norwegian parliament) passed a motion three times it became law despite the monarch's objection. In 1821 the *Storting* abolished all aristocratic titles and the King was powerless to do more than delay it. In the 1820s the Norwegians began to celebrate 17 May as their national day, and when in 1829 the authorities tried to dampen down festivities it became an anti-Swedish celebration, which the Swedish Governor Baltsar von Platen ordered the army to disperse. The outcome was the recall of the Governor and an undertaking that only Norwegians would occupy the post in future.

Disagreements between Norway and Sweden were irritations rather than discord from 1814 until the 1870s. The two main bones of contention remained the office of Governor and the fact that foreign policy was always directed from Stockholm. The Norwegian merchant fleet had grown enormously since 1814 and yet Norway had no consular service of her own. Attitudes began to harden; some conservatives in *Riksdag* (q.v.) felt that too much ground had been given to Norway, while in Norway the liberal Ventre party began to push for parliamentarianism in contravention of the King's power of veto. When the *Ventre* party gained a majority after the 1883 election the *Storting* voted the Prime Minister out of office. Oscar II (q.v.) refused to accept his resignation but found it impossible to form a conservative goverment and had to give way and accept Johan Sverdrup, leader of the Ventre party, as Prime Minister. It was another

20 years before Sweden reached this stage in parliamentary democracy.

In 1892 the *Storting* decided to set up its own Norwegian consular service, contravening the Act of Union. Oscar and his Swedish Prime Minister Boström (q.v.) were prepared to be conciliatory, but there were strong dissenting voices in *Riksdag* urging the King to use his veto. Kaiser Wilhelm, who visited Stockholm that year, advised Oscar to be firm with Norway. The Norwegians found it prudent to let matters rest for a while, but they were not to be intimidated. The *Storting* voted to build fortifications along their southern border with Sweden and to remove the Swedish flag from the emblem of the Union. A Norwegian-Swedish Committee proposed in 1902 that Norway should have her own consular service but on condition that the Swedish Foreign Minister would control both the Norwegian and the Swedish consular services. In 1904 the Norwegians rejected this compromise out of hand and Oscar therefore declared negotiations at an end.

Boström was receiving flak from both the Norwegians and the conservative members of *Riksdag* and resigned. In May 1905 the *Storting* voted again to set up a Norwegian consular service without relations with the Foreign Office, Oscar refused to sanction the motion and the Norwegian government en masse proferred its resignation. Oscar refused to accept the resignation, knowing that he would not be able to form another government, at which point the *Storting* declared on 7 June that the King ''had ceased to function as the Norwegian king'' and that the Union was therefore dissolved. Many Swedes, including Crown Prince Gustav (later Gustav V) (q.v.) realized that Norway was united on this issue and that there was no point in trying to force the prolongation of the Union, but *Riksdag* was reluctant to accept what it considered to be an ultimatum. A special meeting of *Riksdag* was held, which set up a special committee, which in turn drew up a list of Swedish conditions for a dissolution.

On 31 August 1905 representatives from both sides met in Karlstad, Värmland, and began negotiations that were far from amicable. Both countries had mobilized their armed forces, but fortunately no outside power was eager to lend assistance. After some hard bargaining it was agreed that Oscar would resign as Norwegian King, and Sweden would recognize Norway's full sovereignty on condition that Norwegian frontier fortifications were dismantled and that Swedish nomadic Lapps (q.v.) could graze their reindeer on both sides of the border. A Norwegian proposal that a Bernadotte prince be invited to become King of Norway was rejected by the Swedes. Instead, Prince Carl of Denmark was elected. He adopted the name Håkon VII, thus linking Norway with her historical past before the Kalmar Union.

UNIVERSITIES see EDUCATION

UPPSALA (Population in 1991 167,508) The town of Uppsala on Fyrisån (i.e., Fyris River) was originally the port for Gamla (Old) Uppsala and was called Arosa (i.e., river mouth). Gamla Uppsala, three kilometers north of the modern town, was the center of the Svea Kings and their pagan religion, and the meeting place for the Assembly, or Thing. Three burial mounds can be seen today, marking the graves of early Svea Kings. Towards the end of the Viking (q.v.) period (c. 800–1060) Uppsala had a great heathen temple, serving the rest of Scandinavia not yet converted to Christianity, where every nine years a great religious festival demanded human sacrifice. As late as 1080 the Svear banished their King Inge for refusing to perform the pagan rites and they installed Blót (i.e., Sacrifice) Swein instead. Inge regained control, however, the temple at Uppsala was subsequently demolished and a Christian church built on its site.

The see of Sigtuna (q.v.) was transferred to Uppsala, which became a bishopric and in 1164 was raised to an archbishopric. In 1273 it was decided to build a cathedral fit to house the relics of St Erik (d. 1160), Sweden's patron saint. The Archbishop's see was moved in 1276 to what is now modern Uppsala, and the cathedral, Sweden's first Gothic church, was built. From 1287 to c. 1300 the work was led by Etienne de Bonneuil from Paris. The cathedral was finally consecrated in 1435. It has been repaired and restored numerous times, drastically in 1885–93 by Helgo Zettervall after extensive fire damage. During restoration in 1926 the remains of a wooden building presumed to be the original heathen temple was discovered. The latest restoration was completed in 1976 when the cathedral was reconsecrated.

Incipient nationalism during the Kalmar Union (q.v.) helped the cause of a Swedish university at Uppsala. The regent Sten Sture (q.v.) and his government learnt of plans to establish Copenhagen University and founded a Swedish university at Uppsala in 1477, the first university in Scandinavia. It was soon in difficulty and teaching ceased during the civil wars towards the end of the Union. With Gustav Vasa (q.v.) came political stability, but he had little interest in higher education. It fell to his son Erik XIV (q.v.) to reopen the university in 1566. Fourteen years later it closed again, this time because of the staff's opposition to Johan III's (q.v.) Red Book, a liturgy with Catholic leanings. It started up again in 1595 but by 1607 had been suppressed by the ruthless Karl IX (q.v.) who disapproved of the staff's independent views.

Gustav II Adolf (q.v.) to all intents and purposes re-founded the university. He gave it financial independence in 1624 by donating 300 royal estates, he appointed the first Chancellor, created new Chairs and bequeathed his own fine book collection, which formed the nucleus of the University Library, the famous *Carolina rediviva,* founded in 1620. The library was enlarged by war booty after 1648, including the *Codex argenteus* or Silver Bible, a 6th century Gothic translation of the New Testament, a rare document on display today at the library. As early as 1692 Uppsala University library became a copyright library. The University went on to achieve international status as a seat of learning. Carl Linnaeus (q.v.) was Professor there from 1741 to 1778. The Linnaeus museum celebrates his life and achievements and the gardens at Uppsala are laid out as in his own time.

To consolidate his position Gustav Vasa built a series of castles at strategic points. Work on Uppsala Castle started in the 1540s and was completed in 1616. It is a typical Vasa construction, a solid edifice meant to be a fort as well as a prestigious residence. It was damaged by fire on several occasions and was renovated in the 1740s after severe damaged sustained in 1702. It is now the Provincial Governor's residence.

While several industries have been built up around Uppsala during this century, including book printing, machine and mechanical engineering, brick works and textiles, Uppsala's fame remains as an ecclesiastic and educational center. Besides the University, there is a teacher training college, a teaching hospital and Ultuna Agricultural College.

-V-

VADSTENA (Population in 1991 7,557). An idyllic small Swedish town on Lake Vättern. In 1346 Birgitta Birgersdotter (later St Birgitta) (q.v.), persuaded King Magnus Eriksson to donate Vadstena estate, where she wished to build a convent. In 1370 she obtained Pope Urban's permission to found the Birgittian Order (within the Augustinian Order). She died in Rome in 1373 and her remains were taken to Vadstena where her new convent, led by her daughter Katarina, was consecrated in 1384. It soon became a place of pilgrimage. Queen Margareta (q.v.) granted Vadstena town privileges in 1400 and the Town Hall, the oldest in Sweden, was built. By 1430 a convent church had been consecrated. The Order received many substantial donations, its library became the largest in Scandinavia, and Vadstena itself became a Scandinavian spiritual and cultural center. Bishops of Linköping often visited, and soon had a house built in Vadstena. Bishop Henrik Tidemansson's house from 1473 is still standing.

At Vadstena in 1521, after defeating Christian II of Denmark, Gustav Vasa (q.v.) was proclaimed Regent. He had a castle built there, the work being started in 1545 and finally completed in 1620. His sons Johan (later Johan III) (q.v.) and Magnus both lived there, but then it fell into disrepair, being used as a granary and a warehouse. It now houses national archives.

With the Reformation, Vadstena's cultural significance declined. Since many of the nuns came from the most important families in the country, the convent was not closed until 1597, the last in Sweden. The convent buildings were used by military personnel from 1637 to 1783 and then as a mental hospital from 1829 to 1951. They have now been restored and offer a guest house and a conference center with an ecumenical atmosphere. There is also a Vadstena Academy which performs·operas and concerts in the summer, helping to restore Vadstena in some degree as a cultural center.

VIKINGS Norse or Scandinavian seafaring warriors, colonists and traders active mainly from the 9th to the 11th century. Many interpretations have been given to the word "Viking" which could be derived from *vik,* i.e., bay, *vig,* i.e., fight, or *vikjan,* i.e., to settle. Nor is there a single reason given for the rather spectacular entrance of the Vikings onto the European scene. A period of relative prosperity in Scandinavia may have led to overpopulation at home, coinciding with the period after the death of Charlemagne in 814 when European defenses were low. The pagan Scandinavian seafarers found the rich, vulnerable towns, churches and monasteries in Christian countries to the west and south irresistible. In Scandinavia during the Viking period (c. 800–1060) ambitious chieftains and powerful families were struggling for supremacy regionally and nationally, and some chieftains and their followers chose to go on Viking expeditions rather than remain at home under another man's rule. Once a pattern had been set some Vikings simply set off to find lucrative adventure and to establish a reputation. Not least tempting were the prospects of rewarding trade expeditions.

For the Vikings waterways were the most obvious means of transport, and although Vikings from all three Scandinavian countries participated in expeditions irrespective of nationality, they tended to set out on the sea that washed the shores of their own country. Thus it was largely the Norwegians and Danes who settled, raided or conquered Iceland, the Faroes, Orkney and Shetland, the Isle of Man, parts of Ireland and the Scottish mainland, England, northern France, and even Greenland and America, while the Swedes, broadly speaking, turned their attention eastwards.

Archeological sources show that there had already been considerable contact between Scandinavia and the Eastern Mediterranean by way of the Vistula and other East European rivers throughout the Roman Iron Age (AD 0–400). The remains of a Swedish colony dating from the 7th and 8th centuries have been found near Libau in Latvia, proving Swedish connections with the southern Baltic before the Vikings. At the height of the Viking period, Swedish seafarers-cum-traders journeyed east and south and established trade routes through Russia and right down to the Caspian, the Black Sea and the Byzantine Empire.

The Vikings developed different routes to Russia. One was from bases on Lake Ladoga, along the river Volkhov to Lake Ilmen and from there along the Dnjeper to the Black Sea and Constantinople, capital of the Eastern Roman Emperor. Several of the Viking warriors enlisted in the Emperor's Varangian (Viking) Guard, a formidable band of mercenaries. Along this route lay the towns of Novgorod, Smolensk (or its precursor) and Kiev, and a large amount of Viking archeological material has been found there. Another route went further east along the Volga, down to the Caspian Sea from where traders could reach Baghdad and come into contact with the 8,000-kilometer silk road to China. They met and traded too with Arabs. A third, slightly less exotic route followed the Oder and Neisse and reached the east-west Maintz-Kiev trade via Cracow and then to the Danube, south and central Europe and the Mediterranean. The intrepid Vikings tackled seven major rapids on the Dnjeper, or dragged their boats overland on rollers to the Volga.

Their merchandise comprised furs, fish, weapons and slaves, which they exchanged for, among other things, exotic wares: precious metals, silk from China and spices from the Arab world.

There is disagreement about the importance of the Viking influence on Russian history. According to the Russian Primary Chronicle, written over two centuries after the alleged events, the Slavs invited the *Rus* to come and bring order to their country, and Rurik and his two brothers accepted the invitation. Rurik founded Novgorod in the mid-9th century and his successor Oleg (or Helge) conquered Kiev. In 880 these principalities were united by Oleg, and the Rus territory extended from the Baltic to the Black Sea. The ''Normanist'' school believes that the Rus were Scandinavians who founded the great city states of Novgorod and Kiev and therefore laid the foundations of the Russian state. The derivation of the word "Rus" is not known definitely, but it could come from *Ruotsi,* the Finnish word for Sweden, or from the Old Norse *rodr* (a rowing-way) or perhaps from *Roslagen,* the area in Uppland, Sweden, where many Swedish Vikings would have come from. The "anti-Normanists" accept a Swedish presence in the 9th century but dispute the scale and the lasting effects, and insist that the Russian state is of Slav origin. Whatever view prevails, there seems little doubt that in the 9th and 10th centuries the Vikings controlled Novgorod, Kiev, Izborsk, Bjeloozero and what is now Smolensk, and developed commercial routes from the Baltic to the Black Sea and beyond.

By the 11th century Viking expeditions ceased. Swedish trade links with the areas around the Caspian and Black Sea were severed, presumably because of migration and uprisings in southern Russia, while central and western European states had become better organized and defended. At home in Scandinavia Christianity had finally been accepted, bringing about a change of attitude, while monarchs had established their authority, leaving little scope for exuberant Viking enterprise.

VISUAL ARTS The Medieval Church was one of the first patrons of the Arts in Sweden, but the Reformation severed many of those links. In this century, frescoes that had been painted over for centuries have been uncovered in several churches.

The Swedish court during the Age of Greatness attracted portrait painters. David Klöker, ennobled as Ehrenstrahl (1628–1698), was born in Germany, but established his reputation in the 1650s as a fashionable court portrait painter. His subjects included Karl XI (q.v.). In the same tradition was David von Krafft (1655–1724), whose portraits of Karl XII (q.v.) soon became famous.

Gustav III (q.v.) attracted artists to his court, and the National Museum in Stockholm (q.v.), also a result of his patronage, exhibits today works bearing witness to the Rococo charm of that period. They include portraits by Carl Gustaf Pilo (1711–1783) and Alexander Roslin (1718–1793), landscapes by Elias Martin (1739–1818) and drawings and sculptures by Johan Tobias Sergel (1740–1814).

From the mid-19th century many talented Swedish artists were tempted to France, including such illustrious names as Carl Larsson (1853–1919), Anders Zorn (1860–1920), Bruno Liljefors (1860–1939), Rickard Bergh (1858–1919) and Karl Nordström (1855–1923). Influenced by French impressionists, these plein-air artists objected to the style and to the allegorical, biblical or historical motifs expected by the Academy of Fine Arts and the Establishment, and on their return to Sweden they became known as "the opponents" and set up Konstnärsförbundet (Artists' Union, 1886–1920).

Zorn, renowned for his portraits and sensual nudes, settled at Mora in Dalarna and painted scenes of rural life, for example *Mora Fair,* 1892 and *Midsummer Dance,* 1897. Larsson set up house at Sandborn, also in Dalarna. His cheerful water colors captured scenes of an idyllic, essentially Swedish country life there, shown best in the *At Home* series from 1899. Liljefors painted animals and landscapes and caught the dynamic, impressive element in nature. Bergh and Nordström moved to Varberg on the west coast south of Gothenberg (q.v.) and there founded the Varberg School. It developed a Neo-Romantic style of painting that caught the atmosphere of Nordic summer lighting, illustrated best by Bergh's own *Nordic Summer Evening* (1899–1900).

Prince Eugen (1865–1947), son of Oscar II (q.v.), was also a gifted painter and befriended the "opponents." He bought many of their works and hung them at his home Waldermarsudde outside Stockholm. He bequeathed the house and its contents to the nation, and they reflect beautifully the National Romantic Movement. Other contemporaries included Carl Fredrik Hill (1849–1911), who lived in France for five years and produced landscapes showing the influence of Corot; Ernst Josephson (1851–1906), an exponent of National Romanticism, who, after a mental breakdown, produced fantastic expressionistic works; and August Strindberg (q.v.), a friend of the "opponents," whose seascapes from the 1890s pointed towards expressionism.

Several other significant associations of Swedish artists were formed after the Artists' Union. Almost all the members of 1909-års Män (Men of 1909) had studied under Matisse in Paris, evidenced in their work. Leading members were Nils

Dardel (1888–1943), Isaac Grünewald (1889–1946), Edvard
Hald (1883–1948) and Sigrid Hjertén (1885–1948). Falangen
(The Falange) followed, founded in 1922. Its members, who
included Dardel, Hilding Linqqvist (1891–1984) and Otte
Sköld (1894–1959), introduced Modernism into Swedish art.
At their initial exhibition in 1926, the Göteborgskolorister (The
Gothenburg colorists) were too far advanced in their expres-
sionistic use of color for the public and did not sell a single
canvas. Now the paintings of this group, especially those of
Inger Schiöler (1908–1971), Ivar Ivarson (1900–1939) and
Waldemar Sjölander (1906–1988), are classics. The members
of Färg och Form (Color and Form, founded in 1932), such as
Bror Hjorth (1894–1968) and Sven Erixson (1899–1970), were
characterized not just by their effective use of color but for
their social commitment.

The highly developed appreciation of visual arts in Sweden extends to more utilitarian objects. Svenska slöjdföreningen (Swedish Handicraft Association) was founded as
early as 1845 to preserve and encourage handicraft traditions
in glass, wood, furniture and clothing. In this century
Swedish design in glass and porcelain, bearing such names
as Kosta, Orrefors, Rörstrand and Gustavsberg, has become
synonymous with good taste. Ingvar Kamprad (1926–)
started his first furniture factory, IKEA, in 1943. The typi-
cally Swedish clean line and high quality have attracted an
international public, and IKEA now has well over 60 outlets
worldwide.

-W-

WAGE EARNER FUNDS see LANDSORGANISATIONEN;
MEIDNER, RUDOLF

WALLENBERG, ANDRÉ OSKAR (1816–1886) Swedish financier and politician. During Sweden's industrial revolution in
the second half of the 19th century, access to large capital for
investment was important, especially in Stockholm (q.v.).
A. O. Wallenberg, who had served as a naval officer and had
captained the *Linköping,* Sweden's first propeller-driven

ship, ran a business in Sundsvall from 1851 to 1855. In 1856 he founded Stockholm's Enskilda Bank, and became a pioneer in the field of modern Swedish banking methods. He took an active part in the thriving business life of the country and also sat as an independent member of *Riksdag* (q.v.) from 1867 until 1886. He and his descendants have had a decisive influence on large industrial concerns and the development of Swedish industrialization.

WALLENBERG, KNUT AGATHON (1853–1938) Swedish financier, politician, and son of André Oskar Wallenberg (q.v.). He succeeded his father as Director of Stockholm's Enskilda Bank, which, under his guidance, continued to take a leading part in Sweden's business world. He helped to found the Banque du Pays du Nord in Paris (1911) and played a leading role in setting up Stockholm's (q.v.) Chamber of Commerce in 1912.

A member of *Riksdag* (q.v.) from 1906 until 1919, Wallenberg served as Foreign Minister in Hammarskjöld's Conservative (qq.v.) government during World War I (q.v.). He took a more pragmatic view of neutrality (q.v.) and a more positive attitude towards Britain and the Allies than his pro-German premier. He and Hammarskjöld disagreed increasingly on trade policy, Wallenberg wanting to reach a trade agreement with Britain in 1916 and Hammarskjöld dogmatically opposing it. This led finally to a split in government and a crisis. Wallenberg believed in cooperation with the rest of Scandinavia in defense matters and had plans for a defense pact with Norway. His cabinet colleagues were lukewarm, however, and Wallenberg had to settle for a much looser agreement. Hammarskjöld was defeated on a defense issue in 1917 and resigned. Swartz became Prime Minister, and Arvid Lindman (q.v.) succeeded Wallenberg as Foreign Minister.

Wallenberg, one of Sweden's richest men, was also one of its greatest benefactors, setting up in 1917 the Wallenberg Foundation, which finances projects for the furtherance of science, culture and education.

WALLENBERG, MARCUS (1899–1982) Swedish financier and son of Marcus Laurentius Wallenberg (q.v.). He was Director of Stockholm's Enskilda Bank from 1948 to 1958 and of Skandinaviska Banken from 1972 to 1976. In the wake of the Kreuger (q.v.) crash in 1932 he helped in the reconstruction of several large companies, and in World War II (q.v.) he was active in keeping trade links with the West open. He played an active role in founding Scandinavian Airline Systems (SAS). Wallenberg was a very proficient yachtsman and also played tennis well enough to appear on the Centre Court at Wimbledon.

WALLENBERG, MARCUS LAURENTIUS (1864–1943) Swedish financier. Wallenberg succeeded his half-brother Knut Wallenberg (q.v.) as Director of Stockholm's Enskilda Bank in 1938. He assisted in the founding and reorganizing of several industrial concerns both at home and abroad, including ASEA and Atlas Copco.

WALLENBERG RAOUL (1912–?) Swedish diplomat. Like Count Folke Bernadotte (q.v.) and Dag Hammarskjöld (q.v.), Wallenberg was thrown into prominence during and immediately after World War II (q.v.) as a Swedish neutral who proved to be the right man at the right time; also like them he sacrificed his own life in helping others. A member of the famous banking family, and nephew of the financier Marcus Wallenberg (q.v.), Raoul Wallenberg graduated from the University of Michigan in 1935 and worked at a bank in Palestine, where he met Jewish refugees from Nazi Germany. In 1936 he entered partnership with K. Lauer, a Hungarian Jew, running an export business. After 1939, this entailed business trips to Germany, Hungary and Nazi-occupied France.

The Nazi occupation of Hungary in 1944 put the Jewish population there at immediate risk, and the American War Refugee Board and the Swedish government sent Wallenberg to Budapest to set up a rescue plan. Working through the Swedish legation, he designed a special passport (*Schutz Pass*) and set up 30 Swedish houses offering Jews refuge. This encouraged other neutrals to set up "safe houses." Using any method he could, including bribery and blackmail threats, and sheer strength of personality and conviction,

Wallenberg saved the lives of thousands of Jews—estimates vary from 30,000 to 100,000—often at great personal danger. The ultimate threat to his life came not from the Nazis or Hungarians, however, but from Soviet forces. In 1945, when Soviet troops occupied Hungary, Wallenberg was taken under escort to Soviet Headquarters and never returned.

Repeated Swedish requests for information, often hampered by strained relations over Soviet encroachment of Swedish waters and air space, elicited from the Soviet authorities in 1957 a document signed by the Head of Ljubyanka prison hospital stating that Wallenberg had died in 1947 of a heart attack. Evidence of former Ljubyanka inmates suggested, however, that he was still alive in the 1950s, while persistent rumors imply that he was still imprisoned in the 1970s. In 1981 he was made an honorary citizen of the United States, in 1985 of Canada and in 1986 of Israel. In the ''Avenue of the Righteous'' in Jerusalem, where 600 trees were planted to honor the memory of non-Jewish individuals who risked their lives to save the Jews from the Nazis, one of the trees was planted in Wallenberg's honor. International interest in his case remains, and films have been made of his life.

WELFARE STATE A small amount of legislation to improve conditions for the most vulnerable members of society dates from the 19th century, such as the 1847 Poor Law, obliging every parish to care for its poor, and the 1871 Act, which made the councils responsible for giving their destitute the bare necessities of life. In 1913 the Old Age Pension was introduced, but the amount was too small to cover even the most basic needs. A new Poor Law in 1918 forbad the hiring out of young orphans and old people, and the following year a 48-hour working week was introduced.

It was after 1932, however, when the Social Democrats (q.v.) under Per Albin Hansson (q.v.) came to power that social conditions began to change more radically. Hansson had a vision of Sweden as *Folkhemmet,* the home of the people, a welfare state. In 1934 a state-supported unemployment insurance scheme was introduced, and the following year the Old Age Pension was raised appreciably, removing shades of the workhouse. A family allowance scheme was accepted in 1937, and two weeks holiday with pay was legislated for in 1938.

Progress was halted during World War II (q.v.), but the two decades immediately after the war saw the realization of Hansson's hopes. He himself died in 1946, but his successor Tage Erlander (q.v.) continued along the same road. Old Age Pensions were raised further and index-linked; in 1953 a national health insurance scheme was introduced, giving every citizen the right to medical treatment almost free of charge; in 1956 a social assistance law was accepted. Erlander's controversial ATP (q.v.), a compulsory national superannuation scheme, was narrowly accepted in 1959; by 1960 the comprehensive school system was in place, with free equal education for all; in 1963 four weeks holiday with pay was stipulated; in 1976 the pensionable age was reduced from 67 to 65, but the law was flexible, allowing a citizen to select a retirement age anywhere between 60 and 70; in 1978 five weeks holiday was established.

Job security was introduced in 1974 with the "Åman laws" (named after Valter Åman, the trade unionist and politician who saw them through). They prevented an employer from dismissing an employee without proving a good cause, and even then gave generous compensation. The campaign for equal opportunities for women (q.v.) had meanwhile helped to establish parent insurance in 1973, which allowed a parent to claim benefit for up to six months after the birth of a child. It was subsequently extended to nine months.

This "cradle to grave" security entailed heavy taxation, but Sweden had become an affluent country with very efficient industries and high output geared to exports, salaries were high and unemployment almost non-existent.

However, Sweden had become dependent on oil in the boom years, and in 1974 was hit extremely hard by the oil crisis, which coincided with the introduction of expensive social legislation. There was growing opposition not just to increased tax burdens but to the way the state was taking responsibility away from the individual. After 44 years of Social Democratic governments, the elections in 1976, 1979 and 1991 led to non-socialist coalitions.

No political party wants to dismantle the welfare state, but the question is how extensive the services should be and how they should be funded. Only the Communist Party (q.v.) denies that the country has been enjoying benefits that it cannot afford in the present economic climate, and with education (q.v.) taking longer and life expectancy rising, the situation unchecked can only deteriorate further, especially when unemployment has started to rise. The Social Democrats accept that it is no longer possible simply to raise taxes even further to finance social welfare, but appear to think that all that is needed is a reining-in slightly until the economy improves. The non-socialist parties are examining the possibility of a higher degree of private insurance, with state pensions serving more often as a safety net. Whatever parties are in power, however, there is little doubt that the electorate wants to retain a large measure of social welfare.

WESTERBERG, BENGT (1942–) Swedish Liberal politician. Westerberg first gained government experience during the non-socialist coalitions in power from 1976 to 1982. He was a Minister in the Department of Industry from 1978 to 1979 and in the Budget Department from 1979 to 1982. The Social Democrats (q.v.) were then returned to power in 1982. The following year Ola Ullsten (q.v.) resigned as Chairman of the Liberal Party (q.v.) and Westerberg became his successor. The handsome, personable appearance of the new leader won extra support for the Liberals in the 1985 general election (the so-called "Westerberg effect"), when the number of Liberal seats in *Riksdag* (q.v.) rose from 21 to 51. This fell back to 44 in 1988 and 31 in 1991. In the 1991 elections the non-socialist parties had a majority, however, and Carl Bildt (q.v.), leader of the Moderate Party (q.v.), formed a four-party coalition with Westerberg as Deputy Prime Minister and Minister of Social Affairs.

WIBBLE, ANNE (1943–) Swedish Liberal politician. The daughter of Professor Bertil Ohlin (q.v.), a former leader of the Liberal Party (q.v.), she took a Masters degree in economics at Stanford University in 1967 and a postgraduate degree in economics at Stockholm University in

1973. She was elected to the Liberal Party's executive committee in 1987, became Chairwoman of the parliamentary Finance Committee in 1990, and when Carl Bildt (q.v.) formed a four-party non-socialist coalition in 1991 was invited to become Finance Minister, the first woman to hold that office.

WIGFORSS, ERNST (1881–1977) Swedish politician and leading member of the Social Democratic Party (q.v.). Wigforss's name is closely linked with Per Albin Hansson (q.v.) and the founding of the welfare state (q.v.). In many ways Hansson's antithesis, Wigforss was an intellectual and an ideologue. A graduate of Lund University and a specialist in Scandinavian philology, he was also interested in economics and was of the same persuasion as the "Stockholm school," which included Gunnar Myrdal (q.v.). Wigforss believed that an economic depression was the result of low consumption, not excessive wages, and that a strong government should stimulate demand through its fiscal policy. Money raised by taxation should be spent upon a welfare program of benefit to all. Hjalmar Branting's (q.v.) and then Rickard Sandler's (q.v.) Social Democratic government, in which Wigforss was Finance Minister for the first time, lasted only from 1925 to 1926.

However, in 1932 when Hansson came to power and assured a working majority by means of an agreement with the Agrarians (q.v.), Wigforss again became Finance Minister (a portfolio he held continuously until his retirement in 1949) and was able to put his Keynesian views to the test. Money was borrowed to launch a huge construction program, which brought down unemployment and stimulated the economy. By raising income tax appreciably but on a progressive scale, imposing corporation tax and death duties and raising indirect taxes on alcohol and tobacco, Wigforss embarked on his policy of wealth redistribution. The Social Democratic election victory of 1936 allowed Wigforss to proceed towards financing the welfare state. The social program was held in check during World War II (q.v.), but towards the end of the war a committee of Social Democrats and trade union (q.v.) representatives under Wigforss' chairmanship drew up a 27-point program towards socialism. By then Wigforss was reputed to be one of the party's most forceful radicals.

Hansson died in 1946 and was succeeded by Tage Erlander (q.v.), who had the unenviable task of making the program acceptable to the more moderate members of his party. Wigforss's first postwar budget with even heavier taxation was clearly aimed at greater wealth redistribution. He maintained that the response to stringent wartime measures had shown that the population would be able to make sacrifices in a good cause. The more ideological measures proposed by Wigforss's committee, however, were held in abeyance. The predicted postwar depression proved instead to be a boom period, and as Swedish industry, undamaged by war, surged ahead, and productivity and profits rose, the standard of living also improved and radical changes were considered unnecessary by the majority of the Social Democratic Party. By his retirement in 1949, Wigforss was revered by hard-core Social Democrats but denounced by many Conservatives (q.v.), who were frightened by his austere, doctrinaire approach. He was and remained much less of a consensus politician than his leaders Branting, Hansson and Erlander, and the latter was said to be relieved when Wigforss retired. He published his memoirs in three volumes (1950–54).

WOMEN'S STATUS IN SWEDEN The Norse sagas reflect a society where some women occupied a position of authority, running the household and enjoying the right of land ownership and inheritance. Throughout Swedish history there have been women who through sheer force of personality have made their mark. In the 14th century St Birgitta (q.v.) criticized immorality at court to King Magnus Eriksson himself, urged the Pope to return from Avignon to Rome and finally persuaded him to approve her new Order, which would have nuns, monks and lay brothers under her authority. Queen Margareta was skillful enough to engineer a Scandinavian Union of Crowns in 1397 (the Kalmar Union [q.v.]) which functioned as long as she was alive. The Swedish Crown usually passed down to the King's eldest son, but Gustav II Adolf (q.v.) left only one child, Kristina (q.v.), who succeeded to the throne, and when Karl XII (q.v.) died without issue in 1718 his sister Ulrika Eleonora (q.v.) was elected Queen. These were exceptional cases, however, and until this century a woman's position was automatically subordinate to a man's.

In the old rural society, where farms were self-sufficient units, men and women had their own defined roles, each doing essential work. The farm would pass from father to son, but if the woman was a widow or her husband went to war she would take over the management.

In towns, women were more or less men's servants and were financially and socially dependent. With the beginning of industrialization and the breakup of the old social patterns, the position of an increasing number of women in society became difficult. Production moved from self-sufficient farms to factories, increasingly both men and unmarried women began to work outside the home, while children went to school rather than learning by example on the farm. Women were needed for new kinds of employment, such as post-mistresses, primary school teachers and telegraphists. This brought into prominence the question of education (q.v.) for women.

In the 19th century liberal politicians took up the issue and made some progress. In 1845 *Riksdag* (q.v.) gave women equal inheritance rights with men. The old guild system was abolished in 1846. *Riksdag* decreed in 1858 that unmarried women could become legally of age when 25 (if they requested it; men reached their majority automatically at 21), and this left the way open for unmarried women to take an active part in economic affairs. If they married, however, they automatically lost their mature status and their husbands became their legal guardians. In 1884 they were at least given the right to choose their own husbands. In 1862 if they had the necessary qualifications they could vote in local elections. In 1861 a teacher training college for women was established. By 1870 women were granted the right to study at university, although barred from the divinity and law faculties. There were few opportunities for girls to study for the matriculation examinations, however.

A growing number of women were entering the labor market from the mid-19th century onwards, but most of the jobs open to them were of the more menial, poorly-paid kind. As the move from the land into towns gathered pace women who had worked more or less as equals with men felt themselves downgraded. At a time when popular movements generally were gathering momentum in Sweden, a significant number of women's associations were set up. In 1873 Föreningen för gift kvinnas äganderätt (Society for the Property Rights of Married Women) was established. The Fredrika Bremer Society (q.v.), founded in 1884, became a strong influence in the campaign for equal rights for women. Trade organizations for female workers were also beginning to form, and all the main political parties formed their own women's association.

In the 1880s there were intense discussions on the subject of equality, and many leading authors played their part. Two earlier Swedish writers had helped to spark the debate. Carl Jonas Love Almquist (q.v.), who contributed to the new liberal paper *Aftonbladet* (q.v.) and identified himself with the Liberals (q.v.), published in 1839 *Det går an* (translated as *Sara Vidbeck*). There he portrayed a very capable young woman, a skilled tradeswoman who as a child had witnessed her mother's degradation in a hopeless marriage and was determined not to share the same fate. She agrees to cohabit with her suitor Albert and will bear his children but will not marry him, a condition Albert accepts. This was a revolutionary thought in 1839 and caused a storm of protest. Fredrika Bremer (q.v.) was the kind of unmarried daughter who could so easily have been trapped by the claustrophic mores of the middle classes, but instead she devoted her life through her writings to the liberation of women and their right to be treated as individuals rather than appendages of their male guardians. Her most influential work from the point of view of women's emancipation was her novel *Hertha* (1856), in which she preaches women's right to adequate education and to professional employment.

By the 1880s, a period when authors were being exhorted by the Danish critic Georg Brandes to debate current social issues in their work, equal rights for women became one of those issues. The Norwegians Henrik Ibsen and Björnstjerne Björnson were well-known in Sweden, and Ibsen's *A Doll's House* (1879) and Björnson's *A Gauntlet* (1883) were seized on gratefully by women activists as proof of their cause. The equally famous Swedish writer August Strindberg (q.v.) entered the fray with *Getting Married* I (1884) where he argued that, although deserving equal status, a woman was designed to be a wife and mother and the home was her natural "career." Among his Scandinavian contemporaries Strindberg was the odd man out, but even so he helped to stoke the fires. Swedish women themselves were not always united on the degree or nature of the liberation they were seeking. Ellen Key (q.v.), an influential figure of the period, wanted to preserve women's warm and "maternal" qualities from the harsh world of competition and examinations, while the equally renowned Elin Wägner supported the independent, liberated professional woman. The division was evident too in the Social Democratic Party (q.v.), the party associated with reform, with the leader Hjalmar Branting (q.v.) himself considering universal male suffrage essential and women's rights of secondary importance.

In 1884 unmarried women became legally of age at 21, on a par with men. By 1906 *Riksdag* began to examine the whole question of women's suffrage. In 1909 women were eligible for election to local councils and, a large step forward, in 1919 *Riksdag* granted the vote to women, a right which came into force in 1921. The first woman member of *Riksdag,* Kerstin Hesselgren (q.v.), took her seat in 1921. Married women were no longer required to seek their husband's permission to work outside the home. By 1923 women were entitled to occupy most senior state posts and in 1927 girls were allowed to study at the same kind of schools as boys, thus facilitating their entrance to university.

Full equality was a slow process. From 1919 women had the same salary as men for equal work within the public sector. In the private sector, however, there were obvious discrepancies which trade unions (q.v.) did nothing to obviate—rather the reverse, for in collective bargaining they arranged lower wages for women than for men, and women received only half benefit in the event of strikes, unemployment or sickness. The situation remained almost stagnant between the wars during the economic depression. There was an improvement in women's financial position in the 1950s, when there was considerable growth in the Swedish economy. More women were employed, and the larger unions, the Tjänstemännens centralorganisation (TCO) (q.v.) and Landsorganisationen (LO) (q.v.), were obliged to put equal wages for equal work on their agenda. In practice the improvement was slight, for no measures were taken to assist married mothers to return to work, while the increased demand for workers was met instead by immigration, a great fund of cheap labor.

Then in the 1960s the position changed. There was a great national debate about male and female roles in society and the political slogan was "equality of opportunity." It led to many more day centers for children and legislation on equal wages in the private as well as the public sector. In 1970 the tax system was altered so that everyone, married and unmarried alike, paid the same basic tax, depriving families with wives and mothers staying at home of their tax advantage. This coincided with a restriction on imported labor, thus enticing women into the labor market.

Radical feminism as found in the United States had repercussions in Sweden in the 1970s. A committee on equality was set up in 1972 and by 1976 put forward proposals ensuring equal opportunity in the public sector. Firms were given subventions to press ahead with equality. LO, TCO and Svenska Arbetsgivareföreningen (SAF, Swedish Federation of Employers [q.v.]) reached agreements embracing equal wages. The government's decision at this point to give low-paid workers priority in wage negotiations also helped women, who were often in low-paid jobs. In 1976 *Riksdag* made sexual discrimination at work illegal.

Changes in attitude became apparant too. Despite bitter opposition from certain clerical quarters, the Church had formally accepted in 1958 women's right to ordination. The first woman was ordained in 1960 and the number gradually increased, but some clerics, notably Bo Giertz, Bishop of Gothenburg, held their entrenched positions and certain dioceses remained closed to women priests. This has gradually changed, and by 1990 there were 700 women priests spread over all 13 dioceses. In 1973 a law on parent insurance was introduced granting six months' paid maternity leave. This was amended later to nine months and fathers as well as mothers could take part of the leave, the aim being to instill in the man a sense of responsibility towards the home and the children as well as letting the mother get on with her career. In 1974 a highly controversial free abortion on demand was introduced.

In the government formed after the 1991 election there were 232 male and 117 female members of *Riksdag*. A woman Speaker (Ingegerd Troedsson [q.v.]) was appointed for the first time and eight women were appointed to the Cabinet, their portfolios including Finance, Foreign Affairs, Justice and Education.

Whether or not full equality is possible, Sweden has advanced further than most countries in that direction. Soon after the new Constitution was established in 1974 an amendment was passed making the monarch's first-born child heir to the throne regardless of sex. It seems symbolic that the present heir is Crown Princess Viktoria.

WORLD WAR I Sweden's neutrality (q.v.) policy had been evolving during Oscar II's (q.v.) reign, and by the time World War I broke out it was nationally accepted. In August 1914 Norway and Sweden declared jointly their neutrality, and then on the initiative of Gustav V (q.v.) of Sweden the Kings of Denmark, Norway and Sweden met in Malmö (q.v.) to indicate their united intention of remaining neutral. These joint meetings continued at a high level throughout the war, the three Scandinavian Prime Ministers meeting frequently and the monarchs meeting again in 1917, in Christiania (present-day Oslo) on that occasion. Although neutral, Sweden could not afford to be isolated, however, for she had become an international trading nation by this time and needed to import and export to survive.

Nor could it be said that the Swedes were completely neutral in their attitude to the warring factions. There was an extreme right-wing activist group supported by Sven Hedin (q.v.) and encouraged by Queen Viktoria (a granddaughter of

Kaiser Wilhelm), who wanted Sweden to enter the war on Germany's side. They were a minority, but there was a great deal of pro-German sentiment in court, officer and Conservative (q.v.) circles. The late King Oscar II had considered the Kaiser an ally and had also married a German princess. His son Gustav V (q.v.), whose consort was also German, was inclined to similar views, while many leading Conservatives considered Germany a bulwark against Slavonic barbarism and Britain's association with Russia a betrayal of Western civilization. The Liberals (q.v.), on the other hand, were drawn to Britain and her parliamentary democracy, which Karl Staaff (q.v.), the Liberal leader, had always admired. The Social Democrats (q.v.), led by Hjalmar Branting (q.v.), had been influenced in the past by German Social Democracy and had moreover received support from the German Workers' Movement during the General Strike (q.v.) in 1909, but ultimately it was Britain, not Germany, that gained their sympathy. Staaff and Branting both assured Hjalmar Hammarskjöld (q.v.), the leader of a moderate Conservative government, that they would support him in his neutrality policy.

Germany made several attempts to activate pro-German sentiment in Sweden, emphasizing the close family ties between their royal families. The German Ministry of War financed the purchase of the Swedish newspaper *Aftonbladet* (q.v.) in an effort to influence Swedish public opinion, while officials at the German Legation to Stockholm were so unsubtle in their attempts to recruit Sweden that Baron von Reichenau had to be recalled to Berlin. The Swedish Minister in Berlin, Arvid Taube, was meanwhile doing his best to bring about a German-Swedish pact. The Swedish government stood by its neutrality, however.

Sweden was not self-sufficient in agricultural products and had to import grain, corn, concentrated cattle foods and artificial fertilizers. She also needed from abroad oil, coal, machines and raw materials for the textile and other industries. To pay for these she had to have foreign markets for her timber, pulp, engineering products and iron ore.

Britain meanwhile was trying to stop imports to Germany and was anxious to prevent neutral states from reexporting raw materials to Germany, and she also put pressure on Sweden, hoping the latter would join the blockade. Hammarskjöld was a highly respected Professor of International Law and believed that a neutral state had the right to prevent its trade from being controlled in any way by a belligerent, a view which did not endear him to Britain. It was particularly important to Britain that goods from America did not reach Germany via Sweden, and she kept a blacklist of Swedish firms with special contacts with Germany; blacklisted firms were shunned by British firms.

For the first few months of the war Sweden did very well. Exports to Germany not just of iron ore but even foodstuffs increased, and when British coal supplies fell German coal was imported instead. But then as imports from the west dropped, serious shortages of grain, oil, paraffin and animal foodstuffs arose. Poor harvests exacerbated the situation and prices soared, despite government intervention. Profiteering and blackmarketing were rife. By January 1917, sugar, bread and flour were rationed. In February the situation deteriorated further when Germany launched her policy of unrestricted submarine warfare. Some 280 Swedish ships and 800 lives were lost at sea during the war. When the United States entered the way in 1917, pressure on Sweden not to trade with Germany was increased further.

New trade negotiations had been started with Britain, but Hammarskjöld was reluctant and meanwhile the food situation in Sweden was becoming desperate. Hammarskjöld, now nicknamed ''Hungerskjöld,'' was losing support, the other political parties were no longer prepared to postpone opposition, and even within his own party the Prime Minister was meeting resistance. The government was defeated in *Riksdag* (q.v.) in March 1917, Hammarskjöld resigned and King Gustav invited a right-wing Conservative, Ernst Trygger (q.v.), to form a government. Trygger was forced to admit with annoyance that he was unable to do so, and it was the moderate Conservative Carl Swartz who became Prime Minister instead. By May the much more flexible Swartz had reached an agreement that allowed 19 Swedish ships being held in American ports and 14 in British ports to return home with their cargoes, while a number of Allied vessels with timber on board, trapped in the Baltic, were escorted by Swedish warships through minefields in the Sound. This brought some relief, but soon the bread ration had to be reduced and rationing was extended to include potatoes.

The international situation and the complexion of internal politics changed at this point with the outbreak of the Russian Revolution. Left-wing groups in Sweden already incensed by the acute food shortages, which hit the industrial workers in urban areas the hardest, were encouraged by communist successes to go on protest marches and demonstrations. On 5 June some 20,000 workers gathered near the *Riksdag* in Stockholm and had to be dispersed by the police. The election campaign in the autumn in 1917 was carried on against a background of such disturbances and brought into prominence the struggle for real political, democratic reform.

The government ran into further trouble in September when it came to light that Count von Luxburg, the German chargé d'affaires in Buenos Aires, had been using Swedish diplomatic channels to send coded telegrams to Berlin about shipping movements.

In the ensuing election the Conservatives lost heavily, gaining only 57 seats compared with the Liberals' 62 and the Social Democrats' 86. With such a clear majority against the Conservatives Swartz resigned and King Gustav invited the new Liberal leader, Nils Edén (q.v.), to form a government, the first to include Social Democratic ministers. It had to deal with a crisis immediately upon taking office. The cost of living had doubled since 1914, fuel, dairy produce and meat were in very short supply and the harvest in 1917 was poor. Shortages were leading to profiteering on a large scale. Meanwhile Swedish ships were still being torpedoed. Edén negotiated with the Allies and reached an agreement that allowed grain, fertilizers, oil and coffee to be imported into Sweden with the proviso that they would not be reshipped to Germany. Swedish iron ore exports were greatly reduced to Germany and increased to the Allies, and Swedish merchant ships were leased to the Allies. The war ended in November 1918 before the measures had had time to have much effect.

Although not a belligerent, Sweden had been changed politically and socially by the war. By 1918 many aspects of

Liberal policy were being enacted, the Social Democrats had become a parliamentary force to be reckoned with and universal suffrage was accepted. Swedish neutrality remained cross-party policy, but events had shown that strict neutrality was extremely difficult to sustain.

WORLD WAR II The Swedish Social Democrats were traditionally opposed to large defense budgets and in the 1920s looked to the League of Nations to preserve the peace. By the early 1930s, however, it was becoming clear that the League was impotent when faced with determined totalitarian states. When Hitler withdrew from the League in October 1933 and started rearming, alarm bells began to sound in Scandinavia, and there was renewed interest in some form of a Nordic defense treaty, but with negative results: Sweden had close ties with Finland (q.v.) and saw danger from the east, Norway relied on keeping contacts with the West, and Denmark was reluctant to get entangled with her immediate neighbor in the south, an increasingly threatening Germany. The Danish Prime Minister Thorvald Stauning stated in 1937 that Denmark was not going to be made Scandinavia's watchdog. When Hitler offered the Scandinavian countries a non-aggression pact in 1939, Denmark was the only one to accept.

When Germany attacked Poland in September 1939, a European war was obviously inevitable, and, as in World War I (q.v.), the Kings of Denmark, Norway and Sweden, and now the President of Finland, publicly declared Scandinavian neutrality (q.v.). This time, however, matters were taken out of their hands and of the four countries only Sweden was allowed to remain neutral, although constantly under threat.

Events in Finland proved to be Swedish neutrality's first great test. Having signed a pact with Germany in August 1939, Soviet Russia had a free hand in the Baltic and demanded that the Finns withdraw from the border area to allow a more effective Russian defense of the approach to what was then Leningrad. The Finns refused and looked to Scandinavia for help. Sweden was caught in a difficult position. She had started to rearm on a small scale in 1936, and *Riksdag* (q.v.) had in 1938 approved a large increase in the defense budget, but her defenses had not yet been built up. When Russia attacked Finland in November 1939, many Swedes wanted to go to Finland's defense. A National Coalition government was set up in December 1939 under Per Albin Hansen's (q.v.) premiership, with Ernst Wigforss (q.v.) as Finance Minister and Christian Günther as Foreign Minister. The former Foreign Minister, Rickard Sandler (q.v.), had already resigned over what he considered Sweden's betrayal of Finland, Wigforss, eager to build up the welfare state (q.v.), had opposed Sandler's efforts to deviate from strict neutrality, while Günther was a career diplomat. Despite strong pro-Finnish sentiment in the country, especially among military leaders, the Conservatives (q.v.) and academics, but also evident in most walks of life, the government came down on the side of non-belligerence, sending money and arms to Finland, arranging credit for her, allowing Swedish volunteers to fight for Finland but not entering the war officially. Fighting against overwhelming odds in the Winter War, the Finns eventually had to sue for peace and with the help of Swedish mediation the Peace of Moscow was signed by Russia and Finland in March 1940.

The next decisive blow to Scandinavian neutrality fell on April 9, 1940, when without warning Germany invaded Denmark and Norway. The latter made a desperate heroic stand but by early summer the Nazis were in full control. Sweden again declared her neutrality. Hitler's invasion had been to secure the supply of iron ore, so essential to his great modern war machine, from northern Sweden via the Norwegian port of Narvik, and he would have rated Sweden's declared neutrality no more sacred than Denmark's or Norway's. There is evidence indeed that plans had been prepared to invade northern Sweden if necessary. However, a personal letter from Gustav V (q.v.) assuring Hitler of strict neutrality in the conflict with Norway seemed to have reassured him.

Sweden was under constant pressure during the war, first from Germany and then from Britain and her allies, to deviate from neutrality. During the German invasion of Norway, King Håkon, Crown Prince Olav, and the members of the Norwegian government requested permission to move freely in Sweden and return to Norway when circumstances allowed. The Swedish government decided that this would certainly provoke a German invasion of Sweden, and reluctantly refused. The exiled Norwegian government escaped to England instead. While the Norwegians kept up organized resistance to the German invaders, Sweden refused to allow transit of German troops through Sweden to Norway, but under increasing German pressure she permitted ''humanitarian'' transport (medical personnel and supplies) to pass through Sweden to German troops in Narvik, and 800 German sailors, civilians and wounded soldiers returned to Germany by that route.

By June, when Norway and Denmark, France, Holland and Belgium were in German hands and Britain's hopes of withstanding a German invasion seemed slim, Germany stepped up her demands for permission to send troops and supplies to Norway through Sweden, and this time there was little resistance. The infamous ''transit traffic'' began and lasted for three bitter years. Munitions and a continuous stream of uniformed but unarmed German soldiers travelled by rail from southern to northern Norway via Swedish provinces. These common sense, if unheroic, decisions soured relations between Norway and Sweden for many years to come.

When Hitler turned on his former ally Russia in the summer of 1941, the Finns sought German help in recovering territory lost in the Winter War. Once more Finland was at war and seeking Swedish aid, and this time the situation was even more complex, for the Swedish mood was undoubtedly anti-Nazi. Swedish volunteers went to Finland, but there was little genuine enthusiasm for the Finnish cause at this stage of the war. Germany made new demands on Sweden in 1941, requesting that the Engelbrecht Division, 18,000 men stationed in Norway, be allowed transit to Finland via Sweden. The request was, of course, supported by Finland. Within the Swedish cabinet, four Social Democratic ministers, including Wigforss, wanted to withhold permission and others, including Hansson and Günther, were convinced that Sweden had no choice. It was finally decided that permission would be granted but on a strict understanding that it was for one occasion only. Finland's fortunes were now linked to the fate of Nazi Germany, and by 1944 there was a genuine risk that she would be swallowed up and like the Baltic states become part of the USSR. Through Swedish diplomacy a separate armistice was arranged between Helsinki and Moscow in September 1944. Finland had to pay an enormous indemnity but did at least retain her independence.

As Hitler's position deteriorated, the threat to Swedish neutrality from the other side increased. In August 1943 the agreement to allow German transit traffic was cancelled. By early 1944 the United States demanded that Sweden go further and cease trading with Germany. The supply of ball-bearings to Germany was a particularly sore point, for the Allies were convinced that the German war effort would literally grind to a halt without them. Such intense pressure amounting to open threats was exerted on the Swedish government and SKF (the Swedish Ball Bearing Company) that Sweden felt obliged to resist. However, trade between Sweden and Germany was reduced during the second half of 1944 and had ceased altogether by the beginning of 1945.

On a purely material level Sweden fared better in the Second than in the First World War. She was more self-sufficient in agricultural produce and several essential goods (e.g., fertilizers and combustible oils) could be manufactured at home. Substitutes were found for other commodities hitherto imported—cellulose, for instance, replaced woolen fabrics and fodder—and distribution was better organized. Government control was effective and a fair system of rationing was introduced soon after the outbreak of the war. Sweden was still dependent on overseas trade, however, which meant dependence on Germany's goodwill after April 1940. Germany needed Swedish iron ore, timber products and ball-bearings and was prepared to send fertilizers, solid fuel and industrial products in return. Britain understood the position and had, moreover, an interest in keeping Sweden independent, for she was a source of essential products, such as ball-bearings, and much information. Agreements with Britain and Germany towards the end of 1940 ensured that a number of Swedish merchant ships on specified routes could ply between Gothenburg (q.v.) and non-belligerent countries, including Latin America, thus guaranteeing supplies of rice, coffee, grain, cotton and mineral oil. A Swedish State

Commission controlled prices and aligned wages with the cost of living, going so far as to impose a price and wages freeze in 1942. The excessive profiteering and blackmarketing of World War I (q.v.) was thus avoided.

The hardships Sweden suffered were of a more psychological nature, being surrounded by German-occupied countries and never sure that Hitler would not turn on them. Reservists were mobilized and sent to defend Sweden's borders for an unspecified time. The German Foreign Office took great interest in the Swedish press and was immediately informed by the German Legation in Stockholm of any articles critical of Nazism. Hitler himself was extremely sensitive to adverse criticism, and King Gustav had to pacify him on occasion. The government felt compelled to introduce censorship and confiscated several editions of newspapers carrying alleged offensive material. Torgny Segerstedt, editor of the liberal Gothenburg daily *Göteborgs Handels- och Sjöfartstidning,* was a thorn in the government's flesh, for he bitterly attacked the cowardly way the government gave in to Germany. As a neutral country Sweden became a listening post and meeting place for the belligerents, but citizens were exhorted to hold their tongue and keep their own counsel.

As a neutral Sweden became a safe haven for thousands of refugees during the war, especially in its last phases. When Danish Jews were to be deported to Germany, most of them, over 6,500, escaped into Sweden. By 1945 some 15,000 Danes and 36,000 Norwegians had found refuge there. In 1944, when the Russians were advancing, 55,000 Finns fled to Sweden, and when the Russians marched into the Baltic states well over 30,000 refugees from there found their way into Sweden. Plagued by legal aspects of neutrality to the last, Sweden was asked to return 167 Baltic refugees to the USSR at the end of the war. Unlike the others these detainees had arrived in German uniform and had to be handed over. The government honored international law and surrendered them to the Russians, despite hunger strikes, one suicide and national and international outcry.

Once the war was over the coalition government was dissolved, and at the end of July 1945 a purely Social Democratic government under P.A. Hansson was formed.

SELECTED BIBLIOGRAPHY:
INTRODUCTION

As in the Dictionary, the Swedish characters å, ä and ö are treated alphabetically as a, a and o respectively.

As a rule this bibliography lists works in English, although in a few cases Swedish seminal studies not translated into English have been cited. Some publications in French or German have also been included.

It has obviously not been possible to provide a completely comprehensive list, but the first section offers bibliographies, consultation of which should help to deal with omissions here.

The bibliographical sections are as follows:

Bibliographies.
Introductions to Sweden. Ephemeral material and dated guides have been excluded.
General History and Surveys.
More specific historical periods, viz.
    Prehistory, the Viking Period and the Middle Ages.
    The Vasa Period and the Age of Greatness.
    The Age of Liberty.
    The Gustavian Period.
    19th and 20th Centuries.
Economics, Politics and Social Studies. It is admitted that the dividing line between this rather large section and the 19th and 20th centuries section is sometimes difficult to discern.
Language. This is not intended to cover Swedish philology but is included as an aid to readers who may feel the urge to embark on the reading of Swedish texts.
Education.
Emigration.

Geography. Dated tourist guide books and insubstantial accounts of holidays in Scandinavia have been omitted.

Religious History.

Arts and Media. This includes basic reference works on Swedish art, literature, cinema, etc., but material which lies outside the scope of a history book can be obtained through the initial bibliographical section.

A biographical section was deemed unnecessary, but biographies are included in the historical period to which the subject belongs. Linnaeus, for instance, is in the Age of Liberty section, while Bernadotte will be found in the 19th and 20th centuries section.

Mention should also be made of the valuable information service offered in English by the Swedish Institute, Box 7434, S-103 91. Stockholm, Sweden, which commissions and distributes up-to-date publications on many aspects of Swedish cultural and political life.

Bibliographies

Afzelius, Nils Arvid. *Books in English on Sweden.* Stockholm: Swedish Institute, 1951. 56pp.

Bring, S.E. *Bibliografisk handbok till Sveriges historia.* Stockholm, 1934. 780pp.

Eliassen, Kjell A. & Pedersen, Mogens N. *Scandinavian Political Institutions and Political Behavior 1970–1984: An Annotated Bibliography.* Odense: Odense Universitetsforlag, 1985. 158pp.

Erickson, E. Walfred. *Swedish-American Periodicals. A Selective and Descriptive Bibliography.* (Scandinavians in America). New York: Arno Press, 1979.

Excerpta Historica Nordica. International Committee of Historical Sciences. Copenhagen: Gyldendal, 1955– (Summaries, usually in English, of recent historical publications in North-ern Europe. Biennial or Triennial).

Geddes, Tom. *Sweden: Books in English 1963–1978: a Bibliography of English translations of Swedish literature and books on Sweden in English published in Great Britain.* London: Swedish Embassy, 1979. 78pp.

————. "Scandinavian Publications since the Mid-70's" in *Women's Studies.* Papers presented at a colloquium . . . 1989, pp 75–84. London: British Library, 1990. (British Library Occasional Papers 12). 189pp.

————. "Recent Books published in Non-Scandinavian Languages". Compiled by Tom Geddes in *Scandivica,* an International Journal of Scandinavian Studies, Norwich, England published annually. 1962–

Guide to Nordic Bibliography (General ed. E. Munch-Petersen). Copenhagen: Nordisk Ministerråd, 1984. 235pp.

Haugen, Eva L. *A Bibliography of Scandinavian Dictionaries.* New York: Kraus International Publications, 1984. 387pp.

Hoglund, A. William. *Immigrants and Their Children in the United States: a Bibliography of Doctoral Dissertations, 1885–1982.* New York: Garland, 1986. 491pp.

Holmbäck, Bure. *About Sweden: a Bibliographical Outline 1900–1963.* Stockholm: Sweden Illustrated, 1968. 94pp.

Index Nordicus. A Cumulative Index to English-Language Periodicals on Scandinavian Studies. Compiled by Janet Kvamme. Boston: G.K. Hall, 1980. 601pp.

Kvavik, Robert B. *Scandinavian Government and Politics: A Bibliography of Materials in English.* Minneapolis: University of Minnesota, 1984. 21pp.

Ng, Matia & Batts, Michael. *Scandinavian Literature in English Translation 1928–1977.* Vancouver: CAUTG, 1978. 95pp.

Oakley, Stewart P. *Scandinavian History 1520–1970: a List of Books and Articles in English.* (Help for Students of History 91). London: Historical Association, 1984. 232pp.

Publications on Sweden. Stockholm: Swedish Institute. (Annual)

Ries, Tomas. *Bibliography on the Nordic Military-Strategic Situation.* Oslo: Norsk Utenrikspolitisk Institutt, 1988. (NUPI rapport, 114). 319pp.

Sather, Leland B. & Swanson, Alan (eds). *Sweden.* Oxford: Clio Press, 1987. 390pp. (World Bibliographical Series 80).

Svecana Extranea 1963–1966. Books on Sweden and Swedish Literature in Foreign Languages. Stockholm: Royal Library. 1967.

Svecana Extranea. Books on Sweden and Swedish Literature in Foreign Languages. Edited by the Bibliographical Department and published annually by the Royal Library, Stockholm, 1967–

Svensk Bokförteckning. The Swedish National Bibliography. Edited by the Bibliographical Department at the Royal Library, Stockholm. Annual volume 1961– (1866–1960: 10-year and 5-year volumes with title *Svensk bokkatalog*).

Swedish Historical Bibliography 1971–1975. Stockholm: Almqvist & Wiksell, 1988. 552pp.

Tiblin, Mariann & Larson-Fleming, Susan. *Scandinavia in English . . . 1978.* Minneapolis: University of Minnesota, 1980. 149pp.

Warmholtz, Carl G. *Bibliotecha historica sveo-gothica.* 15 vols in 8. 1782–1817. Reprint. Copenhagen: Rosenskile og Bagger, 1966–68.

General Introductions

Austin, P. Britten. *On Being Swedish: Reflections towards a Better Understanding of the Swedish Character.* London: Secker & Warburg; Coral Gables: University of Miami Press, 1968. 182pp.

Brown, Mules & Sinclair, Mick. *The Real Guide: Scandinavia.* New York: Prentice Hall, 1990. 675pp.

Connery, D. *The Scandinavians.* London: Eyre & Spottiswoode, 1966. 590pp.

Di Niscemi, Maita. *Manor Houses and Castles of Sweden: Voyage through Five Centuries.* Woodbridge, England: Antique Collectors' Club, 1988. 216pp.

Elstob, Eric. *Sweden: a Political and Cultural History.* Totowa, N.J.: Rowman & Littlefield, 1980. 211pp.

Fleisher, Frederic. *The New Sweden. The Challenge of a Disciplined Democracy.* New York: David Mackay Co., 1968. 365pp.

Fleisher, W. *Sweden: the Welfare State.* New York, 1956. 255pp.

Gravier, Maurice. *Les Scandinaves.* Paris: Lidis, 1984. 688pp

Hadenius, Stig. *On Sweden.* Stockholm: Swedish Institute, 1992. 110pp.

Heywood, Terence. *Background to Sweden.* London: Constable, 1951. 332pp.

Huntsford, Roland. *The New Totalitarians.* London: Allen Lane; New York: Stein & Day, 1975 (new ed). 354pp.

Jenkins, David. *Sweden and the Price of Progress.* New York:

Robert Hale, 1968; London (title *Sweden: the Progress Machine*): 1969. 286pp.

Lane, Jan-Erik (ed). *Understanding the Swedish Model.* London: Cass, 1991. 210pp.

Kurian, George Thomas. *Scandinavia.* New York: Facts on File, 1990. 457pp.

Leach, Henry Goddard. *Scandinavia of the Scandinavians.* London: Pitman; New York: Scribner, 1915. 332pp. Princeton, N.J.: Princeton University Press, 1959. 298pp.

Mead, W.R. & Hall, Wendy. *Scandinavia.* New York: Walker, 1972. 208pp.

Nott, Kathleen. *A Clean Well-lighted Place.* London: Heinemann, 1961. 207pp.

Scandinavia between East and West. Edited by H. Friis. Ithaca, N.Y.: Cornell University, 1950. 388pp.

Scobbie, Irene. *Sweden. Nation of the Modern World.* London: Ernest Benn, 1972. 254pp.

Shirer, W.L. *The Challenge of Scandinavia.* Boston: Little, Brown & Co, 1955; London: Hale, 1956. 437pp.

Sweden: A General Introduction for Immigrants. Translated by Roger Tanner. Norrkoping: Statens invandrarverk, 1987. 246pp.

Taylor, Doreen. *Insight Guide to Sweden.* Hong Kong: APA Publications, 1991. 345pp.

Tomasson, Rickard F. *Sweden: Prototype of Modern Society.* New York: Random House, 1970. 303pp.

Wadensjö, Gösta. *Meet Sweden.* Malmö: Liber Hermods, 1983. 238pp.

General Histories

Åberg, Alf. *A Concise History of Sweden*. Translated by Gordon Elliot. Stockholm: Natur och Kultur, 1991. 103pp.

Ahnlund, Nils. (ed). *Den svenska utrikspolitikens historia*. 10 vols. Stockholm, 1951–61.

Andersson, Ingvar. *A History of Sweden*. Translated by C. Hannay. Westport, Conn.: Greenwood Press; London: Weidenfeld & Nicolson; New York: Praeger, 1962. 461pp.

Andersson, Ingvar & Weibull, J. *Swedish History in Brief*. Stockholm: Swedish Institute, 1988. 72pp.

Bain, R. Nisbet. *Scandinavia. A Political History of Denmark, Norway and Sweden from 1513 to 1900*. Cambridge: Cambridge University Press, 1905. 460pp.

Berg, Jonas & Lagerkrantz, Bo. *Scots in Sweden*. With an introduction by Eric Linklater and an essay by Frans G. Bengtsson. Edinburgh: Royal Scottish Museum, 1962. 101pp.

Bukdahl, J. *et al.* (eds). *Scandinavia Past and Present*. 3 vols. Odense: Arnkrone, 1959.

Carlsson, S. & Rosén, J. *Svensk historia*. 2 vols. Stockholm: Bonniers, 1977–79. Vol I–580pp. Vol II–648pp.

Collinder, Björn. *The Lapps*. Princeton, N.J.: Princeton University Press, American Scandinavian Foundation, 1949. 252pp.

Derry, T.K. *The History of Scandinavia: Norway, Sweden, Denmark, Finland and Iceland*. London: Allen & Unwin, 1979. 447pp.

Fischer, Ernst Ludvig. *The Scots in Sweden*. Being a contribution to the history of the Scots abroad. Edinburgh: O. Schultze, 1907. 278pp.

Griffiths, Tony. *Scandinavia.* Kent Town, Australia: Wakefield Press, 1991. 212pp.

Grimberg, Carl. *A History of Sweden.* Translated and adapted by C.W. Foss. Rock Island, Ill.: Augustana, 1935. 428pp.

Hallendorff, C. & Schück, A. *A History of Sweden.* Translated by L. Yapp. London: Cassell; Stockholm: Fritze, 1938. 466pp.

Heeres, W.G. *et al.* (eds). *From Dunkirk to Danzig: Shipping and Trade in the North Sea and the Baltic, 1350–1850.* Essays in honour of J.A. Faber. Hilversum: Verloren, 1988. 499pp.

Herlitz, Nils. *Sweden: a Modern Democracy on Ancient Foundations.* Minneapolis: Universsity of Minnesota, 1935; Oxford: Oxford University Press, 1939. 127pp.

Hill, Charles Edward. *The Danish Sound Dues and Command of the Baltic. A Study of International Relations.* Durham, N.C.: Duke University Press, 1926.

Hinshaw, David. *Sweden: Champion of Peace.* New York: Putnam. 1949. 309pp.

Hovde, Brynjolf J. *The Scandinavian Countries, 1720–1865: the Rise of the Middle Classes.* Ithaca, N.Y.: Cornell University Press, 1948. 823pp.

Kirby, David. *Northern Europe in the Early Modern Period: the Baltic World 1492–1772.* London: Longman, 1990. 443pp.

Koblik, Steven (ed). *Sweden's Development from Poverty to Affluence 1750–1970.* Translated by Joanne Johnson. Minneapolis: University of Minnesota Press, 1975. 380pp.

Konopczynski, Wladyslaw. *Poland and Sweden.* Torun, Poland: Baltic Institute, 1935; London: Alvin Redman, 1962. 252pp.

Lindroth, Sten (ed). *Swedish Men of Science, 1650–1950.* Stockholm: Swedish Institute/Almqvist & Wiksell, 1952. 292pp.

Metcalf, Michael F. (ed). *The Riksdag: a History of the Swedish Parliament.* Stockholm: Bank of Sweden Tercentenary Foundation, 1988.

Moberg, Vilhelm. *A History of the Swedish People: from Prehistory to the Renaissance.* London & New York: Pantheon, 1972.

———. *A History of the Swedish People: from Renaissance to Revolution.* New York: Pantheon, 1973.

Nordström, Byron J. *A Dictionary of Scandinavian History.* Westport, Conn.: Greenwood Press, 1986. 705pp.

Oakley, Stewart. *The Story of Sweden.* London: Faber & Faber, 1966. 292pp.

———. *War and Peace in the Baltic, 1560–1790.* London: Routledge, 1993. 222pp.

Rydberg, Sven. *The Great Copper Mountain: the STORA Story.* Translated by Jeremy Lamb. Stockholm: Stora Kopparberg, 1988. 244pp.

Samuelson, Kurt. *From Great Power to Welfare State: 300 Years of Swedish Social Development.* London: Allen & Unwin, 1968. 304pp.

Scandinavian Democracy. Development of Democratic Thought and Institutions in Denmark, Norway and Sweden. Edited by J.A. Lauwerys. Copenhagen: Danish Institute, Norwegian Office of Cultural Relations, Swedish Institute and American-Scandinavian Foundation, 1958. 437pp.

Schück, Herman. *The Riksdag: a History of the Swedish Parliament.* New York: St Martin's Press, 1987. 347pp.

Science in Sweden: the Royal Swedish Academy of Sciences, 1739–1989. Edited by T. Frängsmyr. Canton, Mass.: Science History Publications, 1989. 291pp.

Scott, Franklin D. *Scandinavia.* Cambridge, Mass.: Harvard University Press, 1975. 359pp.

————. *Sweden: the Nation's History* (with Epilogue by Steven Koblik). Carbondale: Southern Illinois University Press, 1988. 686 pp.

————. *The United States and Scandinavia.* Cambridge, Mass.: Harvard University, 1950. 359pp.

Sichel, Marion. *Scandinavia.* London: Batsford, 1987. (National Costume Reference Series). 64pp.

Simpson, Grant G. (ed). *Scotland and Scandinavia 800–1800.* Edinburgh: John Donald, 1990. 154pp.

The Slavic World and Scandinavia: Cultural Relations. Edited by Kjeld Björnager *et al.* Aarhus: Aarhus University Press, 1988. 191 pp.

Söderberg, Johan, *et al. A Stagnating Metropolis: the Economy and Demography of Stockholm, 1750–1850.* Cambridge: Cambridge University Press. 1991. 234pp.

Stomberg, Andrew A. *A History of Sweden.* New York: Macmillan, 1931. 823pp.

Svanström, Ragnar & Palmstierna, Karl Fredrik. *A Short History of Sweden.* Translated by Joan Bulman. Oxford: Clarendon Press, 1934. 443pp.

Svenska Män och Kvinnor. Biografisk uppslagsbok. (Swedish National Biographical Dictionary). 8 vols. Stockholm: Bonniers. 1942–1955.

Todd, Malcolm. *The Northern Barbarians.* Oxford: Blackwell, 1988 (rev. ed.) 224pp.

Wahlbäck, Krister. *The Roots of Swedish Neutrality.* Translated by T. Munch-Petersen. Stockholm: Swedish Institute. 1986. 80pp.

Prehistory. Viking Period. Middle Ages

Ahnlund, Nils G. *Från medeltid och vasatid. Historia och kulturhistoria.* Stockholm: Hugo Gebers förlag, 1933.

————. *Stockholms historia före Gustav Vasa.* Stockholm: Stockholms stad, 1953. 571pp.

Andersson, Aron. *St Bridget of Sweden.* London: Catholic Truth Society, 1980. 141pp.

Arbman, H. *The Vikings.* Translated by A. Binns. London: Thames & Hudson, 1961. 212pp.

Arne, T.J. *La Suède et l'Orient. Etudes archéologiques sur les relations de la Suède et de L'Orient pendant l'age des vikings.* Uppsala: Archives d'études orientales, 1914.

Becker, C.J. (ed). *Studies in Northern Coinages of the Eleventh Century.* Copenhagen: Det Kongelige Danske Videnskabernes Selskab, 1981. 175pp.

Benedictow, Ole J. *The Medieval Demographic System of the Nordic Countries.* Oslo: Middelalderforlaget, 1992.

————. *Plague in the Late Medieval Nordic Countries.* Oslo: Middelalderforlaget, 1992.

Bergquist, Lars. *Saint Birgitta.* Stockholm: Swedish Institute, 1991. 31pp. (Swedish Portraits).

Bertilson, Ulf. *The Rock Carvings of Northern Bohuslän: Spatial Structures and Social Symbols.* Stockholm: Stockholm University, 1987. 381pp.

Birgitta. *Birgitta, Life and Selected Revelations.* Edited by M. Tjäder Harris. New York: Paulist Press, 1990.

Boyer, Régis. *Le Christ de Barbares: le monde nordique, IXe-XIIIe siècle.* Paris: Cerf, 1987. 160pp.

———. *Les Vikings: histoire et civilisation.* Paris: Plon, 1992. 442pp

Brönstedt, J. *The Vikings.* Translated by E. Bannister-Good. London: Penguin Books, 1960. 320pp.

Coles, John. *Images of the Past: a Guide to the Rock Carvings and other Ancient Monuments of Northern Bohuslän.* Uddevalla: Bohusläns Museum, 1990. 95pp.

Davidson, Hilda R. Ellis. *The Viking Road to Byzantium.* London: Allen & Unwin, 1976. 341pp.

Dreijer, Matts. *The History of the Åland People.* Vol. I: *From the Stone Age to Gustavus Wasa.* Stockholm: Almqvist & Wiksell, 1986. 561pp.

Elliott, Ralph W.V.S. *Runes: an Introduction.* Manchester: University Press; New York: St Martin's Press, 1989. 151pp.

Farrell, R.T. (ed). *The Vikings.* London & Chichester: Phillimore, 1982. 306pp.

Foote, P.G. & Wilson, D.W. *The Viking Achievement.* London: Sidgwick & Jackson; New York: Praeger. 1970. 481pp. (New ed. with supplement, 1980).

Graham-Campbell, James. *The Viking World.* London: Frances Lincoln, 1991. 220pp.

Gissel, Sven *et al. Desertion and Land Colonization in the Nordic Countries c. 1300–1600.* Stockholm: Almqvist & Wiksell International, 1981. 304pp.

Holm, Lena. *The Use of Stone and Hunting of Reindeer in the Central Scandes c.6000–1 B.C.* Umeå, Sweden: University, 1991. 142pp.

Holmqvist, Wilhelm. *Swedish Vikings on Helgö and Birka.* Stockholm: Swedish Booksellers Association, 1980. 140pp.

Jansson, Sven B.F. *The Runes of Sweden.* Translated by P. Foote. Stockholm: Gidlund, 1987. 187pp.

Jesch, Judith. *Women in the Viking Age.* Woodbridge, England: Boydell & Brewer, 1991. 239pp.

Jones, Gwyn. *A History of the Vikings.* Oxford: Oxford University Press, 504pp.

Jorgensen, Johannes. *St Bridget of Sweden.* Translated by Ingeborg Lund. 2 vols. London: Longman, Green, 1954.

Karras, Ruth Mazo. *Slavery and Society in Medieval Scandinavia.* New Haven, Conn. & London: Yale University Press, 1988. 352pp.

Kendrick, T.D. *A History of the Vikings.* London: Frank Cass, 1968. 412pp.

Klindt-Jensen, Ole. *A History of Scandinavian Archeology.* Translated by G. Russell Poole. London: Thames & Hudson, 1975.

Kristiansen, Kristian (ed). *Settlement and Economy in Later Scandinavian Prehistory.* Oxford: British Archeological Reports. International Series, 211, B.A.R., 1984. 224pp.

Larsson, T.B. & Lundmark, H. (eds). *Approaches to Swedish Prehistory. A Spectrum of Problems and Perspectives in Contemporary Research.* Oxford: B.A.R., 1989. 393pp.

Logan, F. Donald. *The Vikings in History.* London: Hutchinson, 1983. 2nd ed. New York: Routledge, Chapman & Hall, 1992. 224pp.

Lönnroth, Erik. *Från svensk medeltid.* (Swedish Middle Ages). Stockholm: Aldis/Bonniers, 1959. 222pp.

Montelius, Oscar. *Dating the Bronze Age, with Special Reference to Scandinavia.* Stockholm: Vitterhets-historie- och anti-kvitetsakademien, 1986. 148pp.

Munch, Peter Andreas. *Norse Mythology: Legends of Gods and Heroes.* New York: American-Scandinavian Foundation, 1954.

Musset, Lucien. *Les Peuples Scandinaves au Moyen Age.* Paris: Presses Universitaires de France, 1951. 342pp.

Nylén, Erik. *Stones, Ships and Symbols: the Picture Stones of Gotland from the Viking Age and Before.* Hedemora, Sweden: Gidlund, 1988. 209pp.

Odenstedt, Bengt. *On the Origin and Early History of the Runic Script.* Stockholm: Almqvist & Wiksell International, 1990. 181 pp. (Acta Regiae Gustavi Adolphi, 59).

Olrik, Axel. *Viking Civilization.* New York: American-Scandinavian Foundation/Norton, 1930.

Österberg, Eva & Lindström, Dag. *Crime and Social Control in Medieval and Early Modern Swedish Towns.* Uppsala: University; Stockholm: Almqvist & Wiksell, 1988. 169pp.

Pálsson, Hermann & Edwards, Paul. *Vikings in Russia. Yngvar's Saga and Eymund's Saga.* Translated and introduced by H.

Pálsson and P. Edwards. Edinburgh: Edinburgh University Press, 1989. 102pp.

Peters, Jan. *Die alten Schweden: Uber Wikingerkrieger, Bauernrebellen und Heldenkönige.* Berlin: Deutscher Verlag der Wissenschaften. 200pp.

Roesdahl, Else. *The Vikings.* Translated by S.M. Margeson & K. Williams. New York: Viking Penguin, 1991. 324pp.

Sawyer, Peter H. *The Age of the Vikings.* London: Edward Arnold, 1962. (new ed. 1971). 254pp.

————. *Kings and Vikings: Scandinavia and Europe AD 700–1100.* London: Methuen, 1982. 182pp.

————. *The Making of Sweden.* Gothenburg: University, 1988. 60pp. (Occasional Papers on Medieval Topics 3).

Shetelig, Haakon & Falk, Hjalmar. *Scandinavian Archeology.* Translated by E.V. Gordon. Oxford: Clarendon Press, 1937. 458pp.

Social Approaches to Viking Studies. Edited by Ross Samson. Glasgow: Cruithne Press, 1991. 240pp.

Stenberger, Mårten. *Sten brons järn.* (Swedish Prehistory). Stockholm: Aldus/Bonniers, 1969. 276pp.

————. *Sweden.* Translated by A. Binns. London: Thames & Hudson, 1962. 229pp. (Ancient Peoples and Places).

Svenska Landskapslagar. (Swedish Provincial Laws). (Interpreted and explained for present-day Sweden by A. Holmbäck and E. Wessén. Series 1–5). Stockholm: Gebers. 1933–46.

Turville-Petre, E.O.G. *The Heroic Age of Scandinavia.* London: Hutchinson, 1951. 196pp.

Vestergaard, Elisabeth (ed). *Continuity and Change: Political Institutions and Literary Monuments in the Middle Ages. A Symposium.* Odense: Odense University Press, 1986. 134pp.

Wilson, David W. *Civil and Military Engineering in Viking Age Scandinavia.* London: National Maritime Museum, 1978. (Occasional Lectures, 1). 27pp.

————. *The Vikings and their Origins. Scandinavia in the First Millenium.* London: Thames & Hudson, 1989 (rev. ed.). New York: McGraw, 1970. 144pp.

VASA PERIOD. AGE OF GREATNESS

Åberg, Alf. *The People of New Sweden: Our Colony on the Delaware River 1638–1655.* Translated by Roger Tanner. Stockholm: Natur och Kultur, 1988. 203pp.

Åkerman, Susanna. *Queen Christina of Sweden and Her Circle.* Leiden & New York: Brill, 1991. 339pp.

Andersson, Ingvar. *Erik XIV.* (in Swedish) Stockholm: Wahlström & Widstrand, 1948. 319pp.

Barudio, Günter. *Gustav Adolf—der Grosse: eine politische Biographie.* Frankfurt: Fischer, 1985. 723pp.

Bell, James. *Queen Elizabeth and a Swedish Princess. Being an account of the visit of Princess Cecilia of Sweden to England in 1565.* From the original manuscript. Edited by E. Seaton. London: F. Etchells & H. Macdonald, 1926. 89pp.

Bengtsson, Frans G. *The Life of Charles XII, King of Sweden 1697–1718.* Translated by Naomi Walford. With an introduction by Eric Linklater. London & New York: St Martin's Press, 1960. 495pp.

Berg, Jonas & Lagercrantz, Bo. *Scots in Sweden.* Stockholm: Nordiska Museet/Swedish Institute, 1962. 101pp.

Berner, Felix. *Gustav Adolf: der Löwe aus Mitternacht.* Munich: Heyne, 1985. 607pp. (Heyne Biographien, 132).

Borgenstam, Curt & Sandström, Anders. *Why Wasa Capsized.* Stockholm: Statens Sjöhistoriska Museum, 1985. 79pp. (Wasa Studies, 13).

Coyet, Peter J. *Swedish Diplomats at Cromwell's Court, 1655–1656: The Missions of P.J. Coyet and Chr. Bonde.* Translated and edited by Michael Roberts. London: Royal Historical Society, 1988. 344pp.

Dahlgren, Stellan & Norman, Hans. *The Rise and Fall of New Sweden. Governor Johan Risingh's Journal 1654–1655 in its Historical Context.* Uppsala: University, 1988. 304pp. (Acta Bibliothecae R. Universitatis Upsaliensis, 27).

Dunsdorfs, Edgars. *The Livonian Estates of Axel Oxenstierna.* Stockholm: Almqvist & Wiksell International, 1981. 248pp.

Englund, Peter. *The Battle of Poltava.* Translated by Peter Hale. London: Gollancz, 1993.

Erskine of Mar. *The Great Baltic Bubble.* (On Jacobite attempts to enlist Swedish aid, 1715–1718). London: International Pub. Co., 1940. 122pp.

Franzén, Anders. *Vasa. The Brief Story of a Swedish Warship from 1628.* Translated by Anthony Baird. Stockholm, 1962. 64pp.

Garstein, Oskar. *Rome and the Counter-Reformation in Scandinavia: the Age of Gustavus Adolphus and Queen Christina of Sweden 1622–1656.* Leiden: Brill, 1992. 833pp. (Studies in the History of Christian Thought, 47).

Godley, The Hon. Eveline. *Charles XII of Sweden: a Study in Kingship.* London: W. Collins & Sons, 1928. 254pp.

Goldsmith, Margaret L. *Christina of Sweden. A Psychological Biography.* London: Barker, 1933, 254pp.

Gribble, Francis. *The Court of Christina of Sweden and the Later Adventures of the Queen in Exile.* London: E. Nash, 1913. 356pp.

Haintz, O. *König Karl XII von Schweden.* 3 vols. Berlin: Gruyter, 1958.

Harrison, Ada. "Christina of Sweden (1626–1689)," in *Six Women of the World.* London: G. Howe, 1929. pp. 7–95.

Hatton, Ragnhild. *Charles XII of Sweden.* London: Weidenfeld & Nicolson; New York: Welbright & Talley, 1968.

———. *Europe in the Age of Louis XIV.* London: Thames & Hudson, 1969. 263pp.

Haythornthwaite, Philip J. *Invincible Generals: Gustavus Adolphus, Marlborough, Frederick the Great, George Washington, Wellington.* Poole, England: Firebird, 1990. 240pp.

Johannesson, Kurt. *The Renaissance of the Goths in Sixteenth-Century Sweden: Johannes and Olaus Magnus as Politicians and Historians.* Translated by James Larson. Berkeley: University of California Press, 1991. 282pp.

Jones, G. *The Diplomatic Relations between Cromwell and Charles X Gustavus of Sweden.* Lincoln, Neb., 1907. 89pp

Landström, Björn. *The Royal Warship Vasa.* Translated by Jeremy Franks. Stockholm: Interpublishing, 1988. 157pp. (Architectura navalis).

Lewis, Paul. *Queen of Caprice. A Biography of Kristina of Sweden.* London: Alvin Redman, 1962. 252pp.

Lisk, J. *The Struggle for Supremacy in the Baltic 1600–1725.* London: University; New York: Funk & Wagnalls, 1967. 232pp.

Mackenzie, Faith C. *The Sibyl of the North. The Tale of Christina, Queen of Sweden.* London: Cassell, 1931. 262pp.

Macmunn, George. *Gustavus Adolphus: the Northern Hurricane.* London: Hodder & Stoughton, 1930. 318pp. New ed. entitled *Gustavus Adolphus: the Lion of the North.* New York: R.M. McBridge, 1931. 319pp.

Mellander, Karl & Prestage, Edgar. *The Diplomatic and Commercial Relations of Sweden and Portugal from 1641 to 1670.* Watford, England: Voss & Michael, 1930. 123pp.

Monroe, Harriet. *History of the Life of Gustavus Adolphus II, the Hero-General of the Reformation.* Philadelphia: Lutheran Publ. Soc., 1910. 139pp.

Neumann, Alfred. *The Life of Christina of Sweden.* London: Hutchinson, 1935. 287pp.

Noel, Edward. *Gustaf Adolf, King of Sweden. The Father of Modern War.* London: J. Hale, 1905. 113pp.

Oakley, Stewart. *William III and the Northern Crowns during the Nine Years War, 1689–1697.* London & New York: Garland, 1987.

Ohrelius, Bengt. *Vasa. The King's Ship.* Translated by Maurice Michael. Stockholm, 1962. 124pp.

Roberts, Michael. *The Early Vasas. A History of Sweden 1523–1611.* Cambridge: Cambridge University Press, 1968. 509pp

———. *From Oxenstierna to Charles XII: Four Studies.* Cambridge: Cambridge University Press, 1991. 203pp.

————. *Gustavus Adolphus*. London: Longmans, 1992. (Profiles in Power).

————. *The Swedish Imperial Experience, 1560–1718*. Cambridge: Cambridge University Press, 1984. 156pp. (Reissue).

————. (ed). *Sweden as a Great Power 1611–1697. Government, Society, Foreign Policy*. London & New York: St Martin's Press, 1968. 183pp.

————. *Sweden's Age of Greatness 1632–1718*. New York: St Martin's Press, 1973.

Rosén, Jerker. "Scandinavia and the Baltic" in *New Cambridge Modern History* Vol V (1648–88). Cambridge: Cambridge University Press, 1961. pp 519–542

Rystad, Göran (ed). *Europe and Scandinavia: Aspects of the Process of Integration in the 17th Century*. Lund: Esselte, 1984. 300pp. (Lund Studies in International History, 18).

Soop, Hans. *The Power and the Glory: the Sculptures of the Warship Wasa*. Stockholm: Kungl Vitterhets- historie- och antikvitetsakademien/Almqvist & Wiksell. 270pp.

Stiles, Andrina. *Sweden and the Baltic, 1523–72*. London: Hodder & Stoughton, 1992. 137pp.

Stolpe, Sten. *Christina of Sweden*. Translated by A. Randall & R.M. Bethell. London: Burns & Oates; New York: Macmillan, 1966. 360pp.

Svalenius, Ivan. *Gustav Vasa* (in Swedish). Stockholm: Wahlström & Widstrand, 1963. 271pp.

Taylor, Ida. *Christina of Sweden*. London: Hutchinson, 1909. (reissued 1929). 336pp.

Voltaire. *Lion of the North. Charles XII of Sweden*. Translated by M.F.O. Jenkins. Rutherford, N.J.: Fairleigh Dickinson University Press; London & Toronto: Associated University Presses, 1981. 270pp.

Ward, Christopher. *The Dutch and Swedes on the Delaware 1609–1664.* Philadelphia: University of Pennsylvania, 1930. 393pp.

Watson, P.B. *The Swedish Revolution under Gustaf Vasa.* London, 1989.

Wedgewood, C.V. *The Thirty Years War.* London: J. Cape; New Haven, Conn.: Yale University Press, 1938.

Weibull, C. *Christina of Sweden.* Translated by A. Tapsell. Stockholm: Bonniers, 1966. 186pp.

Weslager, Clinton Alfred. *The Swedes and Dutch at New Castle: with Highlights in the History of the Delaware Valley, 1638–1664.* Wilmington, Del.: Middle Atlantic Press, 1987. 240pp.

AGE OF LIBERTY

Barton, H. Arnold. *Scandinavia in the Revolutionary Era 1760–1815.* Minneapolis: University of Minnesota Press, 1986. 447pp. (Nordic Series, v. 12).

Bergquist, Lars. *Emanuel Swedenborg.* Stockholm: Swedish Institute, 1986. 19pp. (Swedish Portraits).

Broberg, Gunnar (ed). *Linnaeus. Progress and Prospects in Linnaean Research.* Stockholm: Almqvist & Wiksell International; Pittsburg, Pa.: Hunt Institute for Botanical Documentation, 1980. 317pp.

Cieslak, E. & Olszewski, H. (eds). *Changes in Two Baltic Countries: Poland and Sweden in the XVIIIth Century.*

Poznan: Wyd Naukowe Uniw. im Adama Mickiewicaz, 1990.

Frängsmyr, Tore (ed). *Linnaeus: the Man and his Work.* Los Angeles: University of California Press. 203pp.

Gage, A.T. & Stearnes, W.T. *A Bicentenary History of the Linnaean Society of London.* London: Academic Press, 1988. 242pp.

Hagberg, Knut. *Carl Linnaeus.* London: Jonathan Cape, 1952; New York: E. P. Dutton, 1953. 264pp.

Hatton, Ragnhild M. "Scandinavia and the Baltic," in *New Cambridge Modern History,* Vol. VII 1713–1763. Cambridge: Cambridge University Press, 1957. pp 648–680.

Hovde, B.J. *The Scandinavian Countries 1720–1865. The Rise of the Middle Classes.* 2 vols Ithaca: Cornell University Press, 1948.

Hyde, James. *A Bibliography of the Works of Emanuel Swedenborg, Original and Translated.* London: Swedenborg Society, 1906. 742pp.

Kent, H.S.K. *War and Trade in Northern Seas. Anglo-Scandinavian Economic Relations in the Mid-Eighteenth Century.* Cambridge: Cambridge University Press, 1973.

Larsen, Robin *et al.* (eds). *Emanuel Swedenborg: a Continuing Vision. Pictorial Biography and Anthology of Essays and Poetry.* New York: Swedenborg Foundation, 1988.

Roberts, Michael. *The Age of Liberty: Sweden 1719–1772.* Cambridge: Cambridge University Press, 1986. 233pp.

———. *British Diplomacy and Swedish Politics 1758–1773.* Minneapolis: University of Minnesota Press, 1980. 528pp. (The Nordic Series 1).

————. *Swedish and English Parliamentarianism in the Eighteenth Century.* Belfast: Queens University, 1973.

Trobridge, George. *Swedenborg, Life and Teaching.* New York: Swedenborg Foundation, 1962. 298pp.

Uggla, Arvid Hj. *Linnaeus.* Stockholm: Swedish Institute, 1957. 18pp.

Wallenberg, Jacob. *My Son on the Galley.* Translated by Peter Graves. (An account of a journey in 1770 on a Swedish East India Company vessel). Norwich, England: Norvik Press, 1994. 192pp.

Weinstock, John (ed). *Contemporary Perspectives on Linnaeus.* London: University Press of America, 1985. 193pp.

GUSTAVIAN PERIOD

Austin, P. Britten. *The Life and Songs of Carl Michael Bellman, Genius of the Swedish Rococo.* Malmö: Allhem Publishers, 1967. 181pp.

Bain, Robert N. *Gustavus III and his Contemporaries: an Overlooked Chapter of Eighteenth Century History.* 2 vols. London: K. Paul, Trench, Trubner, 1894.

Barton, H. Arnold. *Count Hans Axel von Fersen: Aristocrat in the Age of Revolution.* Boston: Twayne, 1975. 530pp

————. "Gustav III of Sweden and the East Baltic 1771–1772," in *Journal of Baltic Studies* 7, 1976.

————. *Scandinavia in the Revolutionary Era. 1760–1815.* Minneapolis: University of Minnesota Press, 1986. 447pp.

Carr, R. "Gustavus IV and the British Government 1804–9," in *English Historical Review.* Vol 60, 1945.

Fersen, Axel von. *The Letters of Marie Antoinette, Fersen and Barnave.* Edited and translated by W. Stephens & Mrs W. Jackson. London: J. Lane, 1926. 244pp.

Geffroy, A. *Gustave III et la Cour de France.* 2 vols. Paris: Didier et Cie, 1867.

Gustavian Opera: Swedish Opera, Dance and Theater 1771–1809. Stockholm: Royal Academy of Music/Almqvist & Wiksell, 1991. 492pp.

Gustavus III. *Gustave III par ses lettres* (Swedish Academy *handlingar* 1786). Stockholm: Norstedts/Swedish Academy, 1986.

Hilleström, Gustaf. *The Royal Opera, Stockholm. A Presentation of the Royal Swedish Opera and its History.* Stockholm: Swedish Institute, 1960. 83pp.

Kermina, Francoise. *Hans-Axel de Fersen.* Paris: Perrin, 1985. 428pp.

Martenson, Jan. *Drottningholm: the Palace by the Lakeside.* Stockholm: Wahlström & Widstrand, 1985.

Nordmann, Claude. *Gustave III: un démocrate couronné.* Lille: Presses Universitaires. 307pp.

Oakley, Stewart. ''Gustavus III of Sweden,'' in *Studies in History and Politics,* Vol 1V, 1984.

Sahlberg, Gardar. *Murder at the Masked Ball. The Assassination of Gustavus III.* London: Macdonald, 1974.

NINETEENTH AND TWENTIETH CENTURIES

Allen, Trevor. *Ivar Kreuger, Match King, Croesus and Crook.* London: J. Long, 1932. 255pp.

Almdal, Preben. *Aspects of European Integration. A View of the European Community and the Nordic Countries.* Odense: Odense University Press, 1986. 108pp.

Amelunxen, Clemens. *Jean-Baptiste Bernadotte: Marshall Napoleons: König von Schweden.* Cologne: Heymann, 1991. 142pp.

Ander, O. Fritiof. *The Building of Modern Sweden: the Reign of Gustav V 1907–1950.* Rock Island, Ill.: Augustana Book Concern, 1958. 271pp.

Anderson, Edgar. "The Crimean War in the Baltic Area," in *Journal of Baltic Studies* 5. (1974).

Anderson, Stanley V. *The Nordic Council: a Study of Scandinavian Regionalism.* Seattle: University of Washington Press/American Scandinavian Foundation, 1967. 194pp.

Barros, J. *The Åland Island Question: its Settlement by the League of Nations.* New Haven, Conn.: Yale University Press, 1968. 362pp.

Barton, Dunbar Plunket. *The Amazing Career of Bernadotte. 1763–1844.* London: J. Murray, 1929. 396pp.

———. *Bernadotte and Napoleon 1763–1810.* London: J. Murray, 1921. 343pp.

———. *Bernadotte, Prince and King. 1810–1844.* London: J. Murray; Dublin: Hodges Figgis, 1925. 248pp.

———. *Bernadotte. The First Phase 1763–1799.* London: J. Murray; Dublin: Hodges Figgis; New York: Scribner, 1914. 532pp.

Bensen, Adolph B. *Sweden and the American Revolution.* New Haven: Tuttle, Morehouse & Taylor, 1926. 216pp.

Bergengren, Erik. *Alfred Nobel. The Man and his Work.* With a supplement on the Nobel institutions and the Nobel prizes by Nils K. Ståhle. Translated by Alan Blair. London: Thomas Nelson & Sons, 1962. 221pp.

Bernadotte, Folke. *Instead of Arms. Autobiographical Notes.* Stockholm & New York: Bonniers, 1948. 228pp.

Bierman, John. *Righteous Gentile: the Story of Raoul Wallenberg, Missing Hero of the Holocaust.* (Reissue). Harmondsworth: Penguin, 1982. 218pp.

Bok, Sissela. *Alva Myrdal: a Daughter's Memoir.* Reading, Mass.: Addison-Wesley, 1991. 375pp.

Bremer, Fredrika. *Hertha.* Translated by Mary Howitt, London & New York: A. Hall, Virtue & Co., 1856. 394pp.

————. *Works.* Translated by Mary Howitt. London & New York, 1892–1909.

Carlbom, Terry. *Rethinking Swedish Neutrality.* Lampeter, Wales: St David's College Swedish Unit, 1989. 29pp.

Childs, Marquis W. *Sweden: the Middle Way.* New Haven, Conn.: Yale University Press, 1936; New York: Penguin Books, 1948. 171pp.

————. *Sweden: the Middle Way on Trial.* New Haven, Conn. & London: Yale University Press, 1980. 179pp

Churchill, Allen. *The Incredible Ivar Kreuger.* London: Weidenfeld & Nicolson; New York: Rinehart, 1956. 269pp.

Cruikshank, Charles G. *SOE (i.e. Special Operations Executive) in Scandinavia.* Oxford: Oxford University Press. 1986. 292pp.

Denham, H.M. *Inside the Nazi Ring: a Naval Attaché in Sweden.* 1940–1945. London: Murray, 1984. 174pp.

Deterrence and Defense in the North. Edited by Johan J. Holst *et al.* Oslo: Universitetsforlag, 1985. 244pp. (Norwegian Foreign Policy Studies, 54).

Evlanoff, Michael. *Nobel-prize Donor. Inventor of Dynamite. Advocate of Peace.* Philadelphia: Blaiston; New York & London: F.H. Revell, 1943. 190pp.

Frängsmyr, Tore (ed). *History of Science in Sweden. The Growth of a Discipline, 1932–1982.* Uppsala: University, 1984. 64pp. (Uppsala Studies in History of Science, 2).

Fredriksson, Gunnar. *Olof Palme.* Stockholm: Swedish Institute, 1986. 16pp. (Swedish Portraits).

Freeman, Ruth. *Death of a Statesman: the Solution to the Murder of Olof Palme.* London: Hale, 1989. 205pp.

Fritz, Martin. *German Steel and Swedish Iron Ore 1939–1945.* Gothenburg: Institute of Economic History, 1974.

——— et al. *The Adaptable Nation: Essays in Swedish Economy during the Second World War.* Stockholm: Almqvist & Wiksell International, 1982. 109pp.

Futrell, Michael. *Northern Underground. Episodes of Russian Revolutionary Transport and Communications through Scandinavia and Finland, 1863–1917.* London: Faber & Faber, 1963. 240pp.

Gavshon, Arthur L. *The Mysterious Death of Dag Hammarskjöld.* New York: Walker, 1962. 243pp.

Girod de L'Ain, Gabriel. *Bernadotte: chef de guerre et chef d'état.* Paris: Librairie académique Perrin, 1968. 665pp.

Grell, Detlef. *Die Auflösung der Schwedisch-Norwegischen Union 1905 im Spiegel der Europäischen Grossmachtspolitik: Unter besonderer Berücksicht der Akten des auswärtigen Amtes.* Essen: Verlag die blaue Eule, 1984. 171pp.

Häkli, Esko. *A.E. Nordenskiöld. A Scientist and his Library.* Helsinki: Helsinki University Library, 1980. 80pp.

Halasz, Nicholas. *Nobel. A Biography.* London: Robert Hale, 1960. 189pp.

Heckscher, Eli F., Bergendahl, K., Keilhau, W., Cohn, E., & Thorsteinsson, T. *Sweden, Norway, Denmark and Iceland in the World War.* New Haven: Yale University; London: Oxford University, 1930. 593pp. (Economic and Social History of the World War, 7).

Hedin, Sven. *My Life as an Explorer.* Translated by A. Huebsch. Oxford: Oxford University Press, 1991 (reprint). 498pp.

Hellberg, Thomas & Jansson, L.M. *Alfred Nobel.* Sölvesborg: Lagerblad, 1986. 141pp.

Hershey, Burnet. *Dag Hammarskjold, Soldier of Peace.* Chicago: Encyclopaedia Britannica Press, 1961. 191pp.

Hewins, Ralph. *Count Folke Bernadotte: his Life and Work.* London & New York: Hutchinson, 1950. 264pp. Minneapolis: T.S. Denison, 1950. 279pp.

Höglund, Zeth. *Hjalmar Branting och hans livsgärning.* 2 vols. Stockholm: Tiden, 1928–29.

Hovde, B.J. *Diplomatic Relations of the United States with Sweden and Norway 1814–1905.* Iowa City: University of Iowa, 1921. 70pp.

Jägerskiöld, Stig. *Mannerheim, Marshal of Finland.* London: Hurst, 1986. 210pp.

Jones, S. Shepard. *The Scandinavian States and the League of Nations.* Princeton, N.J.: Princeton University, 1939. 298pp.

Jorgenson, Theodore. *Norway's Relation to Scandinavian Unionism 1815–1871.* Northfield, Minn.: St Olaf College, 1935. 530pp.

Kanger, Thomas. *Wer erchoss Olof Palme? Polizeifahndung auf Abwegen.* Translated by Robt Bohn. Kiel: Neuer Malik Verlag, 1988. 224pp.

Katz, Peter. *Nathan Söderblom, a Prophet of Christian Unity.* London: J. Clarke, 1949. 95pp.

Kihlberg, Leif. *Karl Staaff.* (in Swedish). 2 vols. Stockholm: Bonniers, 1962–63.

Knaplund, Paul (ed). *British Views on Norwegian-Swedish Problems 1880–1895: Selection from Diplomatic Correspondence.* Oslo: I Kommisjon hja J. Dybwad, 1952.

Koblik, Steven. *The Stones Cry Out: Sweden's Response to the Persecution of the Jews 1933–1945.* Translated by Jeremy Franks. New York: Holocaust Publications, 1989. 305pp.

———. *Sweden: the Neutral Victor: Sweden and the Western Powers 1917–1918.* Lund: Läromedelsförlagen, 1972.

Levai, Jeno. *Raoul Wallenberg: his Remarkable Life, Heroic Battles and the Secret of his Mysterious Disappearance.* Melbourne: White Ant Occasional Publications, 1989. 313pp.

Lindberg, Folke. *Scandinavia in Great Power Politics 1905–1908.* Stockholm: University, 1958. 329pp. (Stockholm Studies in History).

Lindgren, R. E. *Norway-Sweden Union, Disunion and Scandinavian Integration.* Princeton, N.J.: Princeton University Press, 1959. 298pp.

Lindström, Ulf. *Fascism in Scandinavia 1920–1940.* Stockholm: Almqvist & Wiksell, 1985. 196pp.

Lundestad, Geir. *America, Scandinavia and the Cold War 1945–1949*. Oslo: Universitetsforlaget, 1980. 434pp.

Lowell, Briant Lindsay. *Scandinavian Exodus: Demography and Social Development of 19th-Century Rural Communities*. Boulder, Col.: Westview, 1987. 262pp.

Lutzhöft, H.-J. *Deutsche Militärpolitik und Schwedische Neutralität 1939–1942*. Newmünster: Karl Wachholtz Verlag, 1981. 255pp. (Skandinavistische Studien, Band 15).

Marton, Kati. *Wallenberg*. New York: Random House, 1982. 243pp.

Miller, Richard L. *Dag Hammarskjöld and Crisis Diplomacy*. New York: Oceana Publications, 1961. 344pp.

Miller, Roger & Gerger, Torvald. *Social Change in 19th-Century Swedish Agrarian Society*. Stockholm: Almqvist & Wiksell, 1986. 130pp. (Stockholm Studies in Human Geography, 5).

Misgeld, Klaus. *Sozialdemokratie und Aussenpolitik in Schweden: Sozialistische Internationale, Europapolitik und die Deutschlandfrage 1945–1955*. Frankfurt: Campus Verlag, 1982. 563pp.

Mosey, Chris. *Cruel Awakening: Sweden and the Killing of Olof Palme*. New York: St Martin's Press, 1991. 200pp.

Mousson-Lestang, Jean-Pierre. *La Scandinavie et L'Europe de 1945 à nos jours*. Paris: Presses Universitaires de France, 1990. 205pp.

Munch-Petersen, Thomas. *The Strategy of Phoney War. Britain, Sweden and the Iron Ore Question 1939–1940*. Stockholm: Militärhistoriska förlaget, 1981. 296pp. (Militärhistoriska studier, 5).

Nansen, Fridtjof. *Norway and the Union with Sweden*. London & New York: Macmillan, 1905. 96pp.

Nelson, Marie C. *Bitter Bread: the Famine in Norrbotten, 1867–68.* Uppsala: Universitetet; Stockholm: Almqvist & Wiksell, 1988. 192pp. (Studia historica Upsaliensia, 153).

Nissen, Henrik (ed). *Scandinavia during the Second World War.* Translated by T. Munch-Petersen. Minneapolis: University of Minnesota Press, 1983. 407pp.

Nordlund, Karl. *The Swedish-Norwegian Union Crisis. A History with Documents.* Uppsala & Stockholm: Almqvist & Wiksell; London: D. Nutt, 1905. 107pp.

Palmer, Alan. *Bernadotte: Napoleon's Marshal, Sweden's King.* London: Murray, 1990. 285pp.

Pauli, Herta E. *Alfred Nobel, Dynamite King—Architect of Peace.* New York: Fischer, 1942; London & Brussels: Nicholson & Watson, 1947. 323pp.

Ruin, Olof. *Tage Erlander: Serving the Welfare State, 1946–1969.* Translated by Michael F. Metcalf. Pittsburgh, Pa.: University of Pittsburgh Press, 1990. 367pp.

Russell of Liverpool, Lord. *Bernadotte: Marshal of France and King of Sweden.* London: Assent Books, 1981. 193pp.

Schück, Henrik. *Nobel. The Man and his Prizes.* Edited by O. von Feilitzen. Stockholm: Sohlman, 1950. 620pp. 2nd rev. ed. Stockholm: The Nobel Foundation; Amsterdam: Elsevier, 1962. 690pp.

Scott, Franklin D. *Bernadotte and the fall of Napoleon.* Cambridge, Mass.: Harvard University Press, 1935, 190pp.

———. *The United States and Scandinavia.* Cambridge, Mass.: Harvard University Press, 1950.

The Swedish Armed Forces and Foreign Influence 1870–1945. Edited by Göran Rystad. Stockholm: Militärhistoriska förlaget, 1992.

Shaplen, Robert. *Kreuger, Genius and Swindler.* With an introduction by J.K. Galbraith. New York: Knopf, 1960. 251pp.

Sheldon, Richard N. *Dag Hammarskjöld.* New York: Chelsea
House, 1987. 112pp.

Slettin, V. *Five Northern Countries Pull Together.* Copenhagen:
Nordic Council, 1967.

Smith, Danny. *Wallenberg: Lost Hero.* Basingstoke, England:
Marshall Pickering, 1986. 192pp.

Sohlman, Ragnar. *The Legacy of Alfred Nobel, the Story behind
the Nobel Prizes.* London: Bodley Head, 1983. 144pp.

Soloveytchik, George. *The Financier. The Life of Ivar Kreuger.*
London: P. Davies, 1933. 195pp.

Stoneman, William H. *The Life and Death of Ivar Kreuger.*
Indianapolis, Ind.: Bobbs-Merrill, 1932. 289pp.

La Suède et la Russie. Documents et Matériaux 1809–1818.
Stockholm: Vitterhets- historie- och antikvitetsakademien,
1986. 406pp.

Sweden and the United Nations. Report by a special study group
of the Swedish Institute for International Affairs. Prepared
for the Carnegie Endowment for International Peace. New
York: Manhattan, 1956. 315pp.

Tolf, Robert W. *The Russian Rockefellers. The Saga of the Nobel
Family and the Russian Oil Industry.* Stanford, Cal.: Hoover
Institution Press, 1976. 269pp.

Toynbee, A.J. & V.M. (eds). *The War and the Neutrals.* London:
Oxford University, 1956. 738pp.

Uggla, John. *The Åland Question: Résumé of arguments and
points of view in defence of Finland's right to the Åland
archipelago.* Helsinki: Statsrådets tr., 1919. 20pp.

Raoul Wallenberg. Stockholm: Swedish Institute, 1988. (English and German text). 52pp.

Wencker-Wildberg, Friedrich. *Bernadotte. A Biography.* Translated from the German by K. Kirkness. London: Jarrolds, 1936. 316pp.

Wendt, Frantz. *Co-operation in the Nordic Countries. Achievements and Obstacles.* Stockholm: Almqvist & Wiksell International, 1981. 408pp.

Economics, Politics, Social Studies

Abrahamson, Peter (ed). *Welfare States in Crisis: the Crumbling of the Scandinavian Model.* Copenhagen: Sociologi, 1988. 229pp.

Ahrne, Göran *et al. Class and Social Organisation in Finland, Sweden and Norway.* Uppsala: University; Stockholm: Almqvist & Wiksell, 1988. 154pp. (Studia sociologica Upsaliensia, 28).

Allardt, Erik *et al. Nordic Democracy: Ideas, Issues and Institutions in Politics, Economy, Education, Social and Cultural Affairs of Denmark, Finland, Iceland, Norway and Sweden.* Copenhagen: Det Danske Selskab, 1981. 780pp.

Ålund, Aleksandra & Schierup, Carl-Ulrik. *Paradoxes of Multiculturalism: Essays on Swedish Society.* Aldershot, England: Avebury, 1991. 192pp.

Andrén, Nils. *Government and Politics in the Nordic Countries. Denmark-Finland-Iceland-Norway-Sweden.* Stockholm: Almqvist & Wiksell, 1964. 241pp.

————. *Modern Swedish Government.* Stockholm: Swedish Institute, 1968. 252pp.

————. *Power Balance and Non-Alignment: a Perspective of Swedish Foreign Policy.* Stockholm: Almqvist & Wiksell, 1967. 212pp.

Arbitration in Sweden. Stockholm: Chamber of Commerce, 1984. 276pp.

Arter, David. *The Nordic Parliaments. A Comparative Analysis.* London: Hurst, 1984. 421pp.

Bagge, G., Lundberg, E. & Svennilsson, I. *Wages in Sweden 1860–1930.* 2 vols, London: P.S. King; Stockholm: Stockholm Economic Studies, 1933–35.

Berner, Örjan. *Soviet Policies Toward the Nordic Countries.* Lanham, Md. & London: University Press of America, 1986. 192pp.

Bexelius, Alfred. *The Swedish Institution of the Justitie-Ombudsman.* Stockholm: Swedish Institute, 1966.

Blake, D. *Swedish Trade Unions and the Social Democratic Party: the Formative Years.* Berkeley, Cal. 1961.

Boalt, Gunnar & Bergryd, Ulla. *Political Value Patterns and Parties in Sweden.* Stockholm: Almqvist & Wiksell, 1981. 134pp.

Boalt, Gunnar, *et al.* (eds). *Professionalization and Democratization in Sweden. Studies in Memoirs and Biographies.* Stockholm: Almqvist & Wiksell International, 1980. 264pp.

Böök, Sven A. & Johansson, Tore. *The Co-operative Movement in Sweden.* Stockholm: Swedish Society for Cooperative Studies. Brevskolan, 1988. 193pp.

Bosworth, Barry P. & Rivlin, Alice (eds). *The Swedish Economy.* Washington, D.C.: Brookings Institute, 1986. 338pp.

Carlgren, Wilhelm M. *Swedish Foreign Policy during the Second World War.* Translated by Arthur Spencer. London: Ernest Benn, 1977.

Carlsnaes, Walter. *Energy Vulnerability and National Security: the Energy Crisis, Domestic Policy Responses and the Logic of Swedish Neutrality.* London: Pinter, 1988. 136pp.

Carlson, Allan Constantin. *The Swedish Experiment in Family Politics: the Myrdals and the Interwar Population Crisis.* New Brunswick, N.J.: Transaction, 1990. 235pp.

Carlson, B. *Trade Unions in Sweden.* Stockholm, 1969.

Childs, Marquis W. *This is Democracy. Collective Bargaining in Scandinavia.* New Haven, Conn.: Yale University, 1938. 169pp.

Constitutional Documents of Sweden: The Instrument of Government, the Riksdag Act, the Act of Succession, the Freedom of the Press Act. Stockholm: Swedish Riksdag, 1981. 164pp.

Damgaard, Erik (ed). *Parliamentary Changes in the Nordic Countries.* Oxford: Oxford University Press, 1992. 256pp. Oslo: Scandinavian University Press, 1992. 224pp.

Davidson, Alexander. *Two Models of Welfare: the Origins and Development of the Welfare State in Sweden and New Zealand, 1888–1988.* Uppsala: University, 1989. 432pp. (Publications of the Political Science Association in Uppsala, 108).

Dohlman, Ebba. *National Welfare and Economic Interdependence: the Case of Sweden's Foreign Trade Policy.* Oxford & New York: Oxford University Press, 1989. 254pp.

Eckerberg, Katrina. *Environmental Protection in Swedish Forestry.* Aldershot, England: Avebury, 1990. 179pp.

Edlund, Sten & Nyström, Birgitta. *Developments in Swedish Labour Law.* Stockholm: Swedish Institute, 1988. 87pp.

Einhorn, Eric S. *Modern Welfare States: Politics and Policies in Social Democratic Scandinavia.* New York: Praeger, 1989. 340pp.

Elder, Neil. *The Consensual Democracies? The Government and Policies of the Scandinavian State.* Oxford: Blackwell, 1988. 248pp.

————. *Government in Sweden: the Executive at Work.* Oxford: Pergamon, 1970.

Erikson, Robert *et al.* (eds). *The Scandinavian Model: Welfare States and Welfare Research.* Armonk, N.Y. & London: M.E. Sharpe, 1987. 251pp. (Comparative Public Policy Analysis).

Erikson, Robert & Åberg, Rune. *Welfare in Transition: a Survey of Living Conditions in Sweden 1968–1981.* Oxford: Clarendon, 1987. 297pp.

Esping-Andersen, Gösta. *Politics against Markets: the Social Democratic Road to Power.* Princeton; Guildford: Princeton University Press, 1985. 366pp.

Fitzmaurice, John. *Security and Politics in the Nordic Area.* Aldershot, England: Avebury, 1987. 191pp.

Flora, Peter (ed). *Growth to Limits: the Western European Welfare State since World War II.* Vol. 1: *Sweden, Norway, Finland, Denmark.* Berlin & New York: de Gruyter, 1986. 383pp.

Fry, John (ed). *Towards a Democratic Rationality: Making the Case for Swedish Labour.* Aldershot, England: Gower, 1986. 281pp.

Fulcher, James. *Labour Movements, Employers and the State: Conflict and Co-operation in Britain and Sweden.* Oxford: Clarendon Press, 1990. 367pp.

Furuland, Lars. *Literacy in Sweden: Two Essays.* Minneapolis: University of Minnesota, 1991.

Gellhorn, W. *The Ombudsman and Others. Citizens' Protectors in Nine Countries.* Cambridge, Mass.: Harvard University Press, 1966.

Gendell, M. *Swedish Working Wives.* Totawa, N.J., 1966.

Gjöres, Axel. *Cooperation in Sweden.* Translated by J. Downie. Manchester: Cooperative Union, 1937. 197pp.

Goldmann, Kjell *et al.* (eds). *Democracy and Foreign Policy: the Case of Sweden.* Aldershot, England: Gower, 1986. 206pp.

Gould, Arthur. *Conflict and Control in Welfare Policy: the Swedish Experience.* London: Longman, 1988. 193pp.

Granberg, Donald & Holmberg, S. *The Political System Matters: Social Psychology and Voting Behaviour in Sweden and the United States.* Cambridge: Cambridge University Press, 1988. 254pp. (European Monographs in Social Psychology).

Graudbard, Stephen R. (ed). *Norden: the Passion for Equality.* Oslo: Norwegian University Press, 1986. 323pp.

Growth or Stagnation? The Swedish Economy 1981–1985. Stockholm: Ministry of Economic Affairs, 1982. 286pp.

Gustavson, Carl G. *The Small Giant: Sweden Enters the Industrial Era.* Athens, Ohio: University Press, 1986. 364pp.

Haavio-Mannila, Elina *et al.* (eds). *Unfinished Democracy: Women in Nordic Politics.* Translated by Christine Badcock. Oxford: Pergamon Press, 1985. 206pp.

Hadenius, Stig. *A Crisis of the Welfare State? Opinions about Taxes and Public Expenditure in Sweden.* Stockholm: Almqvist & Wiksell, 1986. 152pp.

————. *Swedish Politics during the 20th Century.* Stockholm: Swedish Institute, 1988. 184pp.

Hamilton, Malcolm B. *Democratic Socialism in Britain and Sweden.* Basingstoke, England: Macmillan, 1989. 270pp. (University of Reading European and International Studies).

Hancock, M. Donald. *Sweden: the Politics of Post-Industrial Change.* Hinsdale, N.Y.: Dryden Press, 1972.

Håstad, Elis. *The Parliament of Sweden.* London: Hansard Society for Parliamentary Government, 1957. 165pp.

Heckscher, Eli F. *An Economic History of Sweden.* Translated by G. Ohlin, with supplement by Gunnar Heckscher. Cambridge, Mass., 1954. 308pp.

Heckscher, Eli F. *et al. Sweden, Norway, Denmark and Iceland in the World War.* New Haven, Conn.: Yale University Press, 1930. 593pp. (Economic and Social History of the World War, 7).

Heckscher, Gunnar. *The Welfare State and Beyond. Success and Problems in Scandinavia.* Minneapolis: University of Minnesota Press, 1984. 273pp.

Heclo, Hugh & Madsen, Henrik. *Policy and Politics in Sweden: Principled Pragmatism.* Philadelphia: Temple University, 1987. 348pp.

Henden, H. *Suicide and Scandinavia: a Psychological Study of Culture and Character.* New York & London: Grune & Stratton, 1964. 153pp.

Henriksson, Benny. *Not for Sale. Young People in Society.* Translated by Susan Davies & Irene Scobbie. Aberdeen: Aberdeen University Press, 1983. 224pp.

Hörnell, Erik & Vahlne, Jan-Erik. *Multinationals: the Swedish Case.* London: Croom Helm, 1986. 190pp.

Horváth, Dezsö J. & Daly, Donald J. *Small Countries in the World Economy: the Case of Sweden. What Canada can learn from the Swedish Experience.* Halifax, Nova Scotia: Institute for Research on Public Policy, 1989. 120pp.

Inequality in Sweden: Trends and Current Situation. Stockholm: Statistics Sweden, 1988. 512pp. (Living Conditions, 58; Sveriges officiella statistik).

Isacson, Maths & Magnusson, Lars. *Proto-Industrialisation in Scandinavia: Craft Skills in the Industrial Revolution.* Leamington Spa, England: Berg, 1987. 151pp.

Jangenäs, Bo. *The Swedish Approach to Labor Market Policy.* Stockholm: Swedish Institute, 1985. 69pp.

Jasper, James M. *Nuclear Politics: Energy and the State in the United States, Sweden and France.* Princeton, N.J. & London: Princeton University Press, 1990. 327pp.

Jervas, Gunnar. *Sweden Between the Power Blocs: a New Strategic Position?* Stockholm: Swedish Institute, 1986. 48pp.

Johnston, T.L. *Collective Bargaining in Sweden: a Study of the Labour Market and its Institution.* London: Allen & Unwin, 1962. 258pp.

Jones, S.S. *The Scandinavian States and the League of Nations.* Princeton, N.J., 1939.

Jonung, Lars. *The Political Economy of Price Controls: the Swedish Experience 1970–1987.* Aldershot, England: Avebury, 1990. 217pp.

Jörberg, Lennart. "The Nordic Countries 1850–1914," translated by P. Britten Austin, in *Fontana Economic History of Europe. The Emergence of Industrial Societies*-2. London: Fontana, 1973. pp 375–485.

Kallberg, Sture. *Off the Middle Way.* New York, 1972.

Kälvemark, Ann-Sofie. *More Children of Better Equality? Aspects of Swedish Population Policy in the 1930's.* Uppsala: University; Stockholm: Almqvist & Wiksell International, 1980. 160pp. (Studia Historica Upsaliensia, 115).

Kalvesten, Anne-Lisa. *The Social Structures of Sweden.* Stockholm: Almqvist & Wiksell, 1965.

KF: Konsum. Consumer Cooperatives in Sweden. Stockholm: KF/Konsum, 1985.

Lamming, Norman. *Sweden's Co-operative Enterprise.* Manchester: Co-operative Union, 1940. 220pp.

Lawerys, J.A. (ed). *Scandinavian Democracy: Development of Democratic Thought and Institutions in Denmark, Norway and Sweden.* Copenhagen: Danish Institute, 1958.

Lawrence, Peter & Spybey, Tony. *Management and Society in Sweden.* London: Routledge & Kegan, 1986. 146pp.

Level of Living and Inequality in the Nordic Countries. Stockholm: Nordic Council; Liber, 1984. 226pp.

Lewin, Leif. *Governing Trade Unions in Sweden.* Cambridge, Mass. & London: Harvard University Press, 180pp.

Lindahl, Ingemar. *The Soviet Union and the Nordic Nuclear-Weapons-Free-Zone Proposal.* Basingstoke, England: Macmillan, 1988. 227pp.

Lindbeck, Assar. *Swedish Economic Policy.* Berkeley: University of California Press, 1974.

Lindström, Eric. *The Swedish Parliamentary System. How responsibilities are divided and decisions made.* Stockholm: Swedish Institute, 1982. 97pp.

Linnér, Birgitta. *Sex and Society in Sweden.* New York: Random House, 1967. 204pp.

Lundberg, E., Meidner, R., Rehn, G. & Wickman, K. *Wages Policy under Full Employment.* London, 1952.

Lundberg Lithman, Eva. *Immigration and Immigrant Policy in Sweden.* Stockholm: Swedish Institute, 1987. 70pp.

Meyer, Donald. *Sex and Power: the Rise of Women in America, Russia, Sweden and Italy.* Middletown, Ct.: Wesleyan University Press, 1987. 721pp.

Meyerson, Per-Martin. *The Welfare State in Crisis: the Case of Sweden. A Critical Examination of Some Central Problems in the Swedish Economy and Political System.* Stockholm: Federation of Swedish Industries. 66pp.

Milner, Henry. *Sweden: Social Democracy in Practice.* Oxford: Oxford University Press, 1990. 260pp.

Moen, Phyllis. *Working Parents: Transformations in Gender Roles and Public Policies in Sweden.* Madison: University of Wisconsin Press; London: Adamantine, 1989. 181pp.

Montgomery, Arthur. *How Sweden Overcame the Depression.* Stockholm: Bonniers, 1938. 91pp.

————. *The Rise of Modern Industry in Sweden.* Stockholm: Norstedts, 1939. 285pp. (Stockholm Economics Studies, 8).

Mörner, Magnus & Svensson Thommy (eds). *Classes, Strata and Elites: Essays on Social Stratification in Nordic and Third World History.* Gothenburg: University, 1988. 269pp. (Report from the Department of History, 34).

Myrdal, Alva. *The Game of Disarmament.* New York, Pantheon, 1977. 399pp.

———. *Nation and Family. The Swedish Experiment in Democratic Family and Population Policy.* New York & London: Harpers, 1941 441pp.

Nicolin, Curt. *Private Industry in a Public World.* Reading, Mass.: Addison-Wesley, 1977.

Norgren, M. & C. *Industrial Sweden.* Stockholm: Swedish Institute, 1971.

Nuclear Power in Sweden. Stockholm: SwedPower, 1985. 147pp.

Olsen, Gregg (ed). *Industrial Change and Labour Adjustment in Sweden and Canada.* Toronto: Garamond, 1988. 248pp.

Olsen, Marvin E. *Participatory Pluralism: Political Participation and Influence in the United States and Sweden.* Chicago: Nelson-Hall, 1982. 318pp.

Olson, Björn. *The Saab-Scania Story.* Translated by Tom Byrne. Stockholm: Steiffert, 1987. 167pp.

Olson, Sven E. *Social Policy and Welfare State in Sweden.* Lund: Arkiv, 1990. 348pp.

Östblom, Göran. *Structural Change: the Swedish Economy.* Stockholm: University, 1986. 136pp.

Persson, Inga (ed). *Generating Equality in the Welfare State: the Swedish Experience.* Oslo: Norwegian University Press, 1990. 345pp.

Population Movements and Industralization: Swedish Counties 1895–1930. Institute of Social Services, Vol. II. Stockholm: Stockholm Economic Studies 10:2, 1941

Portocarero, Lucienne. *Social Mobility in Industrial Societies: Women in France and Sweden.* Stockholm: SNS förlag, 1986. 156pp.

The Postwar Programme of Swedish Labour. Summary in 27 points and comments. Stockholm: LO, 1948 (2nd ed). 151pp.

Reade, Eric (ed). *Britain and Sweden: Current Issues in Local Government.* Gävle: National Swedish Institute for Building Research, 1989. 170pp.

Ross, John F.L. *Neutrality and International Sanctions: Sweden, Switzerland and Collective Security.* New York: Praeger, 1989. 248pp.

Rowat, D.C. (ed). *The Ombudsman. Citizens' Defender.* London: Allen & Unwin, 1968. 384pp.

Ruggie, Mary. *The State and Working Women: a Comparative Study of Britain and Sweden.* Princeton, N.J.: Princeton University Press, 1984. 361pp.

Runeby, S. Cho & N. (eds). *Traditional Thought and Ideological Change: Sweden and Japan in the Age of Industrialisation.* Stockholm: University Press, 1988. 259pp.

Rustow, D.A. *The Politics of Compromise. A Study of Parties and Cabinet Government in Sweden.* Princeton, N.J.: Princeton University Press., 1955. 257pp.

Rydén, Bengt & Bergström, Villy (eds). *Sweden: Choices for Economic and Social Policy.* London: Allen & Unwin, 1982. 257pp.

Sandelin, Bo (ed). *The History of Swedish Economic Thought.* London: Routledge, 1991. 248pp. (Routledge History of Economic Thought Series).

Sandlund, M.B. *The Status of Women in Sweden.* (Report to the United Nations). Stockholm: Swedish Institute/Almqvist & Wiksell, 1968.

The Scandinavian States and Finland. A Political and Economic Survey. London & New York: Royal Institute of International Affairs, 1951. 312pp.

Schmidt, F. *The Law on Labor Relations in Sweden.* Cambridge, Mass. & Stockholm: Almqvist & Wiksell, 1962. 343pp.

Schwartz, Eli. *Trouble in Eden: a Comparison of the British and Swedish Economies.* New York: Praeger, 1980.

Side by Side: A Report on Equality Between Women and Men in Sweden 1985. Stockholm: Arbetsmarknadsdepartmentet, 1985. 113pp.

Sjöberg, B., Hancock, M.D. & Orion, W. *Politics in the Post-Welfare State: a Comparison of the United States and Sweden.* Bloomington, Ind., 1967.

Sjöblom, Gunnar. *Political Parties and Public Administration in Sweden.* Copenhagen: Copenhagen University, 1986. 71pp.

Söderlund, Ernst. *Swedish Timber Exports 1850–1950.* Stockholm: Almqvist & Wiksell, 1952.

Söderqvist, Thomas. *The Ecologists: from Merry Naturalists to Saviours of the Nation. A Survey of the Ecologization of Sweden 1895–1975.* Stockholm: Almqvist & Wiksell International, 1986. 330pp.

Ströholm, Stig (ed). *An Introduction of Swedish Law.* Stockholm, Norstedts, 1988. 532pp. (Institutet för rättsvetenskaplig forskning, 108).

Sundelius, Bengt (ed). *The Committed Neutral: Sweden's Foreign Policy.* Boulder, Col.: Westview Press, 1989. 214pp.

Tarschys, Daniel. *Government Growth: the Case of Sweden 1523–1983.* Glasgow: University of Strathclyde, 1984. 28pp. (Studies in Public Policy, 121).

Taylor, William J. & Cole, Paul M. *Nordic Defense: Comparative Decision Making.* Lexington, Mass.: Lexington Books, 1985. 218pp.

Thomas, Dorothy Swaine. *Social and Economic Aspects of Swedish Population Movement 1750–1933.* New York: Macmillan, 1941. 487pp.

Tilton, Timothy Alan. *The Political Theory of Swedish Social Democracy: through the Welfare State to Socialism.* Oxford: Clarendon Press, 1990. 298pp.

Tingsten, Herbert. *The Debate on the Foreign Policy of Sweden 1918–1939.* Translated by Joan Bulman. London, New York & Toronto: Oxford University Press, 1949. 326pp.

———. *The Swedish Social Democrats.* Totowa, N.J.: Bedminster Press, 1973.

Tomasson, Richard F. *Sweden. Prototype of Modern Society.* New York: Random House, 1970. 302pp.

Verney, D.V. *Parliamentary Reform in Sweden 1866–1921.* Oxford: Oxford University Press, 1957. 295pp.

———. *Public Enterprise in Sweden.* Liverpool: Liverpool University Press, 1959. 132pp.

Vogel, Joachim *et al. Inequality in Sweden: Trends and Current Situation: Living Conditions 1975–1985.* Stockholm: Statistics Sweden, 1988. 512pp.

Volvo 1927–1987. Gothenburg: Volvo, 1987. 80pp.

Wendt, F. *The Nordic Council and Cooperation in Scandinavia.* Translated by A.A. Anslev. Copenhagen: Nordic Council, 1959. 247pp.

Westerlund, E. & Beckman, R. *Sweden's Economy.* Translated by C. Stephenson. Stockholm: Swedish Institute, 1965.

Wilson, Dorothy. *The Welfare State in Sweden.* London: Heinemann, 1979. 173pp.

Wistrand, Birgitta. *Swedish Women on the Move.* Translated by Jeanne Rosen. Stockholm: Swedish Institute, 1981. 112pp.

Swedish Language

Beite, Ann-Marie *et al. Basic Swedish Grammar.* Stockholm: Almqvist & Wiksell, 1963. 168pp.

Bergman, Gösta. *A Short History of the Swedish Language.* Stockholm: Swedish Institute, 1947. 106pp.

Björkhagen, Im. *Modern Swedish Grammar.* Stockholm: Nordstedts, 1956. 194pp.

Bonniers engelsk-svenska ordbok. English-Swedish Dictionary. Glasgow: Collins; Stockholm: Bonniers, 1987. 512pp.

Borland, Harold H. *Swedish for Students.* London: Harrap; Heidelberg: Julius Gross Verlang, 1970. 288pp.

Chrystal, Judith-Ann. *Engelska i svensk dagspress* (English in Swedish Daily Newspapers, with an Abstract in English). Stockholm: Svenska Språknämnden, 1988. 246pp. Abstract pp197–202.

Haugen, Einar. *The Scandinavian Languages. An Introduction to their History.* London: Faber & Faber, 1976. 507pp.

————. *Scandinavian Language Structures. A Comparative Historical Survey.* Tübingen: Niemeyer; Minneapolis: University of Minnesota Press, 1982. 225pp. (Nordic Series, 9).

Haugen, Einar & Markey, T.L. *The Scandinavian Languages: 50 Years of Linguistic Research (1918–1968).* The Hague: Mouton, 1973.

Hellquist, Elof. *Svensk etymologisk ordbok.* 2 vols. Lund, 1935–39.

Hird, Gladys. *Swedish: an Elementary Grammar Reader* (2nd ed). Cambridge: Cambridge University Press, 1980. 270pp.

Holmes, Philip & Hinchliffe, I. *Swedish: a Comprehensive Grammar.* London & New York: Routledge, 1994. 628 pp.

Holmes, Philip & Serin, Gunilla. *Colloquial Swedish.* London: Routledge, 1990. 337pp. (with cassette tape).

Johnson, Walter. *Basic Swedish.* Chicago: Covenant Press, 1983. 279pp.

Lundell, T. *et al. Modern svenska-Swedish.* Los Angeles: University of California, 1972. 169pp.

Prisma's Swedish-English & English-Swedish Dictionary. (4th rev. ed.). Minneapolis: University of Minnesota Press; Stockholm: Prisma, 1989. 613pp.

Stora svensk-engelska ordboken. A Comprehensive Swedish-English Dictionary. Stockholm: Esselte Studium, 1988. 1108pp.

Svenska Akademiens ordbok. Ordbok över svenska språket. Lund, 1898– (The Swedish Academy's Dictionary, still in progress).

Education

Abrahamsson, Kenneth. *Adult Participation in Swedish Higher Education.* Stockholm: Almqvist & Wiksell, 1985. 122pp. (Studies in Higher Education in Sweden, 7).

Ahlström, Karl-Georg. *The University and Teacher Training.* Uppsala: University, 1988. 24pp. (Skrifter rörande Uppsala universitet 1c, 56).

Arvidsson, Stellan. *Education in Sweden.* Translated by P. Öberg. Stockholm: Swedish Institute/Forum, 1955. 106pp.

Axelsson, Rune. *Upper Secondary School in Retrospect: the View of Former Students (on Sweden).* Uppsala: University, 1989. 224pp. (Uppsala Series in Education, 30).

Ball, Stephen J. & Larsson, Staffan (eds). *The Struggle for Democratic Education: Equality and Participation in Sweden.* New York: Falmer Press, 1989. 224pp.

Bedoire, Fredric & Thullberg, Per. *Stockholm University: a History.* Stockholm: University, 1987. 143pp.

Bergevin, Paul. *Adult Education in Sweden. An Introduction.* Bloomington, Indiana: Indiana University, 1961. (Adult Education Monograph Series).

———. *School in Sweden.* Stockholm: Board of Education.

Boli, John. *New Citizens for a New Society: the Institutional Origins of Mass Schooling in Sweden.* Oxford: Pergamon Press, 1989. 296pp. (Comparative and International Education Series, 9)

Brattset, Hallgjerd. *Training of Adult Educators in the Nordic Countries (North Europe).* Trondheim: Norwegian Institute of Adult Education, 1985. 21pp.

292 / Selected Bibliography

Düring, Ingemar. *The Swedish School Reform 1950. A Summary of the Government Bill edited at the request of the 1946 School Commission.* Stockholm: Nord. bokh., 1951. 171pp.

Fagerlind, Ingemar & Saha, Lawrence. *Education and National Development.* London: Pergamon Press, 1989. 320pp.

Fehrman, Carl. *Lund and Learning: an Informal History of Lund University.* Translated by Alan Crozier. Lund: University Press; Bromley: Chartwell-Bratt, 1987. 208pp.

Fleisher, Frederic. *Folk High Schools in Sweden.* Stockholm: Swedish Institute, 1968. 103pp.

Heseltine, Elisabeth (ed). *Alice in Academe: the Place of Women in Higher Education.* Stockholm: Swedish National Board of Universities, 1987. 67pp.

Husén, Torsten (ed). *Differentiation and Guidance in the Comprehensive School.* Stockholm: Almqvist & Wiksell, 1959. 195pp.

Jense, Göran. *The Swedish Academic Marketplace. The Case of Science and Technology.* Lund: University, 1979. 242pp. (Lund Studies in Sociology, 26).

Johannisson, Karin. *A Life of Learning: Uppsala University during Five Centuries.* Uppsala: University Press, 1989. 135pp

Key, Ellen. *The Century of the Child.* Translated by F. Baro & M. Franzos. New York & London: Putnam, 1909. 339pp.

———. *The Younger Generation.* Translated by A.G. Chater. New York & London: Putnam, 1914. 270pp.

Lindblom, Johannes. *The University of Lund.* Lund: Gleerups, 1948. 83pp.

Marklund, Inger. *Formulating a National Educational Research Programme: the Case of Sweden.* A Paper presented at the Scottish Council for Research in Education, 1984. Edinburgh: Scottish Council for Research in Education, 1984. 39pp.

Marklund, Sixten & Bergendal, Gunnar. *Trends in Swedish Educational Policy.* Stockholm: Swedish Institute, 1979. 55pp.

Matshazi, M.J. *In Search for a Distance Education Model: a Look at Practices and Experiences in the Scandinavian Countries.* Oslo: University Center for International Development Studies, 1988. 94pp.

Neave, Guy & Jenkinson, Sally. *Research on Higher Education in Sweden. An Analysis and an Evaluation.* Stockholm: Almqvist & Wiksell International, 1984. 112pp. (Studies in Higher Education in Sweden, 3).

Öhrström, Lilian. *Research: the Swedish Approach.* Stockholm: Swedish Institute, 1991. 128pp.

Orring, Jonas. *Comprehensive School and Continuation Schools in Sweden. A summary of the principal recommendations of the 1957 School Commission.* Stockholm: Board of Education, 1962. 153pp.

―――. *School in Sweden.* Translated by K. Bradfield. Stockholm: Board of Education, 1968. 162pp.

Ottoson, David (ed). *Higher Education in Sweden in a European Perspective: Symposium.* Stockholm: Wenner-Gren Center, 1991. 131pp.

Paulston, Rolland. *Educational Change in Sweden: Planning and Accepting the Comprehensive School Reform.* New York: Teachers College Press, 1968.

Pedersen, Mogens N. & Hunter, Howard O. *Recent Reforms in Swedish Higher Education.* Stockholm: Ratio, 1980. 65pp.

Pramling, Ingrid. *Learning to Learn: a Study of Swedish Preschool Children.* Translated by Gillian Thylander. New York: Springer, 1990. 120pp. (Recent Research in Psychology).

Premfors, Rune. *The Politics of Higher Education in a Comparative Perspective: France, Sweden, United Kingdom.* Stockholm: University, 1980. 260pp. (Stockholm Studies in Politics, 15).

Shapiro, Howard Stephen. *Recurrent Education in Sweden and the Concept of Life-Learning.* Ann Arbor, Mich.: University Microfilms International, 1989. 194pp.

Simon, Erica. *Réveil national et culture populaire en Scandinavie: La gènese de la Hojskole Nordique 1844–1874.* Paris: Presses Universitaires de France, 1960.

Stenholm, Britta. *Education in Sweden.* Stockholm: Swedish Institute, 1970. 133pp.

————. *The Swedish School System.* Stockholm: Swedish Institute, 1984. 133pp.

Svensson, Lennart G. *Higher Education and the State in Swedish History.* Stockholm: Almqvist & Wiksell International, 1987. 254pp.

Tengström, Emin *et al.* (eds). *University of Göteborg: Past, Present, Future.* Translated by David Isitt. Gothenburg: University, 1991. 68pp.

Willén, Birgitta. *Distance Education at Swedish Universities. An Evaluation of the Experimental Programme and a Follow-up Study.* Stockholm: Almqvist & Wiksell International, 1981. 302pp.

Emigration

Anders, John Olson. *The Origin and History of Swedish Religious Organizations in Minnesota 1853–1885.* Rock Island, Ill.: Augustana, 1932. 101pp.

Andersen, P.J. & Blanck, D. (eds). *Swedish-American Life in Chicago. Cultural and Urban Aspects of an Immigrant People, 1850–1930.* Uppsala: Acta Universitatis, 1991. 394pp.

A:son-Palmqvist, Lena. *Building Traditions among Swedish Settlers in Rural Minnesota.* Stockholm: Nordiska museet, 1984. 124pp.

Bäcklund, Jonas Oscar. *A Pioneer Trio. Fredrik Olaus Nilsson, Gustaf Palmqvist, Anders Wiberg. Leaders in the First Decade of Swedish American Baptists.* Chicago: Conference, 1942. 128pp.

Barton, H. Arnold (ed). *Letters from the Promised Land.* Minneapolis & Chicago: Swedish Pioneer Historical Society, 1975. 344pp.

———. *Scandinavians and Americans.* Essays presented to Franklin D. Scott. Chicago: Swedish Pioneer Historical Society, 1974.

Beijbom, Ulf. *Swedes in Chicago: a Demographic and Social Study of the 1846–1880 Immigration.* Stockholm: Läromedelsförlaget, 1971. 381pp.

Bensen, Adolph Burnett. *Farm, Forge and Philosophy. Chapters from a Swedish Immigrant's Life in America.* Chicago: Swedish Pioneer Historical Society, 1961. 162pp.

Bensen, Adolph Burnett & Hedin, Naboth (eds). *Swedes in America 1638–1935.* New Haven, Ct.: Yale University Press, 1938. 614pp.

Biörck, Tobias Eric. *The Planting of the Swedish Church in America*. Translated by I.O. Nothstein. Rock Island, Ill.: Augustana, 1943. 39pp.

Carlsson, Sten. *Swedes in North America, 1638–1988. Technical, Cultural and Political Achievements*. Stockholm: Streiffert, 1988. 136pp.

Christianson, J.R. (eds). *Scandinavians in America: Literary Life*. Decorah, Iowa: Symra Literary Society, 1985. 342pp.

Dahlie, Jorgen. *A Social History of Scandinavian Immigration, Washington State. 1895–1910*. New York: Arno Press, 1980. 186pp.

Fleischer, Eric & Weibull, Jörgen. *Viking Times to Modern. The Story of Swedish Exploring and Settlement in America and the Development of Trade and Shipping from the Vikings to Our Times*. Stockholm: Almqvist & Wiksell, 1953; Minneapolis: Minnesota University, 1954. 115pp.

Forsbeck, Filip A. *New Upsala, the First Swedish Settlement in Wisconsin*. Milwaukee, Wis., 1936. 102pp.

Hokonson, Nels. *Swedish Immigrants in Lincoln's Time*. With a foreword by C. Sandburg. New York: Arno Press, 1979. 259pp. (Scandinavians in America).

Howard, Irene. *Vancouver's Svenskar. A History of the Swedish Community in Vancouver*. Vancouver, Canada: Vancouver Historical Society, 1970.

Janson, F.E. *The Background to Swedish Immigration 1840–1930*. Chicago, 1931.

Johnson, Amandus. *The Swedish Settlements on the Delaware*. Vols 1 & 2. Philadelphia: University of Pennsylvania Press, 1911. 879pp.

Kastrup, Allan. *The Swedish Heritage in America.* Minneapolis: Swedish Council of America, 1975.

Koivukangas, Olavi & Martin, J.S. *The Scandinavians in Australia.* Melbourne: A.E. Press, 1986. 232pp.

Landelius, Otto Robert. *Swedish Place-Names in North America.* Edited by R. Järvi, translated by Karin Franzén. Carbondale: Southern Illinois Press, 1985. 372pp.

Letters relating to Gustav Unionus and the early Swedish Settlers in Wisconsin. Translated and edited by G.M. Stephenson. Rock Island, Ill.: Augustana, 1937. 151pp. (Augustana Historical Society Publications. Vol 7).

Lindberg, John S. *The Background of Swedish Emigration to the United States. An Economic and Sociological Study in the Dynamics of Migration.* Minneapolis: Minnesota University, 1930. 272pp.

Lindmark, Sture. *Swedish America 1914–1932. Studies in Ethnicity with Emphasis on Illinois and Minnesota.* Stockholm: Läromedelsförlaget, 1971.

Lowell, Briant Lindsay. *Scandinavian Exodus: Demography and Social Development of 19th Century Rural Communities.* Boulder, Col.: Westview, 1987.

Lyng, Jens. *The Scandinavians in Australia, New Zealand and the Western Pacific.* London: Oxford University Press; Melbourne: Melbourne University, 1939. 207pp.

Moberg, Vilhelm. *The Unknown Swedes: a Book about Swedes and America, Past and Present.* Translated by Roger McKnight. Carbondale: Southern Illinois University Press, 1988. 182pp.

Nelson, Helge. *The Swedes and the Swedish Settlements in North America.* New York: Arno Press, 1979. 441pp. (Scandinavian America).

Norman, Hans & Runblom, Harald. *Transatlantic Connections: Nordic Migrations to the New World after 1800.* Oslo: Norwegian University Press; Oxford: Oxford University Press, 1988. 335pp.

Olson, Ernst. W. (with Schon, A. & Engberg, M.J.). *History of the Swedes of Illinois.* New York: Arno Press, 1979 (rev. ed.). 268pp.

Olsson, Nils William. *Swedish Passenger Arrivals in New York 1820–1850.* Chicago, 1967.

Ostergren, Robert C. *A Community Transplanted: the Transatlantic Experience of a Swedish Immigrant Settlement in the Upper Middle West, 1835–1915.* Uppsala: University, 1990. 400pp. (Studia Multiethnica Upsaliensia, 4).

Runblom, Harald & Norman, Hans (eds). *From Sweden to America. A History of the Migration.* Minneapolis: University of Minnesota Press; Uppsala: University, 1976. 391pp. (Studia Historica Upsaliensia, 74).

Scando-Americana. Papers on Scandinavian Emigration to the United States. Edited by Ingrid Semmingsen & Per Seyersted. Oslo: Oslo University, American Institute, 1980. 213pp.

Scott, Franklin D. *Trans-Atlantica: Essays on Scandinavian Migration and Culture.* New York: Arno Press, 1979. 208pp. (Scandinavians in America).

Stephenson, George M. *The Religious Aspects of Swedish Immigration. A Study of Swedish Immigrant Churches.* Minneapolis: Minnesota University, 1932. 542pp.

―――. (ed. and trans). *Letters relating to Gustaf Unonius and the Early Swedish Settlers in Wisconsin.* Rock Island, Ill.: Augustana Historical Society, 1937. 151pp.

Strand, Algot E. *A History of the Swedish Americans of Minnesota. With the valuable collaboration of numerous authors and contributors.* Vols 1–2. Chicago: Lewis, 1910.

Swedish Life in American Cities. Edited by Dag Blanck & Harald Runblom. Uppsala: University, 1991. 131pp. (Uppsala Multiethnic Papers, 21).

Unonius, Gustaf E.M. *A Pioneer in North-west America, 1841–1858. The Memoirs of Gustaf Unonius.* Translated by J.O. Backlund, with an introduction by G.M. Stephenson. Minneapolis: Swedish Pioneer Historical Society, 1950. 1,419pp.

Utvandrarnas hus. The House of Emigrants: a Presentation of the Emigrant Institute. Edited by Ulf Beijbom. Växjö: Institute, 1985. 40pp. (Parallel text in Swedish and English).

Westman, Erik G. & Johnson, E.G. *The Scandinavian Element in America.* 4 vols. Chicago: Swedish-American Biographical Society, 1931–34.

Wheeler, Wayne Leland. *An analysis of Social Change in a Swedish-Emigrant Community: the Case of Lindsborg, Kansas.* New York: AMS, 1986. 386pp.

Wulff, Reinhold. *Die Anfangsphase der Emigration aus Schweden in die USA, 1820–1850: Gesamtdarstellung anhand der amerikanischen Passagierlisten.* Frankfurt: Lang, 1987. 348pp.

Geography

Andersson, Henrik O. & Bedoire, Frederic. *Stockholm: Architecture and Townscape.* Translated by Roger Tanner & Henrik O. Andersson. Stockholm: Prisma, 1988. 412pp.

Barlett, N.R. & Rosenwald, A. *Stockholm Public Transport.* Chelmsford, England: Westbury Marketing, 1986. 64 pp

Cowie, Peter (ed). *The Scandinavian Guide 1988.* London: Tantivy Press; New York: Zoetrope, 1989. 296 pp.

Fullerton, Brian & Williams, Alan F. *Scandinavia.* London: Chatto & Windus, 1975. 375pp.

Geographers of Norden: Reflections on Career Experiences. Edited by Torsten Hägerstrand & Anne Buttimer. Lund: University Press; Bromley, England: Chartwell-Bratt, 1988. 216pp. (Lund Studies in Geography, B. 52).

Glase, Beatrice. *The Old Town: a Guide to Gamla Stan, the Royal Palace and Riddarholmen.* Stockholm: Trevi, 1978. 159pp.

Gothenburg: a City of Change and Renewal. Texts by G. Blomé *et al.*, photos by P. Gullers *et al.* Stockholm: Gullers, 1990. 127pp.

Haglund, Sven. *Life among the Lapps. On the Spring Trek with Köngämä Lapps.* Translated by W. Savage. London: D. Archer, 1935. 252pp.

Halfar, Wolfgang. *Gotland: Glück und Unglück einer Insel.* Husum: Husum Druck- und Verlaggesellschaft, 1981. 238pp.

Hulth, Johan M. *Swedish Arctic and Antarctic Explorations, 1758–1910. A Bibliography.* Uppsala & Stockholm: KVA, 1910. 189pp.

John, Brian S. *Scandinavia: a New Geography.* London: Longman, 1984, 365pp.

Karlkvist, Anders (ed). *Sweden and Antarctica.* Stockholm: Swedish Polar Research Secretariat, 1985. 95pp.

Lund One Thousand Years: a Cultural Guide. Edited by Lars Ingvar, translated by Murial Spalding-Larsson. Lund: Kommun, 1990. 163pp.

Lundquist, Gösta. *Lapland. Reindeer, Lapps and Midnight Sun.* Foreword by Dag Hammarskjöld, edited by Olof Thaning. Stockholm, 1960.

Manker, Ernst. *The Nomadism of the Swedish Mountain Lapps. The Siidas and their Migratory Routes in 1945.* Translated by R.N. Pehrson. Stockholm: Geber; Nordiska Museet, 1953. 261pp.

―――. *People of Eight Seasons.* Gothenburg, 1963. 214pp.

Mead, W.R. *An Economic Geography of the Scandinavian States and Finland.* London: University Press, 1969. 302pp.

―――. *A Historical Geography of Scandinavia.* London: Academic Press, 1981. 313pp.

―――. *Sweden: the Land of Today.* Guildford, England: Colour Library Books, 1991. 142pp.

Mingroot, Erik van *et al. Scandinavia in Old Maps and Prints.* Knokke, Belgium: Mappamundi, 1987. 143pp.

National Atlas of Sweden. 17 vols. Edited by Leif Wastenson. Stockholm: SNA, 1990– (Principals are Lantmäteriverket, i.e. National Land Survey of Sweden; Central Bureau of Statistics, and Swedish Society for Anthropology and Geography).

Nyström, Per. *Mary Wollstonecraft's Scandinavian Journey.* Gothenburg: Kungl. Vetenskaps- och Vitterhets-Samhället, 1980. 51 pp.

O'Dell, A.C. *The Scandinavian World.* London: Longmans, 1963. 549pp. (Geographies for Advanced Studies Series).

Rönn, Gunnar. *The Land of the Lapps.* Translated by I. Broström & H. Bergesén. Stockholm: 1961. 111pp.

Ruong, Israel. *The Lapps in Sweden.* Stockholm: Swedish Institute, 1967.

Skåne: a Book on Scania. Texts by G. Blomé, photos by P. Gullers *et al.* Stockholm: Gullers, 1988. 128pp.

Småland - Land of Innovation. Texts by J. Rydén *et al.*, photos by P. Gullers *et al.* Stockholm: Gullers, 1989. 128pp.

Sömme, Axel. *A Geography of Norden.* Stockholm: Svenska bokförlaget, 1968. 363pp.

Sverige: Land och Folk. 3 vols. Stockholm: Natur och Kultur, 1966.

Wollstonecraft, Mary. *Letters written during a short residence in Sweden, Norway and Denmark.* Edited with an introduction by C.H. Poston. Lincoln & London: University of Nebraska Press, 1976. 201pp.

RELIGIOUS HISTORY

Ahlbäck, Tore (ed). *Saami Religion.* (Symposium, Åbo, 1984). Åbo: Donner Institute for Research in Religious and Cultural History; Stockholm: Almqvist & Wiksell, 1987. 293pp.

Andersson, Aron. *St Bridget of Sweden.* London: Catholic Truth Society, 1980. 141pp.

Barrett, Clive. *The Viking Gods: Pagan Myths of the Nordic Peoples.* Wellingborough, England: Aquarian Press, 1989. 175pp.

Bergendoff, C.J.I. *Olaus Petri and the Ecclesiastical Transformation in Sweden 1521–1552. A Study in the Swedish Reformation.* New York: Macmillan, 1928. 264pp.

Cnattingius, Hans. *Studies in the Order of St Bridget of Sweden.* Stockholm: University, 1963. 198pp. (Stockholm Studies in History, Acta Universitatis Stockholmiensis 7).

Craigie, Williams A. *The Religion of Ancient Scandinavia.* London: Constable, 1906. 71pp.

Davidson, H.R. Ellis. *Myths and Symbols in Pagan Europe: Early Scandinavian and Celtic Religions.* Manchester: University Press, 1989. 268pp.

———. *Pagan Scandinavia.* London: Thames & Hudson, 1967. (Ancient Peoples and Places, 58).

———. *The Road to Hel. A Study of the Conception of the Dead in Old Norse Literature.* Cambridge: Cambridge University Press, 1943. 208pp.

———. *Scandinavian Mythology.* (rev. ed.). New York: Peter Bedrick Books, 1986. 143pp. (Library of the World's Myths and Legends).

Dumézil, Georges. *Gods of the Ancient Norsemen.* Edited by Einar Haugen. Berkeley: University of California Press, 1973.

Garstein, Oskar. *Rome and the Counter-Reformation in Scandinavia: Until the Establishment of the S. Congregatio de Propaganda Fide in 1622.* Oslo: Universitetsforlaget; Copenhagen: Munksgaard, 1980. 626pp.

———. *Rome and the Counter-Reformation in Scandinavia: the Age of Gustavus Adolphus and Queen Christina of Sweden 1622–1656.* Leiden: Brill, 1992. 833pp. (Studies in the History of Christian Thought 47).

Hamberg, Eva M. *Studies in the Prevalence of Religious Beliefs and Religious Practice in Contemporary Sweden.* Uppsala: University, 1990. 62pp. (Psychologia et Sociologia Religionum, 4).

Holm, Nils G. *Scandinavian Psychology of Religion.* Åbo: Åbo Academy, 1987. 162pp. (Religionsvetenskapliga skrifter, 15).

Hunter, L.S. (ed). *Scandinavian Churches: a Picture of the Development and Life of the Churches of Denmark, Finland, Iceland, Norway and Sweden.* London: Faber & Faber, 1965.

Macculloch, John A. *The Celtic and Scandinavian Religions.* London: Hutchinson, 1948. 180pp. (World Religions, 10).

Murray, Robert. *A Brief History of the Church of Sweden: Origins and Modern Structure.* Translated by Nils G. Sahlin. Stockholm: Verbum. 1961. 124pp.

———. (ed). *The Church of Sweden: Past and Present.* Translated by Nils G. Sahlin. Malmö: Allhem, 1960. 286pp.

Ottosen, Knud. *A Short History of the Churches of Scandinavia.* Århus: Århus University. 80pp.

Sawyer, Birgit (ed). *The Christianization of Scandinavia: Report of a Symposium, 1985.* Alingsås: Viktoria, 1987. 130pp.

Sharpe, Eric J. *Nathan Söderblom and the Study of Religion.* Chapel Hill: University of North Carolina Press, 1990. 258pp.

Smith, C. Howard. *Scandinavian Hymnody from the Reformation to the Present.* Metuchen, N.J.: Scarecrow Press (ATLA Monograph, 23) 1987. 325pp.

Stromberg, Peter G. *Symbols of Community: the Cultural System of a Swedish Church.* Tucson: University of Arizona Press, 1986. 127pp.

Turville-Petre, E.O.G. *Myth and Religion of the North. The Religion of Ancient Scandinavia.* London: Weidenfeld & Nicolson, 1964. 340pp. (History of Religion Series).

Waddams, Herbert M. *The Swedish Church.* London: SPCK, 1946. 70pp.

Wordsworth, J. *The National Church in Sweden.* The Hale Lectures, 1910. London: Mowbray, 1911.

ARTS AND MEDIA

Algulin, Ingemar. *Contemporary Swedish Prose.* Stockholm: Swedish Institute, 1983. 95pp.

————. *A History of Swedish Literature.* Stockholm: Swedish Institute, 1989. 287pp.

Brask, Per (ed). *Scandinavia* (in Drama Contemporary Series). New York: PAJ Publications, 1989. 216pp.

Cornell, Henrik. *Den svenska konstens historia.* 2 vols. (The History of Swedish Art). Stockholm: Bonniers, 1944–45. New ed. Aldus, 1959, 271 & 245pp.

Cowie, Peter. *Ingmar Bergman: a Critical Biography.* (rev. ed.) London: Deutsch, 1992. 401 pp.

————. *Scandinavian Cinema.* London: Tantivy Press/ Scandinavian Films; Hollywood: Samuel French Trade, 1992. 288pp.

————. *Swedish Cinema from Ingeborg Holm to Fanny and Alexander.* Stockholm: Swedish Institute, 1985. 160pp.

The Cultural Heritage in Sweden. Stockholm: Central Board of National Antiquities and Swedish National Committee of ICOMOS, 1981. 385pp. (ICOMOS Bulletin, 1981:6).

Design in Sweden. Stockholm: Swedish Institute, 1985. 142pp.

Donnelly, Marian C. *Architecture in the Scandinavian Countries.* Cambridge, Mass.: MIT Press, 1992. 401pp.

Edam, Carl Thomas *et al.* (eds). *Scandinavian Modernism: Paintings in Denmark, Iceland, Norway and Sweden 1910–1920.* Gothenburg: Göteborgs Konstmuseum; Copenhagen: Nordic Council of Ministers; New York: Rizzoli, 1989. 262pp.

Espmark, Kjell. *The Nobel Prize in Literature: a Study of the Criteria behind the Choices.* Boston: G.K. Hall, 1991. 211pp.

Groth, Håkon & Schulenburg, Fritz von der. *Neoclassicism in the North: Swedish Furniture and Interiors 1770–1850.* London: Thames & Hudson, 1990. 224pp.

Gustafson, Alrik. *History of Swedish Literature.* Minneapolis: University of Minnesota Press/American Scandinavian Foundation, 1961. 708pp.

Hawkins Opie, Jennifer. *Scandinavia: Ceramics and Glass in the Twentieth Century.* London: Victoria & Albert Museum; New York: Rizzoli, 1990. 184pp.

Hodgson, Antony. *Scandinavian Music: Finland and Sweden.* Rutherford, N.J.: Fairleigh Dickinson University Press, 1984. 224pp.

Jacobsson, Stig & Peterson, Hans-Gunnar. *Swedish Composers of the 20th Century: Members of the Society of Swedish Composers. Biographies.* Stockholm: Swedish Music Information Center, 1988. 205pp.

Johnsson, Ulf G. *Masterpieces from Gripsholm Castle: the Swedish National Portrait Collection.* Stockholm: National Swedish Art Museum, 1988. 134pp.

Kent, Neil. *Light and Nature in the Late 19th Century Nordic Art and Literature.* Stockholm: Almqvist & Wiksell, 1990. 92 pp.

————. *The Triumph of Light and Nature: Nordic Art 1740–1940.* London: Thames & Hudson, 1987. 240pp.

Lindgren, Mereth *et al.* (eds). *A History of Swedish Art.* Translated by Roger Tanner. Lund: Signum, 1987. 277pp.

McIlroy, Brian. *Sweden.* London: Flicks Books, 1986. 184pp. (World Cinema, 2).

Manor Houses and Royal Castles in Sweden. Text by Bengt G. Söderberg, photos by Erik Liljeroth *et al.* (In English, German and French). Malmö: Allhems förlag, 1975. 346pp.

Marker, Frederick J. & Lise, Lone. *Ingmar Bergman: Four Decades in the Theater.* Cambridge: Cambridge University Press, 1982. 262pp. (Directors in Perspective).

Mårtenson, Jan. *Drottningholm: The Palace by the Lakeside.* Stockholm: Wahlström & Widstrand, 1985. 177pp.

Mattson, Inger (ed). *Gustavian Opera: an Interdisciplinary Reader in Swedish Opera, Dance and Theatre, 1771–1809.* Uppsala: Almqvist & Wiksell International, 1991. 492pp. (Royal Swedish Academy of Music no. 66, 1991).

Meyer, Michael. *Strindberg: a Biography.* London: Secker & Warburg, 1985. 652pp.

Peterson, Bo. *Media, Minds and Men. A History of Media in Sweden.* Stockholm: Almqvist & Wiksell, 1988. 366pp.

Rossel, Sven H. *A History of Scandinavian Literature.* Minneapolis: University of Minnesota Press, 1982. 492pp.

Scobbie, Irene (ed). *Aspects of Modern Swedish Literature.* Norwich, England: Norvik Press, 1988. 373pp.

Senelick, Laurence (ed). *National Theatre in Northern and Eastern Europe, 1746–1900.* Cambridge: Cambridge University Press, 1991. 480pp.

Sjögren, Henrik. *Stage and Society in Sweden: Aspects of Swedish Theatre since 1945.* Translated by P. Britten Austin. Stockholm: Swedish Institute, 1979. 181pp.

Skuncke, Marie-Christine. *Sweden and European Drama 1772–1796. A Study of Translations and Adaptations.* Uppsala: University; Stockholm: Almqvist & Wiksell International, 1981. 238pp. (Acta Universitatis Upsaliensis. Historia litterarum, 10).

Steene, Birgitta. *Ingmar Bergman: a Guide to References and Resources.* Boston, Mass.: G.K. Hall, 1987. 342pp.

Swedish Cultural Policy: a Review of State Cultural Policies and Practices. Translated by Stephen Croall. Stockholm: Swedish National Council for Cultural Affairs, 1990. 134pp.

Varnedoe, Kirk. *Northern Light: Nordic Art at the Turn of the Century.* New Haven, Conn. & London: Yale University Press, 1988. 288pp.

Waldekrantz, Rune. *Swedish Cinema.* Stockholm: Swedish Institute, 1959. 71pp.

Walker, Alexander. *Garbo: a Portrait.* London: Weidenfeld & Nicolson, 1990. 192pp.

Zorn: Paintings, Graphics and Sculpture. By Douglas K.S. Hyland & Hans Henrik Brummer; catalog by Marguerite J Harbert. Birmingham, Alabama: Museum of Art, 1986. 100pp.

Zuck, Virpi (ed. in chief). *Dictionary of Scandinavian Literature.* New York; Westport, Conn. & London: Greenwood Press, 1990. 792pp.

PERIODICALS

American-Scandinavian Review. American-Scandinavian Foundation. New York, 1913–1974.

Artes. Kvartalskrift för konst, litteratur och musik. Stockholm: Musikaliska akademien, Konstakademien, Svenska akademien, Norstedts, 1975–

Documents on Swedish Foreign Policy. Annual translations of foreign policy documents from 1950. Stockholm: Royal Ministry for Foreign Affairs (Fritze).

Economy and History. Institute of Economic History and the Economic History Association. University of Lund, 1958–

Historisk Tidskrift. Stockholm: Swedish History Association, 1881–

Kontur. Swedish Design Annual. Svenska slöjdföreningen. Stockholm, 1950–

Industria. International Organ of the Swedish Employers' Confederation. Annual. Stockholm, 1949–

Nordisk kontakt. Nordiska Rådet (Nordic Council). Stockholm, 1955–

Nordisk tidskrift för vetenskap, konst och industri. Letterstedtska föreningen. Stockholm, 1878–

Northern Studies. Journal of the Scottish Society for Northern Studies. Edinburgh University. Annual, 1973–

Saga-Book of the Viking Society for Northern Research. London, 1895–

Scandia. Tidskrift för historisk forskning. Lund, 1928–

Scandinavian-Canadian Studies. Ottawa, 1988–

Scandinavian Economic History Review. Scandinavian Society for Economic and Social History and Historical Geography. Stockholm, 1928–

Scandinavian Journal of History. The Historical Associations of Denmark, Finland, Norway and Sweden. Stockholm: Almqvist & Wiksell, 1976–

Scandinavian Political Studies. Yearbook of the Political Science Associations in Denmark, Finland, Norway and Sweden. Helsinki, New York & London, 1966–

Scandinavian Review. American-Scandinavian Foundation. New York, 1975–

Scandinavian Studies. Society for Advancement of Scandinavian Studies. Lawrence, Kansas, 1911–

Scandinavica. An International Journal of Scandinavian Studies. Norwich, University of East Anglia, 1962–

Statistical Abstract. Annual published by the National Central Bureau of Statistics, Stockholm: Nordisk bokhandel, 1914–

Swedish Book Review. Swedish-English Literary Translators' Association. Bi-annual. Lampeter, Wales: St David's University College, 1983–

Sweden Now. Ingenjörsforlaget. Stockholm, 1967–

Swedish Pioneer Historical Quarterly. Swedish Pioneer Historical Society. Chicago, 1950–

APPENDIX 1.

SWEDISH RULERS

Erik Segersäll (the Victorious)	d. before 994
Olof Skötkonung	c. 994–1022
Anund Jakob	c. 1022–50
Emund	c. 1050–60
Stenkil	c. 1060–66
Halsten and Inge	c. 1080–1110
Filip and Inge	c. 1110–22
Ragnvald	d. c. 1130
Sverker the Elder	c. 1130–56
Erik (IX; St Erik)	c. 1156–60
Karl (VII) Sverkersson	1161–67
Knut Eriksson	1167–96
Sverker the Younger Karlsson	1196–1208
Erik (X) Knutsson	1208–16
Johan (I) Sverkersson	1216–22
Erik (XI) Eriksson	1222–29; 1234–50
Knut Långe	1229–34
Birger Jarl (Regent)	1250–66
Valdemar	1250–75
Magnus Ladulås	1275–90
Torgils Knutsson (Regent)	1290–98
Birger Magnusson	1290–1318
Magnus Eriksson	1319–65
Erik (XII)	1357–59
Håkon	1362–71
Albrekt of Mecklenburg	1363–89
Margareta (Regent)	1389–1412
Erik (XIII) of Pomerania	1389–1439
Engelbrekt Engelbrektsson (Regent)	1435–36
Karl Knutsson (Regent)	1436–40

Kristoffer of Bavaria	1440–48
Karl (VIII) Knutsson	1448–57, 1464–65, 1467–70
Sten Sture the Elder (Regent)	1470–97, 1501–03
Hans (Johan II)	1497–1501
Svante Sture (Regent)	1504–12
Sten Sture the Younger (Regent)	1512–20
Kristian II (of Denmark)	1520–21
Gustav 1 (Regent)	1521–23; (King) 1523–60
Erik XIV	1560–68
Johan III	1568–92
Sigismund	1592–99
Karl IX	Regent until 1604; King 1604–11
Gustav II Adolf (Gustavus Adolphus)	1611–32
Kristina	1632–54
Karl X Gustav	1654–60
Karl XI	1660–97
Karl XII (Charles XII)	1697–1718
Ulrika Eleonora	1719–20
Fredrik I of Hessen	1720–51
Adolf Fredrik	1751–71
Gustav III	1771–92
Gustav IV Adolf	1792–1809
Karl XIII	1809–18
Karl XIV Johan (Bernadotte)	1818–44
Oscar I	1844–59
Karl XV	1859–72
Oscar II	1872–1907
Gustav V	1907–50
Gustav VI Adolf	1950–73
Carl XVI Gustaf	1973–

APPENDIX 2.

SWEDISH PRIME MINISTERS

1876	De Geer, Louis
1880	Posse, Arvid
1883	Thyselius, Carl Johan
1884	Themptander, Robert
1888	Bildt, Gillis
1889	Åkerhielm, Gustaf
1891	Boström, Erik Gustaf
1900	Von Otter, Fredrik
1902	Boström, Erik Gustaf
1905	Ramstedt, Johan
1905	Lundeberg, Christian
1905	Staaf, Karl (Liberal)
1906	Lindman, Arvid (Conservative)
1911	Staaff, Karl, (Liberal)
1914	Hammerskjöld, Hjalmar
1917	Swartz, Carl (Conservative)
1917	Edén, Nils (Liberal)
1920	Branting, Hjalmar (Social Democrat)
1920	De Geer, Louis
1921	Von Sydow, Oscar
1921	Branting, Hjalmar (Social Democrat)
1923	Trygger, Ernst (Conservative)
1924	Branting, Hjalmar (Social Democrat)
1925	Sandler, Rickard (Social Democrat)
1926	Ekman, Carl Gustaf (Liberal)
1928	Lindman, Arvid (Conservative)
1930	Ekman, Carl Gustaf (Liberal)
1932	Hamrin, Felix (Liberal)
1932	Hansson, Per Albin (Social Democrat)
1936	Pehrsson-Bramstorp, Axel (Agrarian)

1936	Hansson, Per Albin (Social Democrat)
1946	Erlander, Tage (Social Democrat)
1969	Palme, Olof (Social Democrat)
1976	Fälldin, Thorbjörn (Centerist)
1978	Ullsten, Ola (Liberal)
1979	Fälldin, Thorbjörn (Centerist)
1982	Palme, Olof (Social Democrat)
1986	Carlsson, Ingvar (Social Democrat)
1991	Bildt, Carl (Moderate)

ABOUT THE AUTHOR

Irene Scobbie (B.A. Durham; M.A. [Hon] Cambridge) graduated in German and then Scandinavian Studies and worked for three years as English Secretary in the Swedish Cultural Attaché's office in London before doing research in modern Swedish literature at London University. As a lecturer she taught Swedish at Cambridge University, and as Reader (full professor) she subsequently ran the Scandinavian Department at Aberdeen University and then Edinburgh University. As well as teaching and research she has directed her energies at the dissemination of Swedish culture, organizing and hosting the first Conference of University Teachers of Scandinavian Studies in Great Britain, lecturing to a wide variety of groups and institutions, editing the Edinburgh-based *Northern Studies* and joining the editorial boards of Scandinavian journals. Her undergraduate course entailed a six-month study period in Sweden, and she has spent part of every year in Sweden ever since. Her publications include specialized studies in modern Swedish literature and more general works on Swedish history and society. In 1988 Sweden acknowledged her efforts by awarding her the Polar Star for services to Swedish literature and culture.